A Concise History of New Zealand Aotearoa

Third Edition

PHILIPPA MEIN SMITH

Shaftesbury Road, Cambridge CB2 8EA, United Kingdom

One Liberty Plaza, 20th Floor, New York, NY 10006, USA

477 Williamstown Road, Port Melbourne, VIC 3207, Australia

314–321, 3rd Floor, Plot 3, Splendor Forum, Jasola District Centre, New Delhi – 110025, India

103 Penang Road, #05–06/07, Visioncrest Commercial, Singapore 238467

Cambridge University Press is part of Cambridge University Press & Assessment, a department of the University of Cambridge.

We share the University's mission to contribute to society through the pursuit of education, learning and research at the highest international levels of excellence.

www.cambridge.org
Information on this title: www.cambridge.org/9781009716734

© Philippa Mein Smith 2005, 2012, 2026

This publication is copyright. Subject to statutory exception and to the provisions of relevant collective licensing agreements, no reproduction of any part may take place without the written permission of Cambridge University Press & Assessment.

First published 2005
Second edition 2012
Third edition 2026

Cover designed by Anne-Marie Reeves
Typeset by Lumina Datamatics Ltd

A catalogue record for this publication is available from the British Library

A catalogue record for this book is available from the National Library of Australia

ISBN 978-1-009-71673-4 Paperback

Reproduction and communication for educational purposes
The Australian *Copyright Act 1968* (the Act) allows a maximum of one chapter or 10% of the pages of this work, whichever is the greater, to be reproduced and/or communicated by any educational institution for its educational purposes provided that the educational institution (or the body that administers it) has given a remuneration notice to Copyright Agency Limited (CAL) under the Act.

For details of the CAL licence for educational institutions contact:

Copyright Agency Limited
Level 12, 66 Goulburn Street
Sydney NSW 2000
Telephone: (02) 9394 7600
Facsimile: (02) 9394 7601
E-mail: memberservices@copyright.com.au

Reproduction and communication for other purposes
Except as permitted under the Act (for example a fair dealing for the purposes of study, research, criticism or review) no part of this publication may be reproduced, stored in a retrieval system, communicated or transmitted in any form or by any means without prior written permission. All inquiries should be made to the publisher at the address above.

Cambridge University Press & Assessment has no responsibility for the persistence or accuracy of URLs for external or third-party internet websites referred to in this publication and does not guarantee that any content on such websites is, or will remain, accurate or appropriate.

For EU product safety concerns, contact us at Calle de José Abascal, 56, 1°, 28003 Madrid, Spain, or email eugpsr@cambridge.org.

A CONCISE HISTORY OF NEW ZEALAND AOTEAROA

Third Edition

New Zealand was the last major landmass, other than Antarctica, to be settled by humans. In *A Concise History of New Zealand Aotearoa*, Philippa Mein Smith beautifully narrates the story of this rugged and dynamic land, from its origins in Gondwana, between 60 and 100 million years ago, its late settlement by Polynesian voyagers, and its colonisation by Europeans (and the exchanges that made these peoples Māori and Pākehā) to the dramatic struggles over land and efforts to manage global forces into the twenty-first century.

A Concise History of New Zealand Aotearoa places New Zealand in its global and regional contexts, linked to Britain, immersed in the Pacific, and part of Australasia, highlighting the effects of the country's smallness and isolation. The third edition continues to analyse key moments in distant and recent history – the signing and continuation of the Treaty of Waitangi (Te Tiriti o Waitangi), the Gallipoli landings, the sinking of the *Rainbow Warrior*, and earthquakes – showing their roles in nation-building myths and connecting them with the less dramatic forces, economic and social, that have shaped contemporary New Zealand.

PHILIPPA MEIN SMITH is Emeritus Professor of History at the University of Canterbury, Christchurch, New Zealand. In Australia, she taught at Flinders University, South Australia, and later at the University of Tasmania. Her first two books were based on her MA and PhD theses: *Maternity in Dispute: New Zealand, 1920–1939* (1986) and *Mothers and King Baby: Infant Survival and Welfare in an Imperial World; Australia, 1880–1950* (1997). She co-authored *A History of Australia, New Zealand and the Pacific* (2000) with Donald Denoon and *Remaking the Tasman World* (2008) with Peter Hempenstall and Shaun Goldfinch. The first two editions of *A Concise History of New Zealand* were published in 2005 and 2012 respectively.

CAMBRIDGE CONCISE HISTORIES

Cambridge Concise Histories offer general introductions to a wide range of subjects. A series of authoritative overviews written by expert authors, these books make the histories of countries, events and topics accessible to both students and general readers.

A full list of titles in the series can be found at:
www.cambridge.org/concisehistories

* * *

Cambridge University Press acknowledges the Australian Aboriginal and Torres Strait Islander peoples of this nation. We acknowledge the traditional custodians of the lands on which our company is located and where we conduct our business. We pay our respects to ancestors and Elders, past and present. Cambridge University Press is committed to honouring Australian Aboriginal and Torres Strait Islander peoples' unique cultural and spiritual relationships to the land, waters and seas and their rich contribution to society.

Cambridge University Press acknowledges the Māori people as tangata whenua of Aotearoa New Zealand.

We pay our respects to the First Nation Elders of Australia and New Zealand, past, present and emerging.

In memory of my mother, Barbara Ann Staff,
whose stories and library
contributed to this book

CONTENTS

List of illustrations	page viii
Acknowledgements	x
Preface	xiii
A note on names	xv

1	Waka across a watery world	1
2	Beachcrossers 1769–1839	21
3	Claiming the land 1840–1860	49
4	Remoter Australasia 1861–1890	77
5	Managing globalisation 1891–1913	106
6	'All flesh is as grass' 1914–1929	135
7	Making New Zealand 1930–1949	165
8	Golden weather 1950–1972	193
9	Latest experiments 1973–1996	221
10	Treaty revival 1973–1999	249
11	Shaky ground 2000–2016	275
12	Beached 2017–2025	300

Glossary of Māori words	327
Timeline	331
Sources of quotations	347
Guide to further reading	361
Index	392

ILLUSTRATIONS

MAPS AND FIGURES

1.1	New Zealand: principal mountains, regions, and towns	page 2
1.2	Zealandia: the sunken eighth continent	3
1.3	A watery world: the South Pacific Ocean	10
2.1	Locations of Māori tribes (iwi), c. 1839	22
2.2	James Cook, *Carte de la Nle Zélande* ..., 1774	25
2.3	George F. Dashwood, *Maoris*, 1832	31
2.4	James Barry, *The Rev. Thomas Kendall and ... Hongi and Waikato*, 1820	36
2.5	George F. Angas, *Motupoi pah with Tongariro*, 1844	42
3.1.1	Eruera Pātuone, 1856–62	51
3.1.2	Tāmati Wāka Nene, 1870	52
3.2	William Mein Smith, *From the pah Pipitea, Port Nicholson* ..., 1840	63
3.3	William Strutt, *Settler putting out chimney fire*, 1855/6	66
3.4	Thomas B. Collinson, *Hosey's battle 1847* ..., 1848	74
4.1	P. E. jnr, *For diver's reasons*, 1881	85
4.2	Population growth components, 1860–2000	89
4.3	Population pyramids, 1874 and 1891 (European only)	90
4.4	Sew Hoy dredge gold mining, 1890s	92
4.5	Helen Connon, 1881	98
5.1	House in Bealey Avenue, Christchurch, c. 1895	110
5.2	*The summit at last*, 1894	115
5.3	Scatz, *How we see it*, 1900	125
5.4	John C. Blomfield, *Still they come*, 1905	130
6.1	Lijssenthoek Military Cemetery, Belgium, 2004	143
6.2	A. Rule, '*In Blighty!*' *A thing we dream about*, 1916	144
6.3.1	Captain P. P. Tāhiwi, 1916	145

List of illustrations

6.3.2	Captain H. S. Tremewan and Mrs M. Mylrea, 1916	146
6.4	Health class, 1926	153
6.5	Californian bungalow, Nelson, 2004	156
6.6	Drain layers milking the cow for morning tea, Christchurch, c. 1920s	158
7.1	May Day demonstration, Christchurch, 1932	168
7.2	G. E. G. Minhinnick, *The medicine man*, 1938	174
7.3	Men from 28 (Māori) Battalion, Alexandria, 1941	182
7.4	*Making New Zealand* pictorial survey histories, 1939–40	190
7.5	G. E. G. Minhinnick, *The invincibility of the All Blacks*, c. 1947	191
8.1	Nevile S. Lodge, *Needmore Power Project*, 1963/4	201
8.2	Toddler in sandpit, Palmerston North, c. 1959	207
8.3	'The kids are already too radio-active', 1956	210
8.4	Eric W. Heath, *Big 3 ANZUS meeting*, 1974	214
8.5	G. E. G. Minhinnick, *Tails you lose!*, 1966	218
9.1	Proportion of total exports going to different markets, 1860–1989	223
9.2	Robert Muldoon and Malcolm Fraser, 1980	227
9.3	Eric W. Heath, *ANZUS*, 1985	243
9.4	The stricken *Rainbow Warrior*, Auckland Harbour, 1985	244
10.1	Justice Edward Taihākurei Durie, c. 2003	256
10.2	Prime Minister Helen Clark, 2003	264
11.1	Meadowlands Shopping Centre, South Auckland, 2011	290
11.2	Christ Church Cathedral, 2006	293
11.3	Christ Church Cathedral, after 22 February 2011	294
11.4	Prince William greeting locals, Christchurch, 2011	296
12.1	Bouquets and messages for victims of Christchurch massacre, 2019	302
12.2	Te Hīkoi mō te Tiriti, Hastings Hīkoi, 16 November 2024	306
12.3	Te Hīkoi mō te Tiriti, Wellington, 19 November 2024	307
12.4	Zealandia Te Māra a Tāne, Wellington, 2024	313

TABLES

4.1	Population trends and Māori land ownership, 1840–1911	94
9.1	New Zealander votes on ANZUS alliance or nuclear-free New Zealand, 1986	246

ACKNOWLEDGEMENTS

A *Concise History* incurs many debts. I owe the largest to my family, especially Richard Tremewan for his steadfast support, my son Alex, and my brother Jeff Mein Smith for his superb photography and care. My niece Jessica Mein Smith and nephew Mark Tremewan supplied photographs for the second edition, while my late mother, Barbara, to whom this book is dedicated, left me engaging source material. My relative Barry allowed me to copy transcripts years ago of ancestral journals now held in the Alexander Turnbull Library. New Zealand is a small society, and readers may notice that in some ways this is a family history.

I am grateful to Kim Armitage of Cambridge University Press, who commissioned this book, to managing editor Lauren Magee for her project management and sensitive editing, copy editor Penny Mansley, Steph Huddleston, and the Cambridge team in Melbourne. Two anonymous referees commented encouragingly on the book proposal and made helpful suggestions. New Zealand historians will see the extent of reliance on their work in this edition as in the earlier ones. The guide to further reading and sources of quotations suggest my principal obligations; in revisions for this edition, I learnt much from the work of Atholl Anderson, Vincent O'Malley, and Anne Salmond. Thanks as ever are due to colleagues at the University of Canterbury, especially Rawiri Te Maire Tau and Paul Schwalger at the Ngāi Tahu Research Centre, Katie Pickles, and Ann Parsonson for feedback on Māori history.

This edition has been revised extensively to take account of new historical research and to bring the text up to date. All the chapters have been modified, especially in the first half and towards the end, where a new chapter brings the narrative into 2025. The link between research and teaching is a precious one, and I thank my present postgraduate students in History and the Ngāi Tahu Research Centre, Ereni Pūtere and Thomas Gilmour, for their collegiality and commitment; as well as previous History postgraduate students, of whom Rosemary Baird, Hayley Brown, Helena Dillon, Stephen Hicks, Matt Morris, Rebecca Priestley, Gary Whitcher, and Megan Woods contributed to the knowledge base underpinning this book.

Finding illustrations was a key task, eased for the first edition by the expertise of Marian Minson and David Small at the Alexander Turnbull Library. Duncan Shaw-Brown turned images into digital files, and Tim Nolan prepared graphs and maps, which he revised and updated for the third edition. I am especially grateful to copyright holders for permission to reproduce material. They are acknowledged in the captions to the illustrations. Donna Hall and the late Benjamin Pittman supplied family photographs, and the late Jack Tait lent me his father's 'soldier' magazines. Photographers Paul Taylor and Kevin Peng generously provided images of the country's largest ever protest march. Special thanks are due to Shane Cotton and the Gow Langsford Gallery, in Auckland, for permission to reproduce Shane's striking painting *Ahuaiti's Cave* on the cover. Shane Cotton's artwork explores themes of biculturalism, Māori and Pākehā cultural history, collective identity, and life and death, themes that weave through this history.

Philippa Mein Smith
May 2025

PREFACE

It is a pleasure to introduce this history to readers who may know little about New Zealand other than that it is in the Southern Hemisphere, somewhere near Australia. Often people are surprised to find how far New Zealand is from Australia. They may know the country from film; sometimes from art, music or novels, sport, or business that takes them there; or from travel. Some are familiar with national brands, such as the All Blacks.

Local readers have their own expectations of how the country's history should be written. The narrative that they require is of equal relevance to the visitor. I wrote this concise history for my students; I also kept in mind friends overseas and people I met while travelling. The revisions for the third edition continue this pattern. Emphases reflect my understanding and interests; but they also indicate where gaps exist in histories of New Zealand. Certain themes, such as literature, are already covered elsewhere. This is not an alternative history so much as a broadening of the histories that have already been written.

Neither is this an isolated history; the aim is to place New Zealand history in global and Pacific contexts. This requires a comparative element, especially concerning interactions with Australia. Globalisation is a core theme of this book, first driven by the British Empire and now by China. One objective is to explore the persistent tension in New Zealand's short history between domestic politics and global and regional pressures and to examine the importance of the effects of smallness and remoteness. Health and social issues are central to this country's international reputation and continue to inform beliefs about national identity. Demographic contours are often ignored. Here population and defence issues are treated together, alongside economic problems that have consistently beleaguered a country dependent on exports. Māori–European engagements are pivotal, but their internal dynamics, prominent at home, need to be balanced alongside global trends.

My approach is to highlight themes that explain what happened. I try to unravel the ways in which key moments and episodes in New Zealand history contribute to the country's national myths. Such events include the Treaty of Waitangi signing and the Anzacs' landing at Gallipoli. There is more to history than war: sex (women and children, fertility) and money (economic history) drive societies. There is more to myth-making than war. Migrants know little of Anzac legends but often come here because of myths about New Zealand as a good place to bring up children, as an Arcadia, and as a social laboratory. Frequently the stuff of marketing exercises, it is often these New Zealand myths that people overseas first encounter. They therefore invite inquiry.

A NOTE ON NAMES

The name New Zealand derived from the European age of exploration. A Dutch cartographer labelled the archipelago 'Nova Zeelandia' after Abel Tasman's visit, and James Cook anglicised the name to New Zealand in the eighteenth century. Today, as communities decolonise, a growing number of New Zealanders associate this English name with colonisation by the British empire and the development of the nation state.

While New Zealand is the country's formal name, Aotearoa today is the commonly accepted Māori name. But Māori did not use this word for the whole country before Europeans turned up. In some traditions, Aotearoa was another term for the North Island. Pākehā writers who liked the word, and the story about the ancestral adventurer Kupe connected with it, were the agents who popularised 'Aotearoa' through the school system from the late 1890s, by ensuring children learnt that Aotearoa was the Māori name for New Zealand.

Naming exerts power and is fluid, as demonstrated by a familiar response in the South Island, where I live. The South Island is where Aotearoa is least likely to be accepted as a formal alternative name, not simply because of its origins, but since there is another Māori word for New Zealand: Nu Tireni, the transliteration in the Treaty of Waitangi. The issue of New Zealand's name is highly politicised; political parties on the right insist on 'New Zealand', centrist or left-of-centre parties use 'Aotearoa New Zealand', while the Māori Party advocates for an official name change to 'Aotearoa'. New Zealand money and passports use both names, only in the order 'New Zealand/Aotearoa'. 'Aotearoa New Zealand' represents what New Zealand is now, 'Aotearoa' what it is becoming, and both acknowledge Māori while recognising New Zealand's place and connections in the Pacific.

For these reasons the book cover features both names. This is important as a way of showing respect for Shane Cotton's remarkable painting. Throughout the text New Zealand is mostly used, as in previous editions, while Aotearoa appears until chapter 3, which addresses when the country was formally colonised, and reappears from chapter 10 as it decolonised. This choice to vary with context was a historical, not political decision. Politically my aim is to chart a respectful middle course while awaiting renewed debate on an official name change. I also sought to consider overseas readers who may recognise the name 'New Zealand' but not yet 'Aotearoa'.

1

Waka across a watery world

How and when did New Zealand Aotearoa begin? In human history the short answer is recently. New Zealand was the last major landmass settled by people, which is fundamental to understanding New Zealand's distinctiveness. Before humans arrived, birds and lizards were the dominant land animals. Archaeologists have agreed, after decades of debate, that the first humans arrived from the late thirteenth century, about 750 years ago. These adventurers undertook epic oceanic voyages in large, double-hulled waka hourua (voyaging canoes) from their legendary homeland of Hawaiki, in East Polynesia, southwards to the temperate region of 'South Polynesia', a term coined to encompass both New Zealand's main islands and its outlying islands. Today, the indigenous people trace their ancestors to over 40 celebrated waka (canoes). South Polynesia as a concept reminds us that New Zealand is a far-flung archipelago that stretches from Raoul Island, in the subtropical Kermadec group, to the subantarctic Auckland Islands, and to the Chatham Islands, which lie 800 kilometres to the east of the South Island. The three main islands – the North Island (Te Ika-a-Māui), South Island (Te Waipounamu), and Stewart Island (Rakiura) – account for almost 99 per cent of the land area of 270 000 square kilometres (see figure 1.1). South Polynesia distinguishes New Zealand from and links it to tropical Polynesia, connecting the indigenous people, the Māori, and the Moriori of the Chatham Islands, to their Pacific origins.

European migrants arrived very late indeed, establishing planned settlements (towns) only from 1840. The two waves of people from East Polynesia and Europe, principally Great Britain,

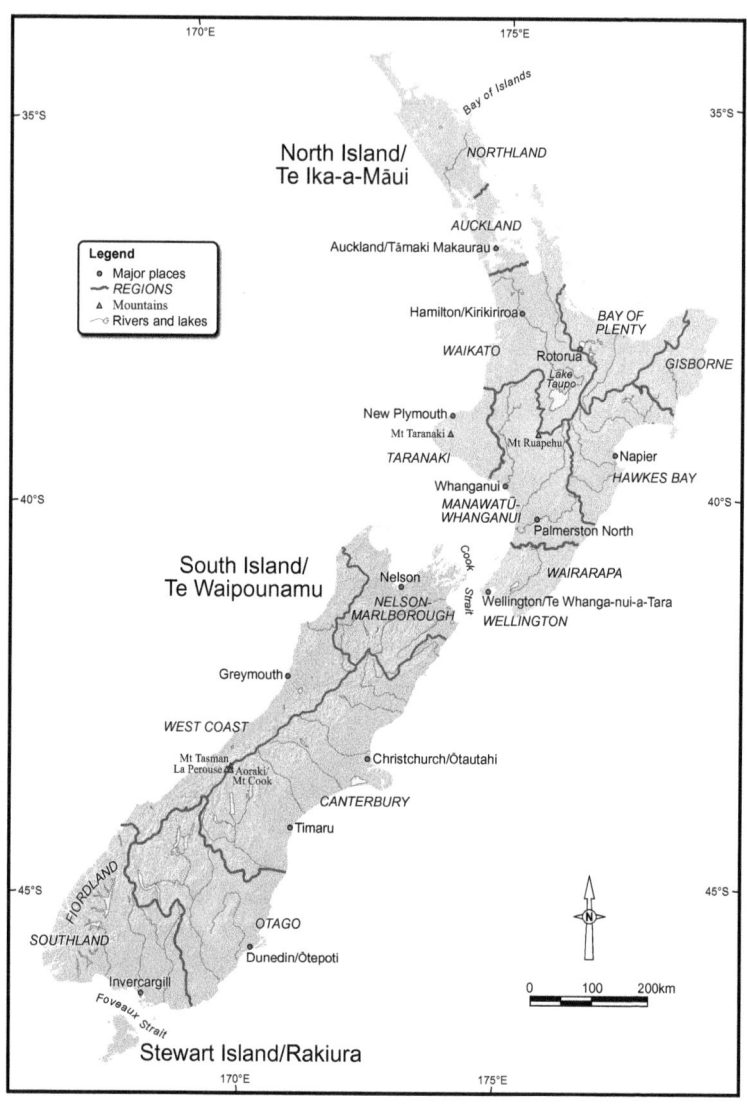

1.1 New Zealand: principal mountains, regions, and towns
Cartographer Tim Nolan

in a flash of time transformed the land and remade the landscapes. These simple facts of place and time help explain why the environment is so much associated with the nation's culture and identity.

TIME BEFORE HUMANS

Geology proffers a different answer to the questions of how and when New Zealand began. Scientists discovered recently that New Zealand's islands sit atop a drowned continent, which they finished mapping in 2023 and named Zealandia (figure 1.2). Today, only c. 5 per cent of this mysterious, submerged continent is above water. New Zealand is the largest part and New Caledonia the second largest piece of Zealandia currently above sea level. Shaped by tectonic activity, Zealandia is half the size of Australia. Its Māori name is Te Riu-a-Māui, or the hills, valleys, and plains of Māui, in honour of the mischievous cultural hero who stars in Pacific stories and genealogies.

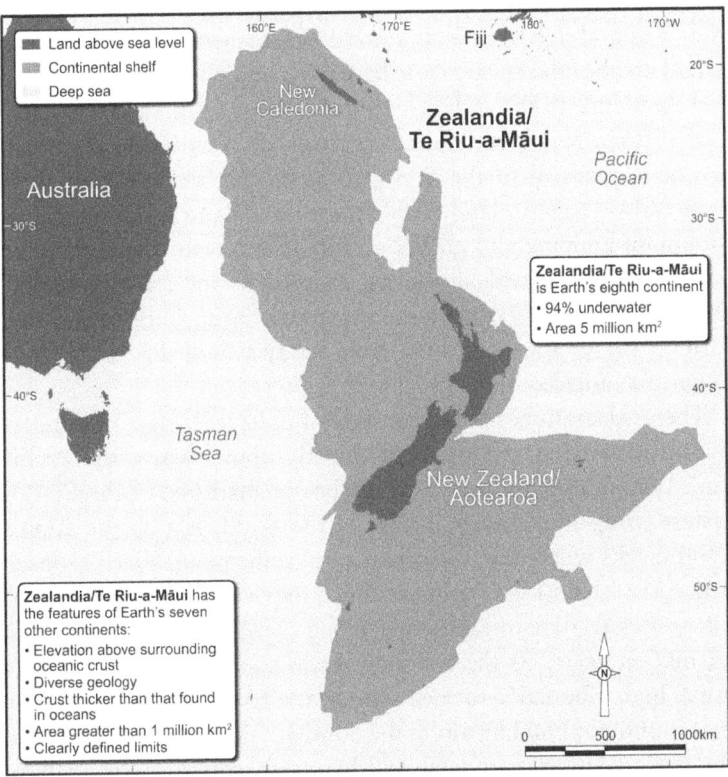

1.2 Zealandia: the sunken eighth continent
Cartographer Tim Nolan

Zealandia broke away from the southern continent of Gondwana (and thus from Australia) between 60 and 100 million years ago, stretching and thinning as it did so. It also rifted from Antarctica. In part, Zealandia's separation from Gondwana was driven by volcanic activity between the two landmasses that thrust Zealandia into the future Tasman Sea. Once isolated by ocean, ancestral New Zealand slowly sank. By 25 million years ago it was mostly under water. Dinosaurs lived on the chain of small islands that remained above sea level, as did crocodiles, frogs, and the three-eyed reptile the tuatara. Geologists were surprised to discover that Zealandia is over a billion years old and big enough to warrant acknowledgement as the Earth's eighth continent.

The mountains which are part of the nation's identity thrust upwards millions of years later, and various parts of the future New Zealand shifted around, moved by plate tectonics as the continental crust of the Pacific Plate began to collide with the Australian Plate underneath the archipelago from about 25 million years ago. Gondwanan rocks, the oldest segments of New Zealand's crust, are now confined to the West Coast of the South Island, from west Nelson to Fiordland. While the South Island evolved through mountain building and glacial activity, the North Island acquired its contours from volcanoes that erupted as the crust crumpled. Exceptions are the extinct large volcanoes in the South Island that formed the Otago Peninsula, near today's Dunedin, and Banks Peninsula, adjacent to Christchurch.

The land continues to be in a state of upheaval. New Zealanders live in a dynamic environment directly above where the Pacific and Australian plates meet, which has created one of the Earth's fastest rising mountain systems. In the South Island, the Alpine Fault marks where the Australian and Pacific plates slide past each other; the island's two segments have moved by an estimated 500 kilometres relative to each other along the Alpine Fault in the last 25 million years. As the colliding plates squeezed New Zealand's crust, high mountains formed right at the coast. Geologists believe that mountain building along the Southern Alps has accelerated in the last 5 million years, matched by rapid erosion. As recently as 1991, the distinctive tip of New Zealand's highest peak, Mount Cook – increasingly known by its Māori name of Aoraki (cloud piercer) – tumbled into the Tasman Glacier below. (It was officially renamed Aoraki Mount Cook in statute in 1998.)

So much for the certainty imparted to schoolchildren that Mount Cook stood at 12 349 feet before metric replaced imperial measures in the 1960s. Even the phrase 'solid as rock' calls for scepticism when a national icon, a towering environmental landmark, is shortened by 10.5 metres (to its current elevation of 3724 metres) in an avalanche. Site and self are shaken: the summit shifts, and with it the vista, the imaginary, that which is sacred.

Because of this seismic history, New Zealand is no ancient Gondwanan ark. Certainly, it was a Gondwanan fragment, at least in the west and south of the South Island, its forests populated by podocarps under whose forebears dinosaurs sought shelter. But the land itself is a dynamic force, anything but solid and permanent, such as when it sank in the Oligocene before the mountains thrust skywards. Pollen records suggest that almost all New Zealand's flora arrived after Zealandia had drifted off into isolation. The native flora resulted from recolonisation after the breakup of Gondwana, which suggests a pattern of plant dispersal from Australia followed by adaptation to local ecological and climatic conditions, and by extinction for some plants. Botanists have found that Tasmania and New Zealand share 200 plant species, while the case of the *Nothofagus* beech, which has Gondwanan origins, can be explained by long-distance dispersal (it is also found in Chile). The origins of the beech tree remain contested. New Zealand kauri (*Agathis australis*, a forest tree), which can live for 2000 years, originated in Antarctica. Many animals were recent migrants, too, and are migratory; for example, seabirds such as the white-faced heron and the royal spoonbill flew from Australia across the Tasman Sea, both by the 1940s.

Palaeontologists have questioned how New Zealand's fauna thrived in isolation for about 85–100 million years, and why that fauna proved so vulnerable to humans. Before people arrived, New Zealand was distinctive for its birds, many uniquely large, naive, and flightless, that occupied ecological niches filled by mammals elsewhere. Prominent among them were the kiwi, which the country adopted as an informal national symbol in the twentieth century, and nine species of moa, whose fossils have fascinated

Europeans since they first discovered them, in the 1840s. As for who, or what, killed the moa, which ranged from the size of a turkey to over 3 metres in height, naturalists in the nineteenth century thought that people did. By the 1950s the accepted view was that climate change had rendered the moa and other flightless birds extinct before the first people arrived. Today, zoologists consider that the continental focus of Northern Hemisphere–trained scientists overrode the initial insights into the disappearance of island faunas. In their view, about half of New Zealand's post-glacial bird species became extinct after humans disturbed their environment. That is, predators were responsible: the first people and the rats that accompanied them in their voyaging waka. Recent research by archaeologists suggests that moa became extinct rapidly: within 100 years of human arrival. Having hunted down the big game, the people had to adapt their ways of living and their diet to include more fish and marine mammals, such as fur seals, sea lions, and elephant seals. By adapting, they became New Zealand Māori.

NAVIGATORS UNDER THE SOUTHERN CROSS

As mentioned at the start of this chapter, the tangata whenua (people of the land, a concept with maritime kin connections throughout the Pacific) are descended from East Polynesian adventurers who voyaged to New Zealand in double-hulled ocean-going waka, which they navigated without instruments. Polynesian captains had to be charismatic leaders to take people with them and resilient and experienced in reading environmental cues to reach Aotearoa, in the South Pacific. Navigators followed the paths of migratory land-based birds, observed the currents and lapa (the underwater phosphorescence that appeared as flashes or streaks of light 50–130 kilometres from land), and sailed towards the clouds that appeared stationary above islands far ahead (hence the meaning of Aotearoa: the long white cloud). The Southern Cross constellation was their guide south of the Equator, and they voyaged southwards in the summer, when the winds grew favourable by turning easterly and the red-flowered pōhutukawa (the New Zealand Christmas tree) was in bloom. Sailing along a narrow corridor of stars, they took their main direction from Venus, with the Southern Cross to the port side, always pointing to Aotearoa. According to one story, the navigator of the Te Arawa canoe (from which the tribe Te Arawa takes its name) 'understood the language of the stars, the children of the lord of light, Tane-nui-a-rangi; he conversed with the moon, Hinauri; and he kept the prow of Te Arawa pointed in a direction that was a little to the left of the setting sun'.

Over the following centuries, generations passed down stories of dangerous voyages from the ancestral homeland of Hawaiki, and of arrival, dispersal, and settlement in these southern islands. To establish their authority over the land, the first settlers 'brought with them the intellectual order, the mental maps, of the Polynesian world', peopling the spiritual fabric of the new land and seas with their names, gods, and creation stories. Historian Te Maire Tau elaborates: first a priest secured the land so it was pervaded by 'the spirit of his god and ancestors', and then the people 'went about establishing the "mental world" for the people to live within, by planting their atua and ancestors upon the landscape'.

The North Island, the first landing place, they named Te Ika-a-Māui after a myth from East Polynesia in which the mythic ancestor Māui fished up islands. In the New Zealand version, Māui stood on the South Island and hooked a great fish, which the sun turned solid, as the North Island. The eye of the fish is Lake Taupo and the tail is Northland (see figure 1.1). The first people gave the South Island the Māori name Te Waipounamu (waters of greenstone) to recognise the value of the nephrite jade found in West Coast rivers, which artists carved into tools such as fine chisels, as well as weapons and ornaments. Sometimes the South Island is Te Waka o Māui (the canoe of Māui), while people who migrated to the South Island seeded it with ancestors, naming it Te Waka o Aoraki (the canoe of Aoraki), after their ancestor who is the highest mountain. The first settlers would not have used the name Aotearoa for New Zealand, because they had no word for the whole country. Instead, they gave names to islands, with Aotearoa originally becoming another name for the North Island.

The first voyagers from the Pacific were boat people, a role and experience with which subsequent European migrants could identify. Undoubtedly their bold sailing ventures were deliberate. But the feats of migration, ocean navigation, and settlement from East Polynesia continue to generate scholarly debate about precisely when, how, and from where the first navigators arrived.

Anthropologists currently surmise that the first people settled New Zealand from around 1280 to 1300. Another hypothesis proposes a time span of 1250–75 for initial settlement in the North Island and 1280–95 for the South Island. According to archaeologists, there is no evidence of human habitation before about 1250. Subsequently New Zealand Polynesians migrated to the Chatham Islands in the sixteenth century, later than previously thought, and they established there the Moriori culture and society.

The first settlers' name for their homeland, Hawaiki, probably referred to the Marquesas or Society Islands and perhaps to the southern Cook Islands, where a beach on Rarotonga is signposted as a departure point. Research has shown these people were descended from Austronesians whose ancestors were from China and who had sailed from Southeast Asia into the Pacific Ocean. Like other East Polynesians, these first New Zealanders were more directly the descendants of central Pacific Lapita people, who were agriculturalists and maritime traders. An 'ancestral genetic trail' can be traced from China and Southeast Asia to New Guinea, West Polynesia, and to the central and eastern Pacific islands. Atholl Anderson argues that Polynesian culture developed in West Polynesia before voyagers sailed to East Polynesia, and thus Hawaiki, but finds the evidence 'inconclusive' that East Polynesians reached South America. Voyages southwards to the cold and treacherous waters around New Zealand completed this remarkable oceanic exploration.

Anthropologists in the decade to 2025 advanced a radical new model for the settlement of East Polynesia which suggests that this oceanic dispersal was more rapid and recent than previously recognised. According to this model, Easter Island and even Hawaii were colonised 'in one major pulse' at about the same time as New Zealand. Based on high-precision radiocarbon dating, the model suggests that the colonisation of East Polynesia occurred in two phases: first out of West Polynesia to the Society Islands around 1025 to 1120; and second in one 'pulse' to the remote islands, including New Zealand. The significance for Polynesian voyages southwards is that these then occurred alongside – not after – migration northwards and eastwards across the Pacific. A shorter chronology of this sort may explain the uniformities found in East Polynesian culture and language and compels a rethink of human impacts on rapid environmental change in the islands.

There are several possible reasons for New Zealand's late settlement. If Pacific colonisation occurred in one 'pulse', possibly in a mass-migration event, then people may have been driven to leave their home islands by a catastrophe, whether famine, climate change, or drought, or by an environmental disaster, such as a major earthquake or volcanic eruption. A sense of adventure would not have sufficed. Traditional stories also tell of family conflict. Those who left demonstrated that they possessed the skills necessary for oceanic migration: familiarity with maritime technology in the form of the double-hulled or dugout canoes stabilised by outriggers and with a lateen sail that allowed long-distance travel across the Pacific; and expertise in agriculture, the use of crops, and domesticated animals. Whether their urge to migrate was religious, entrepreneurial, or desperate, and motivated by scarcity or calamity, it took more than technological innovation for Māori ancestors to navigate such a vast watery world (see figure 1.3).

TRADITIONAL STORIES

Oral traditions are mythic narratives, not historical texts, whose purposes are to give meaning and validate a family's claims to knowledge. Which ancestor a storyteller chooses to emphasise depends on the story's objective and which ancestor's life or exploits place the family and the storyteller in the best light. Stories of return voyaging by ancestral heroes are not factual; they refer metaphorically to constellations of stars as canoes crossing the heavens, which descendants greet in the present when they see the ancestral canoe appear to travel across the sky before them. Western history, on the other hand, requires evidence, and the absence of archaeological evidence in tropical East Polynesia in

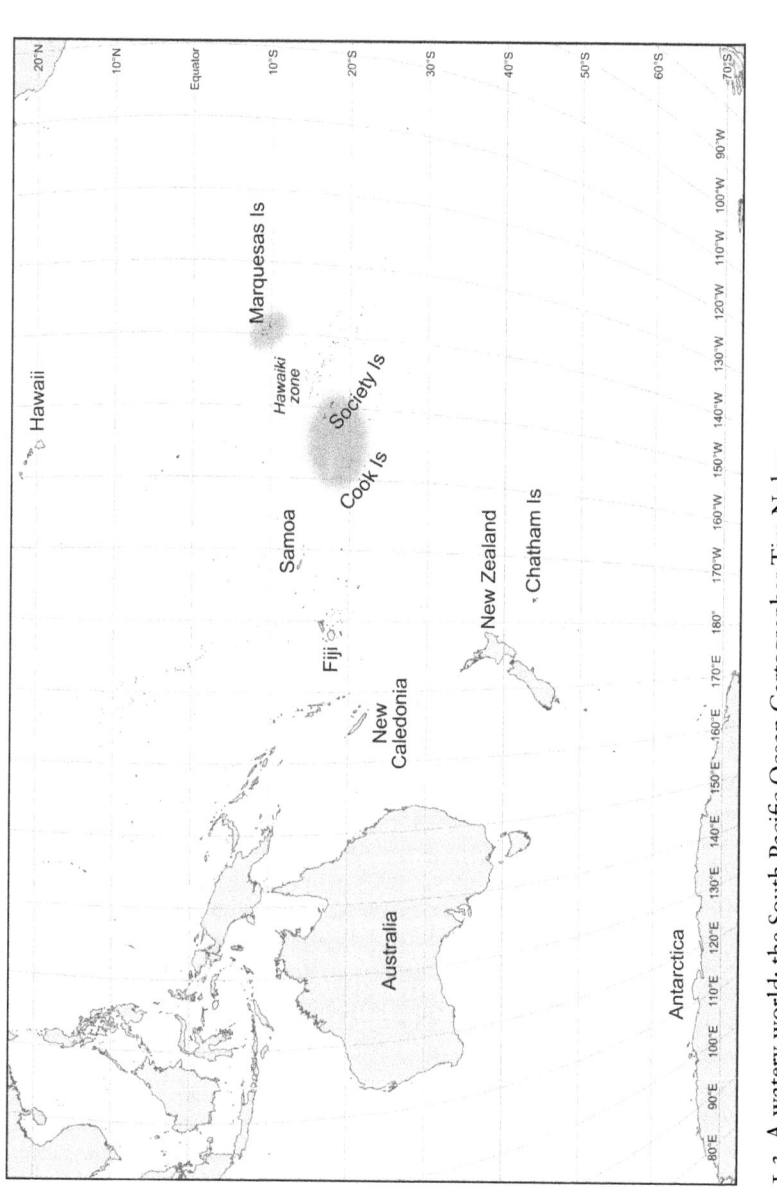

1.3 A watery world: the South Pacific Ocean Cartographer Tim Nolan

the form of stone implements brought back from South Polynesia suggests there was no successful return voyaging. Possibly this is because New Zealand's first colonists established a viable population. One intriguing question is whether and when there was mass migration. Another question, yet to be answered, is when the last of the migrant voyagers arrived.

Despite differences of detail, there are striking consistencies in oral traditions across East Polynesia, which a pattern of late Pacific migration and settlement may explain. For example, the tangata whenua's world was determined by whakapapa (genealogy), which they used to interpret and interact with their landscape. Whakapapa ordered space and time differently from European models and bound the living with the dead, as Te Maire Tau, historian of the South Island tribe Ngāi Tahu, outlines,

If whakapapa was the backbone, oral traditions, chants, wananga [knowledge], incantations and other arts could attach themselves as the flesh to the skeletal structure of genealogy. Thus, the earth (Papatuanuku) and sky (Raki) were understood as the original parents of humankind, with the sea, flora, fauna and other elements of the natural world connected by a web of kinship.

Oral traditions explained kin relationships with the land and nature in particular cultural contexts, which evolved with the generations. A problem for Te Maire Tau's tribe in the present is that people immersed in the 'old' world view know that traditions are not irrefutable accounts of actual historical events, or forever unchanged, whereas new entrants returning to the tribe want traditions to affirm their discovery of indigenous identity. Indigenous knowledge can be applied most effectively in its local context, in terms of knowing the environment – for example, learning how and when to catch eels or birds.

Waka traditions were not just origin stories but prescribed boundary markers of identity, proprietorship, and kin networks. Stories of origin, settlement, and exploration contained familiar role models from Polynesian mythology, whose exploits set the pattern for people to follow. They did not distinguish between the supernatural and the human, between the earliest ancestral 'gods' and later 'heroes', because all were remembered as tūpuna (ancestors) who, while invisible, continued to walk alongside people in the present. Polynesians carried their stories with them, peopling each island with their own genealogy to establish a cosmological and social order. Laid as a mental map across the land, whakapapa acted as a cultural marker, so that the land also became the people's ancestor.

The landing places of canoes helped to establish people's authority in a region. Claiming the land began with naming, and the people planted 'archetypal images' from mythology across the landscape and became tangata whenua in the process. The interaction of tradition and landmark reinforced their beliefs. While myths explained the presence of a landmark, the existence of a landmark associated with a story of waka migration would be invoked to confirm that story's truth.

Ancestral stories evolved as narrators adapted them to fit their new environments and to record local landmarks as they travelled. Accounts across Polynesia shared the names of Hawaiki and of important figures – for example, Māui, the navigator who fished up islands. Names acquired new meanings as traditions shifted and stretched to cover diverse landscapes, as Ngāi Tahu authority Sir Tipene O'Regan elaborated: 'Each time we voyaged onwards we rolled up our legends, our whakapapa and our place names, and carried them with us to be unrolled in a new place and fitted to a new landscape'.

The ancestors were both women and men in waka traditions, indicative of pioneering voyages. As historical narratives expanded to include women in the late twentieth century, historians of gender grew conscious that male narrators of stories – Māori and Pākehā (European New Zealanders) – selected masculine heroes and captains by preference. Traditional stories cast women as helpmeets associated with the natural world, such as when they brought fire and planted kumara (sweet potato). Alternatively, waka women unleashed disaster and violence.

Traditions of his Ngāti Porou people collected by Sir Āpirana Ngata, the pre-eminent twentieth-century Māori leader, relate how their ancestor Māui fished the North Island out of the ocean, naming it Te Ika-a-Māui. Kupe is remembered as a founding ancestor in the west of the North Island, and Toi, another seafarer, in the east. In Te Arawa traditions from around Rotorua, Toi was an ancestor living in Hawaiki before the mariner Tama Te Kapua and Tama's people sailed to New Zealand. In other traditions, Toi lived in New Zealand and was associated with fetching kumara from Hawaiki. He is also known in Rarotonga.

All stories about Paikea, the founding ancestor of the North Island's East Coast tribes, have in common that he travelled to New Zealand on the back of a whale. In the most accepted version of the story, a vessel set sail from Hawaiki with 70 sons of chiefs on board, only to be deceived by the paramount chief's younger son Ruatapu, who avenged an insult from his father by boring a hole in the hull to try to kill his brother Paikea. When the vessel overturned, only Ruatapu and Paikea did not drown. Paikea survived by invoking his heritage as the 'son of the sea', and over generations the metaphor of his summoning the sea to 'lift him "as a great fish" to shore' became a whale that bore him through the surf. Eventually Paikea reached home and later migrated to New Zealand. Most recently the story of the whale rider has been retold by the writer Witi Ihimaera, who is from the East Coast, in his novel *Whale Rider*, and in a subsequent internationally acclaimed film.

A EUROPEAN SEARCH FOR ORIGINS

Problematically, because they were imperialists and typical human beings, Europeans imposed their frameworks on traditional Māori stories. Not only did they rename physical features, but they reclassified Pacific peoples as Polynesians (meaning 'of many islands') and Melanesians and ordered them into hierarchies based on skin colour. According to this racial template New Zealand's (brown) Polynesians ranked more highly than (black) Melanesians and were judged as superior to Indigenous Australians, who were relegated to the bottom of the scale. Ethnographers also found power-holding arrangements less obscure among Polynesians, including Māori, whose entrepreneurial qualities and status awareness European researchers understood.

Europeans developed their own myths about Māori origins that melded diverse stories into tidy legends. Influenced by Bible stories about Noah as a righteous human ancestor, nineteenth-century missionaries preached that the 'New Zealand race' was 'one of the lost tribes of Israel', an idea taken up by the Mormons and by Māori prophet movements. The model of the Aryan Polynesian and, locally, the Aryan Māori gained common currency in the nineteenth century as Pacific scholars sought clues about human origins. With the rise of Darwinism, the concept of Caucasian Māori or Māori of European origin replaced the biblical idea of Semitic Māori. Edward Tregear, a surveyor and public servant, claimed in 1885, in his book *The Aryan Maori*, that Māori and European shared an Aryan origin, an idea that persisted into the twentieth century because it augmented beliefs associated with the eugenics movement.

In 1938 Te Rangi Hiroa (Sir Peter Buck), then Director of the Bishop Museum in Honolulu, published his popular work *Vikings of the Sunrise*. A Māori account of Polynesian settlement written according to the principles of Western scholarship, *Vikings of the Sunrise* brought to the world's attention that the first voyagers to New Zealand, Tonga, and other Pacific islands were among the greatest of all oceanic seafarers. Buck portrayed Polynesian navigators as Pacific Vikings for three reasons: he was Māori, a medical graduate, and a professional anthropologist who lived in two worlds. Likewise the idea of shared origins in human antiquity increased the mana (prestige) of Māori as well as Europeans and usefully complemented New Zealand's distinctive identity as 'Māoriland'. A popular alternative name for the country in the late nineteenth and early twentieth centuries, this rendered New Zealand exotic.

ENVIRONMENT TRANSFORMED

The 'cultural habits of humanity' have always made room for environmentalism or the 'sacredness of nature', and so it is with Māori. During the process of settling claims for redress by iwi (tribes) in the 1980s for past losses because of British colonisation, the Waitangi Tribunal (which from 1985 onwards heard historical grievances back to 1840) suggested that Māori were more ecologically minded than Pākehā and had suffered for that outlook. Tangata whenua saw themselves as part of their environment, not dominating or subduing it; they were its guardians who held resources in trust as taonga (treasures) for future generations. They had to guard and protect the land, lakes, rivers, and sea as gifts from their ancestors. The tribunal stated in 1985,

> Although there is some opinion that the Maori did not come to a full environmental awareness until several generations after his arrival in Aotearoa, it also seems clear that the Maori brought with him a magico-religious world view of the environment that readily lent itself to the conservation of the earth's natural resources.

The tribunal was 'introduced to rules' about how Māori used the sea and land; it was 'told how local tribes taught a respect for the sea' such that Māori treated the sea as a farm, whereas Pākehā cast their waste into it. The people had to be conservationists to survive. Accepting that species were depleted by overuse or accident before Europeans arrived, the Waitangi Tribunal nevertheless concluded that the scale was minor compared to environmental change since European colonisation, from 1840.

Ecologists project a different view. They have portrayed the first Polynesian settlers not as environmentalists but as humans who generated anthropogenic impacts and exploited nature's bounty to survive, who exterminated the moa and decimated marine life before they intensified food production. Ecologically, the late settlement of New Zealand presents a case study of how humans plundered their environment, its flora and fauna, until they learnt to reach an accommodation with it. Australia provides the contrast of people reconciled to their land and ecosystems, because Aboriginal Australians have lived there for at least 60 000 years. In this interpretation, New Zealand's first settlers were 'optimal foragers' who initially hunted moa and seals because these activities required the least effort for the greatest return.

Similarly, evolutionary biologists have attributed Eurasia's global dominance to environments favourable to technological advances. Environmental variables determined that people could continue to practise horticulture as 'hunter-gardeners' and warriors in New Zealand. Other environments shaped a different future; the Moriori of the Chatham Islands, for example, were constrained by the cold to being hunter-gatherers.

Palaeobiologists have concluded that 'the New Zealand avifauna has been decimated by introduced mammalian predators, including people'. After surviving glacial–interglacial cycles, ecosystems vanished 'in a geologic instant, after humans arrived'. Key agents in the extinction of indigenous fauna were 12 species of predators foreign to New Zealand's ecosystem as well as the humans who brought them. In this theory, the Pacific rat came with the first Polynesian settlers and their dogs from the Cook Islands and Society Islands; the rest arrived after Captain James Cook's first visit, in 1769. While Europeans brought the most animal predators, Māori precipitated most extinctions of native birds and animals before that. New Zealand therefore serves as a model of how predators acted as agents of extinction on islands.

There is general agreement that the first East Polynesian settlers were primarily responsible for the extinction of the moa within 100 years or so of human settlement by overkilling and destruction of habitat. Radiocarbon dating of moa eggs, too, strongly suggests that Māori ancestors first arrived by 1300. Humans also precipitated the disappearance of 40 per cent of the forest cover by fire after 1300, whether deliberately or unintentionally, and the extinction of perhaps half the animals, before Europeans in turn transformed the landscape. Forests in Aotearoa lacked resistance to fire, and climate change could have contributed to deforestation. But fern and tussock thrived with firing, so human intrusion to ensnare moa, for example, led to forest loss and erosion, especially in the east of the South Island where open forests gave way to tussock grassland. In the North Island, fire from swidden agriculture transformed the landscape, as fern and scrub replaced the forest cover, offering more scope for harvesting bracken fern root and for kumara gardens.

Over time the climate grew harsher. Probably the wind and the weather restricted the initial choice of settlements to a few coastal districts. Patterns of archaeological sites suggest that people were initially drawn to the leeward zone, in the southern North Island and eastern half of the South Island, with its more open landscape, big game, and easier foraging. Once human-induced changes to the environment forced people to adapt, settlements shifted to the windward, likely reinforced by cooler temperatures in the seventeenth century. Continued migrations reversed the pattern, with late migrations into the eastern North Island, first into Hawkes Bay and the Wairarapa, then into Wellington and across to the South Island. By about the late sixteenth century some Ngāti Mamoe people had begun to settle in the South Island. Ngāti Kahungunu moved into the Wairarapa soon after, motivating other groups to cross Cook Strait. Probably at this time the population in general felt pressure on land and resources. After several migrations Ngāi Tahu consolidated as an iwi in the South Island in the nineteenth century, to combat threats from the north. These migrations were continuing as Europeans arrived.

CREATING AN INDIGENOUS CULTURE

Who Māori were before they encountered Europe is not the same as who Māori were in the nineteenth or twentieth century. The term 'Māori' entered general use in the 1860s, to distinguish 'ordinary people', as Māori saw themselves, from the European, mainly British, newcomers, at the very moment when the first people's descendants found themselves outnumbered by Europeans. One problem with history as a discipline is that it begins not just with human societies but with the written record, so that people who possess an oral culture become people without a history. Risk attaches to any attempt to transcribe knowledge transmitted orally, as happened with waka traditions. Consequently, the pre-European Māori past was frozen in time. Schooling imparted constructs of *The Maori as He Was* (ethnographer Elsdon Best's 1934 book) reminiscent of the dying Māori as a museum artefact, not Māori as adaptive, resilient, stubborn survivors, even if Europeans respected the indigenous people as warriors, entrepreneurs, and agriculturalists.

A historical best guess is that it took generations for the first people to learn what effort would yield the best return in a seasonal environment with a variable climate, and to develop conservation practices in areas where the climate and environment constrained horticulture. In Aotearoa they found the largest and coldest land in Polynesia, much more diverse than the small tropical islands of their ancestors, with unpredictable seasonal extremes that stretched adaptability to the limit. Aotearoa proved a graveyard instead of a garden for the standard Polynesian foods of coconut, breadfruit, and bananas. Cycles of abundance and dearth demanded inventiveness in adapting tropical agriculture to a temperate climate. Kumara grew no further south than Banks Peninsula, on the South Island's east coast, and became economically prominent only in the north, where in turn taro and yam only just tolerated the climate.

Kumara became the staple, as in Hawaii, because of adaptations in technique. Originally from Peru, this sweet potato could have been the key to successful settlement when imported tropical foods failed and large game such as moa and sea lions disappeared. The people who became Māori developed unique food-storage methods, building insulated underground storage pits to provide kumara for winter meals and for seed tubers to plant in spring. They also warmed the soil to grow kumara by adding gravel, planting the sweet potato under stones covered with soot to absorb the heat. Fish, sea lettuce, and wild plants and fruits such as karaka berries were dried and stored, and fish and birds were caught young, when they were plump, and stored in their fat to carry the people through seasonal cycles.

There was much regional variation because of New Zealand's size and diversity. Gardening was a communal activity in which the women planted, weeded, fetched, and carried, while the men dug the ground. Where the climate did not allow extensive cultivation, such as in the south, the people transformed what were famine foods elsewhere in Polynesia into staples – notably, fern root. Bitter, even toxic, plants became 'festive fare' in 'a remarkable example of "added value"', using methods of prolonged cooking and soaking that were practised across the Pacific. Southern Māori carried out seasonal harvesting of fish, birds, seals, and rats, as well as plants and their fruits, stems, and roots. Different groups exchanged foods, such as muttonbirds (sooty shearwaters) from the southern South Island and offshore islands for a dish made from the head of the ti-kōuka (*Cordyline australis*, cabbage tree) and different types of seafood. Throughout New Zealand fish and shellfish formed a major part of the diet and fishing a key part of the economy. In the North Island shellfish and crayfish were especially important.

Part of becoming Māori entailed applying Polynesian crafts to local resources. Women worked the native flax. They selected special shells to scrape the tough flax leaves and wove the strands into mats and intricate cloaks for clothing and to cover floors of houses; they also wove baskets, thatch for roofs, rope, and netting. Fibre fishing nets could be 1.5–3.0 kilometres long. Men built houses and canoes. The land was abundant in tall timber, such as totara and kauri in Northland, ideal for hollowing out logs to build single-hulled canoes. The waka made in New Zealand were long, narrow, and fast, designed for river and coastal travel rather than epic oceanic voyages.

By about 1500 the leading features of Māori culture and society were established. At their core were concepts of collective identity with descent as the primary bond, in which membership of an iwi or hapū (subtribe) derived from direct descent from a founding ancestor. The dynamic culture that evolved mapped territorial boundaries as the population grew, fostering concepts of land ownership and defence. Geographical features such as rivers and mountains, distinctive rock formations, or even trees served as boundary markers. The whole of New Zealand became known and explored, bringing new encounters, such as with wild rivers and snow. On the West Coast of the South Island, explorers discovered pounamu (greenstone), which became a treasured item of trade.

From the early sixteenth century, settlements centred on elaborate pā (fortified villages or forts), which were symptomatic of sporadic warfare, except in the lower half of the South Island, where members of the sparse population were mainly hunter-gatherers. Pā became a distinguishing feature of New Zealand, possibly because the building of pā was associated with developing notions of resource conservation; it became more difficult to feed on flesh or fat because of their scarcity. One estimate is that Māori built 6500 pā between 1500 and Captain Cook's first visit, in 1769. With food storage, the evolving warrior culture grew more specialised. A stratified society saw a flowering of art, especially wood carving, and public buildings, such as marae.

Māori created a competitive society in which iwi contended among themselves, each community held together by land and kinship and by clusters of values that elevated obligations to kin above all else. While Māori developed into fiercely competitive groups with a warrior class and culture, a splinter group, Moriori, found its way from the South Island to the Chatham Islands in about 1500. This youngest group of East Polynesians gathered food in autumn and summer to preserve for the cold months. The harsh environment limited their food resources and shaped a simplified material culture whose efficiency (like that of Indigenous Australians) both Pākehā and Māori misunderstood. In contrast to Māori, Moriori adapted to be nonviolent, sedentary hunter-gatherers who lived amid their key resource, the fur seal, which they supplemented with shellfish, fish, birds, and fern root. These peaceful people were enslaved and butchered by displaced Taranaki Māori in 1835, who caught a ride to the Chatham Islands on a European brig which was based at Sydney.

Despite such differences of environment and climate, the first people spoke one language, although there were minor variations of dialect, and so people from alien territories could communicate with one another. Importantly, one language eventually made it easier for tangata whenua to converse with Europeans.

In the eighteenth century, people lived in hapū-based communities. As far as we know, Māori society centred on hapū before the challenges of European colonisation compelled larger groupings of iwi descended from a common ancestor. From the eighteenth century, political and demographic fortunes of descent groups fluctuated. Some tribes, such as Tainui, who had interests from the Waikato to Auckland and further north, and Te Arawa, who lived among the geysers and hot springs of the central North Island, stayed in the regions where their ancestral waka had landed. Elsewhere hapū responded to warfare with enemies by migrating to new territory. Generally younger sons and daughters were the ones who moved on. Intermarriage followed between migrants and tangata whenua, with an exchange of women by the highest-ranking men a standard practice during peace negotiations. The next generation inherited their mana over the people from the conquering group of superior warriors and mana over the land from the tangata whenua. Marriage alliances ensured mana over both the people and the land: equilibrium, and peace, required women as well as men.

2

Beachcrossers 1769–1839

So deep was Aotearoa in the watery world of the Pacific that it remained for a long time unknown to Europeans, other than as a part of the mythical great southern land, Terra Australis. Surely there had to be a continent in the South Pacific to balance the weight of land in the Northern Hemisphere? As it proved, there was not. New Zealand is immersed in the Pacific, surrounded by 2000 kilometres of ocean, a fact that is reflected in Māori waka (canoe) traditions. Only in the late eighteenth century did its full outline register in European consciousness through the process of physical discovery.

In 1500 no European had seen the world's largest ocean. Once they ventured into the Pacific, European sailors had great difficulty navigating its expanse, devoid as it was of landmarks other than scattered islands and numerous uncharted reefs, and unpredictable in its treacherous currents, winds, and weather. Geography and navigation remained uncertain. There were no reliable sea routes, other than within the narrow limits of latitude used by Spanish fleets from Acapulco in the Americas to Manila in Southeast Asia. For two centuries Europeans crisscrossed the Pacific Ocean along this track without charting the imagined southern continent.

The European history of New Zealand can be located within a second phase of imperial expansion. Nearly three centuries after the colonisation of the Americas, neo-Europes were transplanted in the Pacific to produce new nations and polities through colonialism. The delay in incorporating the South Pacific into European maps and power systems was significant. Spaniards, seeking Terra Australis from the late sixteenth century,

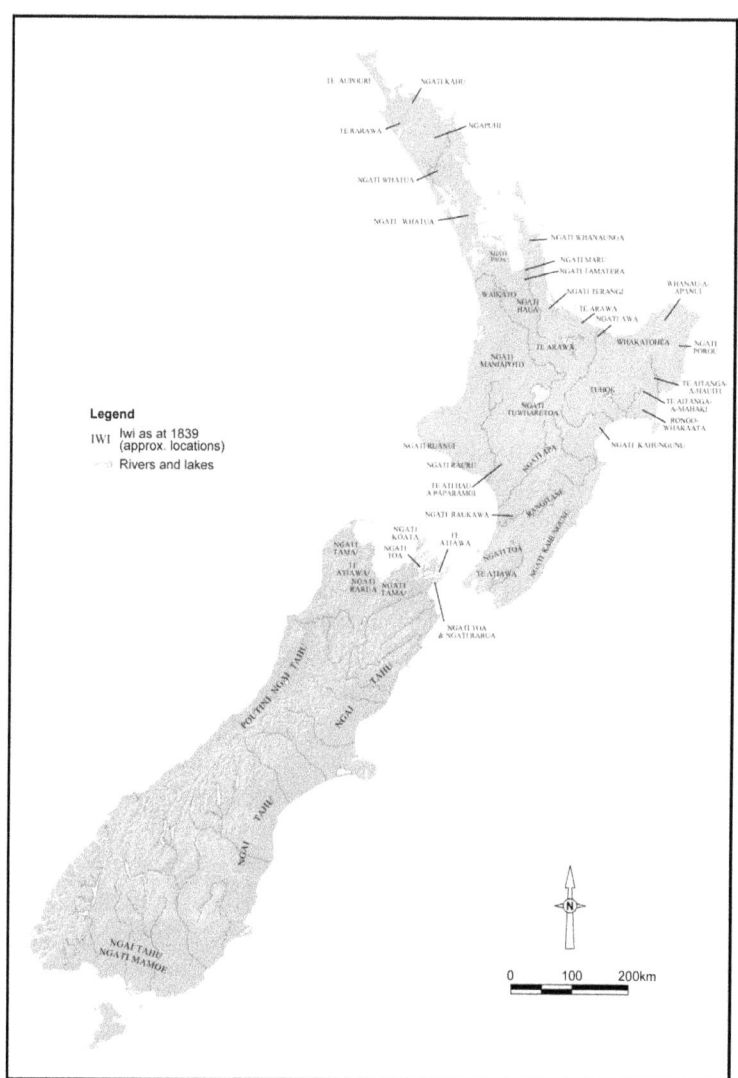

2.1 Locations of Māori tribes (iwi), c. 1839
Cartographer Tim Nolan

sailed through Torres Strait without identifying Australia. Their ventures sparked the belief that sailors from a lost Spanish caravel discovered New Zealand. Dutch explorers sought Terra Australis in the seventeenth century. Because of the inaccuracies in establishing coordinates – longitude as well as latitude – in navigation, numerous Dutch East India Company ships were wrecked along the Western Australian coast, far from their objective of Batavia (Jakarta). Only in 1642 did Abel Tasman head eastwards from Batavia to Tasmania, which he named Van Diemen's Land, and from there to New Zealand, named by Dutch authorities. Hence New Zealand acquired a Dutch name, and schoolchildren learnt to recite that in 1642 Abel Tasman 'sailed the ocean blue' and discovered New Zealand for Europe.

In one view, it was fortunate for Māori that they escaped a rapacious first era in European imperialism. Now Europe was obsessed less with conquest than with commerce. But New Zealand scholars argue that Māori were active in postponing their encounter with Europe (see figure 2.1 for Māori iwi (tribes) in 1839). In Tasman's experience, Māori controlled the first contact, and so – consistent with his instructions, which distinguished 'civilised' men from 'wild savages' – he constructed them not as the 'noble savage' but as violent. Tasman's whole object was to learn 'whether there is anything profitable to be got or effected', which is suggestive of the profit motive, central to capitalism. He decided the answer was no, interpreting the Māori challenge to fight as evidence that they were the 'opposite footers' who Europeans fancied ought to live in the Antipodes. Using speed and surprise, the local people of Golden Bay, where Tasman attempted to land, rammed a boat and killed four sailors, which prevented the Dutch from doing so. In response, the Dutch shot at least one Māori. It was this repulsion by the 'Southlanders' that entered European consciousness and prompted Tasman to name the site Murderers Bay. This story and subsequent tales rendered the Māori frightening to Europe.

CAPTAIN COOK

Explorers had to cross beaches to engage in encounters that involved talk with strangers. The concept of beach crossing implies that meetings were dangerous, volatile, and uncertain. Likewise, the foreshore, the stretch of beach between the low-tide and high-tide marks, is ever changing, unpredictable, and in flux.

Unlike Tasman, Captain James Cook crossed New Zealand beaches, literally and metaphorically, and in the process became New Zealand's Pākehā (European New Zealander) storybook ancestor. Like the Māori mythical ancestors Māui, Kupe, and Paikea, Cook was a great navigator, explorer, and supreme leader. This parallel made him a model for nation-building. But his Britishness made him infinitely more suitable than Tasman as a founding ancestor for a future British colony, and he has contributed enormously to the country's national myth-making. Lieutenant James Cook (as he was on his first visit) literally put New Zealand on the world map. A noted cartographer, he was the first person to chart its full outline.

Cook spent nearly a year exploring the coastline during his four stays in New Zealand. On his critical first voyage he and his men stayed for six months while he drew his famous chart, which is astonishingly accurate but for the sketch of Stewart Island as a peninsula and Banks Peninsula as an island, which may be blamed on stormy weather during which the *Endeavour* had to retreat out to sea (figure 2.2). His maps and journals recording the land's and the sea's resources in timber, flax, and sea life precipitated the process that led to British colonisation. The knowledge which he, the botanist Joseph Banks, and his ships' artists assembled still informs international scholarship and general understanding of what New Zealand was like in the eighteenth century.

Ostensibly subsequent British settlement, more than his voyages, determined that Cook would be esteemed as the founding ancestor, because settlement from Britain allowed New Zealanders (and Australians) to look back to the *Endeavour* voyage of 1769–70 as the opening chapter of their founding stories. Yet the timing of Cook's epic explorations rendered him a new type of hero for European expansion and Pacific imperialism in the late eighteenth century. Cook was an Enlightenment hero, making him an ideal model for the classroom; he was a Christian paragon of humble origins. A self-made man who represented a New World freedom to get on, he rose to fame through merit and promulgated a message of free trade, enlarged scientific knowledge, and civilised behaviour. As explorer and surveyor, he commanded new technologies and expanded the contemporary information age by publishing his

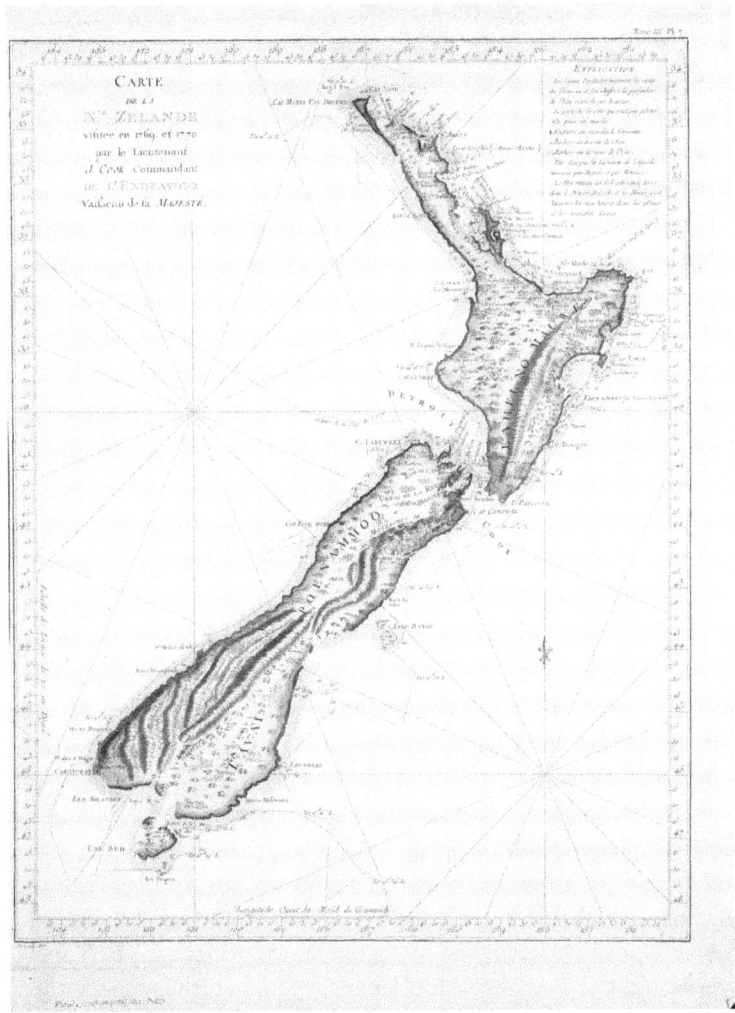

2.2 James Cook, *Carte de la Nle Zélande visitée en 1769 et 1770 par le lieutenant J. Cook commandant de l'Endeavour vaisseau de sa majesté*, 1774. The French version of Cook's chart Published by Saillant et Nyon, Paris. Alexander Turnbull Library, Wellington, 39323

journals. A plain man, he upgraded homely virtues to evoke professionalism and skill, just in time to become the 'new hero of free and civilised trading'. He embodied the parallel breakthroughs in

European printing and exploration, the innovation by a 'large class of mechanical tinkerers' that produced the 'European miracle' of economic development and made the British Empire. His voyages ensured that he did not just belong to New Zealand; he became Cook of Australia and, in Canada, Cook of Quebec and Cook of coastal British Columbia.

The 'humanist myth' of Cook as a product of the Enlightenment surprises some readers, since it is so prevalent in New Zealand. The foremost Cook scholars have been New Zealanders, among whom J. C. Beaglehole, editor of Cook's journals and his biographer, was his greatest panegyrist. Beaglehole's Cook was a 'man of action' who left nothing unattempted. He more than fulfilled his instructions, to observe the transit of Venus in Tahiti; to discover the southern continent; and, if that failed, to explore the coast of Tasman's New Zealand. 'He was the genius of the matter of fact', a 'profoundly competent' seaman, 'completely professional' as an explorer; but above all he was a navigator who discovered and mapped the country for Britain. He was also humanitarian. Aware that Cook was different on his third voyage – harsh, with outbursts of rage – Beaglehole attributed this conflicting evidence to a physical cause. Geography and navigation were his memorials. The Māori memory of Cook, he concluded, confirmed the view that Cook was a great man.

This viewpoint fits well with the belief that New Zealand set an example in relations with indigenous peoples. In fact, Cook owed his reputation to the Tahitian intermediary and beachcrosser Tupaia, a high priest and chief from the island of Raiatea who joined Cook's first voyage in Tahiti in 1769. Because of Tupaia, who could translate the Māori language and in turn be understood, some passengers aboard the *Endeavour* were able to speak with Māori, who Tupaia realised shared a source of origin with other Polynesians. On his first two voyages Cook received help to act as a man of the Enlightenment from Pacific Islanders who were themselves scholars, and Māori appeared to respect him as a leader.

Initially remembered as the consummate imperial explorer, memorialised in print and (in 1967) on the nation's first 50 cent coin, Cook became a white founding father and a hero for an increasingly bicultural New Zealand. Iwi stories of first meetings, positive or negative, focused on Cook; their ancestors had met Cook; his ships connected Māori and other Pacific Islanders to the European world and 'began the process of making the world a global village'. Captain Cook stories and places he named acquired significance for Māori as well as for Pākehā. One example, named for the cabin boy Nicholas Young, is Young Nick's Head, whose purchase by an American investor local iwi opposed in 2002, arguing that the headland was a historic site of national importance. In contrast to Indigenous Australians who tossed back goods, such as inedible ships' biscuits, Māori seized Cook's knowledge selectively, just as he and his passengers keenly observed Māori.

Until recently the most famous encounter of Māori with Cook was that of Horeta Te Taniwha. Every major New Zealand history used to cite the story of a small boy who was given a nail by Cook. A version written in 1888 recorded,

> There was one supreme man in that ship. We knew that he was the lord of the whole by his perfect gentlemanly and noble demeanour. He seldom spoke, but some of the goblins spoke much ... He was a very good man, and came to us – the children – and patted our cheeks, and gently touched our heads.

Critics of the humanist myth of Cook argue that this story cannot represent reality, if only because a missionary first recorded Te Taniwha's account in his extreme old age, more than 80 years after the event. Rather it signifies the triumph of a white over a subaltern voice. Some anthropologists argue that the story illustrates the European myth of the apotheosis of Captain Cook: Europeans needed Cook to be a god and so had him deified by Polynesians. Yet this story is an example of collaboration, as it contains evidence of Māori input and a Māori world view. Cook is certainly remembered as a paternalistic father figure. But it was not he but his ship the *Endeavour* that was described as a god. The 'supreme man' was perceived as a chief. Tellingly, his men were termed 'goblins'. Unlike gods, goblins could be tricked or overpowered; they could be less, not more, than human and therefore easy to manage or dupe. Such perceptions reduced the power and status of the newcomers, and the level of threat tangata whenua (people of the land) felt.

At times Cook did react violently to the bizarreness of contact and was disconcerted by Māori resistance, even in the face of European firepower. On his first visit, in 1769, he left without a sailor killed or wounded, while Māori suffered 10 men killed and many wounded. Nine deaths occurred during the first two days of the *Endeavour*'s landfall at today's Gisborne. Despite Tupaia's presence and Cook's professed peaceful intentions, the European visitors fired muskets and cannon at the slightest excuse, usually due to misunderstanding. Conversely, Māori were offended by European breaches of tapū (religious restrictions), which were believed calamitous.

With colonisation, however, the Enlightenment view gained ground. This has a simple explanation: Cook's triumphant first two voyages – especially the first, in 1769–70 – belong more to New Zealand history than his third, tragic voyage, during which his ships again anchored in Queen Charlotte Sound, in the Marlborough Sounds, in 1777. He died violently in Hawaii two years later, entangled in contradictions.

FRENCH EXPLORERS

A common French view is that Cook brought his fate upon himself through his violent behaviour. This perspective is unsurprising given that France was Britain's enemy until 1815 and a competitor for imperial dominance in the Pacific. French explorers have been neglected in New Zealand. British naming rights decided the hierarchy of the three highest peaks in the Southern Alps visible from the West Coast. These were named, in descending order by height, Cook, Tasman, and La Perouse, after the earliest European explorers to see them. While the first two are familiar to New Zealanders, the name La Perouse is not. Jean-François Galaup de La Pérouse sailed from France on a major Pacific voyage in 1785 and received instructions to report on the newly established British penal settlement at Sydney, which he did early in 1788. Then his two ships vanished. Another explorer, Antoine Bruni d'Entrecasteaux, searched for the lost expedition in the 1790s, tarrying in northern New Zealand in 1793 and finding nothing. The name La Perouse suggests that New Zealand's best memory of the French is of a vanishing act or, less cynically, that French explorers ranked third in importance after their British and Dutch competitors.

It is often forgotten that a French explorer entered New Zealand waters at the same time as Cook. On an unscheduled visit, Jean-François de Surville sought shelter because his crew were succumbing to scurvy; he sighted Northland in December 1769. By coincidence, Cook was sailing up the opposite coast at the same time. The *St Jean-Baptiste* sailed past the *Endeavour* in a gale without the knowledge of either, the British ship blown northwards while the French ship veered southwards.

The resultant encounter between Māori and de Surville's crew proved a negative experience for both sides. Angry that Māori removed a yawl washed up on the beach, in retaliation de Surville's men kidnapped a man who had been kind to crew suffering from scurvy and set fire to buildings. They also formed a more negative view of Māori women than did the English sailors, who had been influenced by earlier exposure to Tahiti. When privateer and explorer Marc-Joseph Marion du Fresne landed at the Bay of Islands in 1772 during his search for Terra Australis, past experience shaped the encounter on both sides. Du Fresne had already observed and formed negative assumptions about Tasmanian Aboriginals, and the local Māori had experience of Europeans with their guns.

Du Fresne's story has served as a parable for how cross-cultural misunderstanding led to violence. Although the Frenchman was a Māoriphile who made great efforts to befriend the tangata whenua, the chief Te Kauri killed him, because he violated a potent death tapū. People throughout Polynesia observed controlling restrictions to order their worlds. In du Fresne's case, he insulted the living and their ancestors by fishing at a tapū cove, where men had drowned. 'To catch these fish was bad enough, but to eat them was tantamount to cannibalism, an attack on the tapu of the corpses and that of their tribe, and on the mana of their tribal gods.' So – like Cook in Hawaii – du Fresne was killed and eaten, to consume his life force and his mana. Thus overpowered, he could not be celebrated in Māori or European narratives. Rather, histories have tended to imply that, as a Frenchman, he deserved his punishment, killed after a 'series of blunders'. His deputy, Julien Crozet, simply confirmed that the French were inhumane relative to the British by seeking revenge through massacre. Anne Salmond's work on cultural encounter, however, has drawn a more nuanced picture, in which du Fresne became caught in Māori rivalries as well as cross-culturally, between worlds.

AUSTRALIAN LINKS

Soon after first contact, Māori discovered a larger world that extended to Australia, encouraged by traders based in Sydney and Hobart who treated New Zealand as their Pacific or eastern frontier. From the 1790s increasing maritime traffic, dominated by vessels involved in sealing and whaling, created a shared Tasman world between New Zealand and New South Wales, the convict colony founded by the British at Sydney in 1788. Māori chiefs soon became enmeshed in British strategic decisions once they started visiting Sydney to engage with the governor of the colony.

The first Māori to visit Australia were Tuki, a priest, and Huru, a warrior, from the Bay of Islands, in 1793. Having adventurously boarded a supply ship, the two young beachcrossers found themselves kidnapped, transported to Norfolk Island to fulfil a request for Māori instructors from Philip King, the future governor of New South Wales, who wanted convicts taught how to dress flax for rope. Dressing flax was women's work. Nevertheless, Tuki and Huru's forced overseas trip evolved into what Māori saw as an alliance between King at Sydney and chiefs in the Bay of Islands. In 1806 a Māori adventurer, Moehanga, visited London. Dozens of Māori sailed to Sydney as heads of state, entrepreneurs, tourists, and students, to acquire new knowledge and technology.

Inevitably, European mental maps helped to shape Māori perceptions of Indigenous Australians, with negative results. As Governor King recorded in 1806, the eminent northern chief Te Pahi, his guest at Government House, and Tuki before him, showed a 'marked contempt' for the 'natives of this country'. Māori were contemptuous of their 'going naked' and of their 'most trifling mode of warfare'. While King believed in the European racial hierarchy, his New Zealand visitors shared disdain for people whom they perceived as nomads rather than as warriors and agriculturalists. They also shared the British military disdain for European convicts, on the basis that they were 'slaves' or war captives. Te Pahi and his four sons returned to the Bay of Islands with numerous presents, including bricks and a prefabricated European-style house, both frontier status symbols.

Visits by young Māori on whaling ships to Sydney stimulated Governor King's interest in New Zealand after 1800 (see figure 2.3). Whalers – hard men who laboured on ships from the United States, Sydney, Hobart, and later France – were the 'largest group of European agents of contact' with New Zealand. They did a brisk trade with Māori, who supplied ships with pork and potatoes initially acquired through their diplomatic relations with New South Wales, until iwi produced these staples. Māori themselves became involved in the business of whaling, notably in Foveaux

2.3 Lieutenant George F. Dashwood, *Maoris*, 1832. Men working on deck are dressed in European clothing and top hats, while the carved prow shows European as well as Māori influences. This ship was likely first owned by Ngāpuhi chiefs who traded with Sydney. Dashwood's sketchbooks, Mitchell Library, State Library of New South Wales, PXA 1679, vol. 2, fol. 89b

Strait, in the south, and the Bay of Islands, in the north, where whalers hunted right whales and sperm whales respectively. Out of concern for Māori and Pacific Island crew who featured in stories of kidnap and brutality, Governor King issued a government order in the *Sydney Gazette* in 1805 giving Māori and other Pacific Islanders some of the civil rights of British subjects: they were not to suffer ill-treatment but were to be protected in property and claims for wages.

In southern New Zealand from the 1790s, sealing gangs – including ex-convicts, escaped convicts, and deserters – landed around the coast to collect skins for the China market. To protect the British monopoly on trade held by the East India Company, which extended as far as Australia and New Zealand, Governor King banned sealing more than 43 degrees south. But Simeon Lord, a rich ex-convict merchant in Sydney, subverted this policy by conniving with American whaling captains and military officers who ran the colonial government. Thus sealers who discovered a new sealing ground in Foveaux Strait in 1804 at first kept the news to themselves, though they soon gained official support. On assuming command of New South Wales after Governor William Bligh's overthrow in 1808, the obscure official Joseph Foveaux, after whom Foveaux Strait is named (along with Foveaux Street in Sydney), allowed sealing gangs to head immediately to this wild strait between Stewart Island and the South Island. Thanks to the military interregnum at Sydney, Stewart Island landmarks bear Australian names left by the sealing rush.

Bay whaling followed sealing from the 1820s, conducted initially by whalers from Sydney and Hobart. This involved the pursuit of whales that entered bays and swam towards coasts to calve. Sydney merchants also profited from selling muskets and gunpowder to tribes, especially to Te Rauparaha of Ngāti Toa, who was secretly planning raids in the South Island.

Relentless hunting drove seals and whales almost to extinction. An estimated seven million seals were killed in New Zealand waters between 1780 and 1830. Yet it is not well known that this plunder shaped the colonial built environment in Sydney, Hobart, and to a lesser extent New Zealand. While 87 heritage sites contain good evidence of New Zealand whaling history, the impact of sealing is more elusive. A Sydney sealing gang and a carpenter built the first European house in New Zealand in 1792, in Dusky Sound (a fiord named by Captain Cook): a 12-metre-long dwelling house, partially prefabricated, with a thatched roof. The gang also erected a drying house, a slipway, and a boat as a backup for escape. Dusky Sound was the only British settlement established in New Zealand before 1800.

As a commercial hub, Sydney briefly flourished as a home base for sealing entrepreneurs, among whom ex-convicts featured prominently. James Underwood, for example, used capital accumulated from sealing to become the biggest shipbuilder in New South Wales. As well as his boatyard in Sydney Cove, he built a substantial Georgian house next door with a 'captain's walk' on the roof, while the richest ex-convict, Simeon Lord, constructed the largest statement house in Sydney in 1803. Other sealers operated out of the Hawkesbury River north of Sydney or from Tasmania.

It was unsurprising that Māori joined sealing gangs, since their ancestors had hunted fur seals. Some engaged in whaling or plundered shore whaling stations and attacked whaling captains in revenge for past slights. Māori responses to sealing and whaling were pragmatic and diverse, depending on the circumstances and how they felt treated. If newcomers launched unauthorised assaults on Māori resources, they were attacked. If they were useful in trade, becoming friends, they might be found wives. In the process, the whaling and sealing industries provided fathers for children of mixed descent, who gained Māori genealogies and identities from their mothers. Around Foveaux Strait, Ngāi Tahu incorporated select sealers and whalers into their communities. The same happened in the Bay of Islands.

Like whalers and beachcombers such as escaped convicts and crew, the Christian Church reached New Zealand from Australia, initially in the form of the Church of England, and followed by the Wesleyan Church. The Anglican mission was delayed when bad relations between whalers and Māori led to trans-Tasman atrocities. Notably the sailing ship *Boyd* was burnt and her crew killed in northern New Zealand in 1809, news of which reached Sydney in 1810. Sadly, Te Pahi was wrongly blamed for this 'massacre', in the process changing in colonial eyes from a 'friendly chief' to a 'treacherous cannibal'. The British fiscal–military state reacted by warning whalers to be vigilant in their dealings with New Zealanders and Pacific Islanders, who were a 'very treacherous race of People, and not to be trusted'. Once again, intersecting worlds provided scope for Māori agency but also Māori tragedy.

Historians and anthropologists have highlighted Māori initiative in the missionaries' arrival in New Zealand; in particular, the trans-Tasman entrepreneur Ruatara of Ngāpuhi befriended Samuel Marsden, the Anglican chaplain based at Parramatta, in New South Wales. By negotiating with Marsden, Ruatara secured a monopoly over the first permanent European settlement in the Bay of Islands, where he managed the Anglican mission and missionaries to enhance his mana. In effect, Ruatara was an early consultant on European relations.

As for Marsden, historians have told of two: Australia's 'flogging parson', loathed by the convicts for his cruelty; and New Zealand's humane missionary. The Anglican chaplain is remembered in the Pākehā story as a good man, the missionary who preached the first Christian sermon to Māori on Christmas Day. He turned to New Zealand in 1814 after failures in the Pacific mission of the Church Missionary Society and among convicts and Indigenous Australians in New South Wales. From Ruatara and other travellers Marsden learnt that rangatira (chiefs) wielded authority over tangata (people). Among such New Zealand clients he saw both trading prospects and an opportunity for his mission of British order. So did northern chiefs, who had their own motives for a Sydney connection – trade above all.

Both sides worked to develop that link. To secure imperial sanction for the Anglican mission to New Zealand, Marsden collected a sheaf of complaints about European aggressions in the Pacific that he placed before the governor. Accordingly, Governor Lachlan Macquarie issued a proclamation in December 1813 that effectively placed Māori 'under the protection of His Majesty' and bound British subjects by British law in their dealings with Māori and Pacific Islanders. The following year, 12 rangatira from the Bay of Islands, including Ruatara of Ngāpuhi; his half-brother Hongi Hika, a Ngāpuhi warrior chief; and Hongi's son, stayed for three months at Parramatta with Marsden, all busy learning English and about European-style agriculture, gardening, and carpentry. This chiefly assemblage returned to New Zealand with Marsden and three missionaries in December 1814. Architecturally and evangelically, the missionary settlement established at Kerikeri, in the Bay of Islands, became a 'pocket Parramatta'. The stone store at Parramatta, built in 1809, provided the plan for what is now New Zealand's oldest heritage building, the stone store at Kerikeri, while Marsden's house at Parramatta, 'Old Rangehoo' (Rangihoua, the name of the first missionary base in New Zealand), became the model for the Kerikeri Mission House. Marsden built the Australian Rangihoua in 1819 as a seminary for high-ranking young Māori. The Anglican mission in New Zealand remained marginal until the 1830s, useful more to northern tribes as an entrée to European technology, literacy, and commerce. Hongi Hika inherited monopolistic control over the first Anglican missionaries from Ruatara. Missionaries in New Zealand before 1830 had the status of Māori property, over whom Hongi Hika retained his monopoly until his death. From his seat in the Bay of Islands, he obliged the missionaries to deal with him on his terms, which included surreptitious trading in muskets.

For Māori, Hongi Hika is more important than Marsden. The one-time seminarian was one among dozens of trans-Tasman Māori travellers and entrepreneurs who engaged closely in trade with colonial New South Wales. Trans-Tasman chiefs are impressive examples of the Māori presence in Australia since the 1800s.

Hongi Hika became famous in New Zealand, however, by venturing in 1820 to London, where he succeeded in his quest to see King George IV; he also assisted a Cambridge professor to compile a Māori dictionary. Hongi sailed to England on a whaling schooner, accompanied by his friend the young lay preacher Thomas Kendall, and Waikato, his aide-de-camp (figure 2.4). Kendall was not authorised to go but was determined to pursue study of the Māori language as a vehicle for conversion. In England, Hongi was feted in society, receiving many valuable gifts, which he traded on the Sydney market the following year for over 300 muskets, powder, and shot. But he did not exchange all his gifts; he kept a suit of armour and a helmet that saved his life on several occasions.

2.4 James Barry, *The Rev. Thomas Kendall and the Māori chiefs Hongi and Waikato*, 1820. Hongi stands in the centre, holding a taiaha (long club) in his right hand and a mere (club) in his left. Alexander Turnbull Library, Wellington, G-618

MUSKET WARS

By the 1800s intertribal warfare was intensifying. Some argue that the Māori population peaked around 1800 and the increased scarcity of resources fuelled hostilities. Tougher resource constraints strengthen the argument for late settlement of Aotearoa, whereby Māori adapted fast to ecological changes caused by human activity. When competition was already intense among rival hapū (kin groups), it was inevitable that European contact would overcook things and unleash unprecedented conflict. The process of using warfare to resolve disputes accelerated between 1815 and 1840, abetted by the trans-Tasman connection, the details of which are complex and controversial. Hitherto Māori tribal warfare had been seasonal and highly ritualistic, with relatively few deaths. European guns – muskets, double-barrelled muskets, and pistols – were more deadly and produced more devastating effects. The musket wars, as they became known, could just as well be called 'land wars', because so much territory changed hands in their wake. Some scholars also attribute the wars' ferocity and extent to the white potato, which was an easier food to grow and for war parties to carry. (The potatoes were grown by slaves – captured enemies.)

Muskets and potatoes are commonly associated with Hongi Hika, because he introduced the musket into intertribal warfare. Offensives began in the north, where Hongi equipped an army and laid waste to opponents on an unparalleled scale. Long-distance raiding did not require guns and potatoes, however. Customarily, warrior victors lived at the expense of their enemies. Hongi aimed to outdo his rivals, not to conquer strangers, and manipulated the new staple items of trade to strengthen Māori values and institutions.

One view is that escaped convicts from Tasmania on the *Venus* triggered the wars in 1806–7, when they kidnapped high-ranking Ngāpuhi women – close kin of Hongi Hika and his ally Te Morenga – whom they dumped at various beaches, to be killed by other tribes. Another is that the core element of reciprocity in Māori cultural relations required utu (repayment) for an offence to any group to avoid loss of mana and to restore balance and order. Therefore, the way the Māori political system operated in seeking restitution for this offence – capture of chiefly kin – and for earlier wars, explained what happened subsequently. Twelve years later Ngāpuhi sought utu from the East Coast peoples, using their new strength in muskets. In 1818 Te Morenga and Hongi Hika led hundreds of warriors on two taua (raids) against hapū in the Bay of Plenty. The very day in 1820 that Hongi left for England, Te Morenga's party returned to the Bay of Islands in 50 canoes with hundreds of dried human heads, about 200 slaves, and all the canoes of a chief who had killed one of the women kidnapped years before.

As a result of the wars, three great warrior chiefs became the most powerful figures in New Zealand: Hongi Hika of Ngāpuhi, Te Wherowhero of the Waikato (the future Māori king), and Te Rauparaha of Ngāti Toa. The campaigns themselves led Ngāti Toa to migrate southwards from Kawhia, first to Taranaki and then to the Wellington region, where Te Rauparaha set out to provide for the future of his people and dominate other tribes.

Scholars who conceptualise the musket wars in terms of the use of guns and potatoes order the wars into three phases. First, tribes acquired a few muskets, mainly from whalers, enough for a shock effect; second, they acquired hundreds of muskets and built an inventory of food to support large armies, thanks to an agricultural revolution in the cultivation of potatoes; and third, tribes accumulated excess guns. At all phases, muskets were acquired through trade in food, women via sex slavery and prostitution, tattooed heads in the 1820s, and, later, dressed flax for the Sydney market. Demand for labour to stockpile trade goods increased the urgency to launch raiding parties who could bring back the slaves required. The embellished workforce in turn made it easier to launch raiding parties as, for a fast-growing food supply, Māori planted potatoes, a job that women or slaves could do while the men went to fight. Not all raid victims were kept for hard labour. A common meat supply for taua was kai-tangata (cannibalism, the term being a combination of the words for 'food' and 'people'), as ritualistic punishment yielded to mass warfare. But the hundreds of surviving slaves, forced to grow more food and earn more weapons, helped tribes to proceed from phase to phase through greater access to Europeans and muskets.

The wars, then, arose from and generated ripple effects. For instance, Hongi Hika returned from England in 1821 with over 300 muskets bought in Sydney, which made Ngāpuhi the most powerful force in New Zealand and left the Auckland area depopulated for fear of raids. In 1822 he invaded the Waikato region, forcing Te Rauparaha and his people to migrate southwards. In turn Ngāti Toa migrants and their allies launched raid after raid against tangata whenua and used the fortress island of Kapiti, north of Wellington, as a base from which to trade with European ships and mount attacks. In 1824 Ngāti Toa leader Te Pehi Kupe emulated Hongi Hika and travelled to England, returning to Kapiti four years later with more arms bought in Sydney. Like Hongi, he traded gifts received in Europe for muskets across the Tasman, which his tribe subsequently used in invasions of the South Island. Ngāi Tahu used muskets for the first time in 1825, against other hapū, escalating internal conflict within the tribe. Waikato musket power balanced that of Ngāpuhi by 1827, and Hongi Hika's death, in 1828, marked the end of unbridled Ngāpuhi power. As hostilities pushed southwards, Te Rauparaha invaded the South Island in the summer of 1827–8, causing much bloodshed when he used muskets against traditional weapons. For the next six years he led campaigns south.

Not all intertribal wars between 1807 and 1840 were musket wars. To be so they would have had to involve Ngāpuhi until the late 1820s, because they had the superior firepower. Yet muskets did not guarantee victory, and the wars were not simply intertribal wars. New ideas and strategies apart from guns disturbed tribal dynamics and called for new institutions to stabilise society. The wars were not merely fought on traditional terms but were a 'modern catastrophe for Māori', demonstrating the full explosive power of Māori–newcomer relations.

Two infamous episodes involved direct European input. The turning point which eventually hooked New Zealand into the British Empire came in 1830, instigated by Te Rauparaha when he approached the English captain John Stewart of the brig *Elizabeth* for assistance with his raids against Ngāi Tahu. In this case Te Rauparaha targeted chief Te Maiharanui in revenge for killing Ngāti Toa's chief Te Pehi Kupe in 1828. Stewart agreed to transport Te Rauparaha and 70–120 armed men (the reported numbers vary) on the *Elizabeth* to Akaroa Harbour in exchange for a cargo of dressed flax. At Akaroa, the passengers at first stayed hidden, to give the impression that the *Elizabeth* was there to trade, before Stewart's crew helped lure an unsuspecting Te Maiharanui into the captain's cabin, where he was handcuffed. The same evening Te Rauparaha's warriors burnt the village on shore, butchering survivors. The false sense of security engendered in Ngāi Tahu by the presence of a European vessel compounded the offence, as did the atrocities committed ashore. After the slaughter Stewart and the *Elizabeth* transported baskets of cooked human flesh back to Kapiti, with the captive Te Maiharanui and his wife. Stewart used the chiefly couple as security for his payment of flax, and on delivery they too suffered a terrible death. Te Rauparaha then sought to capitalise on his *Elizabeth* expedition by attacking the Ngāi Tahu stronghold at Kaiapohia, north of Christchurch, in the summer of 1831–2. After a siege the pā fell. Te Rauparaha pursued refugees to another pā in Akaroa Harbour, where he used chiefly captives from Kaiapohia as a ruse to gain access, ostensibly to discuss peace. Once inside, his warriors fired. Unsurprisingly, Ngāi Tahu long harboured a desire for utu against Ngāti Toa.

In the second notorious episode, in 1835 Ngāti Mutunga and Ngāti Tama from Taranaki invaded the Chatham Islands, having seized a brig and its captain – whose involvement was this time unwilling – in Wellington Harbour. It took two trips to carry the cargo of about 900 people, seed potatoes, and waka to the Chathams. The outcome was tragic. The local Moriori formed a peace council in response to the invaders, who misinterpreted it as a war council, limited by their own cultural constructs that could not conceive of nonviolence, and embarked on a bloody and ruthless campaign to crush them. The Moriori population numbered 1660 in 1835 and 101 by 1862. Thus, encounters with Europe displaced Māori, who used Europeans and European technology to dispossess Moriori.

The musket wars finally ended in the Chatham Islands in 1840, when the feuding Māori were themselves separated by land purchases. The wars also had long-term effects in the Wellington region once Ngāti Mutunga and Ngāti Tama left, because these iwi bequeathed the authority over the land that they claimed in the area to their Te Āti Awa kin Te Wharepouri, who had also led a migration southwards from Taranaki. Insecure in his rights over the land, Te Wharepouri found it expedient not long afterwards to sell the Wellington district to the New Zealand Company, in exchange for goods that included muskets and gunpowder, because the presence of settlers offered protection.

The effects of the musket wars were horrendous. Tribes were redistributed and thousands killed, wounded, or displaced between 1806 and 1845. Massive population displacement, especially the pressure of southward migrations by Ngāti Toa and allied Taranaki tribes, proved devastating around Cook Strait, in the South Island, and in the Chatham Islands. Entire districts were depopulated, making way for future European settlement. Tribal boundaries were redrawn. Victors enjoyed the spoils, ousting tangata whenua from their homelands fewer than 20 years before the Treaty of Waitangi.

The effects still resonate in the present, in current locations of tribes; disputes over tribal authority and resentment about land loss shortly before the Treaty of Waitangi froze the distribution of power. Surveys and land sales inhibited movement and inscribed boundaries after 1840. Musket warfare had devastating effects on the mana of some iwi. New tribes enjoyed dominance, notably Ngāpuhi in the north and Ngāti Toa, who instigated groups' moves to the Kapiti coast, from where they commanded Cook Strait. Iwi who were invaded tended to form more concentrated groupings in self-defence. Large areas were depopulated or left sparsely settled because of disputes over ownership, such as around the future sites of Auckland and Wellington. In these spaces of opportunity European land speculators acquired the disputed land by purchase, to the speculators' advantage, because vulnerable groups sought a Pākehā shield.

Depopulation wrought havoc with land claims. Yet tangata whenua survived the onslaught, many returning to their former territories or intermarrying with invading tribes. Sadly, one response to seeing descendants die was to sell ancestral lands. That at least saw claims vindicated against those of rivals. With the work of the Waitangi Tribunal, however, historians have asked whether the government should recognise boundaries that were set in 1840, based on conquests achieved through European weapons, and about the nature of interests signified by boundaries. To these questions others have replied that many of the intertribal wars would have happened anyway.

For the warfare spiral to subside, a new equilibrium had to be reached that incorporated the newcomers. While missionaries claimed that they had ended the wars, the coming of peace spread Christianity rather than vice versa. Out of the debate over the Māori conversion a consensus has emerged about the role of former slaves, who were captured during the wars, converted to Christianity during their imprisonment, and spread literacy and Māori versions of the gospel to their tribes on returning home. Christianity offered a revolutionary model of governance in which laws created by the state protected peace. In the realm of ideas, Christianity proved revelatory.

Māori seized every opportunity to improve their circumstances and break out of ecological constraints. Once Ngāpuhi had

2.5 George F. Angas, *Motupoi [Motuopuhi] pah with [Mt] Tongariro*, 1844. This Ngāti Tūwharetoa pā was attacked in 1828. Alexander Turnbull Library, Wellington, A-196-022

muskets, the rest of the country had to have them. At one level the wars only ended with a balance of firepower and modern pā designed for musket warfare (see figure 2.5). The wars created a large body of strategists with decades of expertise with guns and the know-how to employ European technology against Europeans. Yet the critical innovation – on the ground – was land purchase.

THE MOVE FROM MINIMUM INTERVENTION

No wonder that historians have described Colonial Office strategy as lethargic in response. Britain had wide-ranging global interests that remained centred on Europe and containing France. Empire comprised a mere fraction of strategic and commercial interests, and Australasia even less. Not that the Colonial Office knew much about it; its mandarins relied on letters and written reports for intelligence from far-flung officials, governors, military officers, and informal agents such as missionaries and their parent societies.

Worried about the impacts of encounter, chiefs from the Bay of Islands in 1831 petitioned King William IV for protection by Britain against its subjects and French ambitions. Token official intervention began in May 1833 in the Bay of Islands with the arrival of James Busby as British resident, reluctantly paid for by the colony of New South Wales. The initiative for Busby's appointment came not from London but from Sydney, to be seen to be doing something about the *Elizabeth* atrocity. Sydney businessmen realised that interracial strife in New Zealand would hurt their profits. Busby and his wife built their home, a prefabricated house designed in Sydney (now called the Treaty House), on a farm that they established at Waitangi. Busby was a civil official, not a military officer with access to an army or navy. In effect the first police officer, he was responsible for the 'maintenance of tranquillity', which included apprehending escaped convicts. Māori soon came to call him 'the watch-dog without teeth', and indigenous law prevailed. Internal dynamics were already asserting their primacy, obliging the colonial government based at Sydney to extend perfunctory policing to New Zealand.

London, meanwhile, supplied the theory of a new Christian imperialism, provided it was done on the cheap. At the Colonial Office, Sir James Stephen held evangelical Christian and humanitarian beliefs that became dominant in discourses of British racial superiority and imperial destiny in the 1830s. 'A clearer racial hierarchy was emerging', underlined by the notion that 'independency' – an idea from the Scottish moral philosophers – was a prerequisite of civic virtue. According to this arrangement, societies moved through stages of development to high civilisation through the application of industry. As modified by evangelicalism, the Christian empire should intervene and speed up this process. The concept of freedom of contract leapt into fashion precisely when this transformation of empire was under way, and Australasia exemplified this global assertion of the 'rights of freeborn Englishmen'.

How would those rights apply in New Zealand? In the mid-1830s the imperial government had no motive to seize sovereignty and in any case had to overcome the inertia imposed by lack of funds. Busby as resident was powerless; his own property was broken into. But he featured in two episodes that had lasting symbolic significance. First, he encouraged northern chiefs to choose a New Zealand flag in 1834 to be flown by Māori shipping so that their ships could freely enter Sydney and other Australian ports rather than be impounded by customs officers for not flying a flag. Aware of what a flag signified collectively, the Ngāpuhi chiefs selected a Church Missionary Society design, white in colour with a red cross and four stars, that became a symbol of Māori sovereignty and identity.

Second, he devised a declaration of independence, signed at Waitangi in October 1835 by 34 chiefs convened as the United Tribes of New Zealand – 52 by July 1839 – that deemed New Zealand an independent state under British protection. Reflective of wider trends, this document is becoming known by its Māori name, He Whakaputanga o te Rangatiratanga o Nu Tireni (The Declaration of Independence of the United Tribes of New Zealand), referring to an emergence of the independence of New Zealand. While He Whakaputanga resembled petitions elsewhere in the Pacific, the signatories, almost all northern rangatira, believed that it declared their sovereignty. The key word in this remarkable document was 'rangatiratanga' (chieftainship), by which it claimed that New Zealand was an independent Māori state in which sovereign power and authority in the land resided with chiefs 'in their collective capacity'. Tribal togetherness was novel, as was the foreshadowed cooperation with the British Crown. While chiefs committed to extend 'friendship and protection' to British subjects, in exchange they requested that King William IV be New Zealand's protector. James Busby, who prepared the English draft, enthused that the agreement was the 'Magna Carta of New Zealand Independence'. When he wrote to the governor of New South Wales, however, he emphasised the declaration's usefulness in making the country dependent, not independent, by its potential to draw New Zealand into the British Empire. Both interpretations were valid.

Today's debates reiterate those of the 1830s about whether He Whakaputanga amounted to a declaration of sovereignty or an assertion of British law. For Busby it might have been both. In New Zealand He Whakaputanga is increasingly seen as the former. Historians agree that Busby intended the declaration would make New Zealand a British protectorate to ward off the French. For some, Busby needed a pretext to convene a meeting of chiefs and found it in a letter from Charles de Thierry in Tahiti saying that he, de Thierry, intended to establish an independent state in New Zealand on land that he believed he had bought from a missionary. Because de Thierry styled himself 'Sovereign Chief of New Zealand', Busby had little trouble persuading local chiefs that he posed a threat. Others argue that Busby was genuinely alarmed. As he explained to Governor Richard Bourke in Sydney, he responded by calling a meeting of chiefs

> in order that they may declare the independence of this country, and assert as a collective body their entire and exclusive right to its sovereignty, and their determination to maintain that right in its integrity, and to treat as a Public Enemy any person who proposes to assume a right of sovereignty within their territories.

Bourke was unimpressed. In retrospect, the Declaration of Independence marked a constitutional step towards the Treaty of Waitangi.

In England the Church Missionary Society opposed colonisation on the grounds that it led to wrongs and injuries to indigenous people. Instead, the Anglicans, and their rival Wesleyans, supported cautious formal British entry. In a mounting fervour, the missionaries pressed 'fatal impact' arguments upon the Colonial Office as a reason to intervene, saying that New Zealand would soon be destitute of aboriginal inhabitants. Imperialism and humanitarianism 'march[ed] together' towards the annexation of New Zealand, with missionaries to the fore. Some see fatal impact as an expedient pretext for the 'fatal necessity' of extending the British Empire to New Zealand.

Modern histories attach less weight to missionaries and more to colonial government and interactions with Māori. But it remains a fact critical for understanding New Zealand history that the timing of formal British intervention coincided with the rise of the humanitarian movement and faith in Christian British imperialism. The world was a different place by 1839 from the late eighteenth century, when British authorities established a convict colony at Sydney.

Religious sectarianism influenced local politics. Roman Catholicism conveyed by priests, and later nuns, from France and

Ireland provided Māori with an alternative politics, a means to compete with their Protestant neighbours and to assert an independent identity. Before the first Catholic priest, Monsignor Pompallier, arrived from France in 1838, northern chiefs had already sent two young Māori to Sydney in 1835 to learn about Catholic teachings, influenced by Irish ex-convicts. A history of New Zealand written in 1896 by Italian priest Dom Felice Vaggioli exemplified the challenge; the British government requested it be suppressed. While it contained factual errors, Vaggioli's book endorsed the Māori right to independence. Vaggioli interpreted the flag of 1834 as a national flag through which the British recognised Māori sovereignty. He scorned the rumour that de Thierry was a French agent when he was a 'pathetic British citizen', and he condemned officials and Protestant missionaries as profiteers and landsharks.

Events, though, began to overtake Colonial Office plans from 1837, as pressures mounted for New Zealand to join the formal empire. The outbreak of another cycle of tribal warfare in the Bay of Islands prompted a petition to Sydney for armed protection. In response, Governor Bourke sent HMS *Rattlesnake* with Captain William Hobson on board. As well as being seen to impose order, this visit produced two despatches – one by Hobson and the other by Busby – that prompted London to end the policy of 'minimum intervention'. Busby wrote in his report of 'the accumulating evils of a permanent anarchy' to persuade the Colonial Office to intervene more strongly. Hobson exercised more influence through his suggestion that Britain acquire sovereignty over at least the parts of New Zealand that contained British settlement. Global politics continued to dominate official thinking. Preoccupied with Europe and especially French ambitions, Britain was also becoming more involved in Asia and the Pacific as eyes for profit turned to China. Belief in British racial superiority only enhanced the confidence with which officials made decisions. When the House of Commons Select Committee on Aborigines in British Settlements in 1837 identified the issues that preoccupied colonial officials for the rest of the century, it 'took for granted Britain's self-evident superiority'. The committee maintained that protection by imperial authorities and Christianity would lead to civilisation, including of Māori, and anticipated the Crown right of pre-emption written into the English text of the Treaty of Waitangi. By this feudal doctrine only the Crown could alienate Māori land by consent; future settlers had to purchase land from the government. In this way both humanitarianism and the need to provide a land bank for a colonial treasury were satisfied.

In 1838 a House of Lords Select Committee on New Zealand endorsed the system of colonisation promoted by the 'notorious and visionary' Edward Gibbon Wakefield (see chapter 3). By 1839 British thinking had moved to advocate restricted, controlled intervention to ensure law and order in British enclaves as Captain Hobson suggested. Letters patent published in June 1839 extended the boundaries of New South Wales to include any ceded lands in New Zealand. Parts of the country settled by Pākehā were to be acquired from chiefs, while tribes were to retain control of their own territories. Governor George Gipps in Sydney had jurisdiction over any land that was appropriated. By July the Colonial Office had come to accept the idea of full sovereignty by Britain. The imperial government appointed Hobson as consul on 30 July 1839, to exercise 'some controlling authority' over the British in New Zealand, and as lieutenant-governor of the part of the New South Wales colony that 'extended over the New Zealand Islands'.

The New Zealand Company resolved to get there first. Formed in 1837 as the New Zealand Association, its advocates of systematic colonisation had fantasised since the 1820s about colonising Australasia with planned settlements settled by selected immigrants. Edward Gibbon Wakefield provided the inspiration for the utopian ideal of making South Australia and New Zealand sites of colonial experiment with a transplanted preindustrial English class structure. In implementing this ideal, however, Wakefield was obliged to lurk in the background and work through propaganda, because of the disgrace that stuck to him following his imprisonment for the abduction of a young heiress. His brother Colonel William Wakefield was besmirched too, as party to the kidnapping. Nonetheless, Colonel Wakefield was appointed the New Zealand Company's agent. He left in haste for New Zealand on the *Tory* in May 1839, to purchase land from Māori as cheaply as possible and secure a monopoly around Cook Strait. Possession, after all, was nine-tenths of the law, and the New Zealand Company's proposed new town of 'Britannia' beside Wellington Harbour / Port Nicholson would be far from the embryonic seat of government in the Bay of Islands.

It was the voyage of the *Tory*, which anchored in the Marlborough Sounds in August 1839, and Colonel William Wakefield's large and dubious land purchases, that motivated the Colonial Office to adopt 1839, not 1840, as the date of cession of New Zealand sovereignty, on the grounds of British settlement. In September the *Tory* sailed into Wellington Harbour and was boarded by the chiefs Te Puni and Te Wharepouri, who sought to establish their claims ahead of other relatively recent arrivals to the Wellington district, especially Te Rauparaha. The barque *Cuba*, carrying the New Zealand Company surveyor-general, survey cadets, and labourers, arrived three months later, followed from January to March 1840 by the first six passenger ships containing the selected migrants. Piloted by American whalers from Kapiti Island, the *Cuba* entered the harbour on 4–5 January 1840 to be greeted by 'three canoe loads of natives' led by 'Warri Podi' and 'Pooni' (Te Wharepouri and Te Puni).

Ever since, the story of the New Zealand Company and its first settlement at Wellington has sat uncomfortably alongside the history of the Treaty of Waitangi as a foundation narrative for New Zealand. Thanks to the New Zealand Company's precipitate action and unscrupulous land deals executed by Sydney developers, Governor Gipps issued a proclamation on 14 January 1840 extending the New South Wales borders to include New Zealand. By 18 January Captain Hobson was on his way from Sydney as lieutenant-governor.

3
Claiming the land 1840–1860

Struggles for land have swirled around the Treaty of Waitangi ever since it was first signed, on 6 February 1840. An instrument unique less in its making than in what it has become, as a constitutional document and guarantee of indigenous rights, it met grand goals at minimal cost. Beforehand, on 30 January, Captain William Hobson, who had landed in the Bay of Islands the previous day, read three announcements at the Anglican Church in Kororāreka (Russell). The first extended the boundaries of New South Wales to include New Zealand, the second declared him lieutenant-governor, and the third established that land titles would derive from the Crown. To secure annexation to the British Empire by consent Hobson next drafted a treaty, as instructed by the Colonial Office.

Europeans on the spot helped with the task. James Busby redrafted Hobson's text to include a promise that Britain would guarantee Māori possession of their lands and other properties, for which British humanitarianism provided precedents in North America and West Africa. Without this assurance Busby knew the chiefs would not sign. Overnight on 4–5 February, the Anglican missionary Henry Williams and his son Edward translated the text into Māori so that chiefs could discuss it, which they did all day at Busby's house on 5 February, until Hobson, several English residents, and about 45 Māori chiefs signed the Māori translation of the Treaty of Waitangi, on 6 February. This initial signing was done in haste; Hobson barely had time to grab his naval uniform's plumed hat from HMS *Herald*.

If for Hobson and Busby the Treaty offered chiefs protection, for the Church of England missionaries it was a covenant between Māori and Queen Victoria as head of the English church and state. For rangatira (chiefs), though, their status demanded equality in rank and power to the new governor, as Tareha declared: 'We chiefs are the rulers and we won't be ruled over. If we were all to have a rank equal to you that might be acceptable. But if we are going to be subordinate to you, then I say get back to your ship and sail away'. Only a few welcomed Hobson as a harbinger of peace and new laws to manage the impact of disease, cultural and social disturbance, and firepower. It remained for Ngāpuhi chief Tāmati Wāka Nene to turn debate in favour of the Treaty with his argument that it was too late to reject Hobson; settlers were already arriving; the governor would be a friend, a judge, and a peacemaker. Such a 'battle of words' did 'justice to the cause', clearing the air before a leader's address ended debate.

Nene and his older brother Pātuone were among the first to sign the Treaty after their relative Hōne Heke, who set the example. As his later photograph suggests, Pātuone, like Nene, bridged two worlds (figure 3.1.1–2). At about six years of age Pātuone met Captain Cook on the *Endeavour*, and in 1814 he and Nene welcomed Reverend Samuel Marsden from New South Wales. A great warrior, Pātuone was one of the first chiefs to be baptised by Henry Williams, and he perceived mutual benefit in treating with the British.

This was not the case for the French bishop Jean-Baptiste Pompallier, who queried whether the assembled chiefs understood that the British intended the Treaty to be an instrument of cession. Pompallier, impressive in splendid robes, interceded to demand a public assurance of religious freedom before any chiefs signed with their names or moko (facial tattoo).

After each rangatira signed, Hobson tried a few words in Māori: 'Hi iwi tahi tātou', he said, for which the usual translation is 'we are now one people'. This assured Christian chiefs that their people and the British would be bound as subjects of the queen and followers of Christ. Ever since, politicians have quoted Hobson's words, which, as with all speech, could hold different meanings for different groups. What did unity entail? Did 'one people' mean

3.1.1 Eruera Pātuone, Treaty of Waitangi signatory, 1856–62.
With his musket and Pākehā (European New Zealander)
gentleman's dress, and the countenance of a warrior chief, Pātuone
bridged two worlds.
Photographer John Nicol Crombie. Courtesy of Benjamin Pittman

all the same, including one law, which in British thought meant civilising and assimilating Māori? Or did it endorse the idea of a new, federal community of Māori and Pākehā (European New Zealanders), ethnic and cultural groups henceforth defined in relation to each other? A more accurate translation is 'we are peoples together', suggestive of the latter.

Nōpera Panakareao, a chief who had signed He Whakaputanga the Declaration of Independence and welcomed European missionaries in Northland, saw the potential for a Christian alliance with Hobson against his less Christian neighbours in which the governor would both apply British laws and 'protect Māori in their own laws', to prevent disputes. He signed to give the people a helmsman: 'Before[,] everyone wanted to be helmsman; one said, let me

3.1.2 Tāmati Wāka Nene, Treaty of Waitangi signatory and Pātuone's brother, 1870
Photographer Elizabeth Pulman. Courtesy of Benjamin Pittman

steer, another, let me steer, and we never went straight'. This suggests that the Treaty was as much about instilling peace and protecting the rights of iwi (tribes) and hapū (subtribes) as about how to manage engagement with Europeans.

THE FOUNDING DOCUMENT

Only recently has the Treaty of Waitangi become central to national life. It always mattered to Māori as a covenant. There are nine documents in all: the original, in English and Māori; seven copies in Māori; and one English reprint. After the gathering at Waitangi the main Māori parchment was taken to other places, first in Northland. Missionaries and naval personnel carried copies of the Māori text around the country; one copy travelled to the

South Island on HMS *Herald*, and some North Island chiefs signed a printed sheet of the English version produced by the Church Missionary Society. Over 500 chiefs signed the Treaty documents, all except 39 of whom signed a Māori version. They signed as representatives not of iwi but of hapū.

Significantly, several powerful non-Christian chiefs, less exposed to European influence, did not sign – notably, Pōtatau Te Wherowhero of Waikato, later anointed as the first Māori king; Te Arawa chiefs; and Mananui Te Heuheu Tūkino II, paramount chief of Ngāti Tūwharetoa, from the central North Island. Wairarapa Māori were not given the opportunity. Te Heuheu, for one, refused to subordinate his mana as first among chiefs to that of a woman, the English queen. (The number of women recognised as signatories had reached 13 by 2025, including Panakareao's wife, who was of high rank.) Two women signed a copy in the Cook Strait region, while women of high status elsewhere were debarred.

Translations of the Treaty of Waitangi and its meaning remain contentious. The Māori text translated by Henry Williams and his son differs from Hobson's English original in subtle yet critical ways. Before the 1970s, national histories – when they referred to the Treaty – relied on the English text to depict a nation founded on full and free consent. New Zealand joined the British Empire on 6 February 1840 as part of the colony of New South Wales. New Zealand became a separate Crown colony from 1841. In this Pākehā story, it took 150 years for the Treaty to grow into a 'founding document'.

Rescued from a fire in 1841, the Treaty sheets were put in storage in 1877, at a time when the Treaty was declared to have no legal status and tribes to have no customary rights enforceable in the courts. Rediscovered in 1911, the documents – especially the parchment signed at Waitangi – were found to be damaged by water and rats and were saved as a relic by the Dominion Museum. In the late twentieth century Māori protested that New Zealand's settler society had neglected the Treaty. Not until the sesquicentennial celebrations, in 1990, were its documents finally arranged on permanent public display, initially at the National Archives, before they moved in 2017 to the National Library of New Zealand, in Wellington.

Now cherished as a heritage artefact, the Treaty sheets continue to mean different things to different groups but have had an evolving official interpretation placed upon them. Elderly New Zealanders are familiar with a settler narrative that did not mention the Treaty at all. The Pākehā narrative that does – and recognises the reality that colonists initially depended on Māori – advances the humanitarian view of government concerned for Māori interests, which affirms that the Crown was present in New Zealand before all but a trickle of settlers and before the making of the nation state. This version is centred in the north of the North Island, on the Treaty ground at Waitangi, with the missionaries and with the governor in Auckland.

In 1841 Hobson shifted the capital from a proposed site at Okiato, in the Bay of Islands, 7 kilometres south of Kororāreka, the whaling port, to Auckland rather than to Wellington. He was persuaded that, as the seat of government for the new colony, Auckland had the advantage of strategic location on the Waitematā Harbour, between the regions of densest Māori population in Northland and the Waikato – as Ngāti Whātua, the tribe that invited Hobson there, pointed out. Tāmaki Makaurau, the Māori name for Auckland, refers to the isthmus (Tāmaki) between the Waitematā and Manukau harbours, where the city developed, and tells how the site was 'much desired' (makaurau).

The rival settler story that downplayed the Treaty grew from Wellington and the five other towns created by the theory of systematic colonisation, invented by Edward Gibbon Wakefield, which left its mark on organised British migration and settlement. Wellington was the first New Zealand town planned according to these principles; and the first New Zealand Company settlers, who reached Wellington between January and March 1840, fully expected that their town would become the capital city. It was the growing tension among Pākehā, between the governor and missionaries in the north and the Wellington settlers, that prompted Hobson to take a further step and proclaim British sovereignty over the whole country on 21 May 1840, when the Treaty documents were still circulating and southern chiefs had yet to sign. Imperial power asserted itself when challenged by its own kind.

From a Māori standpoint the Treaty of Waitangi is the basis of the Crown's authority and legitimised European settlement in New Zealand. Māori narratives came to prominence from the 1970s, and especially in the 1980s, once Treaty jurisprudence established that the Māori rather than the English text of the Treaty had status in international law. Histories known to Māori but not taught in schools revealed there was more to the Treaty than the English version: the document had mana (prestige) as the deed of their tūpuna (ancestors). The Treaty was a living thing, a binding contract, as the missionaries had explained; invoked since 1840 as a source of rights and redress, it stood as a potent symbol for Māori of their rightful constitutional place.

Until the 1970s most appeals to the Treaty were based on the English text translated into Māori rather than on the Māori text, but this changed as Māori scholarship developed. With its legal status affirmed, the Māori text – now known as Te Tiriti o Waitangi – supplanted the English version, and the associated narrative of the Treaty as a founding document grew in political power. In the process, historians began to generate 'a new myth of constitutional foundation' in which Māori had a partnership with the Crown as opposed to a vertical sovereign–subject relationship. This is what rangatira (chiefs) had always understood.

The Treaty comprises three articles. The first extended the Crown's authority over the territory of New Zealand, though there is a question mark over whether chiefs ceded sovereignty, because of the differences between the English and Māori texts. Under article 1 in the English version, the chiefs ceded to the queen 'all the rights and powers of sovereignty' over their land. In the Māori version, te Tiriti, however, the chiefs ceded 'te kāwanatanga katoa' – that is, governance or 'government of all their lands'. The missionary Henry Williams coined the word 'kāwanatanga' from the Māori for 'governor', which his audience interpreted in a biblical context as meaning keeping the peace, as Pontius Pilate did in Israel. By inference, 'kāwanatanga' referred to powers to ensure justice and order, and colonial authority over Europeans. Some therefore argue that for Māori to comprehend British annexation would have required use of the term 'mana', as Williams himself used in his translation of the 1835 He Whakaputanga. Irrespective of terminology, two groups insist that their chiefs did not cede sovereignty: descendants of chiefs who did not sign the Treaty and descendants of northern chiefs who signed the declaration. Chiefs and hapū were nonetheless guaranteed their property rights – that is, collective and individual possession of their lands, villages, and all their treasures. This is specified in article 2, which, in the English text, guaranteed

> to the Chiefs and Tribes of New Zealand and to the respective individuals and families thereof the full exclusive and undisturbed possession of their Lands and Estates Forests and Fisheries and other properties which they may individually or collectively possess so long as it is their wish and desire to retain the same in their possession.

Yet the Māori text signed by most chiefs affirmed unqualified exercise of their rangatiratanga (chieftainship) and that of all hapū and all the people of New Zealand over their land, settlements, and treasures, broadly conceived. The most debated words continue to be 'te tino rangatiratanga'. In the 1865 English translation of te Tiriti (see extract), this crucial phrase is omitted. This translation by Reverend Richard Davis back into English promises 'the Chiefs, the Tribes, and all the people of New Zealand, the entire supremacy of their lands, of their settlements, and of all their personal property'. Today 'te tino rangatiratanga' is translated not as 'entire supremacy' but as 'unqualified chieftainship' or 'independence'. The guarantees of Māori independence in article 2 and of the control by Māori of Māori affairs in their territories retain the power to irk or intimidate some politicians.

The Māori text of article 2 was also silent on the Crown right of pre-emption. It promised the queen 'hokonga' (the buying and selling of land that Māori were willing to part with) but not exclusively, nor even as the highest priority.

A Literal Translation into English, Made in New Zealand, of the Maori Version of the Treaty

Victoria, the Queen of England, in her gracious remembrance of the Chiefs and Tribes of New Zealand, and through her desire to preserve to them their chieftainship and their land, and to preserve peace and quietness to them, has thought it right to send them a gentleman to be her representative to the natives of New Zealand. Let the native Chiefs in all parts of the land and in the islands consent to the Queen's Government. Now, because there are numbers of the people living in this land, and more will be coming, the Queen wishes to appoint a Government, that there may be no cause for strife between the Natives and the Pakeha, who are now without law: It has therefore pleased the Queen to appoint me, WILLIAM HOBSON, a Captain in the Royal Navy, Governor of all parts of New Zealand which shall be ceded now and at the future period to the Queen. She offers to the Chiefs of the Assembly of the Tribes of New Zealand and to the other Chiefs, the following laws:

I. The Chiefs of (i.e. constituting) the Assembly, and all the Chiefs who are absent from the Assembly, shall cede to the Queen of England for ever the government of all their lands.
II. The Queen of England acknowledges and guarantees to the Chiefs, the Tribes, and all the people of New Zealand, the entire supremacy of their lands, of their settlements, and of all their personal property. But the Chiefs of the Assembly, and all other Chiefs, make over to the Queen the purchasing of such lands, which the man who possesses the land is willing to sell, according to prices agreed upon by him, and the purchaser appointed by the Queen to purchase for her.
III. In return for their acknowledging the Government of the Queen, the Queen of England will protect all the natives of New Zealand, and will allow them the same rights as the people of England.

(Signed) WILLIAM HOBSON
Consul, and Lieutenant-Governor

We, the Chiefs of this Assembly of the tribes of New Zealand, now assembled at Waitangi, perceiving the meaning of these words, take and consent to them all. Therefore we sign our names and our marks.

This is done at Waitangi, on the sixth day of February, in the one thousand eight hundred and fortieth year of our Lord.

Was the transition to British rule therefore dependent on devious manipulation of language or did lofty humanitarian motives infuse the Treaty, laying down ground rules for racial harmony? In his study of the English text, Ned Fletcher argues that James Busby distinguished between chiefs' authority over their own people 'in their individual capacity' as chiefs and their 'collective capacity' in negotiations with the British government. Therefore, Busby distinguished in his Treaty revisions between 'governmental power' (kāwanatanga) and 'internal tribal authority' (rangatiratanga). Henry Williams invented these derived nouns to distinguish territorial sovereignty and rule from the person of the ruler – of rangatiratanga (chieftainship) from rangatira (chief), and of kāwanatanga (government) from kāwana (a transliteration of 'governor') – because he thought chiefs would comprehend them. In status terms, too, it mattered that Lieutenant-Governor Hobson was higher in rank than former British Resident Busby but lower than the queen. Hobson was visibly present, whereas the queen was far away in England, a difference that may explain Williams' divergent wording in the Declaration of Independence from that in the Treaty of Waitangi.

Through careful analysis of the English text, Fletcher revived an older, humanitarian interpretation which locates the Treaty within a history of ideas developed over time across the British Empire, as well as in the United States. He maintains that James Stephen at the British Colonial Office was the Treaty's principal author, since Stephen drafted Hobson's official instructions. The drafters of the Treaty, imperial and colonial, unanimously intended chiefs to retain ownership of their land and rights to self-government. Consistent with Colonial Office practice, they recognised that Māori had sovereignty of New Zealand. It follows that, despite ambiguities, the Treaty of Waitangi signified a vote for a peaceful, Christian, Māori and Pākehā future.

To Christian chiefs, the text suggested a kinship model which bound Māori and Pākehā through an imagined shared genealogy that stemmed from God, by which the Treaty made Māori and Pākehā 'friends' as opposed to 'enemies'. Article 3 implied unity as opposed to equal rights. It is likely, then, that Hobson's phrase 'Hi iwi tahi tatou' expressed not merely the Enlightenment belief in a common humanity but also a shared ambition to ensure peace and order. Hobson's phrase may be rendered as 'together we are one nation' as well as 'we are peoples together', both indicative of kinship.

For chiefs such as Tāmati Wāka Nene and Pātuone there was no going back. By 1840 northern chiefs had extensive contact with Europeans and their base at Sydney. In this sense the Treaty denoted a response to globalisation. The tragedy was that Māori could not foresee the arrival from 1840 of thousands of migrants who were to tip the scales of power to the European settler society.

SYSTEMATIC COLONISATION

In retrospect, struggles for land can seem straightforward. In one view, the Māori were out-gunned, as were other indigenous peoples. In another, settler capitalism swept everyone and everything before it. In yet another, the British colonists treated land as a commodity; the tangata whenua (people of the land) in contrast saw it as for the use of their descendants like their ancestors before them. Neither could grasp the other's point of view, though both understood and resented invasion and conquest. It was not only misunderstanding which provoked disputes over land and made them a pivot of New Zealand history. Europeans brought a particular moral perspective to land ownership and management, of 'use it or lose it' (see chapter 5). Backed by the biblical edict to multiply and fill the Earth, colonists believed that those who used the land most productively (their own kind) had the best moral claim to it. European 'civilisation' added value. God gave the world to 'men in Common' but not for the Earth to remain 'common and uncultivated. He gave it to the use of the industrious and rational'. This belief that Europeans – in particular Englishmen – had a God-given right to the world's resources, as espoused by the English philosopher John Locke, spurred the colonisation of New Zealand.

All the main port towns except Auckland grew from the theory of systematic colonisation. This settler capitalist dream entailed a massive colonial experiment between 1840 and 1850 by the New Zealand Company and its offshoots. The New Zealand Company was a vast propaganda machine that set out to create towns and farms that would transplant civilisation to the New World, balance capital and labour, and claim the wilderness as a garden. The theory's chief ideologue, Edward Gibbon Wakefield, was obliged to stay out of sight because of his prison term. In London's Newgate Prison, he wrote *A Letter from Sydney* (1829) in which he outlined his philosophy to export 'a mixture of all classes of society'. Wakefield had never been to Sydney. Similarly, he imagined New Zealand in terms of its 'natural abundance' long before he or his brothers set foot there. He prefabricated the very idea of New Zealand from Arcadian concepts embedded in the European imagination. In 1836, he told the House of Commons Select

Committee on the Disposal of Lands in the [British] Colonies that near to Australia was a country that everyone described 'as the fittest country in the world for colonisation, as the most beautiful country, with the finest climate and the most productive soil'. New Zealand was destined to be a green and pleasant land, to borrow a phrase from William Blake's hymn 'Jerusalem'. In Wakefield's version, land was the central mechanism for the systematic creation of a colonial society that approximated a slice of a romanticised rural England, except with a thin sprinkling of friendly, assimilated 'natives' (his term).

Like all theories of colonisation, this variant, which appeared to derive from the political economy of Adam Smith, presupposed the dispossession of the indigenous people. As Wakefield explained in 1837, he proposed a 'deliberate plan and systematic efforts' to civilise a 'barbarous people'. Although he saw Māori as 'savage' he also labelled them 'superior' and, of all indigenous peoples, the most like Europeans. Their 'peculiar aptitude' for improvement invited prospects of intermarriage with colonists so that future generations of Europeans and 'natives' would 'become one people'. In this way he incorporated the paradigm of a common humanity. Wakefield had his own performer of the 'civilised native' role in the form of Nahiti, a Māori visitor to London who dressed in the latest fashion. Nahiti may have assisted the Wakefield brothers' London performances in the late 1830s, but he was dumped as an interpreter in New Zealand once Edward Wakefield's brother Colonel William Wakefield discovered that he lacked chiefly status. Wakefieldian theory imbibed a common humanity but was class bound, intended to preserve rank and distinctions, because Edward Wakefield was a snob.

The theory's economic basis was to sell land at a 'sufficient price' to ensure the proper balance of land, labour, and capital and so to concentrate settlement and promote civilisation through clustering. The theory prescribed the sale of land at a price high enough to stop labourers from becoming landowners too soon, but not so expensive as to put off worthy settlers. Profits from managed land sales were to subsidise the passages of more migrants. Young married couples were vital to the scheme, because the values of motherhood and family life, fundamental to civilisation, provided a cornerstone of creating a better society. Increasingly, the rising middle classes and respectable working-class people imbibed the evangelical Christian values enshrined in marriage. These were the ideals that Wakefield invoked when he declared, 'As respects morals and manners, it is of little importance what colonial fathers are, in comparison with what the mothers are', a theory based on the support provided by his grandmother, mother, and elder sister to the morally flawed men in his family. The systematic colonisation of New Zealand offered a means to redeem Edward and William Wakefield's reputations, both of which had been tarnished by the abduction offence.

As a colonial experiment, New Zealand provided a contrast with Australia. From the start New Zealand assumed an image of superiority to the Australian colonies, particularly New South Wales, which as the first founded was the 'mother colony' for all the Australasian colonies except Western Australia. No matter that Kororāreka was home to escaped convicts; New Zealand would develop the lessons learnt in Adelaide, the first town planned according to the Wakefieldian dream, and in theory a non-convict settlement. New Zealand Company propaganda promoted the idea of a select type, devoid of the convict stain, who would set the requisite 'standard of morals and manners'.

Demonstrating the power of European templates, the 'colonists' (cabin passengers) bound for Wellington in 1839 mentally possessed themselves of the land before they left home. The New Zealand Company held a lottery of land orders in London before its agent William Wakefield had even arrived in Cook Strait on the *Tory* and drawn up a hasty deed of purchase. The ballot was for land orders rather than land, because in August 1839 the company had no land to sell. Ladies were ostensibly the 'most daring speculators'. There were cheers when 'the Natives' drew a number, and the belief that the game brought about good deeds enhanced the thrill of the flutter: the players believed that their lottery improved the Māori's 'chance of civilisation'. They had no inkling of how much of a lottery settling New Zealand would be in practice.

Meanwhile, across the world, the chiefs Te Puni and Te Wharepouri and rival hapū of Ngāti Toa and Ngāti Raukawa (who named William Wakefield 'Wide-awake'), who had migrated to the

Wellington area because of the musket wars, had no idea that the New Zealand Company had already possessed and renamed their territory. They found out one week after the *Tory* entered the harbour on 20 September 1839, when Wakefield presented a deed of purchase to gathered chiefs. Among the list of goods in 'payment' for millions of acres of land were 100 red blankets and 100 muskets, plus 1200 fishhooks and a dozen umbrellas.

In November, still in rough seas on the *Cuba*, the company's surveyor-general Captain William Mein Smith (named 'Kapene Mete', or 'Captain Measure', by Māori) read Edward Wakefield's *England and America* and liked his reasoning. Realising the dream would be another matter. The idea that Mein Smith was handed a concept plan – the 'Cobham plan' – in London for the imagined town of 'Britannia' is a myth constructed after the event. Nowhere in his journal is there any mention of such a plan. It is more likely that designs of a town laid out in a grid pattern intersected by a wide and navigable river were used in panoramas exhibited in London to promote emigration. The planning of Wellington was left to Mein Smith by the New Zealand Company. He was a teacher and administrator with 26 years' experience in the Royal Artillery who was teaching plan drawing at Woolwich when the company approached him and was accustomed to following orders and presiding at courts martial. Accordingly, he followed the directors' instructions to the letter. His difficulty was that the topography around Wellington Harbour / Port Nicholson was more akin to the Rock of Gibraltar, where he had served with the Royal Artillery from 1829 to 1836, than to the grasslands suited to the grid pattern of the British colonial town. He had experience of the latter in North America, at the British fort town of Kingston, Ontario. Somehow at Port Nicholson he and his assistants had to lay out 1100 town sections of 1 acre (0.4 hectares) each and, more absurdly, find room for parks, boulevards, and 100-acre (40-hectare) country sections for the investors who had paid £101 for each fictitious package of a town section and country section. As he reported, he laid out Wellington 'under every species of difficulty; the incessant importunities of a large body of Settlers who had arrived by this time, a winter of unusual inclemency, no office or place of residence but a tent, and frequent hindrance from the Natives'.

Colonel William Wakefield proved another hindrance. His hostility to the surveyors charged with realising the dream captured the incongruity between the theory of colonisation and what was practicable. Mein Smith and his cadets surveyed two towns in six months, because the principal agent interfered and instructed him to shift the survey from Petone (Pito-one), on the harbour's northern shore, to Pipitea, the current site of downtown Wellington, in April 1840 (see figure 3.2). Mein Smith decided to locate the town on the flat ground at Petone, not at Pipitea, where Wakefield had left stores, because Pipitea, while 'a very nice site for a Town', was too small and too far from potential country sections in the Hutt Valley. Petone, on the other hand, 'afforded abundance of room' to carry out the instructions. The captain reported to the colonel, 'On your return to Port Nicholson you agreed with me in opinion, and I commenced operations'. This was urgent, since settlers began to arrive a mere fortnight after the surveyors. Unfortunately, in March the Hutt River 'rose and overflowed its banks', upsetting everyone's efforts. Mein Smith thought the river could be made

3.2 William Mein Smith, *From the pah Pipitea, Port Nicholson, December 1840*, 1840
Alexander Turnbull Library, Wellington, C-011-005

secure against future floods by clearing away driftwood and cutting channels, but Wakefield refused to provide the funds. Instead he forced a fresh start on the fragments of flat land from Pipitea to past Te Aro, both of which were pā sites.

At Pipitea, former Taranaki people's pā, gardens, and burial grounds occupied the best land, which is now home to the New Zealand parliament. The enforced shift of site exacerbated cross-cultural tensions, because Wakefield claimed that he had bought the land, but residents disagreed. The colonists' host Te Wharepouri presided over and made over for settlement Petone, not today's central Wellington. Compounding the chaos, the 'tenths' reserved for Māori according to the company's instructions were scattered by the ballot system. Some of the 110 acres (44 hectares) of Māori tenths reserves which Mein Smith selected and surveyed were already pā sites and cultivation land, but other occupied foreshore land was claimed for the settlers, presumably because these sites had already been allotted to purchasers who had priority in the London ballot. Consequently, six of nine villages disappeared.

Historians have alternately praised and denounced Edward Gibbon Wakefield and his siblings; only in 2002 did a biography accept the brothers for themselves and acknowledge the importance of their fantasies. But this glossed over the unscrupulous behaviour of William Wakefield, whose undermining of the surveyor-general at Wellington and in reports to London, while not unusual in the world of politics, distorted the story of what happened on the ground. Surveyors were typical of the pragmatic men of the outdoors whose characteristics subsequently evolved into a national type; literally, they made a path for others. Overlooked or judged because their labours overrode indigenous genealogies, the surveyors of the Wakefieldian settlements were following orders deemed right and proper by an imperial script. They used their cross-cultural and military experience to bring the infrastructure for Pākehā New Zealand into being. It is appropriate for this descendant to acknowledge that the New Zealand Company's surveyor-general struggled to realise the colonial dream. He and his staff measured up and made it work.

Nearly 10 000 settlers migrated under company schemes in the 1840s, carrying with them hopes of a better life. Women's domestic labour as wives, mothers, and workers proved critical to the whole venture, not least because there were 1.3 men for every woman. Whole families were transplanted; among these settlers were 3846 children under 13. Some of the colonial elite brought prefabricated houses with them, as did the New Zealand Company. The planning of cities was envisaged from the start, with the town perceived as a symbol of civilising the wilderness – hence the choice of kitset cottages to 'hasten the process'.

Captain William Hobson's house was transported to Auckland to shelter his wife and young family. This greatly disappointed the Wellington settlers, who then realised that their town – conceived and advertised as the principal town – was not to be the capital. William Mein Smith's first houses were small, prefabricated Manning cottages bought by the company and assembled first at Petone and then at Thorndon (Pipitea). He had his private residence, Tinakori Cottage, built in 1841 for his wife, Louisa, and small children. Other Manning cottages made their way to Australia in the 1830s. One became the Pegasus Arms in Christchurch. Migrants expressed pride in their possession of a piglet or a hen to feed their families. The domesticity of the venture is remarkable.

True to Arcadian myth these young people set out to colonise their new land through domesticity and husbandry, by building homes, raising families, rearing imported stock, and planting gardens. In such transplanted narratives scholars have detected the individualism in nineteenth-century Pākehā culture that recurred in a political emphasis on self-reliance. In the backblocks as in towns, dreams of landed independence demanded adaptation to the new environment. This is illustrated in William Strutt's sketch of a back settler's whare (house; figure 3.3). Strutt captured the application of indigenous architecture – the whare, built from timber and ponga logs (fern trunks) – combined with elements of the English country cottage, as resources allowed. Colonial adaptability added the canvas roof. The danger of fire was ever present, as if to confirm that Arcadianism proved its own enemy when faith in 'natural abundance' failed to produce a promised land.

Strutt's image also illustrates the power of the pioneer legend. New Zealand's pioneer mythology paralleled others from the

3.3 William Strutt, *Settler putting out chimney fire*, 1855 or 1856
Alexander Turnbull Library, Wellington, E-453-f-003

frontiers of British settlement. It celebrated settlers as heroes and heroines, the men for their manly virtues of courage, enterprise, hard work, and perseverance; and the women as 'colonial helpmeets' endowed with the feminine versions of these attributes (see chapter 5). Pioneers tamed the land and, they believed, made it productive as God intended. They renamed it and made it home.

A group of French settlers had similar ideas. In 1838 the whaling captain Jean François Langlois returned to France with a deed signed by South Island chiefs that he believed gave him ownership of Banks Peninsula. This deed prompted the French equivalent of the New Zealand Company, the Nanto-Bordelaise Company, to despatch settlers to buy and occupy land in 'Southern New Zealand', because in the French view claiming the land meant occupation. Had the French not sailed into Akaroa Harbour in August to find that local Ngāi Tahu had signed the Treaty of Waitangi in May 1840, the South Island might have become another Quebec. In practice a balance of power prevailed between the tiny French settlement at Akaroa and Ngāi Tahu in the 1840s. But the balance shifted as the European population burgeoned as a result of organised settlement in the South Island from 1848, with the planning of the Otago settlement at Dunedin as a Scottish Presbyterian enclave, and with Christchurch, the principal town of the Canterbury settlement, founded from the end of 1850 as an Anglican stronghold.

No wonder the prior negotiations about land retained and sold led to lasting conversations over indigenous property rights, especially for Ngāi Tahu. Paid a pittance for the vast landholdings and resources that Governor George Grey, appointed in 1845 fresh from the governorship of South Australia, pressured chiefs to relinquish, and misled by Grey's deputy, Ngāi Tahu set conditions for the Canterbury purchase. As their prophet Matiaha Tiramōrehu emphasised, hapū wanted to keep all their mahinga kai (food-gathering places and food resources), kainga nohoanga (seasonal occupation sites) and fisheries. They were also assured of ample reserves. Henry Tacy Kemp, the Crown negotiator, agreed to these demands. But Kemp, like the governor, broke all his promises.

Canterbury provides a case study in settler capitalism. It represented the scheme of systematic colonisation fulfilled, and the identity of its principal town, Christchurch, embodied this precept. Unlike Auckland, which began from Sydney, the Canterbury settlement was intended to be a transplanted England. Founders embraced the goal of civilisation that had been at the heart of British colonisation overseas since the sixteenth century. Christchurch was to have a college and a cathedral.

The Canterbury Association's first four ships reached the port of Lyttelton in December 1850 after a quick passage. They may be better termed the last four ships, because Canterbury was the last Wakefieldian settlement. It was also the most successful. In local history, the Canterbury scheme succeeded because of the calibre of its colonists, assisted by geography, timing, planning, and pastoralism. Like other commercial cities in Australasia, Christchurch had plenty of flat ground and a separate port. Though some land was boggy, environmental obstacles did not pose an immediate hazard: the town site was bordered by large wetlands and separated from the port by hills. There was time for planning. Captain Joseph Thomas, the chief surveyor, a former Royal Engineers officer, and his assistants had completed a trigonometrical survey of the Canterbury block by the end of 1849 and laid out the port of Lyttelton and seaside suburb of Sumner as well as Christchurch in 1850 before the settlers arrived. Canterbury's pilgrims therefore enjoyed an easier start than settlers in the other colonies.

The 'forgotten forty-niners' who built roads, houses, and accommodation barracks for the newcomers comprised 40 northern Māori recruited as roadbuilders, about 30 former Australian convicts, and refugees from Wellington (rocked by an earthquake in 1848) and from Wellington's offshoot of Nelson, which lacked land for farming. Captain Thomas, who had worked on the Whanganui and Otago surveys, astutely managed scarce funds but was denied the role of leader of the settlement once the settlers arrived. That position went to J. R. Godley, whose Oxford College Christ Church provided the name for the colonial town. Ironically, the Catholic Caroline Chisholm and her family colonisation society, which organised migrants to Australia, saved this Church of England settlement. Chisholm ensured that the Canterbury ships were filled with ordinary working people whom she saw as a means of rescuing the project.

Canterbury had an advantage over other Wakefieldian settlements in that pastoralism was allowed from the start. This was possible because Canterbury came into existence relatively late. As happened in other Australasian colonies from 1850, the port and town provided an entrepot for metropolitan culture and at the same time for pastoral expansion in the hinterland. In fact, Godley incorporated pastoralism in the scheme by issuing pasturage regulations, which guaranteed Canterbury's success. The 'advance guard of empire' in the South Island comprised hard-working pastoralists, shrewd and enterprising capitalists with lower-middle-class or working-class origins whose wealth ranked far behind levels found in the United States, Britain, and New South Wales. Wealthy settlers were not a 'gentry' (though they aspired to be) but part of the 'colonial capitalist class', whose assets were built in Canterbury on pastoralism and in Otago on commerce and finance. Most arrived early in the context of late settlement, before the largest immigration wave, in the 1870s. It is striking how, even for the rich, the New Zealand experience was shaped from the start by shortage of money.

CROWN COLONY

Frugality was the first principle of administration by the Colonial Office. New Zealand government was established on the cheap and connoted more ideal than reality. Settlers and Māori thought the governor possessed personal authority as a ruler 'who would protect them from each other'. The colony's viability depended on buying land cheaply from Māori and selling it at a profit to finance further immigration. This explains in part the tense relations between the government in Auckland and the New Zealand Company settlements, because the Treaty of Waitangi threatened the company's land sales through the Crown right of pre-emption, which decreed that the Crown alone could buy land directly from Māori. It also explains why early governments failed to act as protectors of the indigenous people, to provide the guarantees promised in the Treaty, and to intervene to check settler demands.

The Wairau dispute of 1843 became a catalyst. Shortage of land at Port Nicholson prompted a spread of New Zealand Company settlements to Whanganui, New Plymouth and Nelson by 1842, all of which created flashpoints in Māori–Pākehā relations. The dispute resulted from the Nelson settlement's demand for rural sections and especially grasslands suitable for pastoralism. Te Rauparaha and his nephew Te Rangihaeata of Ngāti Toa protested to William Spain, the government commissioner appointed to investigate land sales, that they had not sold the Wairau valley to Colonel William Wakefield. Their own claim to the top of the South Island was dubious and continues to be disputed. But it was foolhardy of Nelson's police magistrate Henry Thompson to decide to travel to the Wairau to arrest the chiefs for arson which had disrupted the survey. Because of this gross misjudgement Thompson, the head of the Nelson settlement Captain Arthur Wakefield – the most honourable of the Wakefield brothers – and their party were killed. Te Rangihaeata felled both men with his greenstone mere after the Pākehā shot his wife, Te Rongo, who was Te Rauparaha's daughter. Wairau left a legacy of embitterment for Pākehā and Māori.

To add to the shock of deaths among them, the Nelson settlers were outraged when Hobson's successor in 1843, Governor Robert FitzRoy, also a naval officer, decided that the settlers were wrong to pursue the survey of the coveted pasture along the Wairau River before Commissioner Spain had investigated the contested claims to ownership. FitzRoy was an aristocrat who hosted Charles Darwin on the voyage of HMS *Beagle* from 1831 to 1836 and had experience of cultural encounter in Tierra del Fuego and other parts of South America, where he aimed to civilise 'savages'. The settlers from Nelson objected, saying that appeasement of the 'savage' exacerbated conflict by encouraging Māori to believe that they owned large uncultivated tracts of land. Incensed at the bloodshed and the governor's response, they hardened their attitudes. Alfred Domett, later the colony's premier, sought revenge for the Wairau episode and subsequently oversaw the confiscation of Māori land in the 1860s.

In the aftermath of the conflict Te Rauparaha and Te Rangihaeata returned to the Wellington side of Cook Strait. Hints about their relations with individual Pākehā can be gleaned from family histories. Charles Hartley, a young gunsmith from Cornwall who arrived in Wellington with his parents and sister in January 1840, became a trader along the Manawatū River and later an interpreter in the Native Land Court. He and his wife, Dinah, cared for Te Rangihaeata when he had serious wounds, so several times Te Rangihaeata warned them of danger in tensions between tribes and with government troops. He also advised settlers to move to Wellington. Dinah is remembered for keeping an axe behind the kitchen door to protect herself, not from her Māori protectors but from Pākehā pit sawyers who became violent when drunk. In the Manawatū, the New Zealand Company claimed to have purchased 25 000 acres (10 120 hectares) of land, but the Māori owners disputed this claim, and the company was eventually allowed only 900 acres (365 hectares). Hasty land deals oblivious to the complexities of tribes were routine even in this district known for its harmonious race relations.

Clashes also erupted in the north over flagpoles and boundary markers. Hōne Heke, who had led the Treaty signing, clearly understood the symbolism of chopping down the British flagpole at Kororāreka / Russell, which he did with his allies four times in 1844 and 1845; and well did the governor understand his challenge. Consequently, the first of the New Zealand Wars broke out in the north between the British, reinforced by military support from New South Wales and Heke's relative Tāmati Wāka Nene; and Heke and the elder chief Kawiti, supported by 'their' Pākehā. In this war Ngāpuhi fought one another. The Anglican church at Kororāreka still bears the scars of gunfire, while, thanks to Heke, Bishop Pompallier's house was saved. By 1845 Heke had largely repudiated the Treaty of Waitangi. His dispute was not with Pākehā in general but with the colonial government, embodied in the governor, over the takeover of chiefs' authority and their land. 'God made this country for us', he wrote to the new governor, George Grey. Heke had agreed to be 'all as one' with the governor, not subordinate, his chiefly authority curtailed. Conversely, other northern chiefs backed the Treaty, and Kawiti's son helped re-erect the flagstaff in 1858 when peace was restored.

Governor Grey failed to capture or crush Heke and Kawiti, who, on balance, outwitted the imperial military. On the contrary, Kawiti surprised government forces by the successful conduct of trench warfare. In the wars of 1845–7, Australia provided most of the military force to quell Māori resistance. Sydney and Hobart supplied arms to both sides; Australian garrisons sent soldiers as well as sailors. The resisters showed who commanded the north, but not just through military strategy. Heke and Kawiti made peace first with Nene, their kin, before they made peace with Grey.

Around the Wellington settlement, power and authority tilted from the Māori world to control by the colonial government. The key moment came in 1846 when Governor Grey arrested Te Rauparaha in his own home, because of rumours of an assault on Wellington, then imprisoned him without charge for 10 months on a naval vessel. Te Rauparaha was not returned to his people at Otaki until 1848. The old warrior's arrest – when he professed to be neutral in local conflicts – destroyed his mana and provided the opportunity for the government to supplant the Ngāti Toa chief in his realm of authority assumed by conquest around Cook Strait, an area that functioned as a highway for shipping, communication, and commerce.

The founding of a settler state followed closely on the establishment of the South Island settlements of Otago and Canterbury. In the Crown colony period from 1841 to 1853 the governor and his executive council ruled the colony. This proved unpopular with the colonists, who sought representative and responsible government. The secretary of state for the colonies Earl Grey produced a constitution in 1846 that created two provinces: New Ulster, most of the North Island; and New Munster, comprising Wellington and the South Island. But the newly knighted Sir George Grey denied self-government on the grounds of injustice to Māori, who were excluded, refusing to give power to a settler minority. As governor he assumed responsibility for Māori affairs. Though he too wished to curb the power of chiefs, he appeared initially to involve Māori in the provision of schools, hospitals, and police; as assessors in magistrates' courts; in gifts of flour mills and equipment; and in making settlers responsible for the trespass of stock.

New Zealand obtained representative government in the form of a governor and two houses of parliament on the Westminster model under the Constitution Act 1852, proclaimed in January 1853, with a Legislative Council nominated by the governor and an elected House of Representatives. The Act also created a system of provincial government established in six provinces: Auckland, the capital and the only non-Wakefieldian settlement; Wellington; Taranaki (centred on the town of New Plymouth); Nelson; Canterbury (Christchurch); and Otago (Dunedin). Settlers secured representative government with a male property vote in the first election, in 1853. In theory there was no racial distinction concerning the franchise; propertied men included Māori men if they held individualised (European) title to land, freehold or leasehold, or lived in a European-style dwelling. In the Wairarapa, for example, Te Manihera, who had invited the first pastoralists to run sheep in the 1840s, voted in 1853 and hosted the local electoral meeting at his house. Edward Gibbon Wakefield himself arrived in Wellington in 1853, cherishing the idea that, with the establishment of constitutional government, he could regain status as a colonial politician. Instead he found that the stigma of his convict past stuck. Responsible government for settlers followed in 1856, in tandem with the rise of early democracy in the Australasian colonies. But in New Zealand this was accompanied by an experiment in excluding native affairs from responsible ministers' control.

If the intent was to pursue a policy of amalgamation, the reality was a mere handful of Māori being qualified to vote in the colony's first election, in 1853. Not by chance, talk about a separate Māori parliament or a Māori king began simultaneously among mission-educated chiefs. Another instance of 'a show of justice' is given in clause 71 of the Constitution Act, which provided for the creation of native districts, set apart from the settler provinces, where Māori could live under customary law. This clause was never implemented. The onus remained with the governor, because despite – and perhaps because of – responsible government, native affairs continued to be his responsibility.

By the late 1850s Māori unease had deepened in response to the government's track record on land purchase and militarism. The pan-tribal Kīngitanga (King movement), centred in the Waikato, rose to the challenge and chose Pōtatau Te Wherowhero as the first Māori king (standing next to Tāmati Wāka Nene in figure 3.4). A decade earlier the Waikato paramount chief had agreed to provide protection for the seat of government at Auckland, as had Pātuone. Te Wherowhero did not see the kingship as opposed to Queen Victoria and sought to cooperate with the government. But escalating land disputes obliged him to oppose the governor, stultifying Crown attempts to purchase land in the Waikato to expand settlement and link the main towns of Auckland and Wellington by road and rail. Te Wherowhero accepted the kingship after other ariki (high chiefs) turned it down and was crowned in 1858. Tribes that joined the Kīngitanga united to resist colonisation and land sales, because together they were determined to protect their lands and communities.

Pastoralism signalled the future in all the Australasian colonies in the 1850s. By 1861 the colonial government had purchased two-thirds of New Zealand, mainly in the South Island, where Grey acquired huge tracts from Ngāi Tahu, such as by Kemp's Deed in 1848 of 20 million acres (8 million hectares) for the Canterbury

3.4 Thomas B. Collinson, *Hosey's battle 1847. Capt[ain] Henderson, Capt[ain E.] Stanley, R. N., Tamati Waka Nene, Potatau Te Wherowhero [the future Māori king]*, 1848. This was a skirmish in the war at Whanganui, where Nene and Te Wherowhero accompanied Governor George Grey 'to stimulate the missionary party to a decided course of action against the hostiles'. James Cowan, *The New Zealand Wars*, vol. 1: *1854–64*, Wellington: Government Printer, 1983, 141 (first published 1922). Original in Alexander Turnbull Library, Wellington, A-292-058

settlement at a price of £2000. Through 10 Ngāi Tahu deeds from 1844 to 1864, the Crown sought to make the tribe's land, waterways, and natural resources available for settler capitalism.

By contrast the government had alienated less than a quarter of the North Island by 1861, thwarting government and settler aspirations. Frustrated, in 1860 Governor Thomas Gore Browne sent in imperial troops to enforce the claim to a disputed purchase of land at Waitara, in Taranaki, long coveted by the New Plymouth settlers. The claim contravened the rights of most owners and in doing so fired the opening round in the New Zealand Wars of the 1860s. Māori were appalled because the government ignored protests that the willing sellers of the Waitara block had no right of sale.

The wrong land purchase at Waitara and the rise of the Kīngitanga combined to return the Treaty to the forefront of discourse about

Claiming the land 1840–1860   75

Māori–Pākehā relations. The issue under debate became how to reconcile the exercise of Māori rights with government authority. In Governor Browne's logic, sovereignty rested neither on Māori rights nor on the rights of Englishmen but was absolute. Perceiving Waitara and the King movement as rebellion, he sought to divide and rule by persuading the rest of Māoridom to attend a month-long conference of chiefs at Kohimarama, near Auckland, in July 1860, with the idea that the chiefs confirm their allegiance to the Crown, and to quash support for the Kīngitanga. He reiterated the humanitarian view that would become a central tenet of relations between Māori and the Crown, not for the benefit of Māori, but to assert sovereignty:

> New Zealand is the only Colony where the Aborigines have been treated with unvarying kindness. It is the only Colony where they have been invited to unite with the Colonists and to become one People under one law ... It is your adoption by Her Majesty as her subjects which makes it impossible that the Maori people should be unjustly dispossessed of their lands or property. Every Maori is a member of the British Nation.

The queen saw Māori 'as a part of her especial people'. But the governor added a threat. If they violated their 'allegiance to the Queen', they would be liable to 'forfeit [their] rights and privileges' as British subjects.

There was no such clause in the Treaty of Waitangi, though such a subtext could be read into it. Donald McLean, who chaired the meeting at Kohimarama, personified the contradictions in the Treaty and in the government's actual dealings with Māori in his combined positions as native secretary and land purchase commissioner. He sought and obtained the chiefs' endorsement of Crown allegiance, including from tribes whose leaders had not signed the Treaty in 1840. Significantly for the future, he also represented the Treaty in Māori, spelling out in the Māori language that article 2 of the Treaty specified rights to possession of their land, forests, and fisheries.

But the chiefs disagreed with the government's policy towards Waitara and the Kīngitanga. Māori believed that Māori (that is, rangatira) and Pākehā leaders should share governmental authority under the queen and stand united but equal, walking in parallel. Such thinking at the time was expressed in religious terms, as equal and united before God. Christianity was politically empowering, because it represented a higher power; and it gave Māori a new voice and a way forwards in what in today's terms would be described as an increasingly cross-cultural and globalising world. What shocked Māori loyalists over Waitara was that the government resorted to force in a civil dispute. They believed that law, not war, was the answer. In the view of Rēnata Tama-ki-Hikurangi of Hawkes Bay, a chief and missionary, the British government breached the Treaty by resorting to violence. The Treaty stood for peace.

4

Remoter Australasia 1861–1890

If the governor's decision to wage war in Taranaki over Waitara in 1860 was heavy-handed and aggressive, the invasion of the Waikato launched by Sir George Grey in July 1863 amounted to a blatant lunge for power. Indeed – as a narrow victory of numbers – it presaged the takeover by settler New Zealand that deluged Māori. From the 1860s the scales of power tipped to the settler society. Within a generation, Māori shrank from being most of the population to a small minority. The amount of land in Māori ownership, already much diminished, halved between 1860 and 1891. But pockets of resistance nurtured a proud legacy that would recalibrate relations a century and more later.

NEW ZEALAND WARS

Thanks to James Belich's scholarship, the New Zealand Wars came to be seen as instances of British 'small wars' of imperial conquest that invaded autonomous Māori sovereignty, played a significant part in defining Pākehā (European New Zealanders) and Māori as 'us' and 'them', and created the national debt. Māori resistance was effective rather than futile until numbers overwhelmed them. 'New Zealand Wars' can include significant battles in the Bay of Islands through 1845–6 (the northern war) as well as clashes on both sides of Cook Strait from 1843 to 1877, notably at Wairau, in Marlborough. But the wars proper raged from 1860 to 1872 across the central North Island, after a decade of peace.

There is vigorous debate about the nature and legacy of these conflicts, fought over land, sovereignty, and rangatiratanga (chieftainship), and begun by the government. Vincent O'Malley calls the Waikato War (1863–4) 'the defining conflict in New Zealand history' and 'the Great War for New Zealand'. Power, propinquity, and possession decreed that war would flare in the North Island, where tribes still owned most of the land in the 1860s. Most Māori lived in the North Island, which remained under tribal control outside the isolated coastal towns. By contrast, the South Island was, in British law, already in settler hands. That left Ngāi Tahu the daunting task of fighting their claim against Crown breaches of the Treaty of Waitangi in writing and later in parliament.

In January 1860 Governor Thomas Gore Browne determined to complete the purchase of the disputed block at Waitara, in Taranaki, and sent in the surveyors. In March the first shots were fired in the Taranaki War after Māori obstructed the survey. Frightened settlers sought refuge from resisters in New Plymouth, British troops burnt the village at Waitara, and farms went up in smoke. For Wiremu Kingi, the offended Te Āti Awa chief, the Kīngitanga (King movement) offered his only chance of support. The ensuing alliance with the Māori king guaranteed that the dispute would widen, even if, after reaching a stalemate, the parties called a truce. Irritated by Browne's clumsiness – or seeking a scapegoat – the British government replaced him with Sir George Grey, recalled from Cape Town to Auckland in 1861. Though the war in Taranaki was over by the time Grey arrived, he was chosen to bring peace to the colony.

On the contrary, Grey brought war. Grey had changed since his first tour of duty in New Zealand. So had the circumstances in which he exercised power: a settler government was installed, while the British military retained 3000 men in the colony. Grey decided to return the contested land at Waitara so that he could turn his attention to the Waikato, where Pōtatau Te Wherowhero's successor as Māori king, King Tāwhiao, was gathering support. But he did not do so before an attack on troops began the second phase of the Taranaki War.

Grey could not tolerate the Kīngitanga's challenge to his authority. Misadvising the British government that his preparations were defensive against an alleged Kingite plot to attack Auckland, Grey built a military road, the Great South Road, from Auckland towards present-day Hamilton, erected the colony's first telegraph line to send military intelligence, and ordered steamboats to patrol the Waikato River. The Kīngitanga warned that the military road must not cross its boundary, and its newspaper announced that the governor's authority over Kingite territory was unacceptable. On 11 July 1863 Grey demanded that Māori who occupied territory up to the designated river boundary declare their allegiance, surrender their weapons, and agree to live in places determined by him as governor. In a pre-emptive strike on 12 July, Grey ordered the British commander Lieutenant-General D. A. Cameron to cross the Mangatāwhiri River, the line which the King movement signalled that the government forces must not pass. Cameron's troops crossed the river before local communities even received the governor's commands. The invasion of the Waikato had begun. As O'Malley states, this was 'a deliberate war of conquest and dispossession'.

The Waikato War, fought between the settler government supported by imperial forces and the Kīngitanga, was the largest and most significant of the New Zealand Wars, which Grey provoked in the hope of smashing the King movement and seizing fertile land. Repeatedly, the Kingite forces slowed the British military advance into the Waikato with a strategy of modern pā and raids, which inflicted substantial losses on the British at Rangiriri, where several women helped defend the pā. Here the elaborate earthworks of trenches, tunnels, and pits astonished the British. Cameron's troops took over 180 prisoners, which startled the Kīngitanga, since they expected peace would follow the fighting.

By February 1864 Cameron's men had come up against a defensive line, built by the warrior chief Rewi Maniapoto, of earthworks that included large pā. It was a lopsided contest. At their peak in 1864, imperial and colonial forces numbered 18 000, against 5000 Māori. A third of the British force comprised volunteers and militia of whom half (3000 volunteers and military settlers) came from the Australian colonies. In the most famous encounter of all, Rewi Maniapoto made his last stand – remembered as 'Rewi's last stand' – at the battle of Ōrākau. This episode encapsulated Pākehā understanding of the wars in general, wherein Māori inevitably lost to the British after putting up a pointless but heroic resistance. A story lives on in film and literature that, when offered a chance to surrender, Rewi responded that he would fight onwards forever. When Cameron invited the women and children to leave, the reply was that they would also die. The British claimed victory at Ōrākau, but Rewi's defiance was mythologised. In fact, Rewi did not make a stand, because the pā was unfinished. Less remembered is that, nearly 20 years later, the government built him a house in the village of Kihikihi and awarded him a pension. This was his reward, since Rewi oversaw the complicated negotiations which led to the breakup of the Rohe Pōtae (King Country). According to writer James Cowan, this recognition by the state 'restored to Rewi a measure of his mana over the old home'. By this time, he was a major celebrity.

From the Waikato, war spread in 1864 to Tauranga, in the Bay of Plenty, and had already reopened in Taranaki, where British forces faced a new foe, in the form of followers of Pai Mārire (goodness and peace), also known to Europeans as Hauhau (the spirit of God, likened to wind). Pai Mārire was a prophet movement that adjusted to colonisation through its fusion of biblical and Māori elements and by resistance to the taking of land. Its leader, Te Ua Haumēne, politicised by the wrongful purchase of the Waitara block, became a Kingite supporter and established the Pai Mārire church, which he believed erased missionary mistakes from Christian teaching. His was the first of several prophet movements to resist oppression and the confiscation of land.

In 1863 the colonial parliament passed the New Zealand Settlements Act, which provided for the taking of land for public purposes and enabled the governor to establish settlements for colonisation in the North Island. This Act was 'just the beginning' of a burgeoning in statute law to allow the confiscation of land for settlement. Consequently, the government confiscated 1.2 million acres (480 000 hectares) of Kīngitanga land in 1865, of which only 314 000 acres (125 600 hectares) were later returned to people deemed 'neutrals' and 'returned rebels'. To add to the offence, military settlers were rewarded with grants of seized land. The confiscation fell unevenly on the government resisters, striking hard at the Waikato tribes while leaving Rewi's people, Ngāti Maniapoto, relatively untouched, as if to confirm that the whole Waikato War had been engineered to secure the most fertile Auckland hinterland for settlement. More accurately, the government confiscated the land it could control, and Maniapoto land in the interior was beyond its grasp. But the King movement lived on, hunkered down in the King Country in the central North Island, where the Māori king strove to retain rangatiratanga and ownership of the land in his name to prevent its being alienated to the settler government.

Worse was to come in the North Island. The main means of extinguishing Māori title to land was not confiscation but purchase. The colonial government had bought over 7 million acres (2.8 million hectares) in the North Island as well as almost all the South Island by 1865. From 1865 to 1890 it bought another 8 million acres (3.2 million hectares) through the Native Land Court, which the settler government established to extinguish customary land rights under the Native Land Acts of 1862 and 1865. It certainly earned its contemporary title of the 'land-taking court'. The court was set up to bring land owned by Māori outside the confiscation areas 'within the reach of colonization' by making it easier to buy, and to effect the 'detribalization of the Natives' to destroy the 'principle of communism' that politicians saw as a 'barrier' to amalgamating Māori into European culture and to government control. Contrary to the court's purpose in statute, which according to Richard Boast was to follow customary law in individualising title to Māori land – a non sequitur, the court exemplified liberal, laissez faire policies.

Effectively the Native Land Court sought a free market in land held by tribes through individualised property titles. The Native Land Acts allowed blocks to be cut up by converting customary title to a form of title in which owners named could sell their individual interests. In one move the court overrode the Treaty of Waitangi (even though the 1862 Act's preamble included reference to the Treaty) by ignoring the constraints of chieftainship, because, in awarding title of tribal land to individuals, it substituted the court's authority for chiefly authority. Since Māori could only sell or lease their land once the Native Land Court had decided its title, they were forced to go to court to establish their claims; and this requirement bogged tribes down in lengthy, expensive legal proceedings. Court hearings ensnared people in a double bind: to ensure the rights to their land they had to secure individualised title, which dealt a blow to customary tenure and to tribal authority. Land loss followed even when tribes refused to sell, because the court limited ownership to a few named individuals. Initially it adopted a '10-owner' rule, registering only 10 owners, regardless of the number who could lay claim to the land. Perhaps more important was how governments and private speculators acquired interests from individuals before title was awarded by the court. Often negotiated to fund surveys, these transfers invariably resulted in land sales.

In the meantime, fighting persisted on the east and west coasts of the North Island. The last campaign conducted by imperial troops was in 1866. Henceforth battles would be fought against Māori 'rebels' by kūpapa (Crown supporters) and colonial forces, including men from the Australian colonies. Kūpapa could be either 'friendlies' who were Queenites, loyal to Queen Victoria, rather than Kingites, or they could use the term to state their neutrality. Either way they were independent-minded. A main motive for tribes such as Te Arawa and Ngāti Porou to stand alongside colonial forces was to look out for their own people and retain their authority and independence. Challenged by change, they took up arms against renegades and religious prophets who posed a threat to traditional and new (Anglican) ideals of what it meant to be Māori.

A new warrior, Riwha Titokowaru, provoked by aggressive tactics and by confiscation of large tracts of land, took up Te Ua Haumēne's cause in Taranaki in the late 1860s. Titokowaru faced seemingly impossible odds when attacked at his stronghold in 1868 by colonial forest rangers, a force that recruited young men with bush experience who sought a 'free and exciting life' by striking 'terror into the marauding natives'. Titokowaru scored a great victory but was written out of history until the 1980s, because he revised the frontier adventure story's expected ending. His stronghold survived, while the colonial forces suffered severe casualties.

Te Kooti Arikirangi Te Turuki, on the other hand, is remembered as a prophet who defied injustice. Whereas Māori in Poverty Bay, on the North Island's East Coast, were neutral during the wars from 1860 to 1864 in Taranaki and the Waikato, from 1865 Te Kooti's iwi (tribe), Rongowhakaata, from Poverty Bay, were split between a government faction of kūpapa Māori and Pai Mārire supporters. The East Coast 'had its own war for its own reasons'. Though Te Kooti had fought on the government's side, he was arrested with hundreds of Pai Mārire followers and imprisoned on the Chatham Islands without trial as a suspected spy. There he founded his own religion, Ringatu (the Upraised Hand), likening his people to the Israelites in the Old Testament, and engineered a brilliant escape with 300 followers in 1868. An attack on Poverty Bay settlers and Māori that horrified the colonial government rendered him the colony's most wanted outlaw. Pursued inland by colonial and kūpapa troops, he waged a guerrilla war, escaping into the remote and rugged Urewera district, until he finally took refuge in the King Country in 1872. Like the Australian bushranger Ned Kelly, Te Kooti was famous at the time for his ability to vanish. Surrounded by ambiguities, neither chief nor tribal leader, he lived in exile yet, unlike other outlaws, received a pardon. He became the subject of narrative fiction, astride his white horse, even before his death. Two of New Zealand's earliest films were *Rewi's Last Stand* (1925) and *The Te Kooti Trail* (1927), both silent movies shot by filmmaker Rudall Hayward.

The New Zealand Wars changed settlement and land-ownership patterns across the central North Island and destroyed the Māori economy in the Waikato that had supplied Auckland. Those opposed to the government often took refuge, as Te Kooti did, in inaccessible areas inland. Confiscation of territory after the wars created grievances that simmered into the twenty-first century. On the North Island's East Coast, the government rewarded military settlers and 'loyal' Māori with confiscated land, often the territory of former enemies, which created new problems, since under Māori tikanga (custom) the newcomers could claim rights after some years in their new locations. Battles then transferred to the Native Land Court, which after 1873 declared all owners to be 'tenants in common' to ensure everyone was included. The outcome, however, was even more intense individualisation of land interests.

After the wars, 'neither the treaty nor the doctrine of aboriginal title came to the rescue of Maori'. On the contrary, tolerance dwindled.

With no protection of customary title in the Native Land Court, there would be no protection in the courts generally. A key judgment in 1877 by Chief Justice James Prendergast declared the Treaty a 'simple nullity'. Prendergast's decision followed from an interpretation of international common law that denied that 'any kind of civil government' or Māori law existed before the Treaty. He argued that the Treaty could not recognise native title that did not exist, since he believed Māori had 'no body politic'; rights could be created only by parliament. So much for the status of He Whakaputanga the Declaration of Independence, which James Busby had promised chiefs would allow them collectively to pass laws.

Given the futility of war, the Te Āti Awa prophet Te Whiti o Rongomai emerged to lead the Taranaki people in new, pacifist methods of resistance. In 1865 the government confiscated Taranaki land as punishment under the New Zealand Settlements Act and in 1878 began the survey of fertile plains in the province. The delay was significant, because in Te Whiti's view the governor should have occupied the confiscated land at the time of conquest. In the meantime, his people reoccupied it and according to custom reaffirmed their rights of ownership. Te Whiti and his supporters – including Titokowaru – symbolically ploughed his moko (face tattoo) across the disputed plains, obstructed newly surveyed roads, and peacefully removed the surveyors. Furious, the government passed special legislation so that it could hold hundreds of protesters without trial and imprison them, with two years' hard labour, in South Island gaols. This it did.

Then, as the prisoners returned, in 1881, the government began to sell off the coveted plains to settlers. Their landholdings taken, dispossessed and distressed Māori throughout the province walked long distances to the village of Parihaka, where Te Whiti established a model community to house them. Through spring, Taranaki people cleared, fenced, and cultivated. The government responded in November 1881 by sending nearly 1600 troops of the armed constabulary and volunteers on horseback to invade Parihaka, where they were greeted by young girls singing and dancing in peaceful defiance. Figure 4.1 depicts the violent response by Minister of Native Affairs John Bryce to this peaceful protest. Bryce, who led the assault, ordered the arrest of Te Whiti and Tohu Kākahi,

4.1 P. E. jnr, *For diver's reasons*, 1881. Bryce is carving up the protester, who wears the white feather headdress of Te Whiti's followers and lies down in passive resistance. Te Whiti's ploughmen, tents of the armed constabulary, and Mount Taranaki are in the background.
Wellington Advertiser Supplement, 19 November 1881. Alexander Turnbull Library, Wellington, A-095-038

the protest's leaders, who were relatives and allies; they 'walked to captivity' with great dignity and were again imprisoned without trial, banished to the South Island until 1883. Bryce ordered the troops to sack Parihaka to break the settlement. The armed constabulary duly ransacked the village, inflicting violence, including sexual violence and trauma, on those who remained.

Parihaka and the King movement were vindicated more than a century later. Both experienced expropriations to make way for small farmers from the 1880s. The government set aside native reserves within the confiscated territories and vested the reserves in the public trustee, who leased them to settlers under 21-year leases with a right of renewal. By setting leases centrally, the public trustee endeavoured to provide better returns for Māori owners. No rental reviews for 21 years, however, reduced leases to peppercorn rentals, while the transfers into leases occurred without Māori consent and often sparked protest.

The land was sliced up, but its people rebuilt Parihaka and continued to wear their symbolic headdress, of two white albatross feathers, in proud defiance. Te Whiti and Tohu retained their following. Not only did their people venerate them, but historians have since cast them as national heroes in an evolving peace tradition. Mahatma Gandhi, too, noted Parihaka's teachings on nonviolence and passive resistance.

King Tāwhiao finally made peace in 1881. Against his advice, Ngāti Maniapoto – who escaped confiscation because it was impossible to invade the King Country – negotiated with Bryce and his successor, the Liberal John Ballance, to allow surveys for the main trunk railway through their territory. That was preferred to the alternative of encroachment by the Native Land Court. This also affected other tribes, because the surveys set the tribal boundaries of the five main Kīngitanga iwi, including Ngāti Tūwharetoa, on the volcanic plateau. Before long, individuals acquired title and sold blocks piecemeal. The King Country's sale also resulted from the complexity of competing tribal interests and confusion over the boundaries set for specific political purposes. The Native Land Court added more layers of difficulty.

The opening of the King Country was soon undermined by government policies, through land agent deals with individuals that exacerbated the rivalries inherent in Māori society. Organised protest grew in the 1880s; King Tāwhiao petitioned Queen Victoria, travelling to England accompanied by other chiefs in 1884 to deliver the petition personally, with its message that Māori people continued to uphold the Treaty of Waitangi. His group was not granted an audience, because the New Zealand government objected. Back home, however, kūpapa chiefs joined calls to honour the Treaty.

POWER IN NUMBERS

Such demands grew once Māori numbers declined and followed the pattern of population loss suffered by every indigenous society during colonisation. New infections – tuberculosis, the biggest killer in the nineteenth century; influenza; and sexually transmitted diseases – ran amok among people with no inherited or acquired immunities. Babies and young children were highly susceptible to gut and respiratory infections; among Te Arawa of the Rotorua district, for example, only half the children born in the late nineteenth century lived to adulthood. By contrast, Pākehā enjoyed high rates of child survival. The infant mortality rate (Pākehā only) declined at least from when official statistics began to be published, in the 1870s, when infant mortality was already very low by world standards, at about 100 deaths in the first year of life per 1000 live births. In settler families, parents saw about four of every five children grow up.

The scales of depopulation and immigration, and of child survival, were such that Pākehā outnumbered Māori by 1860. Captain James Cook was probably about right with his guess that there were 100 000 Māori people in 1769. By 1858 Māori numbered between 56 000 and 62 000, while Pākehā, at 59 000, were poised to tilt the balance of power. By 1878 Māori were dominated demographically by a ratio of 10 to 1, swamped by two successive immigration waves in the 1860s and 1870s. To summarise, Māori numbers fell by more than half by the 1890s, consistent with a pattern of decline in indigenous populations throughout the Pacific, while mainly British migrants arrived by the boatload.

Dispossession hit North Island tribes hard from the 1860s, as did population decline. It is known that land loss, health, and wellbeing are linked by way of poverty, although how these links operate is complex and unclear. In one view, Māori relative poverty in the late nineteenth century resulted from synergies between three main processes: changes in the Māori economy, with shifts to individual property rights and wage labour; loss of resources, especially land and water; and loss of power. From the 1860s the sale of land through the Native Land Court had as radical an impact as the confiscation of land in rendering Māori vulnerable to poverty, disease, and premature death. Most communities lost a resource base, while the land retained proved barely enough for subsistence, let alone development. Sometimes land was sold to obtain capital to develop land elsewhere. Hapū (subtribes) who kept land suffered too, because multiple owners shared blocks that were too small for everyone and were often uneconomic. Even Te Arawa – whose forces fired the last shots in the New Zealand Wars, against a retreating Te Kooti in 1872, and who did relatively well as kūpapa – felt the grip of the Native Land Court.

British migration overwhelmed Māori and provided the numbers to create a settler society. Given that New Zealand was so far – the furthest place – from Britain, the obstacles of distance and cost determined that migrants had to be either adventurous or given the incentive of a free or subsidised fare to journey to the opposite side of the world. Themselves a tiny fraction of the great European diaspora in the nineteenth century, Australasian migrants shipped out to the New World in four main waves. First came the convicts to eastern Australia, and second the boatloads of free migrants that included the 10 000 New Zealand Company settlers. The third and fourth waves, however, proved to be the most significant in numbers and power. From 1850 to 1870 the gold-seekers who ventured from the goldfields of California to Victoria and then New Zealand, and eventually to islands in the South Pacific, brought boom times, towns, and gold fever. After them, from 1860 to 1890, followed a veritable tidal wave of planned, assisted immigration to Australasia, and this wave contained the 100 000 migrants carried to New Zealand by the vision of the business politician and premier Julius Vogel in the 1870s.

Demographic contours illustrate how the migrants in the second half of the nineteenth century proved decisive in shaping Pākehā New Zealand, establishing a settler state and society. Natural increase (births minus deaths) rather than net migration generated most of the population growth from the 1880s until the end of the twentieth century (see figure 4.2). Settler New Zealand was young, vigorous, and suddenly dominant.

The excess of men usual in frontier societies did not generally last long (see figure 4.3). Nor did the imbalance of men over women match that in the United States. The Pākehā population bulged with men, as if the population pyramid grew a beer pot, only until the 1870s. Gold rushes around the Pacific Rim explained this temporary imbalance. Auckland merchants lured gold-seekers to the Coromandel with the offer of a reward in 1852–3, and a brief strike followed in Golden Bay (renamed for the find) in 1856–7. But the real rush to New Zealand from California and Australia began in 1861, when a Tasmanian miner, Gabriel Read, struck gold in Otago, in a gully that now bears his name. Otago proved the bonanza from 1861 to 1863, followed by the West Coast from 1864 to 1867. While war preoccupied the North Island, gold fever consumed the South.

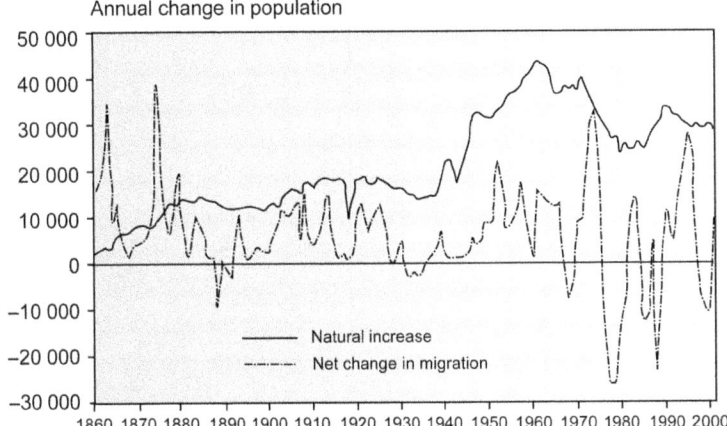

4.2 Population growth components, 1860–2000
After Phil Briggs, *Looking at the Numbers: A View of New Zealand's Economic History*, Wellington: NZ Institute of Economic Research, 2003, 21; 2016, 22

Central Otago's European population soared to about 24 000 between 1861 and 1864 but halved once the swarms of gold-seekers learnt of finds on the rugged West Coast. The first and largest stream of miners, containing many Irish, came from the Australian colonies, and the second from Britain, mainly Cornwall and Devon, while the Scots sought opportunities all over New Zealand. About 37 000 Irish miners reached the West Coast in 1865–7, all of them from Australia, where they had experienced life on the goldfields and to which they retained close connections. Altogether some 195 000 gold-seekers followed the rushes to New Zealand, two-thirds from the Australian colonies and the rest from Britain. Many moved on, however, producing a net population gain from gold of 114 000 in the 1860s.

Gold's geology shaped the pattern of the rushes, as diggers favoured successive types of gold deposits, from alluvial gold in the swift, ice-cold rivers of the South Island, to beach leads and coastal terraces that demanded sluicing, to gold locked in reefs of quartz, dug by deep-shaft mining. Each kind of deposit created a distinctive culture and community, from nomadic hordes under canvas who left ghost towns, to permanent towns during the underground phase, which required capital and permitted family life. Miners dug

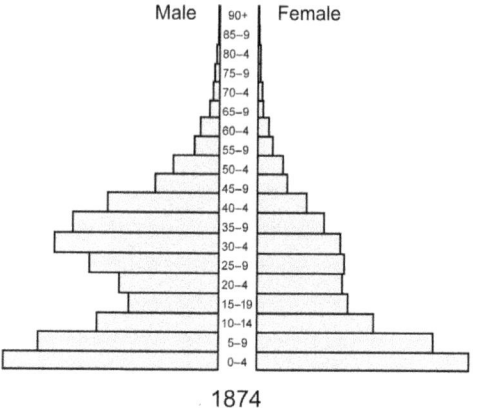

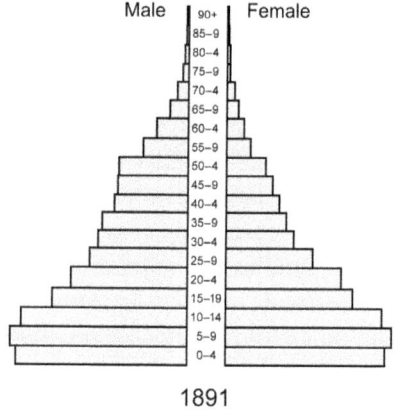

4.3 Population pyramids, 1874 and 1891 (European only)
Tim Nolan, based on Statistics NZ data, www.stats.govt.nz

piles of tailings and, at Ross, on the West Coast, and St Bathans, in Otago, great holes in the ground. Culturally and politically the rushes transformed the landscape through their impetus to early democracy. From Victoria the miners brought the concept of the miner's right and their hard-won democratic traditions, and New Zealand adopted the Victorian system of goldfields administration. In a direct response to the Eureka uprising, at Ballarat, in Victoria, the New Zealand government extended the vote to miners, most of whom would otherwise have been excluded, because they did not meet the property qualification. By 1865 the diggers' presence had led to 15 new electorates.

The gold rushes created communities that were both cosmopolitan and ethnically distinctive. Linguists have found that the New Zealand accent first appeared in mining towns in the South Island and military towns in the North Island, because these places had English speakers from a variety of origins. Census figures for Arrowtown, near Queenstown, show people in roughly equal numbers from England, Ireland, Scotland, and the Australian colonies; their presence influenced early New Zealand English. If not to the same extent as 'Marvellous Melbourne', gold gave a fillip to Dunedin, which temporarily displaced Auckland as New Zealand's largest city and flourished into a banking and business centre, proud of its gold-rush architecture. From Victoria, too, gold lured the future premiers and colonial nationalists Julius Vogel, to start the *Otago Daily Times*, and Richard Seddon, to run a pub on the West Coast.

The gold rushes also fuelled – as in Seddon's case – racial prejudice against the Chinese. At their peak there were 4000 Chinese miners in Otago and 5000 in New Zealand, all from Guangdong province: a tiny proportion compared to the 105 000 in the United States in 1880–1 and the 38 500 in Australia. Most were sojourners who experienced mixed fortunes, remitted money, and eventually returned home. Some stayed on as solitary prospectors, while others entered business and later paid for their wives to join them. Chinese in New Zealand formed part of a Pacific Rim diaspora in the 1850s and 1860s. Invited to Otago by Dunedin businessmen in 1865, when diggers flocked to the West Coast, they proved extremely efficient gold-seekers. As numbers rose, so did prejudice, heightened by anti-Chinese agitation in the Australian colonies in 1888, when Chinese refused entry to Australia were diverted to Greymouth and Dunedin. The colonial government responded with the transfer of immigration restriction policy from the Australian colonies.

Chinese have been remembered as fossickers and small-scale prospectors following behind the European diggers; but the entrepreneur Choie Sew Hoy was a prominent figure in gold dredging. It was Sew Hoy who formed the Shotover Big Beach Gold

4.4 Sew Hoy dredge gold mining, 1890s
Museum of New Zealand Te Papa Tongarewa, Wellington, C.014896

Mining Company, which initiated the first gold-dredging boom of 1889–91. His dredge, which provided the prototype for the New Zealand bucket dredge, worked beaches on the Shotover River near Queenstown, where tourists now go whitewater rafting and for jet boat rides (figure 4.4).

By the 1890s the beer pot in the Pākehā population pyramid had largely worked itself out. Men still outnumbered women, but the numbers of women were starting to catch up as young girls grew to adulthood (figure 4.3). Gold fever and the associated danger of excitement (a condition ascribed to men), however, threatened the image of New Zealand as an ideal society because of the perceived menace posed by greed, excessive or hyper masculinity, and frontier chaos. What subversive forces would the quest for riches unleash, and what might topple the precarious maintenance of order? High rates of loneliness, drunkenness, and interpersonal violence suggested a society short on mutual understanding and social cohesion. The lesson was that an individualistic, harmonious society could not be established 'simply on the basis of material abundance'.

Such problems were not unique to the colony or to the frontiers of British settlement. Internationally, rates of violence, drunkenness, and civil litigation fell and rose in broad U-curve trends from the late nineteenth to the late twentieth century. Perhaps this is why colonists were so determined to restore the yeoman ideal at the core of Arcadian imagery. They realised that their dream was fragile, at risk of failure, because of war, gold fever, and economic downturn. Evidence of disorder merely strengthened collective resolve to experiment with new ways of doing things and to improve old ones.

Contemporaries responded to imagined crises by establishing institutions such as, from 1877, a police force: not a paramilitary force as on the goldfields but a combined civil and military police force. Health institutions developed to counter disturbance in body and mind. Fourteen new hospitals served the goldfields in the 1860s. The first lunatic asylums appeared for the mentally ill; like hospitals, they provided for the care of strangers, usually men without families who would otherwise have been locked in gaol.

More profoundly, colonists developed grand strategies to manage the forces of 'progress'. One such strategy was assisted immigration. The Otago provincial government responded to the gold rush by changing its immigration policy to recruit single women only and imported 1300 in 1862. Canterbury spent almost its entire migration fund on single women in the 1860s, to rectify the 'disproportion of the sexes', with the idea of building a stable province and to protect its myths of settlement. Again, women were seen as vital to the ideal society as wives, mothers, and domestic workers, to create and raise its basis of well-behaved citizens and settled families.

CREATING A SETTLER STATE AND SOCIETY

The period from the 1840s to the 1880s has been described as an era of 'progressive colonisation' in which the neo-British of New Zealand grew explosively. In 40 years, the settlers mined £40 million in gold, sheared £40 million in wool, and borrowed

£70 million on the British market. To keep the show on the road, however – especially after the calamity of the New Zealand Wars – required the establishment of what can be described as an 'entrepreneurial state'. This model of state development entailed a close partnership between colonial government and business, and government borrowing and expenditure in the interests of business, to stimulate economic growth.

By the 1870s the spirit of colonisation needed a hand, and under Julius Vogel as colonial treasurer, government and business cooperated to attract capital and labour. Contrary to the economic orthodoxy of the time, Vogel determined that government enterprise could expand the economy faster than anything the private sector could achieve alone, through borrowing for public works and immigration. Vogel himself moved to London as the colony's agent-general (high commissioner) in 1876 to promote colonisation

Table 4.1 *Population trends and Māori land ownership, 1840–1911*

Year	Estimated Māori population	Non-Māori population	Land owned by Māori (ha)
1840	100 000	2000	26 709 342
1852	59 700	55 762	13 770 000
1860	–	79 000	8 667 000
1874	49 800	295 184	–
1878	47 800	410 207	–
1881	46 750	487 280	–
1886	43 927	576 524	–
1891	44 177	624 474	4 487 000
1896	42 113	701 101	–
1901	43 143	772 719	–
1911	–	–	2 890 000

Source: Adapted from Mason Durie, *Whaiora: Māori Health Development*, 2nd edn, Auckland: Oxford University Press, 1998, 36

Note: The decline in land ownership from 1891 is deceptive, since much of the fall involved earlier purchases that were validated retrospectively after 1894.

in the world centre of finance. By 1880 the government had borrowed £20 million and recruited over 100 000 extra migrants (see figure 4.2 and table 4.1). Isolation still ruled, however; even subsidised passages from Europe were not enough to persuade the desired number of people to take on the expense and distance of travel to New Zealand. The government offered free passages from 1873, after which agricultural labourers migrated in droves. About half of the assisted migrants of the 1870s were English; a fifth came from the west of England, including Cornwall. About a quarter were Scots. The colony also looked to Germany and Scandinavia for workers to develop North Island bush settlements.

Gradually communications began to link isolated settlements, making the connections that allowed people to think nationally. In 1876 a private telegraph cable joined New Zealand to Australia. A great earthquake lifted Wellington sufficiently to preclude building a sea wall and made room for a road around the harbour to Petone in 1855, elevating the town's status. The shift of the capital southwards, from Auckland to Wellington, in 1865 prepared for the centralising of government a decade later. In the South Island the main trunk line increased economic and social integration, linking the port of Bluff, in the far south, to Christchurch. In the North Island the railway began to encroach into the King Country.

In land and infrastructure development, the private sector played a key role. Auckland commercial lawyer Thomas Russell created New Zealand Insurance in 1859 and a national bank, the Bank of New Zealand, in 1861. In partnership with (Sir) Frederick Whitaker he ran the colony's richest legal practice. Whitaker and Russell symbolised the emerging Auckland market, created from speculation in confiscated Māori land as well as from land bought with title individualised through the Native Land Court. Russell, the minister of defence in 1863–4, and Whitaker, the colony's premier from 1863 to 1864 and from 1882 to 1883, profited from their insider knowledge, trading, and extensive networks. Russell led the Auckland business syndicate which bought the Piako Swamp – 86 500 acres (34 600 hectares) of confiscated land in the Waikato – from the government in 1873 for development and to float land deals on the London market. In this speculative venture this vast block passed to Russell 'as a result of clandestine negotiations with the Vogel Ministry', which justified the unlawful sale as expedient. Subsequently the deal almost destroyed Russell's stock and station agent creditors. (Piako Swamp was drained for farmland.) Then, as now, greed and fraud mingled with dash and entrepreneurship in a business community that colluded with politicians.

Although all the colonies with responsible government – the future British White Dominions – adopted the entrepreneurial model of state development, it proved strongest in Australia and New Zealand. From the earlier experience of the New Zealand Company, business politicians learnt the lesson that to make a profit colonial business had to obtain access to capital, for infrastructure and physical improvements, at less than full cost. The problems of distance, low institutional density, and isolation encouraged government and business to get together to diminish expense, risk, and distrust. In turn the colony depended on the network of finance and commercial services that together made the British Empire.

With the end of provincial government in 1876 New Zealand's political institutions suddenly resembled forms in the Australian colonies. Government was unitary and centralised, with two houses, the lower house – the General Assembly – elected on the basis of one man, one vote from 1879, and an appointed upper house of property owners. But in New Zealand Māori gained manhood suffrage 12 years earlier than settlers, with a view to defusing anger from the New Zealand Wars. From 1867 all Māori males aged 21 and over, including 'half castes', could vote for four new Māori seats in parliament. At the time the idea was to include Māori in the political process without undermining settler control. Colonial politicians made the male Māori vote conditional on no 'treason felony or infamous offence', so that 'rebels' in the wars were denied political citizenship. Donald McLean, a former land commissioner who was elected to parliament in 1866, suggested the idea of four Māori seats as a temporary measure, effectively until Māori were assimilated and tribal land was converted into individual title, whereupon Māori men could exercise the same property vote as settlers. For North Island politicians it was also convenient that the four Māori seats balanced the Pākehā electorates created by the gold rushes. The extension of the vote to all men in December 1879, following the introduction of the secret ballot in 1870, made

New Zealand an early democracy. Increased popular participation and national issues began to dominate electoral politics, while class and party politics had their beginnings in the late 1880s. Settlers committed to self-reliance (funded by British capital) expected 'a reasonable share in the fruits of progress'. The Protestant majority saw their colony as Christian in law and ethos but without an established church in which the religion of the Bible was fundamental to morality. Roman Catholics – about 12 per cent of the population – comprised a smaller minority than those across the Tasman.

Education proved to be one area in which religious sectarianism influenced political debate. The Sisters of St Joseph, founded in South Australia, began a network of schools in New Zealand from 1883, while Catholic bishops worked closely with their Australian colleagues to strengthen Roman Catholic identity. Catholicism continued to provide an alternative politics for those who sympathised with Māori grievances. In 1883 the French nun Suzanne Aubert (Mother Mary Joseph) commenced her mission to Māori on the Whanganui River. The government, however, established village primary schools for Māori children a decade before it established the public (state) schools system. Separate 'native schools' from 1867 implemented the policy of amalgamation by teaching in English, and the alternative given children was stark: either 'take to the best European customs' or 'be sure to die out'. If the teachers were mainly Pākehā, assistant teachers were mainly Māori: bright teenage girls, as in state primary schools. A Māori community that aspired to a school provided the land, half the cost of the buildings, and a quarter of the teacher's salary.

At the secondary level, the churches established denominational, single-sex boarding schools for Māori students. Schools such as the Anglican Te Aute College, founded in 1854, would prepare an indigenous elite, fluent in English and Māori, who moved in both worlds.

Like other English-speaking countries, New Zealand introduced free, compulsory, secular primary education in 1877, though elementary education for girls and boys was widespread in towns before the state legislated for compulsory attendance. Education gradually transformed the child's place in the family from a worker and economic asset to a scholar who was precious but not contributing as much, if at all, to the family income. At first there was a high rate of non-attendance, because farming families had more use for children's labour than for schoolwork. The real winners from free, state primary schooling were working-class girls, whose lives changed more than boys'; girls increasingly attended school and later found employment before marriage. Girls and boys still lived by a 'gendered script'; at Taradale School out of Napier an iron fence erected in 1890 divided their playgrounds. In the main towns, in competition with church schools, the state funded separate secondary schools for girls and boys to which bright students could win scholarships. Nelson College was set up as early as 1856, while Otago and Christchurch Boys' high schools served as preparatory schools for the new provincial university colleges, established by acts of parliament, and acquired twin schools for girls: Otago in 1869 and Christchurch in 1877.

4.5 Helen Connon, MA Hons, Canterbury College, 1881
Canterbury Museum

The colony's first university college, Otago (1869), and the second, Canterbury (1873), became the third and fourth Australasian universities, after Sydney and Melbourne. At Canterbury College women were admitted from the start on an equal basis with men, because John Macmillan Brown, one of the foundation professors, insisted that 'true democracy' required that the 'best women as well as the best men' take their rightful place in arts and government. He taught and married Helen Connon (figure 4.5), who became the first woman in the British Empire to graduate with honours when she received a master's degree with first-class honours in Latin and English at Canterbury College in 1881. In 1877 Connon's friend Kate Edger was the first woman to obtain a degree from the University of New Zealand and the first in the British Empire to graduate with a bachelor of arts degree. Since Auckland University College did not open until 1883, Edger graduated through an affiliated boys' school, Auckland College and Grammar School, where she studied with her father's support and the headmaster's permission. These women colleagues were rediscovered in time for the centennial of women's suffrage in 1993, after decades of invisibility.

A role model for earlier generations of schoolgirls, because she married her professor as much as for her cleverness, Helen Macmillan Brown epitomised the new urban woman – genteel, scholarly, and beautiful – who countered arguments by critics of women's higher education that too much study impaired maternity. Her greatest public achievement was as the second principal of Christchurch Girls' High School, whose academic reputation she established by preparing girls for university, while she broke with tradition by working full-time when she was a wife and mother of two small daughters. Similarly, Kate Edger built up Nelson College for Girls as its foundation principal.

The first female graduates proved to be pathbreakers in other ways. Demographically, they led the transition in family size that transformed families across the European world: 55 per cent of Canterbury women graduates in the university's first 50 years remained unmarried, while those like Connon and Edger who did marry had small families. Such statistics appeared to confirm the stereotype that higher education made women less fit to be mothers.

But graduate women thought that it better equipped them to raise superior-quality children (see chapter 5).

If colonists were unexceptional in bringing such inherited ideas and cultural practices with them, in other ways they broke new ground. Motivated by the principles of self-help and family responsibility that drove the fertility decline, settler New Zealand embarked on what some scholars interpret as a colonial welfare experiment, in which independence and voluntarism held sway. The government assisted families through immigration and land settlement rather than through income support. Colonists determined not to adopt Poor Laws, because they assumed such measures were unnecessary in a New World that would be better than the old. Families should care for themselves, and a settled society opted for self-help rather than support for 'shiftless' itinerants who threatened the anticipated respectable order of things.

Instead, as in England and the Australian colonies, the Married Women's Property Act in 1884 allowed wives to own property separate from their husbands. By contrast Māori women traditionally could hold land under Māori customary law. But the assumption held fast that women should be 'economically dependent' on husbands and fathers.

In 1885 the colony established a national system of hospitals and charitable aid under local boards that created a pattern of local autonomy, mixed funding, and discretionary assistance. Widows ranked at the top and unmarried mothers at the bottom of the hierarchy of women who lost a male breadwinner, while unemployed men without families, judged 'undeserving', were expected to fend for themselves. Hospitals were also 'user pays' until 1939.

Such institutional developments reflected a core belief that settlers were blessed by living in an exceptionally healthy country. The image of a healthy outdoors life, especially for children, has consistently infused New Zealand marketing. The colony was promoted as a health spa in the late nineteenth century, foreshadowing the establishment of the Department of Tourist and Health Resorts – itself a world first – in 1901. It was logical for tourism and health to combine, because good health was associated with fresh air and a clean, unspoilt environment.

Māori were central to health spa imagery, especially Te Arawa of the geothermal region. While (Sir) William Fox, an artist politician, urged the government to make the Rotorua district a national park on the Yellowstone model, Te Arawa proposed a township to be laid out around the Rotorua hot springs, with the idea of creating a sanatorium for tourists, who would soak in hot pools and enjoy water treatments. In 1880 local hapū agreed to lease the geyser lands, rather than sell them, and to allow the government to auction 99-year leases on their behalf.

Under the Thermal Springs District Act 1881, however, the government obtained a monopoly on the purchase and lease of areas with hot springs, lakes, or rivers. Consequently, half the Rotorua blocks were sold by the end of the century, and Native Land Court hearings lasted a generation, leaving Te Arawa's economy in a precarious state. The core problem was that the government, not the 'native proprietors', controlled the leases. When lessees defaulted in the depression of the 1880s, government mismanagement through the difficult years compelled forced sales.

By establishing Rotorua as a tourist and health resort, Te Arawa influenced race relations and images of the 'exotic' Māori. Their daughters worked as famous guides and cultural entertainers from the beginning of the tourist industry. As it became easier for tourists to experience the picturesque, travelling by steamship and by rail, a flurry of guidebooks to 'Boiling Water Land' appeared. By the 1880s numbers of tourists travelled from Australia to visit Rotorua and its natural wonders, including geysers and the Pink and White Terraces, New Zealand's top tourist attraction before they were destroyed by the eruption of Mount Tarawera in 1886.

New Zealand's first national park, Tongariro, only came into being because Te Heuheu Tūkino IV, paramount chief of Ngāti Tūwharetoa, gifted the three volcanic peaks of the central North Island, including Mount Ruapehu, to the people of New Zealand in 1887. The Native Land Court partitioned the Tongariro and Ruapehu blocks and awarded the tops of the mountains to Te Heuheu alone. He then gifted the mountain peaks to the people, European and Māori, for a national park.

Intense debate erupted 120 years later over this land transfer, what portion of the national park was a gift, and especially over

Te Heuheu's and the government's motives in negotiating it. A broader view of land alienation throughout the district suggested a government-engineered process that was part of a bigger development program with the goal, 'as always', of 'practical sovereignty and the expansion of settlement'. It suited the government to believe the mountain peaks were entirely Te Heuheu's to give to the nation. This argument diminishes his action's significance. Te Heuheu's agency was pivotal. He acted to protect the mountains, which were tapū – too sacred to be sold – and to keep them sacred. On the other hand, his gifting asserted his mana as paramount chief against challenges by other tribes. He fully expected to have his and his tribe's name forever associated with the park. As his great-great-grandson Dr (Sir) Tumu Te Heuheu explained, 'By inviting the Queen to hold the mountains jointly with Ngāti Tūwharetoa, my great-great grandfather expected that the Crown would act in the true spirit of partnership with Tūwharetoa to respect and protect the tapū of the mountains'. Increasingly, Pākehā as well as Māori began to appreciate New Zealand's beauty and to contemplate scenery preservation, if only in enchanting places less conducive to timber milling and sowing grass.

A FEDERAL AUSTRALASIA?

Ties of family and diverse traffic, including cultural and policy transfer, trade, travel, and communications, connected Australasia in the late nineteenth century. In the 1860s Charles Hursthouse, a former colonist, proposed a federation – indeed, an Australasian republic – of New Zealand and the Australian colonies, excluding Western Australia (which had reintroduced convicts). He reasoned that the 'deep natural Exchequer' of land, minerals, and agricultural resources in this cluster of settler colonies would provide better security for loans on British money markets. By 1890 'Australasia' had come to mean the Australian colonies, New Zealand, Fiji, 'and any other British Colonies or possessions in Australasia'. At the Australasian Federation Conferences in Melbourne in 1890 and in Sydney in 1891, New Zealand's representative, the pastoralist politician Captain William Russell, described the colony as a 'rather remote part of Australasia', distinguishing between the 'more remote colonies of Australasia' and the 'Australian colonies proper'. The big question for Russell was whether Australasia should federate as a British sphere in the South Pacific. Not Australia but Australasia denoted the community to which New Zealand could belong by allowing room for both autonomy and the special nature of Pākehā–Māori interdependence. Ironically the New Zealand Wars reinforced faith in superior cross-cultural relations. Russell repeated in 1891 that questions of 'native title' were 'of very grave moment', and Pākehā–Māori relations 'of the most serious importance'.

New Zealanders contemplated more than the 'crimson thread of kinship' (imperial blood tie) with Australians; politicians pondered the effects of the climate and environment on British racial development, imagining differently what it meant to be British. Russell told Australians that New Zealand was likely to develop a 'distinct national type'. Imperialism and nationalism were not mutually exclusive; often in balance, they might present as Janus-faced. Indeed, imperialism could manifest as nationalism and vice versa, blurring the boundaries of identity. In 1905 Richard Jebb gave this seeming paradox the name of 'colonial nationalism'. The 'soul of the Empire', for Jebb, was 'not one, but two': the one, the awakening patriotism of the native-born in Canada, Australia, South Africa, and New Zealand; and the other, the British imperial 'life-task' of spreading civilisation. Many in New Zealand agreed that their country's future lay with the native-born, a label that settlers appropriated for themselves. Like white Australians, Pākehā were beginning to turn inwards in their search for identity, to perceptions of the landscape – the bush – and a future shaped by the land, even more than by the surrounding ocean. Much of the reason for Australasia's subsequent 'dismemberment' relates to seismic shifts, around 1890, in culture as well as in the economy and political institutions in all the Australasian colonies.

In New Zealand, the economic bubble burst in the 1880s. Whether the colony plunged into 'long depression' from 1885 to 1895 is moot, because the word 'depression' has changed its meaning, and economists argue that real incomes reached a plateau rather than declined. Historians put the Long Depression in capitals because of its effects on people: unemployment, family distress, ragged children and exploited women workers, general business collapse, a crash in the property market, a 10-year banking crisis, bankruptcies, and unstable ministries. They point to new class tensions and moral panic that Old World evils had appeared, such as sweating of women and children in the clothing industry, which prompted a royal commission report in 1890. In a workingman's paradise a provident husband and father would support his family. Was the ideal society tumbling down? Were migrant hopes and myths illusory?

The 1880s and 1890s in New Zealand and Australia have parallels with the 1980s and 1990s: financial institutions failed, big businessmen were bankrupted, politicians were involved in speculation, as was business in government. A 'frenzy of private borrowing' pinpointed the problem of banks' lending by overdraft, in which banks ran their own scheme of borrowing for development parallel to that of colonial governments. In these circumstances, a sharp drop in British capital – the drying up of loans in London – squeezed the trans-Tasman financial structure. Just as borrowing in London inflated the boom of the 1870s, shrinking British credit aggravated the downturn in the 1880s and early 1890s. Loans did not dry up only for external reasons; London financiers took fright at declining profitability in the colonies. In the 1880s New Zealand offered less attractive investment opportunities than across the Tasman, but investment there, too, rapidly dried up. The lesson was that development had to generate sufficient export income or London would tighten its grip on economic life.

Big public spending by local and central government, unpromising business ventures, and excessive house building characterised all the main towns, though Auckland experienced hard times later than Dunedin and Christchurch. In the early 1880s Auckland enjoyed a suburban building boom but by 1886 had 2000 empty houses. Cheap credit and speculation in real estate brought down many in the local business community. It probably also hurt aspiring suburbanites burdened by mortgages and unsellable dream homes.

Hard times, combined with the British example, encouraged the growth of 'new unionism' among unskilled workers in the trans-Tasman labour movement, notably in export-related industries, among seamen, watersiders, shearers, coalminers, and tailoresses. Locally the labour movement boasted 200 unions with

63 000 members by 1890. Both unions and shipowners developed Australasian federations, the seamen and coalminers through the Maritime Council, which affiliated to the Australian Maritime Council in 1889. The Union Steam Ship Company, based in Dunedin, became the archenemy of seamen and miners, because it had a monopoly in the New Zealand coal industry and in trans-Tasman shipping. Employers interpreted the mere establishment of a union as an aggressive act. For the labour movement, however, it was vital to have trade unions recognised, because unskilled men were easily replaced. New unionism asserted a form of social citizenship – the 'closed shop' – against the market liberalism of the employers, who insisted on 'freedom of contract'. Rising tensions in the context of depression triggered the Maritime Strike, which spread from Sydney in September 1890 and involved at least 50 000 workers in Australia and 8000 in New Zealand.

The Maritime Strike did not determine the response of arbitration, although it focused attention on the idea. The crises of depression and industrial conflict together prompted a rethink of the nation-building project, giving impetus to plans to redraft the government's role in mediating between the new settler society and global pressures. As we have seen, isolation and smallness compelled an active role by colonial governments and exerted an enduring impact, shaping the very conditions of settlement. The entrepreneurial state that emerged foreshadowed a new model of state development in which progressive social reforms accompanied the restructuring of the economy. In finding a way out of the mire New Zealand was rescued by the technical advance of refrigeration, as both the Australian colonies and New Zealand responded to crisis by seeking a preferential position in the British market.

5

Managing globalisation 1891–1913

A changed attitude to globalisation emerged out of the aura of crisis: now there was a growing trend to manage it. The Australasian colonies resolved to seize opportunities to develop new commodities for export and to manage the social outcomes by building an edifice of progressive liberal 'state experiments'. Led by Premiers John Ballance (1891–3), Richard Seddon (1893–1906), and Sir Joseph Ward (1906–12) – two of whom were Irish-born and all of whom were immigrants – a series of Liberal governments from 1891 to 1912 set out to transform New Zealand into a democratic social laboratory. In doing so, they enacted an Australasian model of state development.

Political scientists have shown how institutions mediated globalisation through a colonial, democratic citizenship. The 'Australian Settlement', supposedly established at the federation of the Australian colonies, in 1901, had five planks: a white Australia and associated restricted immigration; arbitration; protection; 'state paternalism'; and 'imperial benevolence'. In reality this model extended to New Zealand as a distinctive settler colonial response to guarantee 'domestic defence' against a range of external threats.

Concern about the social consequences of global forces shaped governance and fostered a new liberalism. As outlined by William Pember Reeves, a newspaper editor and Liberal politician who helped fashion this regional model of state development, the 'state experiments' entailed state intervention in pursuit of liberal ideals. Reeves wrote this concept into New Zealand history in his two-volume *State Experiments in Australia and New Zealand* (1902).

The Liberals, as a party of and for the people, promoted populism. They aimed to use state intervention to make it easier to 'get on' and to create a civilised community. The 'experiments' ranged from an entrepreneurial state, women's franchise, liquor laws, and cheap land for development by settlers to management of the effects of capitalism and competition on labour, an old-age pension for elderly pioneers, and the exclusion of aliens and undesirables. Political scientists have characterised the state experiments of the 1890s as social liberalism, while historians have seen them as a renewed effort to fulfil the idea of an ideal society or to build a new, democratic world.

This era brought into sharp relief the tension between forces for exclusion, driven by imperial views of superiority, and those for inclusion, derived from the humanism within Enlightenment thought. The former promoted ethnic solidarity among settlers at the expense of non-Europeans; the latter benefited women. Māori were both included and excluded.

Historians subsequently claimed the state experiments for separate national narratives, according to their own time and perspective. If New Zealand's Liberals were viewed as colonial pragmatists by 1930, as radicals and humanitarians in the 1960s and as technocrats determined to impose social control by the 1970s, late-twentieth-century historians interpreted them as populists and nationalists. In their accounts, the Liberal era was one of centralisation and colonial nationalism which saw the creation of the modern New Zealand state. Society was settling from the 1880s, as Pākehā (people of European descent) born in New Zealand began to outnumber migrants and Māori. Pride in being a 'native-born' European manifested itself in natives' associations designed to strengthen patriotism, co-opting Māori motifs and names for babies, and in musings about New Zealand as 'Māoriland'. As this sense of national identity grew, the idea coalesced of New Zealand as a site of experiment and its people as wont to score 'firsts'.

For neo-imperial historians, a new system grew from the old in the Liberal era. According to Belich, from the 1880s New Zealand tightened links with Britain, rather than striving for national independence. After an era of 'progressive colonisation', links tightened between colony and metropolis through 'recolonisation', joining New Zealand to London, the centre of the British Empire, as effectively as a bridge. Belich has since generalised New Zealand's experience to the Anglo-world. Problematically, this thesis represents the Liberal era merely as a 'transitional' phase between 'progressive colonisation' and 'recolonisation' when Antipodean new liberalism stood for more than the rhythms of boom, bust, and rescue by new export industries. These rhythms, however, did set the scene for local variants of progressive reforms.

Initially, the state experiments served to market the Australasian colonies to an imperial world. It was no accident that Reeves wrote his classic histories in London, while New Zealand's agent-general. Britain was the only serious global power, and London, the centre of world finance. In fact, the refrigeration boom concentrated on Britain, because Britain retained free trade for agricultural produce. The British global economy grew rapidly with innovations in transport that saw a collapse in the cost of sea freight. While steamships allowed the Australasian colonies to export produce to British markets, refrigeration was the key technical advance; New Zealand made its first shipment of frozen meat in 1882. Refrigeration generated revolutionary developments not merely in the economy but in New Zealand culture through marketing and food choices.

The major change to the New Zealand political economy came when agriculture was restructured to export food as well as fibre to the British market. Assisted by British capital, the country pulled out of its economic doldrums from 1895, earlier than the eastern-Australian colonies, which were also beginning to produce food for export. The Australasian colonies faced quite different conditions from those of Europe and North America. With a small, scattered domestic market, and the problems of vulnerability and remoteness from overseas markets and sources of technological change, Australasia would not have found it more efficient to industrialise. British investors, moreover, would not have approved: they believed in Australasia's 'natural resource benefits' as much as did the British settlers. Given the power of European mental maps, there were no credible alternative paths of development. New Zealand's economic expansion was destined to be by family farms, because global capital ingested Arcadian mythology.

Innovations designed to manage export economies from a distance extended beyond government to the business sector. Stock and station agents represented an Australasian response to a history and geography of isolation by reducing the costs of marketing over long distances, transferring information about British capital, and establishing connections through settler society networks. New Zealand, with its small population, relied on such entrepreneurship to temper instability and shocks. Stock and station agencies became business leaders as traders in capital and ideas between local farmers and the global – British – export market.

The export-led economy fostered the economic dependency of settler capitalism. The colony's increasingly bilateral, dependent trading relations with Britain reordered not only the economy but also its physical, social, and cultural landscapes. Refrigeration had dramatic ecological effects, through timber felling, drainage of wetlands, weeds and grass growth, and pollution of waterways. It also encouraged small farming. Indeed, the way that mutton and dairy produce featured in national policies moulded forms of social and political life.

To balance the readjustment of the colony's global relations, Liberal politicians and public servants resolved to create a social laboratory. This comprised what political scientists call a 'social contract': an arrangement among people who recognised their mutual interests in creating a democratic society and behaved accordingly. In New Zealand, as in the Australian colonies, liberals devised a social contract between settler capitalism and the entrepreneurial state. In New Zealand, the social contract was a settler contract, encapsulated in its state experiments. The settler contract balanced the new export economy with a fresh start at consolidating the ideal society after the distress of the 1880s. To contemporaries, 'New World' and 'crisis' were contradictory terms; the very idea of New Zealand entailed escape from Old World evils. Rather, they hoped to make New Zealand a better Britain.

THE SETTLER CONTRACT

The settler contract – fundamentally a deal about land and property ownership – mediated between global forces and the colonial body

5.1 House in Bealey Avenue (possibly the Minson family home near the Carlton Mill Bridge), Christchurch, c. 1895. This spacious villa represented the suburban house to which most New Zealanders aspired. Flags are flying to celebrate Queen Victoria's jubilee, and the verandah is decorated with fashionable Chinese lanterns. Note also the bicycle (a modern symbol), the tī-kōuka (cabbage tree), and the corrugated-iron fence.
Alexander Turnbull Library, Wellington, 1/2-145266-F

politic. Intended for the 'free' settler and workingman, it was based on early democracy and designed for Pākehā families. As we have seen, Māori provided the land. Under the Liberals, settling the land came to be viewed as a panacea to address urban ills. The new export economy was based on an increasingly mechanised dairy industry that revived plans for closer settlement. The idea of an independency, a block of land on which the settler and his family built a home of their own, gained momentum (see figure 5.1).

In the 1890s, Crown lands could not satisfy settler demand. Land prices rose as new land became scarce with the growing settler population and their desire to become landowners. The first Liberal government, formed in 1891 (65 per cent migrants), aimed to make land accessible to settlers, to give them a better chance at life. This goal presumed a collective idea of an archetypal outdoors lifestyle: in effect husbandry would provide for the settler family's independence and material comfort. Areas most suitable for dairying in the North Island were already in government and settler hands. But Māori still owned 11 million acres (4.4 million hectares) in the island, much of which was timbered or hill country suitable only for sheep farming. In the North Island, the Liberal government strove to buy blocks from Māori as cheaply as possible, to establish bush properties for settlers. In the South Island, the Liberals compulsorily purchased large estates for subdivision into smaller farms suited to grain and grazing sheep, to the chagrin of wealthy runholders, such as Allan McLean, forced off his station in South Canterbury, but to the relief of others, like the trustees of the Cheviot Hills estate, in North Canterbury, who were keen to sell in the depression. Among settlers, everyone except South Island pastoralists embraced the Liberal policy of closer settlement as morally worthy.

In this context, 1870–90 proved to be the era of major land loss for tribes in the central North Island. The Liberals bought another 2.7 million acres (1.08 million hectares) between 1892 and 1899, for £775 500, or an average of 5 shillings 9 pence per acre (0.4 hectares), alienated through the Native Land Court. At the same time the government paid 84 shillings per acre for estates in the South Island owned by pastoralists. Settlers acquired a further 423 000 acres (169 200 hectares) privately by 1907. While large areas were purchased retrospectively, an estimated 3 million acres (1.2 million hectares) of Māori land were transferred to settlers because of purchases begun or completed in the 1890s. About 28 per cent of land still held by Māori in 1890 was alienated within a decade. In the process, most remaining first-class land passed into settler hands, and the state engineered this transfer extremely cheaply.

Cheap loans through advances to settlers consolidated the settler contract. To prevent landlordism by the wealthy, the state acted as landlord for the less well off, introducing a lease in perpetuity (999-year lease) in 1892 to provide security for settlers who could not afford to buy freehold land. Instead, landholders reserved any capital for improvements. The Liberal statute that offers the most insight into the settler contract is the Advances to Settlers Act of 1894. State advances for land were for Pākehā only, in the sense that legislators did not think about Māori. As Reeves observed, state loans to settlers constituted another regional experiment that served as a 'special reward' for 'enterprise' at the 'other end of the earth'. With falls in commodity prices and high interest rates, a colonial farmer had to have cheaper finance to live. Advances to settlers also diminished British investors' doubts about the scope for development of New Zealand (and Australian) farming. The winners were small farmers, agricultural labourers, and their families who had access to capital: the 'deserving', judged best able to help themselves, if the ultimate outcome can define them as winners, that is. The isolated bush settlement of Ballance is a product of state advances to settlers; named after the first Liberal premier, John Ballance, it is a dot on the map under the Tararua Range, between Pahiatua and the Manawatū Gorge.

Correspondingly the Liberals introduced an income tax in 1891 to replace the property tax, to relieve hardship on tradesmen and smallholders. This was designed to ensure fairness between groups rather than between individuals, through a simple, progressive tax in three steps.

Most of all, however, the suburban house and garden came to signify the settler contract and the family ideal of land and home ownership in the New World, by adapting the Old World idea of the country in the city. In contrast to their medieval European forebears, low-density suburban houses spread outwards rather than upwards in creating the 'new urban frontier' of New Zealand towns. Descended from the rural cottage rather than the townhouse of Western Europe, the standard New Zealand house by around 1900 was a cottage or villa of four or five rooms, which shared design and layout with houses in cities in Australia and the American West. Local carpenters built houses using pattern books from Australia and California. What made the ordinary New Zealand house distinctive from its Pacific Rim cousins was that it was built mostly in timber (except for in the deep south, in Otago).

From the beginning of New Zealand towns, the suburban ideal existed in the ideas for the Wakefieldian settlements. The ideal was male centred but also family centred, built on skilled-working-class values of respectability; of separate spheres for men and women; of thrift, sobriety, and security. Forty-nine per cent of the Pākehā population lived in urban places of over 2500 people by 1911, compared to 55 per cent in Australia and 46 per cent in the United States. Of this Pākehā population, 31 per cent lived in the four main centres (cities), and 18 per cent in small towns such as Palmerston North. Māori, by contrast, were overwhelmingly rural. Australia and New Zealand had two of the highest home-ownership rates in the world by 1911, of 50 per cent or more, as home ownership became the dominant form of tenure.

We can reconcile the argument that the Liberals espoused skilled-working-class values with the idea that the farmer stood at the top of the Liberal league table and represented the coming man, because the settler contract was intended for the deserving. Realised on the dairy farm, it also found expression in suburbia, in the small house and domestic garden.

WOMEN'S SUFFRAGE

New Zealand is proud of its history of early women's suffrage, which passed in parliament in 1893. Yet the colony was relatively late to adopt marriage reform, introducing restricted equal rights to divorce in 1898, after Britain and the Australian colonies. There was no inconsistency in being early with one measure and late with the other, because New Zealand was a 'man's country', where women were valued as wives and mothers. On the one hand, women's scarcity value offered scope for greater opportunities and potential political equality; on the other, it imposed what feminist scholars have viewed as patriarchal constraints. Historians have therefore debated whether early women's suffrage recognised women's special role in the home and family or changes in women's status sufficient to convince politicians and launch a women's campaign for political citizenship.

These competing arguments emphasise different images of New Zealand women, embodying the two principal themes of colonial feminism: New Women, who stood for freedom from women's 'disabilities', for equality and progress, even equal pay for equal work; and colonial helpmeets, who were society's moral guardians and the 'mothers of the race'. Kate Sheppard of Christchurch, the national leader of the women's suffrage campaign, embodied both New Woman and colonial helpmeet. Rediscovered by women's historians for the celebration of the women's suffrage centennial in 1993, she was resurrected as a national icon, with her image imprinted on the New Zealand $10 note. Religious, tactful, and beautiful, with a questionable private life, Sheppard led a quiet campaign that won cross-spectrum support.

If we blend the arguments in the suffrage debate, it emerges that the women's movement sought equal rights on grounds of difference – that is, equality as women – for the public good. Suffragists argued that the vote would allow women to extend their maternal skills to the public world, to the greater public benefit. Among the reasons for supporting women's suffrage advanced by the Women's Christian Temperance Union in 1891, first on the list were 'because the enfranchisement of women is a question of public well-being' and 'because the votes of women would add weight and power to the more settled and responsible communities'. Suffragists as helpmeets *and* New Women also wanted men to change, to stop drinking and domestic violence. As Anna Stout, wife of the chief justice of New Zealand Sir Robert Stout, explained, 'Our children must have pure and temperate fathers'.

In New Zealand, the vote both was the ambivalent gift of men and had to be fought for by the colonial women's movement. Women's numbers were significant in towns, where most of them lived. Male settler politicians needed their support. The campaign for the vote succeeded because of cooperation between sympathetic men in parliament, such as Stout, and the women's movement outside. Kate Sheppard's dining room, with its extensive table, proved ideal for glueing sheets of women's signatures onto rolls of wallpaper, which suffragists then turned into parliamentary petitions. While women collected the signatures, their conservative advocate Sir John Hall, a Canterbury pastoralist who cooperated with Sheppard, rolled out the petitions – literally – on the floor of parliament, in a powerful public gesture.

Just as one man, one vote included Māori, Pākehā and Māori women gained the vote together in September 1893, just in time for November's election and the election for the Māori seats, held

Managing globalisation 1891–1913 115

separately in December (see figure 5.2). In Australia, white women gained the federal vote at the same time as Indigenous Australians were denied it, in 1902. The contrast suggests that Māori, unlike Indigenous Australians, were included in Liberal concepts of 'the people', and of 'the British race'. But the reality was not so clearcut. Other reforms were a long time coming, while gender divisions remained firmly intact. Women could join the 'women's parliament', the non-party National Council of Women, from 1896, or

5.2 Unknown artist, *The summit at last*, 1894. Amazonian womanhood is assisted to the summit by the liberal man (dressed as a lawyer). Scaling new heights was already firmly embedded in the New Zealand psyche.
New Zealand Graphic and Ladies Journal, 21 July 1894.
Alexander Turnbull Library, Wellington, PUBL-0126-1894-01

if they wished to participate in Liberal politics they were confined to the women's branch of the Liberal Association, established by Maud Reeves, wife of William Pember Reeves. The first woman member of parliament, Elizabeth McCombs, was elected only in 1933, on the death of her husband, a Labour politician.

Put in an international context, women gained the vote early in places where men had also gained manhood suffrage relatively early, ushered in by gold rushes. Generally, too, women's suffrage was won early in colonial settler communities that had dispossessed indigenous peoples, where claiming the land was central to politics. In these men's countries, women's rights came to the fore as reformers waged social purity campaigns, against the 'demon drink' that brought such grief to women and children, and strove to establish new societies. Thus New Zealand became the first self-governing country to enfranchise women. While some supporters advocated equal rights for women, others aspired to counterbalance rough men and to promote respectability in public life. New Zealand was not the first place in the world to approve votes for women: that accolade went to the tiny Pacific island of Pitcairn, in 1838, while three mid-American states preceded New Zealand, and the colonial parliaments in South Australia and Western Australia voted for women's suffrage soon after New Zealand, in 1894 and 1899. In New Zealand, however, gender trumped race: humanism included all women aged 21 and above in the social contract.

ARBITRATION

In Australia and New Zealand, national narratives separately claimed compulsory arbitration as a key institution, reflective of the national psyche. The two countries were pioneers of compulsory industrial conciliation and arbitration, which became the pivot of industrial relations and later their welfare states. In New Zealand, Minister of Labour William Pember Reeves was the architect of the Industrial Conciliation and Arbitration 1894. As often happens in policymaking he pieced together other people's ideas and fitted them for use in the colony, gaining most from a bill drafted by Charles Kingston, the Liberal premier of South Australia, and some from New South Wales and Massachusetts. New Zealand historians maintain that a Liberal–Labour alliance produced the distinctive institution. The New Zealand example, however, supports as readily the argument that liberalism shaped compulsory arbitration as an idea and a system. In liberal thought, arbitration operated for a 'free, prosperous and contented people'. In addition to advances to settlers, state arbitration in industrial disputes formed part of the settler contract, intended for the whole community, not just labour. As John Ballance explained, 'The capitalist equally with the labourer must be identified, by residence and fulfilling all the duties of a colonist, with the progress and destiny of New Zealand'.

Again, the economic focus was to promote export-led development and growth while meeting political and social ends by striving for harmony in the workplace. The Australasian colonies shared this strategy as a means of managing globalisation, because they were too small to influence international trade cycles; instead, when times were tough, they would act to avoid disputes. The arbitration system, which in New Zealand entailed local conciliation boards and an arbitration court, was intended to 'hold the balance' between capital and labour; it recognised unions, yet an amendment to the Act in 1905 made strikes illegal. In theory, the system balanced the unpredictable export economy with workers' desire for security and ensured a 'fair go' for ordinary people.

Some historians suggest that this regional model developed from a context of financial crisis and labour unrest combined with early democracy and ideas of bettering Britain. Long-term trends of settlement patterns and entrepreneurial states that allowed social engineering by middle-class professionals as politicians and public servants proved more significant. Shared and parallel problems and political opportunities invited a pattern of trans-Tasman policy transfer. The classical Australasian form of compulsory arbitration, introduced in New Zealand in 1894, entered the statutes of Western Australia in 1900, although Western Australia enjoyed a gold-rush boom in the 1890s, which also made it reliant on exports. New South Wales followed in 1901, federal Australia in 1904, and South Australia and Queensland by 1912.

In turn, New Zealand adopted most ideas for its legislated arbitration from Australia, as well as later add-on policies of workers' welfare. Arbitration became a device to protect workers' living standards. Migrants travelled across the world to find a better life, and government agents promoted New Zealand as a 'workingman's paradise'. Following the famous Harvester judgment by Australia's new Commonwealth Court of Conciliation and Arbitration in 1907, the New Zealand arbitration court adopted the principle of a 'living wage' – that is, a family wage sufficient to maintain a male breadwinner, a dependent wife, and three children. The living wage was gender based, rendering women and children dependent on Labour policies for male breadwinners. It expressed the principle that the workingman was entitled to marry, have a family, and earn a wage sufficient to keep his family in a small degree of comfort. The living wage supposedly acted as a bulwark against the global market, because it was based not on market rates but on the cost of living.

It is ironic, then, that New Zealand wage-earners fared worse between 1890 and 1913 than workers in Australia, where common forces shaped wage movements, and with which New Zealand shared an integrated labour market. In terms of gross domestic product per capita, New Zealand was not far behind Australia by 1913, and Pākehā New Zealanders had the highest life expectancy in the world. Before 1890, real wage growth was stronger than productivity growth. After 1890, globalisation increased productivity and improved the terms of trade; but workers' wages declined relative to property income. The biggest beneficiaries of the settler contract were landowners, who gained most from technical advances, notably refrigeration, because the export of frozen meat and dairy products increased the relative value of their land. This income redistribution to property might have been greater but for the state experiment with arbitration.

Unsurprisingly, labour militancy mounted as real wages failed to keep pace with workers' expectations and rising working-class respectability. West Coast coalminers, the first to use arbitration, in 1896, turned against it. Miners called a 'tucker time' strike at the local coalmine at Blackball in 1908. Their action heralded the rise of independent labour in the form of the New Zealand Federation of Labour, radical and anti-arbitration. Four of the federation's five key leaders were Australian socialists and unionists, while other leaders had experience on British and American coalfields. Their commitment to class struggle earned them the name 'Red Feds', and they led an assault from the Left on the arbitration system. Goldminers enacted a strike at Waihi in 1912. The wave of unrest culminated in disputes in mines and at ports that merged into the widespread Great Strike of 1913, in which moderate unionists such as carpenters and clerks fought alongside Red Feds, watersiders, and (belatedly) seamen against special constables, employers, and farmers on horseback. This bitter dispute reflected ideological beliefs and global changes in work patterns, but above all the 1913 strike represented a 'battle over democracy'.

Proud to be 'workers', the Red Feds reinforced a competing model of manliness to the family man of artisan craft unionism whom the arbitration system served best: a 'real' man who vaunted his manly independence, evocative of mateship and sweat, and had control of his workplace and his life. The breaking away by the Red Feds, however, helped arbitration to survive. By 1912 the settler contract formed the basis of government. Small farmers successfully transformed New Zealand into the 'Empire's dairy farm', harnessing the yeoman myth in their class interests to achieve political power under Auckland farmer Bill Massey, who was born in Northern Ireland, and the Reform Party that Massey established in 1909. The title 'Reform' avoided the label 'conservative'.

MĀORI LAND LOSS AND PROTEST

In this structural shift, the big losers were Māori. Apart from claims that settlers had honoured the Treaty of Waitangi by recognising Māori land title and buying the land, the Treaty was no longer alive in the Pākehā narrative and the settler parliament. Māori were excluded from the settler contract, dispossessed, and denied capital for farming, left without a resource base to develop. They were underpaid for their land, deprived of their best land, and denied cheap loans to develop the remainder. The remnant barely provided for subsistence, since promised reserves did not materialise. The steep downward trend in Māori land holdings continued into the Liberal era, which witnessed the 'penultimate Maori land grab', and only slowed after 1900. Reeves did not write about this land redistribution in his histories, and most non-Māori New Zealanders were oblivious to it. But the compact for settlers clearly depended on Māori land loss.

In seeking social justice for settlers, then, the Liberals created another set of injustices for Māori. They passed a series of interlocking acts of parliament between 1892 and 1896 which streamlined procedures for alienating land from hapū (subtribes) and largely restored the Crown right of pre-emption. Land purchases became easier under the Department of Lands and Survey. Yet more laws added to the maze concerning tribal land, offering more scope for alternative interpretations and ambiguities, ripe for lawyers and speculators to exploit. In 1892 the Liberal government placed the West Coast Settlement Reserves under lease in perpetuity, in what amounted to a second confiscation. Settler demands prevailed over the Māori right to, and need of, income from remaining land. Under the Native Townships Act 1895, furthermore, European townships could be built on Māori land. Potential tourist towns, and towns on the main trunk line in the central North Island, completed in 1908, were established by this method. The railway township of Taumarunui, in the heart of the King Country, was one example: built to service the main trunk line between Auckland and Wellington and intended to provide benefits to Māori, in fact it did the opposite, by opening up land for settlement.

In the 'bursting up' of the great estates, pastoralists who sold could retain homestead blocks. In the 'bursting up' of the remaining Māori estate, Māori were denied an equivalent right; instead, they were confined to inadequate reserves. The whole system was designed to force hapū to sell. An assumption that only settlers could be successful farmers – and the inability to provide security – denied Māori access to cheap credit for development. According to community attitudes, tribal land was perceived to be 'lying waste and unproductive'. Supporters of the Reform Party resented leases as 'intolerable' and demanded the right to freehold 'all the Native Lands which the Maoris themselves cannot use', a demand the Reform government met with vigour from 1913 (see chapter 6). Where hapū held on to their land through lease, under the public trustee's oversight this increasingly became lease in perpetuity, so that their land was alienated in effect for a diminishing return.

By the close of the nineteenth century, control of most of the North Island had transferred from Māori to Pākehā. According to official figures published in 1911, in 1891, 2.4 million acres (960 000 hectares) of Māori land were leased to Europeans, and by 1911, another million acres (400 000 hectares). An estimated 10.8 million acres (4.32 million hectares) in the North Island (including leased blocks) remained in Māori ownership. To compound the difficulty for iwi (tribes), the most heavily populated districts were left with the least land. Ngāti Tūwharetoa, who retained more land than almost anyone else, did not oppose European settlement around the shores of Lake Taupo but wished to control the process, to generate income from timber milling, and to obtain loans from the government to farm their land themselves.

Tribes fought back against the relentless assaults on their wellbeing. In Wellington the four Māori members of parliament argued that policies breached the Treaty of Waitangi, drawing attention to landlessness and the need for resources to help Māori development. From the 1890s tribal leaders and organisations demanded that the Liberal government stop the purchase of Māori land, address the tangled problems of title, and give Māori access to capital.

The pan-tribal Kotahitanga (unity) movement spearheaded this process, and in 1895 the Kotahitanga organised a boycott of the Native Land Court. From 1897 the movement ran its own newspaper, *Te Puke ki Hikurangi*, whose name referred to a story from Hawaiki about people surviving a flood by seeking refuge on a mountain. The paper, which expressed a new pan-tribal consciousness and exemplified how Māori embraced literacy, moulded political action by venting collective problems, such as the continued alienation of land, a declining population, and government indifference to people's wellbeing.

Kotahitanga sought a new solution: a separate Māori parliament, which it claimed as a right under the Treaty of Waitangi. This Māori parliament met at Papawai, near Greytown, in the Wairarapa, in 1897, in grand buildings erected for the purpose by Ngāti Kahungunu chief Hāmuera Tamahau Mahupuku, who had good relationships with local settlers and was a farmer himself. Papawai hosted Premier Richard Seddon as well as Māori leaders. The Kīngitanga (King movement), too, established a rival parliament.

Both presented petitions and draft bills to the settler government and sought the return of Māori rangatiratanga (chieftainship) over their land. In 1897 the Kotahitanga petitioned Queen Victoria on her jubilee to stop the settler purchase of Māori land. The Young Māori Party – effectively a club of modernising politicians – emerged from these claims to citizenship, led by Āpirana Ngata of Ngati Porou and his mentor, James Carroll, who was of mixed Ngāti Kahungunu and Irish descent. Both these Māori members of parliament were subsequently knighted. Carroll represented a general East Coast electorate from 1893 to 1919. While anti-separatist, he fought hard for Māori advancement. After a secondary education at Te Aute College, Ngata became New Zealand's first Māori university graduate, of Canterbury College, in 1894. Ngata's people ensured that he was educated in Pākehā knowledge, including law, to help them face the challenge of colonisation. After he entered parliament in 1905, he rose to be the greatest Māori leader of the twentieth century and returned to circulation posthumously as a national figure on the $50 note. Backed by Carroll, from the late 1890s Ngata and fellow former students from Te Aute College embarked on a mission to uplift their people through health reform and land development. Ngata wanted Māori included in the policies referred to here as the 'settler contract'. Both he and Carroll engaged with the state as politicians and emphasised Māori's ability to modernise.

Their efforts had some impact. Persuaded by Carroll, politicians and Māori leaders accepted a compromise struck in 1900 wherein the government established Māori land councils to balance iwi demands to hold on to their remaining land against settler demands for land for settlement. Thanks to Carroll, in some areas the councils (later boards) slowed the trend in land loss. Even the Kīngitanga was briefly reconciled to the new system, but the councils lost authority with the government once they were seen to block settlement. A stocktake by a commission of inquiry conducted by Sir Robert Stout and Ngata in 1907 confirmed how little good land was left. After the Native Land Act of 1909 removed restrictions on sales, the rate of land loss sped up. The Act made it easier to transfer property from Māori to settler, though the Native Land Court still oversaw the process. If more than nine people owned a block then owners' meetings were necessary, a system still used by the court in 2025.

INCLUDED AND EXCLUDED MĀORI

This was a crucial period in the history of Māori health, marked by the turnaround from a decline in health and numbers in the nineteenth century to recovery in numbers, health status, and hope. Colonial views of Māori as a dying race continued to colour Pākehā perceptions and to exclude them from 'the people': 'if there was any hope for a future for the Maori, it was that their blood might be perpetuated as a trace in a future strain of blended New Zealander'. The sense of mission felt by the Young Māori Party reformers spread across the country; they saw themselves as 'saviours of a race' who could see 'with the eyes of both races'. Dr Māui Pōmare, Native Health Officer under the Department of Public Health established in 1901, operated a health service for Māori on a shoestring budget relative to the amount spent on turning Rotorua into a health spa for tourists. In his health promotion he used the latest technology, in the form of slide presentations, to scare people about the water they drank. But lack of funding led to disillusionment. Māori communities suffered from typhoid, diarrhoea, respiratory diseases, and relatively high infant mortality.

Ambivalently, hapū were simultaneously included in 'the people' through a post-Enlightenment stereotype of the Aryan Māori. Assembled by Edward Tregear in his book on the subject, this concept offered a 'long and adventurous past for both Maori and Pakeha migrants to New Zealand, and one that linked them to a distant but common ancestry' (see chapter 1). Tregear was Cornish, steeped in classical and Arthurian legend, and imposed his mental maps on Māori in trying to understand their world. In the Antipodes, he believed, the 'Aryan of the West greet[ed] the Aryan of the Eastern Seas'. This search for origins was as much a search for self by Pākehā intellectuals who aspired to create a new community.

The package of Liberal state experiments required such a past for an emerging colonial nationalism that developed alongside shifting relations with the imperial power, Britain, from about 1900. Ever since the propaganda of the New Zealand Company, New

Zealanders had absorbed the myth that New Zealand's 'Better Britons' were superior to the Australian Britons. New Zealanders lacked the taint of convictism (a point that ignored escaped convicts); they were moulded by a vigorous, cooler climate; and they enjoyed relations with a superior type of 'native'. Thus elevating Māori to honorary whites was another way to render Pākehā superior to white Australians, as well as to affirm the long-held belief in a hierarchy of races in which Māori were superior to everyone but Europeans.

WHITHER AUSTRALASIA?

Such beliefs shaped New Zealand sentiment in the decision not to join the Commonwealth of Australia when the Australian colonies federated, on 1 January 1901. The majority view, amid general apathy, is illustrated in figure 5.3. Such views underpinned historian Sir Keith Sinclair's claim that 'most New Zealanders did not want to become Australians'.

In 1968 F. L. W. Wood (an Australian) dismissed as 'emotional fluff' the 'waffle about consummating nationhood' which choked 'sensible' economic and foreign affairs arguments against New Zealand's joining. But a dissenting view, that a widespread belief in 'geographically determined racialism' explained New Zealand's decision not to federate, has regained ground. On both sides of the Tasman Sea, federation was more about sentiment than a business deal. The very act of creating the Commonwealth of Australia stimulated New Zealanders to 'imagine' the distinctive and desirable features of themselves and their colony.

Given that the New Zealand economy pulled out of the difficulties of the 1890s earlier than the Australian colonies and was being restructured as Britain's farm, economics did play a part. Also, the Australian colonies keenest to federate – Victoria, Tasmania, and South Australia – had been the most depressed. Different mail routes across the Pacific and through the Suez Canal since the 1860s underlined the Australasian colonies' different geopolitical and strategic interests. Defence, however, was not a core issue, because Britain determined their global foreign policy. Minds and markets were connected, but minds dominated over markets.

The vanity of nation-building politicians influenced New Zealand's decision not to join the new Commonwealth of Australia.

HOW WE SEE IT

THE OGRE: "Come into these arms."   NEW ZEALAND: "Nay sir, those arms bear chains."

The New South Wales Premier speaking at a Federal League meeting said that as the Colonies were on the eve of federation it was proper for Great Britain to defer linking the South Sea Islands to New Zealand. He also believed that the sentiment of the people of New Zealand would force that Government into the Australian Federation.

New Zealand Graphic, Auckland, Saturday, October 20, 1900. Vol. XXV. – No. XVI. Cartoonist: Scatz.

5.3 Scatz, *How we see it*, 1900. Zealandia, Britannia's daughter, wearing an indigenous feather cloak, holds hands with the 'noble savage' (depicted as a Pacific Islander rather than Māori). She fends off the ogre of convict Australia – who is in chains – to protect her indigenous ward and so opts for a separate destiny in the Pacific. In the background stands her imperial sister Australia. The cartoon suggests that, but for the ogre, Zealandia could have moved closer to Australia and perhaps taught her sister something about settler–indigenous relations.
New Zealand Graphic and Ladies Journal, 20 October 1900.
Alexander Turnbull Library, Wellington, J-040-002

Richard Seddon, aptly nicknamed 'King Dick', shrewdly heeded the apathetic mood and determined not to let it spoil his chances of re-election by inviting discussion on the subject. Nor would he tolerate diminished prestige, as premier of a state third in importance after New South Wales and Victoria; on the contrary, he assumed the title of 'prime minister' in place of 'premier' to place himself on an equal footing with the Australian prime minister. A popular figure on both sides of the Tasman, Seddon attended the federation celebrations in Sydney on 1 January 1901 with an entourage of Māori warriors, attracting the anticipated press coverage.

Australians have influenced New Zealanders' national identity more than has been historically conceded. While federation reinforced that New Zealanders are not Australians, Australia continued to influence New Zealand identities through common stories. The 'Tasman world' of intercolonial traffic and maritime connections did not end in 1901 with the creation of Australia. Moreover, Australasia could extend beyond Australia and New Zealand and continued to function as a region even though its collective name gradually fell into disuse. The French caused a problem by intruding into this British-dominated zone in New Caledonia and the New Hebrides, as did the Germans in Papua New Guinea and Samoa, constraining the concept.

White Australia itself posed a problem to perceived health and security. As the first Australian prime minister, Edmund Barton, told New Zealand's federation commission in March 1901, which was set up to justify New Zealand's decision not to federate,

> On the question of the character of the immigration which should be allowed, I take it that the ideas and sympathies of New Zealand and Australia are practically identical. If one may judge from the conversations I have had with Mr. Seddon, I should think that our objections to alien races and New Zealand's objections are practically the same, and that we have the same desire to preserve the 'European' and 'white' character of the race.

The question as the New Zealanders saw it was which would win: the law of nature or the law of the Commonwealth? How could Australia be white when its northern third was in the tropics? In this mode of thinking, northern Australia was likely to be populated by 'Asiatic races', and Queensland used South Sea Islands labour in its sugar industry. Miscegenation notwithstanding, would not the white race also degenerate in the tropics, so that in a few generations Queensland would become home to the 'mean white', as in the United States? Advocates of the White Australia policy insisted that Australia would show the world that the laws of nature would not limit the white man. New Zealanders, however, believed that nature would make Queensland a blot on White Australia.

New Zealanders were also less sure as to whether the land or the sea defined a community of interest. The notion of a British Australasia in the South Pacific presumed a community bound by a shared expanse of southern ocean and blood ties, and protected by the British navy. By the time of federation, however, the bush held sway in Australian popular culture, which was already looking inwards, and New Zealanders were beginning to imagine a future shaped by their islands. It was commonly believed that New Zealand would produce an island race more British than the Australian type, for being shaped by a geography similar to that of the British Isles. As Dunedin's Reverend William Curzon-Siggers declared, New Zealand was an 'insular nation', while Australia was a 'continental nation', and 'the history of all races shows that continental races and insular races diverge further and further apart'. Some cited the Tasman Sea's '1200 miles of stormy ocean' as an impediment. But the author of this famous phrase, Sir John Hall, continued, 'That does not prevent the existence of a community of interests between us'.

In doing so, Hall gave voice to the New Zealand solution: to retain the community of interests defined by sea, trade, and blood ties through a reciprocal treaty rather than federation. A reciprocal treaty would resolve the tension between the desire for imperial unity and the hope for a grander future within the empire, which politicians thought would be grander as a separate colony. By 1901, New Zealand opinion-makers already saw a precursor of the Closer Economic Relations free trade agreement secured eight decades later as the best means to express and develop trans-Tasman ties (see chapter 9). Seddon established the terms for such a treaty with the Australian prime minister Alfred Deakin on his last trip to Australia, in 1906, and discussed with Deakin joint Australia–New Zealand opposition to an Anglo-French deal in the New Hebrides. But he died on the voyage home.

New Zealand expressed imperial aspirations in the Pacific, by annexing the Cook Islands and Niue in June 1901. Having presumed a destiny to govern Polynesia on Britain's behalf, New Zealand developed a dream to acquire Samoa. But British strategic interests allowed Germany to secure Western Samoa in 1899 in exchange for Britain's acquisition of German New Guinea, to Australia's relief. New Zealand had to settle for the tinies: the Kermadec Islands in 1887, followed by the Cook Islands and Niue as compensation for the deal over Samoa (New Zealand had supplied the British resident in the Cook Islands since 1891). Māori members of parliament supported the Pacific strategy because of Polynesian kinship links, while Pacific Islander chiefs favoured annexation on the understanding that land rights would be preserved, though they too lost control.

RACIAL ANXIETIES

Increasingly, the Pacific came to be seen as a buffer against Asian invasion. By the early twentieth century Asia had displaced Europe as the source of imagined military threat, heightening settler angst about remoteness and a small population. For New Zealand to be a white country, and home to a better British stock, it had to exclude 'alien races'. The discourse of Social Darwinism and a flexing eugenics movement reinforced the policy of 'domestic defence'. In the 1890s New Zealand's anti-Chinese policy hardened. The poll tax on Chinese migrants soared from £10 to £100 in 1896, and the restriction on numbers doubled from one Chinese person for every 100 tons (90 tonnes) of cargo to one Chinese person for every 200 tons. Fears also rose about the awakening might of Japan, which defeated China in 1895. While Chinese people were perceived as the 'archetypal alien', in 1899 the Liberal government extended immigration restrictions to all non-Europeans.

This exclusiveness was not simply a matter of Aryanism; New Zealand and Australian policies were complicated by imperial policies towards China, India, and Japan. In 1896 the Liberals passed an Asiatic Restriction Bill directed as much against Japanese as against Chinese people, after an attempt in 1895 also to exclude Indians failed, because Indians were British subjects. The bill of

1896 did not receive royal assent because it clashed with the Anglo-Japanese Commercial Treaty that so angered Queensland in 1894. In this context the Chinese can be viewed as scapegoats for New Zealand's failure to impose a blanket restriction on all 'Asiatics' in 1896. Faced with disapproval in London, the Australasian colonies reluctantly agreed to an imperial compromise, to use the model of a dictation test to exclude aliens and 'undesirables'. Natal, a province of South Africa, used such a test to restrict Indian indentured labourers, and Joseph Chamberlain of the Colonial Office suggested this device as a way for the Australasian colonies to reconcile their shared anxieties with British foreign policy.

Accordingly, New Zealand's 1899 Immigration Restriction Act prohibited migrants of non-British or Irish parentage who were unable to pass an English-language test. Overtly, this alternative approach caused less offence to Japan, and to India, the jewel in the imperial crown. New Zealand did not abolish the poll tax on Chinese migrants until 1944. From 1907, Chinese migrants also had to pass a reading test, assessed by customs officers, of 100 words in English. Those who were allowed to live in the country were denied citizenship from 1908 to 1952.

British global economic dominance bolstered beliefs in the empire's superiority. While some aspects of Chinese and Japanese culture were admired, even fashionable (for example, the Chinese lanterns in figure 5.1), imperialist arrogance assumed cultural superiority as well. Settlers believed that Asians would not fit into their Christian, democratic society. On the contrary, their cleverness presented a supposed menace to democracy, ethnic solidarity, and civilisation. The Chinese tradition of sojourning was interpreted negatively; the Chinese 'simply did not swim with the mainstream of colonial development'. New Zealand and Australia both shut their doors to Asia at a time when social cohesion and forming a community identity were thought crucial to building strong, new, young nations. Some historians consider that the 'real enemy of the Chinese was the ideal society'. But it remains true that cultivating whiteness was a central feature of creating genealogies for the new settler communities of Australasia. Whether this process is read as colonial nationalism or 'recolonisation', contemporary rhetoric trumpeted that to be pure was to be white. To be superior was to

5.4 John C. Blomfield, *Still they come*, 1905. Chinese or Japanese (to xenophobes they were indistinguishable), depicted as coolies, are pole-vaulting into New Zealand over the barrier of immigration restrictions, to the chagrin of Premier Richard Seddon.
Free Lance, 7 January 1905. Alexander Turnbull Library, Wellington, A-315-3-042

be white. Fears and dreams in remote New Zealand made sure that it would become as white and as British as possible (see figure 5.4).

At the same time, mounting international tensions drew the colonies into British wars. Most settlers felt bound to British kith and kin globally. War strengthened feeling for the empire. War was thought honourable, a means to test and prove virility. The South African (Boer) War (1899–1902) served as New Zealand's rehearsal for the First World War, an opportunity, Seddon pontificated, to 'prove to those of our race and those in the dear Motherland that we were prepared, outside all questions of expense, to help them'. Loyalties to Britain went unquestioned, and the few dissenters, such as the pacifist Wilhelmina Sherriff Bain, were vilified. Some Māori were keen to fight but were excluded on British orders. Loyalists instead volunteered under their English names. For Elizabeth Hawdon, the author of a popular history of New Zealanders and the South African War, this enthusiasm affirmed the warrior Māori as Pākehā brethren, moving her to ask rhetorically, 'Is there any record of white and brown of any other land being on such fraternal terms as the New Zealanders?' The colony sent 10 volunteer contingents to South Africa. Volunteers and their horses were the first to leave, farewelled by a crowd of 40 000; then provincial, and finally government, contingents. Twenty women schoolteachers followed to teach in the world's first concentration camps and earned the nickname the 'Learned Eleventh'.

As on later occasions, 'imperial sentiment masked … a concern for New Zealand's long-term interests'. While the South African War fed anxieties about racial degeneracy, Pacific Rim settlers were nervous about the Anglo-Japanese alliance. Japan's naval victory over Russia at Tsushima in 1905 debunked European race theory's assumption that the Russian navy would win. After Tsushima the 'Yellow Peril' assumed a military shape. The sole consolation about the Anglo-Japanese alliance, renewed in 1905, was that it transformed the British strategic position in the Far East. Even more than Australia, New Zealand looked to Britain as protector.

New Zealand acquired Dominion status in 1907, like the other three White Dominions (Canada, Australia, and South Africa), granted the elevated title of the 'Dominion of New Zealand', along with self-government to prop up the British role as a great power. The New Zealand government borrowed to donate a battle cruiser to the Royal Navy, and HMS *New Zealand*, built at a cost of £1.7 million, was launched in 1911. The government also cooperated more closely on defence issues with Australia.

At the same time, the undercurrent of danger posed by Japan prompted a change in attitude in Australia and New Zealand towards the United States. The 1908 visit of the Great White Fleet, the popular name for the American Grand Fleet, at the invitation of Prime Ministers Alfred Deakin and Joseph Ward, saw both countries join with the United States president Franklin D. Roosevelt to show that 'these colonies [were] white men's country'.

BABY AS BEST IMMIGRANT

As war clouds gathered, population policy extended from the exclusion of non-British or otherwise 'undesirable' migrants to the promotion of New Zealand–born babies. The dominion joined in the international clamour to boost white birth rates and reduce mortality, particularly among children, who acquired a new public importance as central to the empire's and the nation's future. In the early twentieth century the idea that 'our population is best replenished and our empty spaces best filled by our own natural increase: the newborn infant, in other words, is our best immigrant' was axiomatic. Alarmingly, Pākehā parents joined the international trend to smaller families, irrespective of pronatalist rhetoric from the government, the churches, and the medical profession. Together, declining fertility and mortality generated a demographic and health transition that accompanied revolutions in sexuality and the family. The value of the healthy, white child increased, and with that rose the standards and status of motherhood.

The fertility decline was not simply a 'mother's mutiny'. Moralists blamed women's emancipation and higher education for smaller families, and in part they were right; demographers have found that the longer girls stay at school, the fewer children they will have. But effective birth control in the absence of effective birth-control methods required men's cooperation. Couples engineered the halving in size of the average Pākehā family from six children in the 1880s to two or three by the 1920s. The choices and behaviour of ordinary New Zealanders had more in common with colonial feminist beliefs that empire and nation would benefit from fewer, higher quality children than they did with official rhetoric.

Fighting back, armed with the report of a birth rate inquiry in New South Wales in 1904, Seddon launched a public crusade to save the babies with a memorandum on child life preservation in the press. Grace Neill, a nurse and his leading woman public servant, used this opportunity to establish the St Helens Hospitals as state maternity hospitals from 1905 in the principal towns. Shrewdly, she named these hospitals after Seddon's birthplace in Lancashire. The St Helens Hospitals were both training schools for midwives, registered under the Midwives Act 1904, and maternity homes for the deserving, the respectable women married to steady, skilled workers. Single mothers were excluded. Respectable working-class values, coloured by eugenics, defined the terms of inclusion. W. A. Chapple, a doctor politician, also published his *Fertility of the Unfit* in 1904, in which he expressed the anxiety that the 'unfit' – the poor and the degenerate – were outbreeding the 'fit'. Since they could do little beyond making speeches about the birth rate, however, reformers set their sights on reducing the infant mortality rate.

It was not then known that Māori infant death rates were three or four times higher than those of Pākehā, because Māori statistics were incomplete before the 1930s. Nor did reformers acknowledge that Pākehā infant mortality was already declining. When it was the lowest rate in the world, they stressed it was too high, as if to show how much the white baby mattered.

New Zealand's voluntary infant welfare society, the Plunket Society, had its beginnings in Dunedin in 1907, and in Christchurch and Auckland in 1908. Like overseas counterparts this local movement represented a response to the European health transition. While in theory Plunket was available to Māori, in practice it was not, because its clinics were principally urban and so inaccessible to Māori; the government established a separate scheme of public health nurses for rural Māori districts. A woman's movement that appealed particularly to the well-to-do, the society took its popular name from Lady Victoria Plunket, its vice-regal patron. Its paternalist figurehead was the eugenicist and superintendent of the Seacliff Mental Asylum Dr (Sir) Frederic Truby King, who embarked on a mission, supported by his wife, Bella, to 'help the mothers and save the babies' in an effort to counter racial degeneracy. The society's first aim was 'to uphold the Sacredness of the Body and the Duty of Health; to inculcate a lofty view of the responsibilities of maternity and the duty of every mother to fit herself for the ... natural calls of motherhood'.

The Plunket Society was a local example of international concerns, but it gained a reputation, especially among imperial devotees, for its 'systematic pioneering educational health mission' in infant welfare. Imperial women made Truby King famous after the First World War as a figurehead in the campaign to save babies: his wife, who wrote his newspaper articles; the Kings' adopted daughter, Mary, who made his message Australian; Lady Plunket and her imperial sisters (one sister was married to the Australian governor-general); his matrons; and the mothers who carried his feeding routines and mixtures along the trade routes of empire. Correspondingly, King made the Plunket baby famous by taking his mission to London, so that the Truby King baby became a model among those to whom a British imperial identity mattered. The Plunket Society developed into a national icon in the twentieth century, symbolic of New Zealand as a good place to bring up children, because in the national imagination the Plunket baby embodied the better British type.

The 1905 All Blacks exemplified the offspring desired: with 'broad hips, deep chest, square shoulders, good muscles'. In this body-building and nation-building process, the bonny baby grew into the boy scout. The scouting movement developed rapidly from the earlier volunteer and cadet corps trained for defence purposes. By the end of 1908, when Sir Robert Baden-Powell published *Scouting for Boys*, there were 36 scout troops in New Zealand, mostly in Canterbury. Endorsed by Baden-Powell, whom he had met in the South African War, David Cossgrove, the headmaster of Tuahiwi School, organised the New Zealand Boy Scout movement, which aimed to teach boys 'peaceful citizenship' through outdoor activities. It also drilled boys in martial skills. Tuahiwi is a Ngāi Tahu settlement, and Cossgrove as a military officer recognised the compatibility of the Māori warrior stereotype with scouting. Mrs Selina Cossgrove ensured that girls also had their girl peace scouts movement. With compulsory military training introduced under the Defence Act 1909 and a territorial force, New Zealand steeled its youth and prepared to 'produce patriots capable of defending the British Empire'.

6
'All flesh is as grass' 1914–1929

'In New Zealand more than in any country in the world we find justification for the words of the Bible, "All flesh is as grass, and all the goodliness thereof is as the flower of the field".' So began the issue on pasture land of the *Making New Zealand* pictorial survey to mark New Zealand's centennial, in 1940. This biblical phrase had multiple meanings for New Zealanders, in relation to 'ecological imperialism', feeding Britain, and the sacrifice of its best young men in war.

In this era, too, the dominion underwent a grasslands revolution in which farmers turned to pasture plants, such as clovers and ryegrass, to increase agricultural productivity. English grasses were imported to New Zealand, to be re-exported as frozen meat and dairy products, in an imperial food chain. The biblical reference suggests that New Zealand was indeed a land of milk and honey. This reference also became an anthem, sung at Anzac Day services on 25 April, the anniversary of the perilous landing by the Australian and New Zealand Army Corps, or Anzacs, on the Gallipoli Peninsula, in the Ottoman Empire (today's Türkiye), in 1915. (To the Turks it was an invasion.) New Zealand not only processed imperial grass seed into flesh and blood, but the flower of its manhood died for king and country during the First World War, principally at Gallipoli and on the Western Front, in France and Belgium.

Together, New Zealanders and Australians remembered their best and bravest young men as the 'flower[s] of the field', in the Flanders poppy, worn on Anzac Day. Soldiers took to heart the poem 'In Flanders Fields', composed by Canadian doctor John McCrae in 1915, which members of the Allied forces sent to the Western Front made their own:

> *In Flanders fields the poppies blow*
> *Between the crosses, row on row,*
> *That mark our place; and in the sky*
> *The larks, still bravely singing, fly*
> *Scarce heard amid the guns below.*

For New Zealand and Australia, the distant battlefields spawned a story of sacrifice and heroic archetypes of the citizen soldier. Mythmaking helped to make sense of horrendous losses, whose impact at home remains almost too great to comprehend. The First World War is 'arguably the most traumatic event in New Zealand's experience' and left 'a generation of men both physically and mentally scarred'. From an official viewpoint the war obliterated a chunk of the tallest and healthiest 'A1 stock', classified fit for overseas service. Approximately one in five New Zealand men was sent to defend the empire, or 10 per cent of the total population. Of about 120 000 New Zealanders who served (over 101 000 overseas), 18 000 died. A further 3300 served in the British or Australian forces. The casualty rate was high: towards 60 000, or 60 per cent. Nearly all the men who enlisted early and survived were injured. The legacy of grief and trauma proved deep and lasting. Women grieved for loved ones – a generation of cherished youth – for the rest of their lives.

Insights into national identity can also be gained by connecting the First World War with trends in food production and health that shaped New Zealand in its aftermath. Such links showed in wartime when, from 1915, Britain supplied a guaranteed market for New Zealand's primary products. The change of name and status to the Dominion of New Zealand distinguished the country as a self-governing, British White Dominion. People felt no contradiction between nation and empire, between New Zealand and 'Britain overseas', because they were British subjects. For all the siblings in this far-flung imperial family, it was a matter of course that London continued to make the decisions over war, peace, and foreign policy. New Zealand's participation in the First World War logically followed from a defence policy which depended on the power of Great Britain.

When Britain declared war on Germany in August 1914, New Zealand's prime minister, Bill Massey, therefore pledged the expected loyal and immediate support, and New Zealanders responded by volunteering enthusiastically. The government marshalled four expeditionary forces. The first force, assembled within three days, sailed to Samoa, landing on 29 August, and took control of German Samoa without encountering any resistance. This prompt response reflected the degree to which settler governments had long coveted Samoa. Equally it showed how the British resumed command, because the Admiralty directed the territorial force's movements and organised its escort by the battle cruiser *Australia*. The main body, of 8000 men, was ready to send to Egypt on 28 August. However, this expeditionary force – still, in 2025, the largest number of troops to leave New Zealand at one time – had to wait until October for a naval escort. It joined the troopships of the Australian Imperial Force off the coast of Western Australia and arrived in Egypt by the end of the year. There, imperial authorities grouped the two contingents as the New Zealand and Australian Division, which, combined with the 1st Australian Division, formed the Anzacs – the Australian and New Zealand Army Corps – which landed at Gallipoli in April 1915.

So sacred was the experience at Gallipoli that it was embraced as the initial episode in New Zealand's Anzac tradition, which emerged alongside, and yet separate from, the more celebrated Australian Anzac legend. Yet the largest division – the New Zealand Division – served in France from 1916, with the heaviest losses. On the Western Front, along the Somme, and in Flanders at Messines and Passchendaele, in the Ypres salient, New Zealand lost 13 250 men, nearly five times as many as the 2700 killed at Gallipoli and more than the nation's losses in the whole of the Second World War.

Gallipoli became a defining moment for both New Zealand and Australia in 1915 because Gallipoli was the site where their representatives of the 'coming man' were subjected to their first – global – test and proved their manhood. The Anzacs represented the highest form of citizenship: soldiers who passed the test of war. In an age of empires, this test had to be undertaken on the ancient battlefields of Europe, and, given the location of Gallipoli, in northwest Türkiye, the men were likened to Trojan heroes. The campaign also made Australia and New Zealand Anzac neighbours, linking them with, and at the same time distinguishing them from, Great Britain. The Anzacs at Gallipoli demonstrated how the best of British qualities flowered in Australasia; and at Gallipoli the men realised the hellish futility of war. In reality as well as in legend they hung on bravely, although the campaign was a failure. On 5 May 1915 Lieutenant-Colonel Dr Percival Fenwick of the field ambulance recorded in the diary that he wrote for his wife, 'Every day we hear more stories of the heroism of our stretcher bearers', adding despairingly, 'An order came out naming this bay Anzac Bay ... Perhaps it will some day be known as Bloody Beach Bay'.

Gallipoli was a sacred site for the very reason that the men in this war first spilt blood there. Most of the dead have no known graves; their bones still lie in Turkish soil. Already, by the first anniversary of the landing, on 25 April 1916, the first Anzac Day set the tone as a day of mourning. The men quickly adopted the name 'Anzac Beach', or 'Anzac Bay', for the small cove where the troops were mistakenly delivered. In a gracious act to commemorate the 70th anniversary of the campaign, in 1985, Türkiye officially renamed Ari Burnu beach as 'Anzac Cove'. The gesture acknowledged the site's sacred status to expanding numbers of Australian and New Zealand pilgrims and reinforced Türkiye's growing bonds with Australia and New Zealand as more people, young and old, retraced their ancestors' steps to show respect, learn, experience the terrain, and uncover family stories.

So powerful was the tradition invented to commemorate 25 April 1915, and those who served and died in subsequent conflicts, that it was sometimes proposed to make 25 April New Zealand's national day. Anzac Day was made a full public holiday and 'holy day', as if it were a Sunday, in 1922, in response to the public mood. It became 'an expression of sorrow rather than an opportunity to glorify war', at the same time reflective of the Anzac spirit in which some commentators identified the kernel of nationhood.

The main themes of the parallel Australian and New Zealand legends – courage, endurance, duty, love of country, mateship, good humour, and decency in the face of dreadful odds – explain their resonances and the reverence they command. To a loyal public the First World War represented a fight for the world as they knew it: a war between empires, a struggle for the survival of the British Empire and of civilisation. Recruiters implored the first Anzacs to fight in 'the greatest of all causes, the cause of right, of justice, and of liberty'. The Gallipoli campaign was therefore heroic even as a failure. From the start, the Gallipoli catastrophe came to denote sacrifice: by and for local communities, for the nation as well as in defence of the empire, for the British race and the entire imperial family. New Zealanders believed they had shown themselves to be superior specimens to whom Britain now owed a debt. *New Zealand's Roll of Honour* published in 1915 softened the impact of 103 pages of photographs of the fallen with King George V's congratulations 'upon the splendid conduct and bravery displayed by the New Zealand troops at the Dardanelles Strait, who have indeed proved themselves worthy Sons of the Empire'.

In contrast to the uniformed larrikin favoured as Australia's icon, the New Zealand archetype of the pioneer farmer turned soldier was a gentleman. At least, he appeared to be so in the presence of Australians, encouraged by his officers to show by 'neat dress and sobriety that there was a wide difference between the two forces'. He was the quiet New Zealander, depicted by Ormond Burton in *The Silent Division* (1935). A pacifist initially with the ambulance corps and a stretcher bearer, Burton was so moved by the soldiers' conduct that he rejoined his regiment. As members of the smaller partner in the Anzac corps, the New Zealanders defined themselves against both the Australians and the metropolitan British. Together, the identity of Australians and New Zealanders as Anzacs distinguished them from the British Tommies and their officers in their strength, initiative, and resourcefulness. In the trenches of France, the Anzacs also began to describe themselves as 'Diggers'. 'Anzac' was already a more formal, solemn, distinguished term; 'Digger' was a more informal name, reflective of the New Zealand Pioneer Battalion's and engineers' skill in digging trenches and tunnels, as well as the collective experience of trench warfare and a colonial heritage. Diggers were 'war friends', as a soldier wrote in Flanders:

> Digger and cobber, mate and chum –
> Who says there's nothing in a name?

At the same time, the New Zealand soldier who began the war as 'Tommy Fernleaf' had become a 'Kiwi' by 1917, conscious that he was different. As the Australian scholar Ken Inglis explained, 'Anzacs together, Diggers at least in parallel, Aussies and Kiwis apart: the war had given citizens of the southern dominions two words which distinguished them from metropolitan Britons, and another pair which signalled their different nationalities'.

An emphasis on distinctiveness gained ground in the 1980s in the context of conscious assertions of nationhood, in which historians reinvented the Anzac legend consistent with the country's nuclear-free stance and defiance of its United States ally and with its difference from its other ANZUS partner, Australia (see chapter 9). Historians began to pay more attention to the experiences of the men as a corrective to the official version of the legend, which celebrated the superior British colonial type and the glory of the Great Sacrifice. The Anzac survivors told their stories only in old age, just before death; so awful was the slaughter that they tried to block it out for their lifetimes. The 'private' narrative equally built on sacrifice, but with a new purpose: to embalm the horrors of war that the men endured. Both military historian Chris Pugsley and novelist Maurice Shadbolt determined to give the last word to the Gallipoli veterans about what happened, which meant installing the New Zealanders' assault on the strategic hill Chunuk Bair on 8 August 1915 as 'central to the New Zealand experience of Gallipoli'.

In the play *Once on Chunuk Bair* (1982), Shadbolt created his own living memorial to the men, to enshrine the New Zealand experience in the way that Peter Weir's film *Gallipoli* told the Australian story of fighting at Lone Pine and the Nek (Shadbolt's play was made into a film in 1991). The effect was to highlight the 'NZ' in Anzac. In this interpretation, Anzac Day was Australia's day, because the Australians landed first, before dawn on 25 April 1915, while the New Zealanders landed from 9 a.m.; 'the New

Zealand role came later'. Instead Shadbolt and Pugsley proclaimed 8 August as the New Zealanders' day, when they lost their innocence. It was after climbing Chunuk Bair that disillusionment set in with conditions and with the British and that the Kiwi soldiers realised they were different. Aged 88, 'Daredevil Dan' Curham of the Wellington Infantry Battalion recalled that when the Turks retook the summit of Chunuk Bair, 'it was all over'. He continued, 'From then on we knew there was little hope of victory on the peninsula, that all the suffering had been in vain'.

Chunuk Bair had its New Zealand hero, Colonel W. G. Malone, who led the August offensive. A meticulous officer, Malone inspired his men by refusing orders which he judged were suicidal and by saving lives from disease with his standards of hygiene and from machine-gun fire by covering trenches. It was Malone who, with 760 men of the Wellington Battalion and some from the Māori Contingent, took and held Chunuk Bair for 36 hours. The Wellingtons could see the Dardanelles, their ultimate objective, but the British relieved them too late. Unbeknown to New Zealanders, Malone was killed by Allied shellfire, not by Turkish bullets. Worse, he became a British scapegoat. Elevating the Chunuk Bair story, then, amounted to a declaration of independence.

It is telling that the New Zealand Division adopted the Lemon Squeezer hat from 1916, which became part of the army's dress uniform in the Second World War. Previously New Zealanders were instructed to wear the British peaked cap. The Lemon Squeezer, with its four distinctive dents, designed so that the rain ran off, began as the headdress of the 11th Taranaki Rifles, Malone's regiment in the Wellington Battalion. Its adoption can be read as a memorial in uniform, which signifies that the emergence of a New Zealand identity among the men was indeed associated in the soldiers' minds with Malone and Chunuk Bair.

Māori warrior heroes also proved themselves at Gallipoli – the only place they fought as infantry – as members of the 1st Māori Contingent, and in France, in the Pioneer Battalion. As volunteers they, too, represented Britannia's warriors and the chivalric Christian soldier. But they simultaneously invoked the tradition of Tumatauenga, god of war. Māori proved to the British High Command that the 'natives' could excel in war as combat troops and to Pākehā (European New Zealanders) that Māori deserved equality. The four Māori members of parliament Dr Peter Buck (Te Rangi Hiroa), Āpirana Ngata, Dr Māui Pōmare, and Taare Parata, with Sir James Carroll, had determined to train a Māori contingent for this very purpose, to prove Māori equality by emulating their warrior ancestry. On 3 July 1915 the Māori Contingent landed at Anzac Cove, where Buck expressed a sentiment shared with Pākehā: 'Our feet were set on a distant land where our blood was to be shed in the cause of the Empire to which we belonged'. In September 1917 the Pioneer Battalion became a full Māori unit, the New Zealand (Māori) Pioneer Battalion, although, as numbers thinned, it included 200 Niueans and Cook Islanders.

IN FLANDERS FIELDS

The Western Front, in France and Belgium, was the site of most deaths in the First World War but was not mythologised in the manner of Gallipoli. There the New Zealand Division, flanked by British and Australian divisions, experienced the horrors of trench warfare, bogged in mud. At the first Battle of the Somme, in September 1916, they made a successful attack on German trenches, but some units lost over 80 per cent of their men. Reinforced with volunteers and conscripts, the New Zealand Division fought at Messines in June 1917, again successfully, but with severe losses. The story of Passchendaele in 1917 is particularly significant, because there, on 'Black Friday', 12 October, Sergeant W. K. Wilson recorded in his diary, 'Our boys and the Aussies went over at 5.30 and got practically cut to pieces'. Passchendaele remains New Zealand's worst military disaster. David Gallaher, captain of the 1905 All Blacks, died in the assault, which the men knew was hopeless before they started, because the barbed wire was not cut and they lacked artillery support in the rain and mud. Senior commanders failed to learn the lesson of their earlier success: the need to provide artillery support to the infantry against German machine guns.

No wonder the men of the New Zealand Division called their magazine *Shell-Shocks* or that Tyne Cot Cemetery, in Belgium, is

'All flesh is as grass' 1914–1929   143

6.1 'Row on row'. Lijssenthoek Military Cemetery, the second largest New Zealand cemetery in Belgium, 6 June 2004 Quotation from John McCrae, 'In Flanders Fields', 1915. Photographer Richard Tremewan

the largest cemetery tended by the Commonwealth War Graves Commission (figure 6.1 shows the second largest). While trauma robbed soldiers of the ability to talk about the horrors of technological warfare, of mates shelled, gassed, and sunk in mud, the artistically inclined drew revealing cartoons. Figure 6.2, for example, suggests that soldiers dreamt of being invalided with minor wounds to England, to be cared for by New Zealand nurses. Rather than the psychoanalytical view that it was unhealthy to repress their experience, a modern psychiatric view agrees with the Anzac treatment of shell shock: a combination of rest, alcohol, or prescribed drugs, followed by getting on with the job, helps in cases of post-traumatic stress.

Wounded at Gallipoli, Captain P. P. (Pirimi) Tāhiwi of the New Zealand (Māori) Pioneer Battalion led his men in the haka 'Ka Mate, Ka Mate' (it is death) on Chunuk Bair. Figure 6.3.1 shows him at Sling Camp in England in 1916 where the New Zealand

6.2 A. Rule, *'In Blighty!' A thing we dream about*, 1916
Shell Shocks: By the New Zealanders in France, London: Jarrold & Sons, 1916, 29. Courtesy of Jack and Betty Tait

Division trained for warfare in France. Tāhiwi survived the war but his friend Captain H. S. (Spencer) Tremewan (figure 6.3.2) did not. When the latter was shot and killed at the Battle of the Somme in September 1916, aged 23, his company commander wrote to Tremewan's mother, Mary,

> It will be a great comfort to you to know that the very high standard which he set himself to live up to was never diminished, and that all the roughness and hard living of active service left him unspoiled – in fact only strengthened his resolve to live a straight and honourable life.

The subtext suggested is not repression, but resilience, and living an 'honourable life' in defiance of the odds.

6.3.1 Captain P. P. Tāhiwi, Sling Camp, England, July 1916, wearing the British peaked cap
Photographer H. S. Tremewan. Tremewan album, family collection

THE HOME FRONT

Mary Tremewan was one of thousands of women for whom the war denoted sacrifice by giving the life of her son. At his memorial service the minister comforted her with the statement that 'his was the priceless heritage of a Christian mother'. Some mothers lost more than one son; some lost all their sons. The Great Sacrifice included heroic maternal sacrifice. Supporters of the war (the majority) likened soldiers' mothers to Volumnia in William Shakespeare's *Coriolanus* when she professed that, had she a dozen sons, she 'would rather eleven die nobly for their country than one voluptuously surfeit out of action'. An ideal from classical myth to Mary, mother of Jesus, this fed a conviction that all mothers' sons should share the same test of manhood and all families share the burden of grief. Hence most New Zealand women supported

6.3.2 Captain H. S. Tremewan, wearing a Lemon Squeezer hat, and Mrs M. Mylrea, YMCA, Sling Camp, England, July 1916
Tremewan album, family collection

conscription, to ensure equality of sacrifice, to redistribute the pain of having all the sons in one family die or suffer dreadful injury and none in another. In fact, nearly every family experienced the loss.

Unlike Australia, New Zealand introduced conscription in November 1916, to rebuild the shattered New Zealand Division after the Battle of the Somme. Henceforward its reinforcements were a mix of volunteers and conscripts. This contrast with the Australian Anzacs, who were volunteers for the whole war, affected the tenor of the nations' respective legends. The absence of conscripts made the Australian legend more celebratory and more militaristic. New Zealand, on the other hand, asserted a greater loyalty to empire by introducing conscription on the British model, while its legend acquired a mood more funereal and subdued, with greater emphasis on mourning the war dead. Conscription also engendered different outcomes on the home front. It spurred the formation of the New Zealand Labour Party in 1916, whereas the 'no' vote to conscription split the Labor Party in Australia. Anti-conscription did not equate to anti-war sentiment, although these two strands of dissent overlapped. A handful of conscientious objectors refused to fight, preferring prison, because they rejected the war and killing as immoral. Theirs were mainly Irish, socialist, Quaker, and Christian fundamentalist loyalties. Dissent was militant among West Coast miners and the Red Feds, who advanced class arguments for equality of sacrifice. These representatives of a radical, left-wing, peace tradition included unionists who played a key role in the formation of the Labour Party and leaders in Labour politics, the future prime ministers M. J. (Micky) Savage, from Victoria, and Peter Fraser, a Scottish immigrant (see chapter 7). Archibald Baxter, father of poet James K. Baxter and son-in-law of Helen Connon (see chapter 4), was encouraged by his wife to write the book *We Will Not Cease* (1939), which became well known only on its reissue, in the late 1960s, when its pacifism spoke to a generation of anti–Vietnam War protesters.

Iwi (tribe) and hapū (subtribe) loyalties ensured that some Māori were pacifists. The divide in loyalties was created in the nineteenth century by the New Zealand Wars, between tribes who had fought for and against the Crown. Whereas kūpapa (Crown supporters) such as Te Arawa and Ngāti Porou provided volunteers for the Pioneer Battalion, the Kīngitanga (King movement) asserted that its men should not fight, and none did. One of its leaders, Te Puea Hērangi, granddaughter of King Tāwhiao, opposed the support for the war shown by Māori members of parliament. Te Puea also led her Waikato-Tainui people's resistance to conscription. In response to recruitment calls for king and country, she retorted, 'We've got a king. But we haven't got a country', because her Tainui confederation had suffered the unjust confiscation of most of its land. When the government attempted to conscript her people but not other iwi in 1917, Tainui resisted effectively. They ignored this punitive gesture. In the rugged Urewera, the prophet Rua Kēnana, religious heir to Te Kooti, similarly opposed volunteering and was arrested, first on charges of illegally supplying liquor and then for alleged sedition in a police raid, in 1916, on his community, on his Tūhoe tribe's sacred mountain. Rua was imprisoned until 1918 for his defiance.

Women peace activists who shared the sympathies of conscientious objectors co-opted belief in the duty of motherhood to protest that mothers did not bring lives into the world to be used as fodder for capitalists. It was their role to promote peace and arbitration; they did not raise sons to kill other mothers' sons. The Women's International League for Peace and Freedom, established in Christchurch in 1916, argued that as 'mothers of the world' they bore a global responsibility to campaign to end armed conflict.

Some women wanted to volunteer for overseas service. While two women doctors (Agnes Bennett and Elizabeth Gunn) donned uniform, those who ventured closest to the front were nurses, of whom over 600 served overseas in field hospitals and on hospital ships. The nurses' memorial chapel at Christchurch Hospital is the country's only memorial to nurses from the war, built to honour three local nurses who died when a German submarine sank a transport ship, the *Marquette*, in the Aegean Sea, in October 1915. Ten New Zealand nurses died in this disaster, plus 19 medics and 23 Australian nurses.

Confined to non-combatant, maternal roles, women at home joined patriotic societies to raise funds through fairs and concerts and to provide 'comforts' for the soldiers. Of all their patriotic work, knitting had the greatest symbolic significance; for women, a pair of knitting needles replaced the bayonet. *Her Excellency's Knitting Book* (1915) declared on the front cover, 'The men go forth to battle, the women wait – and knit'.

Lady Annette Liverpool, the governor's wife, led the women's war effort in her social role as leader and patron of women's philanthropic organisations. In a gesture of equality on the home front, she and Miria Pōmare (later Lady Pōmare), wife of Dr (Sir) Māui Pōmare, who chaired the Māori recruitment committee, together set up the Lady Liverpool and Mrs Pōmare's Māori Soldiers' Fund to send parcels to the New Zealand (Māori) Pioneer Battalion.

Women as mothers played a special part in remembrance, as mourners, privately and in public. Remembering the war dead in 1925, the *New Zealand Herald* appreciated that families who laid wreaths at the newly built war memorials 'kept their own soldiers' memory green'. As the only place that named a district's dead soldiers, the local war memorial served as a site of mourning for a town's or borough's lost sons, buried so far away, many with no known graves. Given the mobility of New Zealand society, a man's name might appear on more than one monument – where he was born and in the district's main town – aiding community remembrance. A survey conducted around 1990 counted 366 such civic memorials.

Most Anzac memorials were built in stone. About 35 per cent were simple obelisks; 17 per cent were arches or gates, commonly at the entrance to rugby grounds; and a Digger figure stood tall on 10 per cent. With the odd exception, New Zealand's memorials named only the dead, unlike Australia's memorials, which honoured the dead and the living. In Oamaru, residents planted memorial oak trees from 1919 to keep their boys' memory green. An imperial yet personal symbol associated with moral qualities and regeneration, the oaks remembered the district's sons as the 'flower of the field'. In oak and in stone, the imagined community invoked was still both empire and nation.

REPAIRING THE WAR WASTAGE

Inevitably, war heightened emphasis on the sanctity of life; premature deaths of the country's youth and universal grief renewed the value of birth, and of health, and bestowed more attention on the child and the mother. Invited to Australia on his way home from London in 1919 by Lady Victoria Plunket's sister, Lady Helen Munro Ferguson, wife of the Australian governor-general, Dr (Sir) Frederic Truby King lectured that the 'great wastage of manhood, womanhood, and also infant life caused by the war must be made good'. His imperialist rhetoric intoned that women bore a public duty as mothers to 'repair the war wastage' by having more babies and preventing infant deaths. Patriotism for women equated to motherhood. The war also gave renewed urgency to eugenic anxieties about racial degeneracy, because army medical examinations exposed a high level of unfitness. Recruits were assessed for their fitness for overseas service (A1) or otherwise (C2 or C3), and these indexes supplied advocates of eugenics with categories by which to classify children after the war.

The First World War, then, propelled mothers and babies onto the public agenda and advanced the idea that girls and women possessed a maternal duty to the nation and empire. The Plunket Society (see chapter 5) did its bit; New Zealand's version of the infant welfare movement developed its health mission, entering an era of expansion after the war, and King and his devotees claimed the credit for the decline in infant mortality from already low levels. They helped to make New Zealand a model to the world in infant welfare on the grounds that the country with the lowest (white) infant death rate set the example for others to follow. The author has argued elsewhere that mothers deserve more credit for reduced infant mortality and that the rise of the infant welfare movement is better understood as a response to, more than a cause of, the decline in fertility and mortality rates. Similarly, Plunket's historian has reasoned that, 'with raised expectations of survival and smaller families by the 1920s, mothers invested more time and energy in child-rearing. They were "modern" women who wanted "modern" advice, and turned to the nurses for guidance, as well as for support and reassurance'.

In fact, King himself knew little about babies; as his rivals were quick to point out, he was a psychiatrist, not a paediatrician. This criticism was raised on every one of his 10 (or more) trips to Australia between 1919 and 1931. That an elderly New Zealand doctor with a gift for media sound bites provoked a clash of patriotisms in Australia over infant-feeding methods showed how much the white baby mattered politically after the war. New Zealand and Australia competed for the title of social laboratory in health in the 1920s, just as they competed in sport, to display the biggest, strongest Anzac bodies. King's Australian visits confirmed that his real historical significance was as a propagandist. He put mothers and babies on political agendas as much through his invective as through his broad appeal, raising political and public awareness about the value of the child to the empire and the nation. Such zealous personalities have a role in getting things done, provided they do not overstep boundaries and polarise or alienate.

For the government to be seen to be promoting the child, it had to reform public health as well as expand educational opportunities. The devastation of war served as a catalyst, but an insufficient one to jolt politicians. It took the global catastrophe of the 1918 influenza pandemic to prompt the passing of the new Health Act. The flu proved to be New Zealand's worst natural disaster. Worldwide, the pandemic killed at least 25 million, more than double the estimated 10 million war dead. Tragically, it struck hardest at young adults, particularly men aged 25 to 45, the cohorts hurt by the war. At the time Pākehā did not know that the Māori death rate from the flu was one of the highest in the world, seven times the European death rate of 5.8 per 1000. It was highest of all in New Zealand–administered Western Samoa, where a fifth of the population died. By contrast American Samoa stayed free of infection by imposing a strict quarantine.

For strategic reasons, in 1920 New Zealand accepted a League of Nations mandate over Samoa, where it largely continued the pre-war German system of government, as suggested by military administrators who received little help from Wellington. However, the flu unfortunately gave New Zealand rule in Samoa a reputation for incompetence, which – combined with lack of understanding and racial prejudice – fuelled distrust.

Clearly New Zealand had to reform its responses to epidemic disease, whose prevention was the primary purpose of public health. The restructured Department of Public Health, established in 1900, had its focus broadened in 1920 from the environment, sewerage, and sanitation to people and personal health services, which targeted the child as the future citizen. Renamed the Department of Health, the modernised department had seven divisions, including child welfare, school, dental hygiene, and Māori hygiene. Truby King, the incoming director of child welfare, advised the minister of health that his mission would be no less than the 'physical, mental and moral betterment of the race'.

In the 1920s 'the nation's health is the nation's wealth' became a familiar catchcry. An irascible Truby King, already past retirement age, assumed charge of child welfare policy only briefly, before it returned to the Department of Education in 1925. The health of European infants and preschoolers remained in the hands of the Plunket Society. This government-subsidised voluntary organisation enjoyed widespread influence through its class appeal to upright middle-class people, their receptiveness often deepened by imperialist beliefs. It won the support of the wives of businessmen, of mayoresses, and of prime ministers and their wives, including the Masseys and J. G. and Marjorie Coates in the 1920s. The Department of Health, meanwhile, turned its attention to the schoolchild, with the idea of devising complete health records from the start of school to military age.

The open-air school enjoyed its heyday in New Zealand in the 1920s. The concept originated in Germany to expose tubercular children to sunlight and fresh air. Strong winds proved a challenge, such as the Canterbury nor'wester, and in winter the classrooms were freezing. This was a time when poor children walked or rode to school barefoot, and small boys lacked socks and underpants.

School medical inspections began belatedly under the Department of Education, in 1912. Transferred to the Department of Health in 1921, the school doctors targeted defective teeth and tonsils in their search for infection. Dr Elizabeth Gunn, who joined the wartime Medical Corps, intimidated small children in her district by shouting 'Show us your crockery!', war medals bristling on her chest. Toothbrush drill epitomised the era's militarism. The concerns were international, to educate to prevent disease and to influence the parent through the child. But alarm mounted that there should be poorly fed children, with bad teeth, in New Zealand. Officials were reluctant to acknowledge the existence of poverty. Faith in 'natural abundance' demanded that children be demonstratively healthier than those in Britain. How could it be that, in this agricultural country, children ate insufficient meat, vegetables, and dairy products, and that the milk they drank was often condensed milk? Already some school doctors and teachers had begun to experiment with milk in schools (see figure 6.4).

Puny children found themselves sent to health camps to gain weight and to sunbathe on tarpaulins, to acquire a suntan. An appropriate agricultural metaphor captured the campaign objective of 'fattening human stock'. Its eugenic undertones were clear. In December 1919 Gunn, a forthright eugenicist, organised the first health camp for undernourished children on a farm near Whanganui, under ex-army canvas. A description of a camp in 1922 illustrates contemporary attitudes: a local farm was 'fattening more

6.4 'Eat more milk'. Health class, 1926
Ministry of Health, Wellington. In author's possession

valuable stock than it has ever fattened before ... for 95 boys and girls are there under canvas and enjoying wholesome living and fresh air ... nice amiable little boys and girls with arms and legs like matches'. All were underweight. After sunbathing at the camp, however, 'some looked more like A1 than C3. They looked rosy and sunburnt'.

That schoolchildren measured in 1927 were taller and heavier than English and especially Australian children gave gratifying substance to the belief that New Zealand ought ideally to serve as a nursery for British stock. In the 1920s, when officials marketed the dominion as Britain's farm, it was logical to complement advertising of primary products for export to Britain, the world's largest importer of food, with a health campaign to win New Zealand a reputation as the best place to build strong bodies. Building the child, the empire, and the nation acquired a central place in national mythology, because New Zealand demonstrated prowess in producing soldiers, athletes, and commodities such as food and clothing: the raw materials for imperial defence.

After the First World War maternal deaths were chief among concerns about national efficiency, because deaths in childbirth undermined the population imperative of more babies. New Zealand launched a campaign for safe maternity in the 1920s, amid alarm at statistics published internationally that showed the dominion had the second highest maternal mortality rate after the United States. This was embarrassing, to say the least, and anomalous with the nation's proud record of the world's lowest infant mortality rate (excluding Māori). In 1923 five women died from puerperal sepsis (blood poisoning) in a private maternity hospital in Auckland. The public storm of protest compelled a commission of inquiry, which decided that population policy justified state involvement in maternity services.

The dispute that erupted between doctors and midwives in the 1920s over responsibility for the management of childbirth provides another case study of international trends. In New Zealand a midwife system received the backing of departmental medical advisers with British backgrounds, who were also able to demonstrate statistically that midwife deliveries were safer. But family practitioners increasingly ministered to families from birth. The campaign for safe maternity launched by the Department of Health in 1924 prompted an institutionalised response by general practitioners, whom Dr Doris Gordon, who practised with her husband at Stratford in Taranaki, organised into the Obstetrical Society from 1927. General practitioners denied the charge that their 'meddlesome midwifery' accounted for the high maternal death rate. They asserted that, on the contrary, civilisation had made childbirth pathological, as opposed to a normal process that could be left to midwives, and a doctor service was superior precisely because it was more expensive, modern, and scientific.

In the 1920s the New Zealand place of birth shifted from the home to the hospital as new public maternity hospitals and wards opened. The campaign for safe maternity achieved its aim of bringing New Zealand's maternal mortality into line with that of other nations, through better care and training, strict asepsis, and reform of the many private, mixed hospitals which practised both obstetrics and surgery. Rates of puerperal sepsis declined from 1927, before sulphonamide drugs in the 1930s and antibiotics in the 1940s. Since the quality of the carer is crucial in childbirth, improved care and cleanliness saved lives.

The New Zealand mum came into her own from the 1920s. Politically, the women's movement achieved successes. The institution of six o'clock closing in pubs survived from 1917 to 1967. It ensured that men, even if drunk or disorderly, went home for dinner. The public bar became a men-only zone; barmaids were banned. Pressure from the revived National Council of Women won the legislative gain of women being allowed to stand for the House of Representatives in 1919, but women could still not be appointed to the upper house, the Legislative Council. With health an aesthetic goal, for a woman to be beautiful she had to be healthy and meet the 'fit' eugenic, racial ideal of the future wife and mother. Miss New Zealand set the standard for healthy beauty in 1926, following the Miss America and Miss Australia contests. In contrast to more recent years, a married woman could win the title.

Development priorities infused all body politics, including immigration policy. An amendment act in 1920 prescribed an undeclared White New Zealand policy; anyone not of British or Irish birth or parentage was excluded, other than at the discretion of the minister of customs. More precisely, this policy aimed to protect British New Zealand. The group systematically excluded were the Chinese, who were judged a menace to democracy. That wives and children of Gujarati men already in the country were admitted indicated the importance of marriage to ideal citizenship, extending to acceptance of arranged marriages, for this cheap, colonial labour from those who were British subjects. British emigrants arrived under the 1922 Empire Settlement Act, which authorised assisted passages to the White Dominions. The target groups were single agricultural labourers, married couples, young people in their teens, and domestic servants, much as in the 1840s.

New Zealanders were more urban than rural by the 1920s. Suburbs burgeoned on the outskirts of the main towns, and the number of cars on the roads doubled. The Californian bungalow (see figure 6.5) replaced the villa as the desired low-cost suburban house: builders adapted designs from Californian plan books, adding English Arts and Crafts embellishments. Driving the expansion of suburbia were state mortgages. Bill Massey's Reform government continued the Liberal policy of advances to workers,

6.5 Californian bungalow, Wakefield, Nelson, 2004
Photographer Jeff Mein Smith. Family collection

providing to working men and returned soldiers home loans of up to 95 per cent for a suburban house and section. Electric lighting, hot water, and inside toilets eased the lives of families who could afford home ownership. Electricity lit up rooms and showed the dust, inviting marketing strategies of the consumer society. People turned on the radio and flocked to silent movies.

EMPIRE'S DAIRY FARM

The farmer, however, was hailed as the 'backbone of the country', because of reliance on the British economy for a large proportion of national income. The standard of living depended on the export of primary produce. So did the settler contract, which extended to the returned soldier. A rehabilitation scheme rewarded soldiers – including some Māori returned servicemen – with farms. Often the sections surveyed were in the backblocks, in steep, remote bush and hill country, where the soldier settlers faced environmental obstacles and lack of capital.

New Zealand was the most dependent of all the dominions on Britain, the greatest global power. On average it sent at least 75 per cent of its exports to Britain and bought 50 per cent of its imports from Britain in the 1920s. The appropriation of the Australian and New Zealand wool clips by the imperial government from 1916 to 1920 tightened bilateral relations but led to a stockpile not disposed of until 1924 as demand recovered after the war. Postwar dairy production exceeded British requirements, and the country once again faced the problem of export income instability, with prices for produce decided overseas.

From the 1920s to the 1960s New Zealand underwent a 'grasslands revolution' that saw a threefold increase in production based on grass. Much of this expansion depended on phosphate, crucial as fertiliser to grow grass in poor soils, mined on the tiny Pacific island of Nauru. Dairying developed in 'wet' areas, with the climate and soil assumed best for cows' milk supply, and in areas of forest and wetland, including the Waikato, Manawatū, and Taranaki. Global consumerism transformed forest into grass for intensive agriculture, which was seen as modern and the way of the future. Dairying represented science and progress. It also imperialised the landscape, replacing native bush and fern with improved English grasses and European livestock – Friesian and Jersey cows – to feed British consumers. New Zealand supplied half of Britain's cheese and a quarter of its butter in the 1920s.

Unsurprisingly, New Zealanders internalised the image of the 'Empire's Dairy Farm' used in export marketing. Milk became central to images of New Zealand as 'clean and green' and a healthy place to bring up children, and the dairy farmer a masculine type in literature (see figure 6.6). Milk for bodybuilding represented a form of cultural imperialism fashioned by the empire in New Zealand. Medical arguments helped transform milk into an 'essential food', an imperial icon of health, and a medicine to counter racial degeneracy. A children's food, it was associated with health and purity. As consumerism joined science and democracy as part of the New World Order, milk became the food symbolic of nourishment by the mother and the state. But dairy products also acquired masculine qualities in their association with health, strength, and virility; milk had to manifest masculinity to become an empire-builder.

6.6 Milk for muscles. Drain layers milking the cow for morning tea, Christchurch, c. 1920s
Canterbury Historical Association Collection, Canterbury Museum, Christchurch, 2000.198.452

The Dairy Export Control Board, established in 1923, made six films to market dairy products in the 1920s, including *New Zealand: The Empire's Dairy Farm*. All six promoted Fernleaf as the national brand, akin to the soldiers who adopted the Fernleaf as a symbol in the First World War, and began with the words 'Healthy stock – sunbathed pasture – rippling streams – assure ideal production', projecting the vision of 'natural abundance' and a pristine environment. All ended with a 'picturesque' sunset scene of an ocean steamer disappearing over the horizon, carrying produce to Britain. Similarly, the Anchor brand adopted by the New Zealand Co-operative Dairy Company, the country's largest dairy cooperative, signified the connection with the Royal Navy and British shipping.

In effect the films showed how British grasses were exported to New Zealand and re-imported as empire dairy products, whose quality attested to New Zealand's prosperity, successful agricultural development – and Britishness. The film titled *The Dairy Cow as an Empire Builder* opened with a supposedly 'romantic' reference to the transformation of Māori from warrior to worker since the New Zealand Wars: 'Where Maori warriors fifty years ago held at bay English troops – to-day their descendants make a daily round gathering cream cans!' Explicitly, 'butter for Britain wrought the change' from 'former wilderness' to 'to-day's development' of 'prosperous farm homes ... and thriving country towns'. Civilisation of the wilderness and of Māori, then, issued from producing food for British tables.

The films were part of a campaign to educate the British public about New Zealand's dairy industry that, with other marketing pitches, contributed to the reshaping of the physical landscape as well as 'the economic and cultural landscape of New Zealand'. Shown at trade shows in London, Glasgow, and Liverpool, they were pitched at women, who were responsible for buying food and feeding families. With the end of the war commandeer in 1921 and the return to a free market, prices slumped. Dominion dairy farmers had to promote themselves to British consumers rather than rely on the British government. Exposed to the global marketplace, New Zealand sought a united empire with preferential trade within its borders and was disappointed by Britain's opposition to imperial preference. Instead, the Dairy Board turned to a domestic imperialism, because housewives held the 'housekeeping purse': a hope that British housewives would give preference to the 'pure quality foods produced in their own Empire overseas'.

ECONOMIC INSECURITY AND POLITICAL UNCERTAINTY

New Zealand and Australia were vulnerable to external shocks, New Zealand especially so with its more open economy. 'Maximising farm income was an elusive goal' in the 1920s, because British demand set limits on growth. The prosperity expected to continue after the war did not materialise. Policymakers therefore strove to manage income instability by establishing meat and dairy marketing boards, a common device between the wars, and through state finance for farmers. The Meat Producers' Board of 1922 was the first export monopoly board in the world. The Dairy Board sought to control exports, but the Meat Board did not.

While the dominion depended on trade with Britain, it was even more dependent on its ability to borrow for development. Power was concentrated in the hands of an elite who recognised the importance of the British connection and the need to satisfy London's criteria for sound financial management. Faced with this reality, New Zealand became increasingly frustrated that its banking system was tied closely to Australia's. London failed to distinguish between Australia and New Zealand; yet Australia was the biggest borrower in London, in pursuit of an ambitious program to build 'Australia Unlimited'. Saddled with its share of war debt, New Zealand found itself further beholden to London, because of loans, when its export market collapsed in 1929, though it escaped Australia's acute short-term debt crisis.

In such circumstances postwar hopes were dashed. A disillusioned electorate voted for a series of conservative minority governments in the 1920s, the Reform Party having lost its majority in 1922. Under the first-past-the-post voting system, Reform, in government from 1912 to 1928, did not once win half of the votes. The Labour Party gained traction only in the cities, deterring mainstream support until it abandoned its platform of socialisation, especially the nationalisation of land. As historian Michael King observed, few people 'from any background wanted to "smash" the capitalist system: most just hoped to make that system more responsive to their wants and needs'. When Bill Massey died (the new agricultural college in Palmerston North was named after him in 1926), J. G. Coates, a war hero, became prime minister. He too was a dairy farmer, from Kaipara, in Northland. But the election of the elderly Sir Joseph Ward as leader of a revived Liberal government, renamed United (in power from 1928 to 1931), suggested that the people had opted for nostalgia. Ostensibly they voted for Ward due to a mistaken promise: with failing eyesight and subject to diabetic blackouts, he famously misread his speech notes and promised to borrow £70 million instead of £7 million to cure the country's ills. Dream and reality could not have been further apart with the onset of worldwide depression.

MĀORI RECOVERY

Refuting doomsayers, from the early twentieth century Māori health and numbers recovered, despite the ravages of the 1918 influenza pandemic. As family members died from the flu, T. W. Rātana, a Māori farmer who practised Pākehā-style farming near Whanganui, had a vision of the Holy Ghost, which called him to unite and redeem Māori as God's chosen people. Rātana launched a religious revival as the founder of the Rātana Church and political movement, centred on the Bible and the Treaty of Waitangi. His faith healing and his message attracted a large following among the sick and the poor, especially ex-servicemen. Rātana's son had served in Gallipoli and France, where he was badly gassed. The men of the Pioneer Battalion, who fought for equality, lacked equal access to soldier settlement schemes that assisted men to purchase homes and farms, though they were not formally excluded. Yet Māori provided land for soldier settlers. Between 1910 and 1930 another 3.5 million acres (1.4 million hectares) passed out of Māori hands. Rātana held special appeal for ordinary people, increasingly detribalised and landless, who eked out a subsistence living or worked as casual labourers. With a growing population there was too little left for subsistence, despite the popular prejudice about 'idle' land.

The Rātana movement, committed to working with the government and within what followers saw as the straitjacket of traditional iwi leadership, presented a challenge to the tribal establishment. The Rātana Church, registered in 1925, rivalled both the Kīngitanga (King movement) and Anglican tribal leaders of mana (prestige) who had organised the Pioneer Battalion. Indeed, it spurred the Anglican Church to appoint its first Māori bishop of Aotearoa, Reverend Frederick Bennett of Te Arawa, in 1928. Rātana advocated a Māori national identity. He wanted the Treaty recognised in statute, so that it would become operative and 'preserve the ties of brotherhood between Pākehā and Māori for all time'.

In sport, George Nēpia modelled this ideal, dominating the rugby field with his personality and dazzling displays of kicking, tackling, and fielding the ball. As 'New Zealand rugby's first superstar' he attracted large crowds in New Zealand and Australia in the interwar years. In addition to his talent, Nēpia's success reinforced a deliberate policy by Te Aute College and by Sir Āpirana Ngata (knighted in 1927) to promote Māori prowess on the rugby field, to counter prejudice, and to promote equality. His popularity offered hope; he demonstrated how skill in playing what was already the national game opened new worlds for young Māori men.

Tribal leaders such as Te Puea Hērangi of the Kīngitanga were likewise determined for their people to occupy their rightful position. To this end, Ngata campaigned in parliament on diverse fronts. He helped establish the Native Trust Office in 1920 to oversee revenue from the lease of Māori reserves, with the long-term aim of persuading the government to agree to a land-development policy that would deliver equality to Māori. In the 1920s he oversaw a handful of consolidation schemes intended to turn remnants of tribal land into an economic base by creating blocks large enough for dairying. In the process he lifted dairy farming and the idea of New Zealand as Britain's farm into another cultural context. Ngata converted his own iwi, Ngāti Porou, from sheep to dairy farming on established family farms on communally owned land. He set up a training scheme to send young men, including his eldest son, to Hawkesbury Agricultural College, in New South Wales, to learn the latest methods. By 1926 Ngāti Porou owned a cooperative dairy factory.

Conversely, Ngāi Tūhoe, whose homeland of Te Urewera represented the North Island's last frontier, strongly resisted attempts by the Reform government to alienate their picturesque lands of forests and waterways in the 1920s as Richard Seddon had attempted 30 years earlier. The Urewera District Native Reserve Act 1896 had appeared exceptional at the time in promising internal self-government to Ngāi Tūhoe. In practice, the Act was passed in exchange for the iwi's agreement to survey Te Urewera and brought this 'bounded land' under the government's authority. Increasingly the Native Land Court reached into Ngāi Tūhoe territory in the early twentieth century, encouraged by Liberal members of parliament Ngata and Carroll, who used their legal knowledge to make Tūhoe conform. Ngata was particularly contemptuous of the prophet Rua Kēnana, whose imprisonment in 1916 'snuffed out' any group move among Tūhoe to control decisions to sell. Massey's Reform government recommenced land purchasing in the Te Urewera illegally in 1915 and spent £200 000 by 1921 without any land being made available for settlement.

Once the Reform government began alienating land in the Urewera, Ngata worked to consolidate holdings to assist Tūhoe in land development. But the plan to bring dairying to this remote district foundered, with low returns to farmers in the 1920s. Ngata's legacy is complicated, since the Tūhoe consolidation benefited the government more than Tūhoe by accelerating government encroachment into Urewera country. In 1922 the Urewera District Native Reserve was abolished, and five years later the government acquired more than two-thirds of the reserve for future tourism and forestry, thus setting aside the basis of the eventual Urewera National Park.

Politically, Ngata's successes owed much to his friendship with J. G. (Gordon) Coates, the minister of native affairs from 1921 and prime minister from 1925 to 1928. Coates had grown up among Māori. Together, Ngata and Coates oversaw the first attempts to settle grievances in the 1920s. The Te Arawa Lakes agreement of 1922 provided an annuity of £6000 a year in acknowledgement of the iwi's customary rights to the lakes in the thermal districts specified in law in 1881. The Te Arawa Māori Trust Board followed in 1924, to supervise the national cultural revival urged by Ngata by establishing a school of arts and crafts in Rotorua. Ngāti Tūwharetoa reached their agreement with Coates in 1926, when the Tūwharetoa Māori Trust Board was established with an annuity of £3000 from fishing licences (to fish for introduced trout) and campsite rentals at Lake Taupo. In exchange, Tūwharetoa ceded the bed of Lake Taupo for a public reserve. The Kīngitanga, too, began to be heard by the government.

Ever since the New Zealand Wars, tribes forced into poverty by confiscation had sought an inquiry, and the Sim Commission (named for its chairman, W. A. Sim) was established in 1926 to investigate whether the confiscation of three million acres (1.2 million hectares) of land in Taranaki, Waikato, and the Bay of Plenty under the New Zealand Settlements Act 1863 had exceeded 'what was fair and just'. The Sim Commission reported in 1927–8 that the confiscations in Taranaki were 'unjustified' and those in the Waikato were 'excessive', though it considered that tribes who fought in the Waikato War ought to have been punished. By contrast the commission found the Tauranga confiscation was 'justified and not excessive', except in the case of the Whakatōhea iwi, in the Bay of Plenty, where the confiscations were excessive 'but only to a small extent', assessments challenged by the four Māori members of parliament.

But it was as minister of native affairs, from December 1928, in the otherwise lacklustre United government, that Ngata achieved his dream of directing government policy away from alienating land from Māori for Pākehā farmers towards state advances for Māori to develop their own land. Legislation in 1929 authorised him as the minister to advance money to settle and utilise Māori land more effectively and to encourage iwi in the practice of agriculture and self-help. Māori could obtain mortgages for up to 60 per cent of the value of their land, even if Pākehā settlers could borrow up to 90 per cent, because they could provide greater security and it was easier for lenders to deal with single rather than multiple owners. The Act also empowered the minister to gazette land for development. Ngata used his powers to bring land under departmental control: to survey, drain, reclaim, and clear it; to grass, fertilise, and fence it; to construct buildings, buy equipment and livestock, and hand it over to Māori farmers. Through land-development schemes he strove with tribal leaders to create self-sufficient Māori communities. This created problems, since development schemes often rested on consolidation. Yet his quest could not have been more timely, as global depression arrived.

7

Making New Zealand 1930–1949

The 1930s and 1940s witnessed a formative era in nation-building, through the conscious 'making' of New Zealand. At the same time, New Zealanders had to 'make do' through depression and another world war, and these global onslaughts only intensified the quest for security at home and abroad. Making do and creating a nation moved in symbiosis, because, as often happens with the evolution of a sense of national identity, panic, crisis, anxiety, or rupture produces stories and rituals to soothe and explain. This context saw the rise to power of the first Labour government, which resolved to pick up where the 1890s' Liberal model of state development left off. In this era politicians reinvented a tradition of a progressive, decent society that protected ordinary people from the icy winds of international competition and conflict. A geological reminder of living on the edge, the magnitude 7.8 Napier earthquake, in February 1931, which killed 256 people, only added to the sense of fissure and fragility. New Zealand's worst environmental disaster of the twentieth century, the earthquake reinforced the urge to rebuild. An extra 2000 hectares of land uplifted by tectonic fault movement and the sea's drainage from wetlands fortuitously created room for that task.

DEPRESSION

Even before the Wall Street Crash in 1929, global depression and unemployment had cast a pall over the dominion. Already the dependent economy had been hit by the fall in export prices. In the two years from 1928–9 to 1930–1, export income nearly halved. Export values returned to pre-depression levels only from 1936. To maintain funds in London, New Zealand had to adopt a deflationary policy of balanced budgets. A United government led by George Forbes, a North Canterbury farmer, made the economies necessary to meet local interests' insistence on cost-cutting. Reduced debt repayments were unthinkable, because that would have impaired the ability to borrow. The government therefore slashed expenditure. The cuts were particularly severe in education, which consumed nearly half of annual public spending, and in health.

Conservatives sought solidarity to stem the crisis in a United–Reform coalition government from September 1931, which proceeded to pension off the core idea of the 'workingman's paradise'. In 1931 the Arbitration Court reduced award wage rates by 10 per cent; public service wages were also trimmed by 10 per cent, and by a further 10 per cent in 1932. Modest family allowances (introduced in 1926) and widows' and old age pensions were cut. Though offset by falling prices, the reduced pensions provoked anger at the government's seeming indifference to the needs of ordinary people. The principle of 'no pay without work' led to massive public works schemes; simultaneously, the government slashed expenditure, laid off staff, and re-employed them at relief rates. Arbitration in industrial disputes and union membership ceased to be compulsory in 1932, giving more power to employers. Social histories interested in ordinary people and left-wing histories view the coalition government with disdain, reflecting the bitterness of the depression era.

The Depression bit deeply into community life, punishing people in debt and those at the bottom or on the margins of society who lacked a male breadwinner. A strong work ethic offered no escape from worry and frustration. Estimates of the unemployment rate range from 12 to 15 per cent (40 per cent among Māori), yet economic research suggests that nearly 30 per cent of the workforce were not formally employed by 1933. Up to 40 per cent of the male workforce were unemployed in the worst of the crisis. Mass unemployment overwhelmed charities and charitable aid boards, etching images of the soup kitchen in popular memory. The impact of widespread insecurity varied by region; one study saw Canterbury as the most severely deprived.

Depression literature focused on the suffering of the 'worker', the unemployed man subjected to the ignominy of relief work, underpaid and compelled to move to rural relief camps. Distress in the cities erupted in street riots in 1932, precipitated by relief schemes that rotated the unemployed for a few days at a time for pitiful pay. Unemployed men toiled with picks and shovels in harsh conditions to build roads through the Lewis Pass and to Milford Sound, in the South Island, creating the infrastructure for future tourism, while in the North Island workers constructed the East Coast Railway. Such extremity politicised significant sections of the community; an intelligentsia fired by social injustice and inequality spawned a national literature and art that illustrated the international genre of social realism. John Mulgan, who served as a special constable in the 1932 riots, portrayed in his novel *Man Alone* (1939) the acute distress in relief camps felt by the individualistic, strong-willed, egalitarian, hard-drinking, laconic male, who represented the equivalent of the Australian 'lone hand'. Family folklore recalled the humiliation suffered by that other masculine type, the family man, demoralised by the indignity of his inability to provide.

By the 1980s economists began to question the Depression's effects on people and whether life was as tough as claimed. Inevitably a myth of 'the Depression' evolved, because generations tend to collectivise their experiences through storytelling. There was no unified experience of depression, only a unified story that smoothed the rough edges of a national memory of hardship. The Depression was a class experience, which left a gulf between the unemployed and the employed, between workers – especially casual labourers – and the privileged. Among the better off who enjoyed relative prosperity with the rise of consumerism, the slump brought insecurity and disappointment through defaults on mortgages, bad investments, and reduced educational prospects. The effects of the 1920s housing boom and depression showed in declining home ownership and rising levels of renting; in Christchurch, for example, while 32 per cent of houses were rented in 1926, the figure was 46 per cent by 1936. The proportions of unskilled and semiskilled rose, and the gap between richest and poorest widened.

In many ways women bore the brunt of hardship, of which much evidence is hidden. One telling indicator comes from 109 married women who died from (illegal) septic abortions between 1931 and 1935. Their husbands were labourers, drivers, farmers, or farmhands, in shop work and trades vulnerable to downturn. Official unemployment statistics excluded women, youths, and Māori employed on Department of Native Affairs work schemes. Women and youths were not entitled to relief payments, although as wage earners they paid unemployment tax from 1931, with the significant exception of the large group in private domestic service. The novelist Ruth Park observed astutely, 'Women were not supposed to be breadwinners, therefore they were not'.

Out of the gloom, however, emerged promise of change. During the worst of the slump, voters in the working-class electorate of Lyttelton elected New Zealand's first woman member of parliament, Elizabeth McCombs, after the death of her husband, the local Labour member until then. A former suffragist, she resisted the injustice of 'unfair taxation' of low-paid women and youths and led that campaign into parliament (see figure 7.1).

7.1 May Day demonstration led by a small band of women, Christchurch, 1932
Press photograph, Hocken Collections Uare Taoka o Hākena, University of Otago, Dunedin, P1998-028/02-002

In 1933, too, New Zealand began to assert a separate financial identity. At the Imperial Economic Conference at Ottawa in 1932 J. G. Coates and other dominion representatives negotiated a system of imperial preferences – the Ottawa Agreements, a series of bilateral trade agreements between the United Kingdom and the White Dominions – that ensured access to the British market. To help farmers, the government devalued the currency in 1933, against Treasury advice. Encouraged by British experts, it also established a Reserve Bank.

Recent assessment of Coates depicts him as a statesman faced with an impossible task of managing the global downturn at a time when New Zealand had no independent monetary policy and when borrowing was subject to the willingness of Australasian private banks answerable to the Bank of England. Indeed, Coates has been credited with creating a platform for the growth that materialised under the first Labour government. The key to recovery lay with the Reserve Bank, established in 1934, to take control of credit away from the six trading banks, only one of which had its headquarters in New Zealand. Most bank headquarters were in Melbourne. The new monetary regime successfully distinguished New Zealand reserves from those of Australia, and New Zealand from the Australian banking system, establishing the desired financial separateness.

Happily, this intervention ensured that the country's recovery from depression was unusually fast; it raised real gross domestic product per capita by a third by 1938. Often the best policy outcomes are unintended, and ironically such success was unforeseen. The policy's success remained unrecognised until the Labour Party entered office. In a fortunate sequence of events, the credit squeeze imposed in the period of balanced budgets created an unplanned boost to the money supply that, with devaluation, increased reserves held by the Reserve Bank, allowed lavish expenditure by the reformist first Labour government, and lifted national income.

SECURITY AND RECOVERY

In most interpretations, the first Labour government pulled New Zealand out of the doldrums after Labour won the November 1935 election by a landslide, with 47 per cent of the vote and 53 out of 80 seats in parliament. But it is now clear from research into the economic reality, as opposed to political rhetoric, that the new monetary regime already in place by 1935 provided the mechanism for rapid recovery. With confidence and spirits buoyed, the climate of opinion changed. Social priorities were transformed as Labour made manifest Christian and humanist versions of dignity and equality. Immediately, the unemployed received a Christmas bonus. The kindly prime minister Michael Joseph Savage became a legend in his lifetime; already 63 on his election, he died in 1940, his framed photograph hung in remembrance in thousands of living rooms. Savage personified the social security scheme created by the first Labour government in 1938 to raise living standards and provide security and dignity, Labour promised, 'from the cradle to the grave'. This famous promise by the first Labour government – the objective of the 1938 Social Security Act – has entered the New Zealand lexicon. His chief adviser, who admired him, remarked, 'Savage was the most Christ-like figure I have ever known, and an absolute ninny'.

From Ned Kelly country in Victoria and New South Wales, an Irish Catholic with a similar background to the outlaw, Savage identified with the poor, and they loved him. But he joked that he 'did not inherit [Kelly's] methods'. The Labour Party's election manifesto in 1935 proclaimed the objective to use the 'wonderful resources of the Dominion' to restore 'a decent living standard to those who have been deprived of essentials for the past five years'. It promised to restructure the economy to secure not a minimum but a universally comfortable standard of living for the male breadwinner and his dependants, 'with everything necessary to make a "home" and "home life" in the best sense of the meaning of those terms'. In other words, Labour resolved to restore the model of state development established during the 1890s. Only this time it partially included Māori.

For dairy farmers, the contract was rewritten as the right to full employment and a fair and reasonable wage in the form of guaranteed prices for primary products. Sheep farmers at the time opted to stay with the free market. The Dairy Board had already decided to assume control of marketing, but the government took over the export of all butter and cheese in 1936 in return for security for farmers in the form of a guaranteed price, based on production costs. It also provided state advances to help indebted farmers remain on the land. For workers, Labour restored the system of compulsory arbitration and unionism, and reversed depression cuts to award wages, salaries, and pensions. The Industrial Conciliation and Arbitration Amendment Act 1936 empowered the Arbitration Court to set the basic breadwinner wage at a level 'sufficient to maintain an average family, a man and his wife and three children', while continuing to assume that the working woman was single, with no children or elderly parents to support.

Nutrition surveys suggested that the young child suffered in the Depression. The League of Nations urged member countries to institute nutrition inquiries and to promote the new standard of optimum child health and development, for which it prescribed milk consumption of 1.5–2.0 pints (0.8–1.1 litres) daily from the age of two. New Zealand responded with a national school-milk scheme in 1937, followed by dietary surveys of basic wage earners in 1939 and of Māori in the 1940s. School milk had political appeal, because it was intended to benefit both the dairy farmer and the child as future citizen. From 1937 the state supplied a half-pint of pasteurised bottled milk, free, to every child at primary school and kindergarten as far as practicable. For 30 years the half-pint bottle of milk a day signified, with the Plunket Society, that New Zealand was a healthy place to bring up children.

For the urban worker as for the dairy farmer, Labour believed that increasing the purchasing power of the ordinary New Zealander would boost the economy, and it did. The state took over the Reserve Bank to control credit and to finance its program of recovery and security. This government of former Red Feds, once feared as socialists, determined to constrain the powers of bankers, and again it sought to build a civilised community in which ordinary people shared the benefits of science and education. In effect, Labour introduced a variant of 'protection all round': a controlled economy to manage the core problem of economic instability and to safeguard the ideal society, this time in the form of a universal welfare state.

From 1938, then, New Zealand refashioned its version of the Australasian settlement, in which the family wage recovered its pivotal status in a 'workers' welfare state'. The strategy, however, did not comprise 'wage security for the worker rather than social security for the citizen'. Instead it provided worker security supplemented by non-contributory social security, the latter determined by citizenship rather than by ability to pay. New Zealand made social security a right, paid for from tax, Walter Nash, the minister of social security, explained, to give the people the standard of living 'we think they ought to have'.

In the belief that the state could insulate New Zealand from overseas influences, Labour introduced import and exchange controls late in 1938, which the British government and Bank of England opposed. The aim was to manage an exchange rate crisis brought on by the flight of British capital and spiralling demand for imports as the economy recovered. Import licensing also had the intended effect of protection of industry. New Zealand lagged behind Australia in protectionist rhetoric, finally adopting protection of industry in 1938 to ensure worker security. The country grew more tied economically to Britain, which insisted on free trade and discouraged manufacturing in its dominions until the Depression forced a move to imperial preference in an interwar world of tariff barriers. When New Zealand did adopt protection, the logical consequence of the revival of worker protection in 1938, the country met strong British disapproval at the prospect of aspiring to be anything other than the empire's farm. The Australasian model of state development survived, because Britain soon needed all the food that New Zealand could produce to sustain its people through another world war.

The Social Security Act 1938 restored New Zealand's status as a social laboratory. An improved age pension (renamed 'benefit') and an attempt to introduce universal superannuation at age 65 confirmed that removing insecurity beyond working age remained a priority. The Act introduced an unemployment benefit for men and for single women for the first time, to counter workers' loss of paid employment. The entire framework supplemented the family wage. It accepted that single women were moving into paid employment between school and marriage but confirmed married women and children as dependants. To ensure equal medical treatment the Act legislated for a universally free general practitioner service, free hospitals, and free maternity care, paid for by the taxpayer. The second and third eventuated, but not the first, in 1939. Free medical care for childbirth was a notable achievement, secured only because the aims of most doctors, politicians, and women overlapped. The government was obliged to listen to doctors, whom it needed to meet the ultimate objective of a free health service. Labour politicians genuinely believed that care by a doctor, traditionally available only to the wealthy, was the right of all women, and women's groups advised that 'painless maternity is every woman's right'. The Committee of Inquiry into Maternity Services of 1937–8, which included Janet Fraser, the wife of Peter Fraser, the minister of health, recommended that birthing mothers have access to the 'fullest degree of pain-relief consistent with safety to mother and child'. Under Labour, the belief in egalitarianism reinforced the trend to birth managed by a doctor in hospital. Such humanitarianism was also pronatalist, since politicians hoped that financial support, 'modern' pain relief, and a fortnight's rest in hospital, advocated by women's organisations, would encourage women to have more children.

A free general practitioner service, however, fell foul of medical protests (see figure 7.2). Labour's health scheme had its origins in Kurow, a village in Otago, where, during the Depression, the local medical practitioner Dr David McMillan (Labour's first minister of health) and his friend Arnold Nordmeyer, the local Presbyterian minister (also a member of the first Labour government), established a form of contract practice with the unions representing the men building the Waitaki hydroelectric power station on the Waitaki River. McMillan and Nordmeyer wanted a universal health system in which the state acted as paymaster for all doctors. Because of a battle with the British Medical Association's local branch, however, the scheme finally introduced in 1941 acceded to the professional demand of a fee for service; and doctors' visits were henceforth not universally accessible in practice, nor universally free. The doctors' top-up fee reduced the scheme to a mere state subsidy for medical care.

Labour also made the suburban dream accessible to urbanites who fitted the model of the nuclear family. It endorsed the ideal of home ownership, eroded by the Depression, but since low-wage

7.2 G. E. G. Minhinnick, *The medicine man*, 1938. Prime Minister Michael Joseph Savage has had to resort to distributing medicines himself.
New Zealand Herald, 18 August 1938. Alexander Turnbull Library, Wellington, H-723-005. Courtesy of Dion Minhinnick and *New Zealand Herald*

families could not afford to own a home, a refurbished entrepreneurial state built houses for rental from 1937. State houses, compact, well built, comfortable, and financed by Reserve Bank credit, mushroomed in the four main cities. An enterprising builder, James Fletcher, constructed the first houses on contract, establishing his company's reputation for delivery. While better-off workers continued to obtain access to state finance for home ownership, the scheme brought the ideal of a new small house on its own block within reach of ordinary people. Typically, families who did not fit the model missed out.

The scheme was not intended for Māori, who remained geographically separate, second-class citizens. Land-development schemes provided tribes with some new, inferior houses in rural areas. But even among iwi (tribes) who had not lost so much land and resources, the majority lived in rural poverty. Chiefly families might live in bungalows on farms or in towns, but housing on marae (meeting places including buildings) had dirt floors and unsafe water supplies.

Labour promised Māori equality based on need under its political alliance with the Rātana movement. It held two of the Māori seats in parliament and strove to win all four in alliance with Rātana, which it did by 1943, when Sir Āpirana Ngata finally lost office. Māori in theory were equal citizens, but in practice they received social security benefits paid at approximately 25 per cent less than Pākehā (European New Zealander) rates, and that inequality persisted from the introduction of an old age pension in 1898 until 1945. Bureaucrats reasoned that hapū (subtribes) could live off the land, though many were landless and had lost access to traditional food resources. Nonetheless, Māori wellbeing improved dramatically under Labour. As minister of native affairs following on from Coates and Ngata, and as prime minister, Savage expanded land-development schemes. Public health standards improved, and the Department of Health extended health services and stepped up inquiries as to why Māori suffered higher death rates.

Social security went hand in hand with national security. New Zealand increased defence spending by 2.3 times between 1935 and 1938, when overall government expenditure expanded by 1.6 times. It established a tiny air force and recruited volunteers for home defence, which in strategic thinking included forward defence in the Pacific Islands. Internationally, the Labour government advanced the principle of collective security through the League of Nations. New Zealand alone among the dominions criticised Britain for assuaging aggressors. It opposed Britain over Abyssinia (Ethiopia), the Spanish Civil War, and the Japanese invasion of China. Above all it opposed Neville Chamberlain's appeasement of Adolf Hitler. Yet it advocated a negotiated peace after Nazi Germany's conquest of Poland, prompting a new argument that Labour pursued more of an 'independent foreign policy' than a 'moral' one.

There is vigorous debate about the degree of independence from British policy in New Zealand's stance. Was it moral or merely realistic? The government did show independence of interest, and 'loyal opposition' to Britain. Its security problem entailed not just home defence but the protection of trade routes, so reliance on isolation and remoteness did not suffice. By 1938 New Zealand knew that its security depended on Britain's security in Europe. In retrospect, Savage was vindicated in his concern for the security of the Pacific and whether a British fleet could defend Australia and New Zealand in the event of war in Europe. He was also right that because the country was small and isolated, national interests belonged with Britain and its empire.

WAR IN EUROPE

When Britain declared war on Germany on 3 September 1939 the Cabinet committed New Zealand late on the same day (in the middle of the night), only this time independently. From his sickbed on 5 September, the dying Savage, 'for whom war was such a disappointment', broadcast the famous sentiment 'Both with gratitude for the past, and with confidence in the future, we range ourselves without fear beside Britain. Where she goes, we go; where she stands, we stand. We are only a small and young nation, but we march ... to a common destiny'. Truly he spoke for the country. This was a more measured response than that of the dominion in the First World War, and from this stance of traditional support for Britain both loyal and reluctant could gain comfort. Savage died in March 1940, replaced as wartime prime minister by Peter Fraser, an astute politician and a superb strategist.

Some historians highlight Labour's contrasting views of the world wars. The contrast is represented by Fraser himself and by three other ministers who had been imprisoned for opposing conscription during the First World War yet who were in the Cabinet that introduced conscription in June 1940, copying the British regulations. The dissenters had become the establishment. In fact, their thinking followed the Australian more than the New Zealand pattern: the First World War, an imperial conflict, imposed a vast inequality of sacrifice on workers, as cannon fodder. The Second World War entailed war in a just cause, between reason and Nazi brutality. In this way of thinking, only victory could ensure peace and a democratic new order.

New Zealand made a full commitment to the war effort under Labour, which remained in power from the end of 1935 until 1949. Overall, 205 000 served, about one in eight of the population, including more than 10 000 women. The dominion mobilised over 65 per cent of all men aged 18 to 45 to provide one division (the 2nd) for Europe and subsequently a reduced 3rd Division for the Pacific, as well as sailors and aircrew. The Royal New Zealand Air Force played an important role in training pilots as part of the Empire Air Training Scheme; in the Pacific, too, 'air came first'. Not as many died as in the First World War, and this conflict left less of a mark upon the national psyche. This time, 11 671 New Zealanders were killed, the biggest losses being among airmen, particularly in Europe. Soldiers also served in frontline combat units in Greece, the deserts of North Africa, and Italy. The whole country served again as a farm, providing food first for Britain and second for United States marines during the war in the Pacific.

Events fast overtook imperial strategy. In 1940 Hitler's blitzkrieg swept through the Low Countries, leaving Britain alone and under attack from an enemy-occupied Europe. In this context New Zealand introduced conscription, with France overrun and Italy's entry into the war. From June 1940 the fall of France to the German offensive obliged the Second Echelon of the 2nd New Zealand Expeditionary Force to be diverted for training in England, where its troops joined the forces preparing for a German invasion. New Zealanders also fought in the Royal Air Force's Fighter Command and Bomber Command; the best known, Sir Keith Park, led the air defence of London and southeast England in the Battle of Britain.

The First Echelon of army volunteers, on the other hand, went to North Africa, as did the Third Echelon, which arrived just as an Italian force invaded neutral Egypt. The British (Prime Minister Winston Churchill's) decision to send one division each of Australians and New Zealanders to Greece in April 1941 proved disastrous. Hastily evacuated, the Anzacs suffered a serious but narrow defeat in the battle for Crete. Meanwhile Hitler repeated Napoleon's mistake of opening a second front against Russia when his armies invaded the Soviet Union in June 1941.

For New Zealand and Australia the turn of events from June 1940 in Europe bode ill for their own security in the South Pacific.

Japan and China had been at war for years. New Zealand despatched men to Europe and the Mediterranean theatre on the explicit understanding that if Japan were to strike southwards, the mighty British naval base in Singapore, which the country had helped to pay for, would serve as a bulwark. In Asia and the Pacific the entire imperial defence strategy depended on the assumption that the British fleet would defend Singapore if Japan attacked.

In June 1940, therefore, it shocked the Australian and New Zealand governments to learn that Britain could not promise a naval fleet for Singapore: they would have to rely on the United States. Diplomatic historians have described this as a 'momentous admission' of 'almost apocalyptic character'. Fraser's reply seethed with understatement: this advice was a 'departure' from 'repeated and most explicit assurances' about sending the fleet to Singapore which 'formed the basis of the whole of this Dominion's defence preparations'. He asked to send a New Zealand minister to Washington, and his deputy, Walter Nash, arrived in January 1942, in effect as the dominion's first ambassador. By then Japan's offensive against the United States had transformed the war in Europe and the Mediterranean into a truly global conflict. Two issues, long foreshadowed, loomed from 1942: a turn to the United States as protector and the question of whether New Zealand should bring home the 2nd Division to fight in the Pacific war.

WAR IN THE PACIFIC

The Japanese assault on Pearl Harbor, Hawaii, on 7 December 1941, launched simultaneous stunning offensives. Japanese forces drove Americans from most of the Philippines by Christmas and swept southwards to the north coast of New Guinea, in the Dutch East Indies, and Solomon Islands. In a little over two months the Japanese invaded Southeast Asia from Burma (Myanmar) to the Philippines, and to New Guinea, so that Japan controlled not only the Pacific north of the Equator but south from Guam to Rabaul and Bougainville, in the watery world of Australasia.

So much for the imperial strategy centred on the Singapore naval base, assumed to be impregnable: when the Japanese attacked Pearl Harbor, British ships were far from Singapore. Nor could the island withstand the assault from the northwest, since its guns faced the wrong way. The fall of Singapore, in February 1942, led Australia and New Zealand in separate directions. The 8th Australian Division, based in Singapore, was destroyed, almost all its men captured as prisoners of war. Australia suddenly stood on the front line, with bombing raids on Broome and Darwin and the discovery of Japanese midget submarines in Sydney Harbour.

From this point there was no Anzac rerun. Australia recalled its 6th and 7th Divisions from North Africa to meet the Japanese threat and concentrated its war effort in the Pacific, while New Zealand's 2nd Division remained in the Mediterranean. Thus the Australian war narrative centred on prisoners of war and fighting the Japanese in the islands; New Zealand's (although not exclusively) on fighting Hitler and Benito Mussolini. This Anzac divergence had three impacts on national war stories. First, it explained why the Kiwi soldier in the Second World War adopted the image of the 'hard man' and the 'hard case', as opposed to the gentleman, since the Australians no longer served as a reference point. New Zealanders could therefore embrace some stereotypically Australian characteristics. Second, historians have debated the extent to which Allied grand strategy, to defeat Hitler first, best met New Zealand interests. And third, there was deliberation over whether the decision to stay in Europe reflected a colonial or 'recolonial' relationship.

New Zealand's smallness is a factor in understanding these issues. Its larger neighbour split its forces; the 9th Australian Division stayed in the Mediterranean until the victory at El Alamein, while the 6th and 7th returned. New Zealand only had one full division, which precluded a similar strategy. As far as possible, the country split what forces it could marshal. New Zealanders who had taken up forward positions in Pacific islands such as Fiji eventually formed two brigades of a forgotten 3rd Division in the Pacific. Moreover, the threat of invasion passed with the Battle of Midway, in June 1942. New Zealand agreed to keep the 2nd Division in Europe from 1942 on the understanding that United States marines would defend New Zealand if necessary, and the first shipment of Americans arrived in June. Long-serving men also returned home on furlough. Given their different geopolitics, both Australia and

New Zealand made realistic assessments of their respective places on the global chessboard of Anglo-American grand strategy.

War in the Pacific rearranged New Zealand's outlook. Now that the United States was responsible for repelling the Japanese, it was essential for New Zealand to have a voice with the Allied decision-makers. Events soon proved that a Pacific war under United States command with Australia in support best met the community's interests. From 1942 an accord developed, if an uneven one, between great and small white settler societies on opposite sides of the Pacific. Such agreement had been mooted during the Asian scare, over 30 years before, when the American Grand Fleet sailed forth in 1908 to show that the United States planned to keep this vast region safe for white people. Given New Zealand's size and remoteness, it suited it to serve as a minor player, as a rear base for the United States' assault on Japanese forces in Solomon Islands and Papua New Guinea. Churchill's views singly were not persuasive. President Franklin D. Roosevelt's views understandably weighed heavily with the War Cabinet, because the strategy of imperial defence had failed. From 1942 New Zealand and Australia stood or fell with the United States, Britain's most important ally. The United States divided Australasia into separate military zones on the Pacific Rim (itself an American concept). It placed Australia and its forces in a South West Pacific area under the command of General Douglas MacArthur, of the United States army, and New Zealand and its forces in the South Pacific under the command of Vice-Admiral Robert L. Ghormley of the United States navy.

A novel consensus of farmers, business, and the labour movement established that New Zealand could best serve the Allied cause by continuing its major effort in Europe alongside the British, and by leaving to the Americans the Pacific, where New Zealand could help to feed United States forces. It made no sense to bring home an effective force from Egypt, where the troops were needed to fight General Field Marshal Erwin Rommel, and there were no ships to transport them. For the men of the 2nd Division, it was not a case of wanting to fight for Britain but of not wanting to fight in the tropics, combined with the obsession to keep out Asia. The war front was not in New Zealand but in the islands of the Pacific – Australia's 'near north' – which served as a buffer. The Japanese

Making New Zealand 1930–1949   181

sweep into Australasian waters only confirmed such thinking. Anti-Japanese as well as pro-British sentiment, geography, and strategy prompted New Zealand to step up her war effort from 1942, to satisfy the great-power demands of Britain and the United States that on balance decided the form of national security.

WAR FRONT – HOME FRONT

At home, world war overshadowed the country's centennial, in 1940, which celebrated not so much the Treaty of Waitangi but 'pioneers', 'progress', and the history of settlement. The first public remembrance of the Treaty occurred in 1934, after Governor-General Charles Bathurst, Viscount Bledisloe, and his wife, Alina, bought and gifted to the nation British Resident James Busby's house and substantial farm at Waitangi. Māori leaders responded to the gift by arranging a landmark hui (meeting) of all tribes at Waitangi on 6 February. While the Department of Tourist and Publicity hailed the 1934 celebrations, it dated the 'real settlement' of New Zealand from the 'formation of the New Zealand Company ... and the arrival of the pioneers in 1840'. Nationally this interpretation giving precedence to the Wakefieldian narrative continued to dominate. Wellington's *Evening Post* published its centennial issue in November 1939 to advertise the opening of the *New Zealand Centennial Exhibition* and likewise gave priority in its coverage to the settlement of Wellington by the New Zealand Company.

The exhibition cited the dates in its title as '1939–1940', in remembrance of the 'pioneers'. Only at Āpirana Ngata's insistence were carvings created at the Rotorua School of Arts put on display; Māori in general were sidelined. Remembrance of the Treaty at the centennial owed greatly to Ngata's leadership. At a re-enactment of the Treaty signing at Waitangi on 6 February 1940, Ngata led the haka (posture dance, accompanied by a song). For their part, Ngāpuhi had carved a massive waka taua (war canoe) from three kauri (*Agathis australis*, forest trees). Afterwards the governor-general opened the ceremonial carved meeting house built especially for the centennial. Reviewing the previous 100 years, Ngata noted that the Treaty was a 'gentlemen's agreement', which had not been observed too poorly in comparison to the record of

European colonisation elsewhere. But he warned presciently that, with lands gone, chiefly powers crumbled, and with culture broken, land claims had to be settled for Māori to move forwards side by side with Europeans. He made clear that Māori wanted to 'retain [their] individuality as a race'.

Ngata placed his hopes for equality with the 28 (Māori) Battalion (see figure 7.3), organised on a tribal basis, who were all volunteers. Ngāpuhi from North Auckland served mainly in A Company; Te Arawa from the thermal district in B Company; principally Ngāti Porou from Gisborne in C Company; and the rest in D Company. Headquarters Company became the 'Odds and Sods'. This time even Waikato supported the war effort, because of Te Puea's friendship with Peter Fraser, who promised recompense for nineteenth-century land confiscation. Within boundaries set by the

7.3 'Got his man'. All soldiers were souvenir collectors. Here, men from 28 (Māori) Battalion perform for their Australian photographer, George Silk, in Alexandria, 1 June 1941. Māori 'frightened blazes outa the Hun with their bayonet charges ... This one "got his man" and also a decent souvenir, a German iron cross'. Australian War Memorial, Canberra, 007783

settler society, 28 (Māori) Battalion nudged their people closer to equality through their wartime prowess. They fought in Greece, the desert campaigns, and Italy and returned national heroes. Yet they were not allowed their own officers until late in the war.

At home the drive for full citizenship and Māori leadership of Māori affairs created the Māori War Effort Organisation in 1942, arranged into tribal committees that coordinated recruitment, food production, and labour across the country. In some districts freezing works and dairy factories could not have operated without the assistance of the committees. Once the officers of the Māori Battalion returned, their experience and hopes joined with the successes of the Māori War Effort Organisation to imagine how it could evolve into a peacetime structure for postwar reconstruction under tribal leadership. But Māori autonomy that operated so effectively during the war proved to be only for the duration.

For women, too, the war offered new opportunities and adventure, but it did little to change the gender script that decreed a woman's place was in the home. Women volunteered for patriotic duties, as in 1914, knitting, packing parcels for servicemen, in first aid, and as drivers. More than 75 000 enrolled in the Women's War Service Auxiliary, organised by Dr Agnes Bennett and Janet Fraser, to coordinate and direct women in war work. A major task entailed food production: volunteers tended rows of vegetables in home gardens, dug-up lawns, parks, and around schools; 2700 worked on farms as land girls, making women's agricultural work visible. The Pacific war finally saw authorities agree to women's service in uniform. Women's auxiliaries to the armed forces numbered over 10 000 from 1942.

The war also demanded a short-term increase in the number of women in the workforce. Indeed, after the fall of Singapore, women were conscripted to meet the labour shortage. In the food and clothing industries, hospitals, the public service, banks, post and telegraph, the railways and trams, women without young children stepped in for the duration of the war. They worked as clerical assistants and as tram girls, who daringly wore trousers. But trousers did not signal a breakdown of the segmented labour market: women's appearance in the paid workforce was temporary and subordinate.

Trousers were a wartime austerity measure in place of stockings; so were socks for schoolgirls. The depression ethos of 'making do' reached new heights with the fashion for remade, recycled clothing, and eggless cake recipes. Wartime rationing renewed the emphasis on thrift. New Zealand rationed petrol from 1939 until 1950, except for two short breaks. Paper, corrugated iron, liquor, prams, lawnmowers, china, silk stockings, canned foods, and knitting wool disappeared, encouraging ingenuity with the sewing machine, in the kitchen, and with self-provisioning, while the shortages vested more meaning in home preserves. The Japanese attack on Pearl Harbor led to panic buying of sugar and tea, which, with butter, were rationed from 1942 as necessities; and Dr Muriel Bell, the first nutritionist in the Department of Health, advised mothers how to make rosehip syrup to feed families their vitamin C. While meat and canned vegetables were rationed to feed the United States forces in the Pacific, butter was destined for Britain and remained restricted until 1950.

American marines transformed food habits. Their presence in large numbers from 1943 generated a new market for milk, especially milkshakes, Coca-Cola, steak, hamburgers, and vegetables. The threefold impact of the demands of United States troops, the British market, and the school-milk scheme generated a milk inquiry in 1943–4, which exposed that the little milk drunk locally was not subjected to the same checks as exported dairy products and was likely to be bad. In Christchurch, unlike Auckland, most milk was unpasteurised.

The Americans also set feminine hearts aflutter, with their smart uniforms that suggested Hollywood romance. Marines had access to luxury goods, notably tobacco, silk stockings, and chocolates. They proffered gifts, including flowers, and enjoyed women's company and conversation. They were also there when the most marriageable men were absent. From the viewpoint of Kiwi and male rivals, wherever they were stationed, the Yanks were 'over-paid, over-sexed and over here' – usurpers and a threat to local manhood. Among young women, however, the American presence encouraged a shift in ideals of femininity, from grace and refinement to sex appeal and sexual allure, as portrayed in Hollywood movies. An American boyfriend posed opportunities as well as risks in a moment of glamour and adventure.

VISIONS OF POSTWAR RECONSTRUCTION

Foreign relations were obviously tested by the American presence. The Japanese settled the question that New Zealand was 'geographically part of the Pacific', the historian F. L. W. Wood concluded in 1944. The Japanese threat spurred diplomatic representation in Washington, then Ottawa, and the establishment of the Department of External Affairs. It also provided the catalyst for frequent direct contact between Canberra and Wellington to supplement the long-standing system in both of direct ties with London, completing a Britain–Australia–New Zealand triangle. Australia and New Zealand opened high commissions in Wellington and Canberra respectively in 1943, whereas previously New Zealand had only tourist bureaus in Australia. Air travel also made it easier for policymakers to cross the Tasman, increasing government-to-government contact.

An Australia–New Zealand Agreement (Canberra Pact) followed in January 1944. Drafted by the Australians, the agreement asserted the neighbours' long-held belief in their right to participate in all decisions about the South West and South Pacific. Despite some sensitivity about the future of American bases and landing rights – for burgeoning air travel – in the islands, Australia and New Zealand realised that the future security of their region depended on cooperation with the United States. Most importantly, the agreement foreshadowed closer trans-Tasman ties in the postwar world. Australia and New Zealand agreed to cooperate not merely in external policy, but in the 'development of commerce'. Further, they planned to cooperate 'in achieving full employment in Australia and New Zealand and the highest standards of social security both within their borders and throughout the islands of the Pacific', and in encouraging missionary work in the Pacific Islands and territories.

Fraser was deeply affected by his visit to Samoa late in 1944 to investigate the question of trusteeship for League of Nations mandated territories. Expecting to see progress under New Zealand's mandate, he was shocked by the degree of colonialism, especially in education and health, and the neglect of development. With Australia's foreign minister H. V. Evatt, he sought a new commitment to the South Pacific. To this end the South Pacific Commission, foreshadowed by the Canberra Pact, was established in 1947. Samoa changed status to a New Zealand Trust Territory from the end of 1946, and New Zealand adopted a plan for Samoa to prepare for self-government.

Fraser played a leading role at the San Francisco Conference that devised a charter for the United Nations, in 1945. Australia and New Zealand agreed beforehand, first, that the 'territorial integrity and political independence' of members should be preserved against the threat of force and, second, on the principle of trusteeship. New Zealand's commitment to the multilateral model embodied in the United Nations in one sense represented a continuity of the Commonwealth tradition, which allowed a voice for the small and otherwise powerless. In another, it refashioned Labour's principle of collective security. Effectively New Zealand exercised its Dominion status to argue for a democratic structure to safeguard a new order in a postwar world. Having to live with great-power dominance was a fact of New Zealand life. Ever mindful of the conduct of great- and small-power relations, all New Zealand's representatives could do was to influence the drafting of the United Nations charter to reflect humanitarian aspirations that might make global-power politics operate more peacefully.

The war also added democratic principles to the goal of equal opportunity at home. From the Second World War, the Labour government's belief in education as a right rather than a privilege subsumed the 'new', progressive education intended to foster full development of the individual, with its focus on all-round child development from preschool age. In 1939 Dr C. E. Beeby, a psychologist, had laid down the postwar blueprint when he summarised his own idea of education for Peter Fraser, then minister of education, in language that he rightly judged expressed Fraser's objectives. The following statement by Fraser, in its call for equality of opportunity, formed the lodestone of education policy for a generation:

> The Government's objective, broadly expressed, is that every person, whatever his level of academic ability, whether he be rich or poor, whether he live in town or country, has a right, as a citizen, to a free education of the kind for which he is best fitted and to the fullest extent of his powers.

This included the improvement of race relations by educating young Pākehā teachers about Māori culture. At Wellington Teachers' College in 1938-9 the principal, Frank Lopdell, appointed Ngāti Raukawa teacher Kingi Tāhiwi, a skilled interpreter, to teach Māori to interested students, with the goal of increasing tolerance between Māori and Pākehā. The number of kindergartens and parent-run play centres for preschoolers increased, influenced by international ideas. The pull-along toy to promote the toddler's motor development, painted in bright primary colours, took the form of the Buzzy Bee in New Zealand and was improvised from toilet-roll holders in 1948. Secondary-school reforms, a raised school-leaving age, and revised qualifications prepared New Zealand's youth for a future of full employment. Following Australia, the government introduced a universal family benefit in 1945, of a generous 10 shillings a week for each child, payable to the mother. Teachers noticed that the allowance improved the appearance and dress of children at school.

Postwar reconstruction generally focused on the goal of full employment. Labour resolved to avoid the failures of soldier settlement after the First World War by introducing an extensive rehabilitation scheme for returned servicemen. The settler contract lived on in the development of farms for ex-servicemen, complete with houses built on state-house plans and modified for their farmhouse function by including porches for boots and outdoor clothing. In the cities ex-servicemen enjoyed priority for state houses and for jobs, while 'pressure cooker' courses at teachers colleges and universities offered men opportunities unavailable before the war.

For Māori, the 'rehab' scheme signified new opportunities. Until farms became economic, ex-servicemen were paid wages, and the Department of Rehabilitation insisted on more equal housing standards. Fraser hoped that the Māori Social and Economic Advancement Act 1945 would finally bring about equality. A compromise between Māori hopes of full citizenship, raised by the war, and the resolve of the Pākehā-run Department of Native Affairs to remain in control of official policy, the Act replaced the word 'Native' with 'Māori' in official usage. But paternalism persisted, because neither the government nor the public understood the nature and extent of Māori needs. The legislation subordinated the goal of development to an emphasis on welfare, and officers of 28 (Māori) Battalion, experienced leaders, returned to jobs in teaching or as welfare officers in the renamed Department of Māori Affairs. What limited authority they exercised over social, economic, and welfare issues of concern to their people was soon checked by a change of government.

The goal of equal opportunity also encouraged a series of settlements between 1944 and 1946 with iwi whose grievances had remained outstanding since the 1920s. Parliament passed the Waikato-Maniapoto Māori Claims Settlement Act in 1944, under which Tainui received a lump sum of £10 000 and annual payments for the next 45 years as compensation for the vast land confiscations of the nineteenth century. Subsequent settlements allocated £5000 annually to the Taranaki Māori Trust Board for confiscated land and compensation to Ngāi Tahu of £10 000 annually for 30 years. The government was inundated with petitions from other iwi demanding redress of grievances, and the Treaty's absence in these settlements formed a major justification for revising them at the end of the twentieth century.

While Māori were more included in notions of 'the people' from the end of the Second World War, New Zealand continued to restrict entry to migrants on grounds of race. A committee on population in 1946 recommended against mass immigration, in contrast to Australian policy; the profile of the good migrant remained white and British. If immigration of 'other European types' were encouraged, the committee reported, they should be 'of such character as will, within a relatively short space of time, become completely assimilated'. This meant that if other than British migrants were to be accepted, they should come from northern European countries. Non-Māori New Zealanders, 95 per cent of the people, remained 96 per cent British and proud of it.

Consistent with a Commonwealth agreement on citizenship, separate New Zealand nationality came into existence in 1948, on the Canadian model. British subjects born in New Zealand became New Zealand citizens, with New Zealand passports. But few British migrants registered for New Zealand citizenship, because they remained British subjects, which suggests that ethnicity dictated who belonged. At the time no thought was given to Pacific

Islanders in New Zealand–administered territories; by default they became brown New Zealanders.

Nonetheless, a sequence of symbolic moves indicated that the dominion had become a nation by the end of the 1940s. New Zealand finally ratified the Statute of Westminster in 1947 and so attained constitutional independence, five years after Australia did, in response to the fall of Singapore. The 'Dominion of New Zealand' became 'New Zealand' in 1945, and the royal coat of arms disappeared from official letterheads, replaced by the national coat of arms, which contained a Māori warrior and an updated figure of Zealandia. In retrospect the era from 1930 to 1949 proved to be one of cultural nationalism, state sponsored under a long-serving Labour government, from the introduction of public radio, in 1936, to state patronage of the arts, a national museum, an art gallery, and an orchestra.

By 1949 historians and economists were writing books about an emerging nation state. J. B. Condliffe's *New Zealand in the Making* (1930) pursued the theme of economic development through small farming and closer settlement, from the Wakefieldian schemes of the 1840s to dairying. By the Second World War the popular series of pictorial survey histories *Making New Zealand* (1939–40), used by schoolchildren for another 30 years, suggested that making the nation was very much under way (see figure 7.4). Published in wartime, these and other centennial publications were intended to strengthen the sense of nationhood among the Pākehā majority.

The assumption of the time was that making the nation and its history was a settler enterprise, achieved through their efforts. Māori belonged more to the past, serving as a preface to New Zealand history and a support act. In settler New Zealand, fourth and fifth generations who identified with their environment were growing up. The forthright newspaper and literary magazine editor Oliver Duff co-opted the biblical imagery that the country had made its own in his idiosyncratic centennial survey, *New Zealand Now*, to explain the process of adaptation: 'There is of course a sense in which every man springs from the soil. Literally as well as figuratively all flesh is grass. A New Zealander is a man whom New Zealand earth has nourished'. The concept of flesh as grass, while made in New Zealand and masculine, was no longer imperialistic.

7.4 *Making New Zealand* pictorial survey histories, 1939–40 Government Printer, Wellington. Photographer Duncan Shaw-Brown

In 1930 Condliffe had pondered the effects of isolation on imperial sentiment, from his new vantage point as an expatriate in Honolulu. Disillusioned by what he later termed New Zealand's 'intellectual stagnation', he decided that imperfect knowledge lay at the basis of New Zealand's 'mother-complex'. Remoteness precluded analysis of events and encouraged resort to imperial loyalty without the necessary scholarly research.

In the 1920s 'New Zealand's so-called mother complex reached its climax', F. L. W. Wood responded when writing his own survey in 1943. Foreign policy was a 'drama enacted on another planet', and since New Zealand 'could do little or nothing to shape the course of events', there was 'no reason' to 'affront sentiment by any assertion for nationhood'. But that could change; and historians have debated ever since how much dependence on Britain did change after Japan's entry into the war, which propelled the adjustment to 'dual dependency', on the United States as well as Britain. As far as Condliffe and Wood were concerned, New Zealand's future lay with the countries that surrounded the Pacific Ocean, 'the eye of the earth'.

Making New Zealand 1930–1949

"... the invincibility of the All Blacks ..."

7.5 G. E. G. Minhinnick, *The invincibility of the All Blacks*, c. 1947 C. V. Smith, *From N to Z*, illus. G. E. G. Minhinnick, Wellington: Hicks Smith & Wright, c. 1947. Family collection

In a tongue-in-cheek sketch of late 1940s Kiwi culture and upbringing, the popular cartoonist G. E. G. Minhinnick illustrated how everyday actions contributed to the country's myths. He captured the passing-on of a key myth about 'the invincibility of the All Blacks' to a small boy at his mother's knee (see figure 7.5). Mother, not father, relayed the message, illustrating the importance of nurture in the formation of identities. The national obsession with rugby could be read as continuing to play an imperial game; yet the process of telling stories about and attributing meaning to that game happened at home in New Zealand, where mothers instructed children in beliefs and values.

Politically, 1949 proved a turning point, when the principles of private enterprise and freedom, as opposed to regulation and wartime controls, swept Labour from office. Conservatives had rallied to form the National Party in 1936 in response to Labour's election success. Cold War clouds incited a 'yes' vote in a referendum for peacetime conscription, but with a low turnout. Once again, a small nation searched for new ways to balance internal and external security.

8
Golden weather 1950–1972

Wartime controls ended in 1950, allowing New Zealanders to look forward to an era of postwar growth and change. The 1950s and 1960s are often recalled as a 'golden age'. In many respects they were, for the baby boomers born from 1945 to 1961 who enjoyed a childhood unburdened by depression and war, and for the parents responsible for their upbringing. Broadly, however, the internal dynamics of the Pacific region were in flux. Playwright Bruce Mason captured the mood in *The End of the Golden Weather* (first performed in 1960), his dramatic solo performance about a summer in a boy's childhood. At adolescence, he explained,

> This strange and magic light – this *golden weather* – begins to change and, for the first time, some of the troubling weathers of a man's soul are revealed to him … he becomes aware of the thousand changing visages of time, touched with confusion and bewilderment, menaced by terrible depths and enigmas of experience he has never known before.

So it was for New Zealanders in the 1950s and 1960s. The unsettling of settler society had begun, first for Māori, then for future Pacific Island migrants, and lastly for Pākehā (European New Zealanders).

These were years of full employment for men (until 1967) in an economy that increasingly needed married women in the workforce. The significant gap in life expectancy between Māori and Pākehā narrowed rapidly. A new round of culture contact began, with a major movement of Māori to the cities. A generation gap opened between baby boomers and their parents: the latter wanted their children to better themselves through expanding educational opportunities. Sustained growth made possible the consumer society and accompanying changes in etiquette and social norms, from hats and gloves to miniskirts and informality. Communications were transformed, linking New Zealand more strongly to the world. This was an era of social change and new interdependencies.

In art, the visionary Colin McCahon emerged as a seminal figure, though he was treated harshly by the public for his word paintings and abstract landscapes, often done in panels. Darkness was fundamental to his distinctive artwork; in the black of McCahon's landscapes the fleeting passage of time contrasted with the land's seeming permanence. Through his painting he tried to invent a way to see 'something logical, orderly and beautiful belonging to the land and not yet to its peoples', a vision not understood and appreciated until after his death in 1987.

Politically the National Party was supreme. The government of Sidney Holland, from 1949 to 1957, argued for 'freedom' and development, claiming the middle ground of equality of opportunity and endorsement of the settler contract. In theory National embraced the free market, which still meant dependence on Britain, now a declining world power; in practice it continued the Australasian model of state development, whose core business involved managing the economy in an increasingly uncertain and confusing postwar world dominated by the United States. The Holland government of New Zealand–born returned servicemen, loyal to Britain, contained just one woman, Hilda Ross. In 1950 the government abolished the Legislative Council, the appointed upper house, which also contained one woman, Agnes Louisa Weston, wife of the National Party's first president. (Ironically Weston was chosen when Peter Fraser discovered that women had been ineligible in the 1940s, only to become a member of the 'suicide squad' appointed on the understanding that they vote to abolish the Legislative Council.) New Zealand now had a system of unicameral government, which had unintended outcomes in terms of the untrammelled use of executive power during the ruptures of the late twentieth and early twenty-first centuries.

COLD WAR AND NUCLEAR PLAYGROUND

The origins of New Zealand's late-twentieth-century stance against nuclear weapons were already discernible. First, the nation faced the 'Anzac dilemma', having to juggle the expectations of not one but two great-power protectors after the Second World War. To confound this dilemma, the less preferred protector, the United States, was now the dominant Pacific power, replacing Britain, which was in withdrawal and decline. The Antipodes were used to having a voice in British policy; strong ties, economic dependence, trust, and familiarity lowered transaction costs, strategic let-downs notwithstanding. The United States was less familiar and played by different rules, as yet unknown. 'Do as we say' appeared to be the directive.

Second, both Western great powers had divergent interests from small, remote New Zealand. The country's insignificance posed the problem of how to manage the tension between a conservative realist strategy of obediently falling in with the interests of Britain and the United States and the idealism of seeing to its own interests by managing isolation through collective security. In the longer term, New Zealand opted for the higher moral ground of the multilateral formula provided by the United Nations.

The top diplomat of the time, the urbane Alister McIntosh, mused in retrospect that clinging to the British connection 'paid off' as a strategy but was 'perhaps followed for too long' after the war. The war itself had demonstrated that there would be no security without the full support of the United States, which had become the essential 'great and powerful friend'. Prime Minister Sidney Holland understood this 'dual dependence' clearly, stating in parliament in 1955, 'Not only must we justify help from Britain by being prepared to pull our weight in the British boat, but also we must earn the active support of the United States'. After 1945 the external threat of the Cold War shaped defence policy. Indeed the fear of communism drove New Zealand into the Cold War alongside Australia as a small partner in the Western alliance, led by the United States, against countries led by the Soviet Union.

Happily, the Cold War provided a new window of opportunity to keep the United States interested in a region peripheral to the main game while maintaining traditional Commonwealth ties. Both Australia and New Zealand deplored the communist victory in the Chinese Civil War in 1949 and treated the defeated Nationalist regime that sought refuge in Taipei, in Taiwan, as the Chinese government. In the Pacific, both acquiesced in United States actions that denied West Papua (formerly Dutch New Guinea) to the Netherlands. With the outbreak of the Korean War, in 1950, the communist threat seemed real, and the neighbours sent troops, nominally to support the United Nations, but technically as part of a Commonwealth force. In reality New Zealand and Australia supported the United States, which expected not to go into Korea alone. At the same time, the United States sought a soft peace with Japan to ensure its friendship and cooperation while containing the communist threat in Korea and China. This acceptance of a recent wartime enemy required a change in attitude by Australia and New Zealand. The ANZUS alliance of Australia, New Zealand, and the United States, which stipulated that a threat to any of the three partners was a threat to all, proved to be their sizeable reward.

Non-military influence in South and Southeast Asia extended alongside the military through the Colombo Plan from 1950, to encourage economic development and remove the instability that nurtured the conditions for communist influence. Colombo Plan scholarships brought students from newly independent countries to study in Australia and New Zealand, idealistically to aid the Third World (a Cold War term originally used to classify countries that were neither capitalist nor communist) and realistically to commit the United States to funding and regional security.

At bottom, any latitude sought in foreign affairs depended on the American alliance. Drafted in Canberra, the ANZUS Pact was signed in San Francisco in 1951, the first security alliance that New Zealand (or Australia) joined without Britain. The Americans insisted on a tripartite agreement, because they did not want to be subjected to British and French demands as imperial powers in the Pacific. From New Zealand's perspective the alliance also made it possible to help Britain in the Middle East should hostilities erupt into a third world war. ANZUS promised, but did not guarantee, American support in the event of threats from Asia – the old fear dressed up in new Cold War guise. The importance of ANZUS grew with time, because it supplied high-level communication with Washington and easy access to the United States' superpower military intelligence and infrastructure.

Still distrustful of the 'Asian menace', New Zealand and Australia became involved in a series of small wars in Southeast Asia. New Zealand rallied to help Britain in Malaya, contributing to the Malayan Emergency in the 1950s, followed by commitments in Thailand and Malaysia in its confrontation with Indonesia in the 1960s. New Zealand participated in the Malayan Emergency as a signatory to the Southeast Asia Collective Defense Treaty of 1954, which included Britain and France with the ANZUS partners, as well as Thailand, Pakistan, and the Philippines. New Zealand then followed the American lead in turning against President Sukarno in Indonesia only as he lost power in 1966. Finally, New Zealand reluctantly followed Australia into Vietnam.

The Vietnam War was the first in which New Zealand participated without Britain and was the result of external pressures. To avoid any risk to ANZUS, regarded by officials as the pivot of foreign policy, a small New Zealand contingent joined the Australian task force. An artillery battery of 120 men replaced 25 engineers already in Vietnam in 1965, followed by an infantry company sent as part of an Australian battalion in 1967 and medics. Keith Holyoake, the National government's prime minister from 1960 to 1972, however, kept the forces' contribution to a minimum. (Alliteration bestowed on Holyoake the nickname 'Kiwi Keith' to distinguish him from an Australian cousin of the same name, which says much about Kiwi identity.) A mere 3900 New Zealanders, all volunteers, served in rotation between 1965 and 1972 – nearly 600 at the peak. Thirty-seven died.

Far to the south, meanwhile, relations with the United States received a fillip from New Zealand's involvement in Antarctica. Britain had named the Ross Dependency and placed this wedge of Antarctic territory under New Zealand jurisdiction for the British Empire in 1923. But New Zealanders only roused themselves to protect the Antarctic from Cold War rivalries and human exploitation in 1957–8, spurred by International Geophysical Year initiatives and the 1955–8 Commonwealth Trans-Antarctic Expedition, led by Dr (Sir) Vivian Fuchs, who retraced the doomed steps of British explorers Robert Scott and Ernest Shackleton. The United States navy based at McMurdo Sound, in sovereign New Zealand territory, helped New Zealanders establish their base (Scott Base) as 'neighbours' nearby on Ross Island in 1959. Conversely, Christchurch served as, and in 2025 still was, the departure point for the Americans' Operation Deep Freeze, with both the airport and the port involved since 1955 in the resupply of bases on the icy continent.

Back home the Cold War permeated life. National's success at exploiting the domestic effects kept it in office throughout the 1950s and 1960s, an era which saw the remaking of conservatism and a consensus around policies of economic development, Keynesian economic management, security, and social democracy. The bitter waterfront dispute of 1951, which lasted 151 days, brought the issues to the fore, breaking the back of the powerful Waterside Workers' Union and leaving the National Party in the ascendant. Economically, the stoush grabbed headlines, because prosperity depended on the export-led economy. Before relatively cheap air travel New Zealanders relied on shipping and ports to sustain their living standards. But the organisation of work on the waterfront was the preserve of British companies concerned only with a fast turnaround and with cutting costs, which led to constant conflict with waterside workers. During the Korean War the prolonged dispute disrupted exports at a time of record prices for primary products, especially high wool prices.

In one view, the Cold War divided the labour movement between the Federation of Labour, led by F. P. Walsh, a former confidant of Fraser – and the closest the country has had to a mafia godfather – and the more militant Trade Union Congress, including the waterside workers. The militants made the critical mistake of rejecting arbitration, unwisely challenging the power of the state, which proclaimed emergency regulations and ordered armed forces onto the wharves. The refusal to accept arbitration destroyed the union and hurt public confidence in the Labour Party, while the Federation of Labour sided with the government, to their mutual advantage. In a snap election centred on the issue of law and order in 1951, National won decisively.

A more recent view of the dispute argues that Cold War rhetoric had nothing to do with the real underlying causes, which were 'structural and embedded in the labour process'. A history of low wages, insecure employment, and dangerous work practices bred hostility and covert resistance, strategies used to effect against the employers when the economy improved. Management refused to recognise legitimate grievances, and governments were obliged to defer to the shipping lines' market dominance. The employers provoked the dispute and then ducked for cover, allowing the government to capitalise on Cold War hysteria and the populist platform of law and order.

Cold War jitters further spurred nuclear-weapons programs and vice versa. Throughout the polarised contest between communism and capitalism the United States, Britain, and France treated the Pacific, with its sparse populations and minimal political costs, as their 'nuclear playground'. In the wake of the secret Anglo-American Manhattan Project during the Second World War, Britain sought its own nuclear deterrent. The British returned to the region to conduct nuclear tests on uninhabited islands off Western Australia and in outback South Australia in the 1950s and hydrogen bomb tests in Kiribati (formerly the Gilbert Islands) in 1957–8. The United States conducted atmospheric tests of atomic and hydrogen bombs in the Marshall Islands until 1958 and began a final series of tests in 1962 that disturbed New Zealand's telecommunications systems, amid mounting public concern about nuclear fallout. Overall the Americans exploded 66 nuclear devices in the Pacific.

French bomb tests, however, provoked the strongest protest, both because they started in 1966, in violation of the Partial Test Ban Treaty of 1963, and because France used nuclear testing to assert its colonial power in Polynesia – a power long resented in New Zealand. France could not have detonated bombs above and below French Polynesia had the islands been independent. The peace movement, which formed a Campaign for Nuclear Disarmament on the British model in 1959, gathered strength as the bomb tests proliferated. New Zealanders resented experiments with nuclear bombs in what they regarded as their backyard. Concern about the effects on the Cook Islands added to anti-French feeling. Problematically, nuclear weapons also became a key feature of United States military strategy. In such unintended as well as deliberate ways, Cold War tensions refracted into local policy and politics.

The development of nuclear weapons during the Second World War created a demand for uranium and gave rise to hopes of entering the atomic age with a find. A secret wartime search for uranium came to nothing, but in 1955 a publicly promoted search saw a Geiger counter go wild on the West Coast – in an area that is now national park – precipitating a uranium rush reminiscent of the gold rush a century earlier. Thereafter the New Zealand government, the British Atomic Energy Authority, and business spent 25 years searching for uranium on the West Coast, but no viable deposits were ever found. A tantalising teaser remains: What if uranium had been discovered in economic quantities in the 1950s? Would New Zealand have developed a nuclear-free policy? Had economic deposits been located, the country could have followed a different path altogether.

In the 1950s the energy future, then, looked nuclear. Officials agreed on the need for nuclear power stations but debated how to respond to competition between Britain and the United States arising from their efforts to supply atomic equipment to the 'free world'. After signing an agreement with the United States in 1956 (as Iran did in 1957) New Zealand acquired enriched uranium as fuel for research reactors and equipment (the agreement transferred in 1961 to the new International Atomic Energy Agency) and established its Institute of Nuclear Sciences. The United States' 'atoms for peace' program also donated a subcritical nuclear reactor to the University of Canterbury; it was installed in 1961 with the aim of training nuclear-power engineers.

Nuclear power was put on the agenda because power shortages plagued postwar New Zealand. Between 1955 and 1964 electricity generation doubled yet barely kept up with soaring demand. In response, the state built infrastructure to provide electricity, just as it had done with railways. It turned to geothermal electric power after a project to use North Island geothermal steam to produce heavy water for nuclear reactors in Britain proved too costly. Hydroelectric-power projects commanded the waters of the Waikato, the country's longest river, in the 1950s and the Waitaki

8.1 Nevile S. Lodge, *Needmore Power Project*, 1963 or 1964
Alexander Turnbull Library, Wellington, PUBL-0206-081-1.
Courtesy of Debby Edwards

River, in the South Island, in the 1960s. A cable across Cook Strait, laid in 1964, transferred energy from hydroelectric-power stations in the South Island to the power-hungry North Island. Such was the scale of earth moving required for the Benmore Dam, built between 1958 and 1965, that cartoonist Nevile Lodge suggested the argument over which island was the 'mainland' – a title claimed by the South – could be resolved by shifting the two islands together (figure 8.1).

PEOPLING NEW ZEALAND

To the surprise of some, postwar growth did not require as many non-British migrants as expected, and this freed the country from having to compete for them. The baby boom lifted the birth rate, while enough British migrants arrived to supply two-thirds of long-term new arrivals. Assisted migration resumed in 1947 with the 'ten pound Poms', who found it cheaper to migrate than to holiday at home. Dutch people comprised almost half the intake of migrants from continental Europe between 1945 and 1975; in New Zealand minds, as Northern Europeans, they best approximated the British ideal. Between 1945 and 1971 almost 77 000 newcomers arrived from Britain, while about 6200 migrated from the Netherlands. Postwar migration produced a significant Dutch community, which included the de Bres and Borren families, who rose to prominence in social justice issues and in hockey respectively, and Eelco Boswijk, who opened Nelson's Chez Eelco coffee house in 1961. A mere 4500 displaced persons arrived from 1949 to 1971, and 1100 Hungarian refugees, in a total of 90 000 assisted European migrants. Kin migration continued in its historical pattern until the late 1980s; Britain provided nearly half the permanent arrivals, followed by Australia, with about a quarter.

With the postwar need for relationships around the Pacific Rim came the first easing of policy towards 'Asia'. As in Canada, Indians could enter New Zealand as British subjects and were Commonwealth citizens. The poll tax imposed on Chinese migrants was abolished in 1944; in 1952 Chinese New Zealanders regained the right of naturalisation, denied since 1908, and only 1 woman qualified, followed by 20 men in the next two years. In response to the global development of restrictions at the border, the Immigration Amendment Act 1961 required non–New Zealand citizens to have an entry permit. In practice it remained difficult for Chinese and Indian people to gain entry unless they had family links. Even Britons required permits. The exception was Australians, who did not need a permit or even a passport until 1981.

Changes in migration policy accompanied changes in the economy. Whereas Europeans largely met the need for skilled labour, Pacific Islanders and Māori provided a cheap unskilled and semi-skilled workforce. In the biggest postwar shift, the South Pacific supplemented Britain as the leading source of migrants. With decolonisation in the Pacific Islands, the 'good migrant' came to include Islanders. Settler society illusions lasted into the 1970s both that Pacific Islanders and Māori had a place in the nation as Polynesian kin and as an unskilled workforce and that Māori were too 'integrated' to unsettle structures of power and privilege.

The numbers of Pacific Islanders were small (little more than 26 000 in 1966) but proportionally significant. The majority came from New Zealand dependencies the Cook Islands, Niue, and tiny Tokelau, the last of whose population largely relocated to New Zealand in 1966; and from Western Samoa, a trusteeship territory subject to United Nations scrutiny until 1962. Smaller numbers from Tonga, Fiji, and Tahiti claimed real (and imagined) links. Pākehā saw Pacific Islanders as another kind of Māori, a view Māori did not share. At the same time the public remained oblivious to the country's legacy of sub-colonialism in the Pacific. Even politicians were unaware that Pacific Islanders from New Zealand dependencies were New Zealand citizens.

New Zealand decolonised in the South Pacific earlier, but less completely, than other powers. Under New Zealand trusteeship, the Samoan constitution was modified regularly to transfer responsibility in stages to prepare for independence. Full internal self-government came in 1959 and independence in 1962, after which Western Samoans could enter the country under a quota system.

The 'free association' deal reached with the Cook Islands was a world first and a stark contrast to Australian relations with Melanesians at that time. The sequence of events paralleled the pattern in Western Samoa. In 1962 the Cook Islands was offered the choice of integration, independence, or self-government 'in free association' with New Zealand. Cook Islanders chose the last and became fully self-governing in 1965, with New Zealand responsible for foreign affairs. Free association proffered to this scattered island group the advantage of confidence associated with nationhood while tempering the risks of independence when dealing with larger powers. New Zealand was well versed in how to negotiate the best of both worlds, from its own colonial experience of simultaneous dependence in foreign policy and independence in internal affairs, and put this experience into practice in its Pacific territories. Niue, a single coral outcrop, followed a similar path to free association by 1974, and in 2025 Tokelau remained a New Zealand dependency.

While New Zealand exerted an impact on Pacific Islanders, Islanders conversely made an impact on New Zealanders' sense of themselves. Creatives and intellectuals, from economists to poets, musicians, and artists, began to assert a Pacific identity. It is no accident that the nationalist historian Keith Sinclair, who graduated as a University of New Zealand doctor of philosophy from Auckland, adopted a Pacific-centred view in his Penguin *History of New Zealand* in 1959. Sinclair located New Zealand in the Pacific and in the New World. He opposed Britishness, which he saw as part of a South Island myth of settlement, while his rivals quipped that the leftist 'Sinclair School' portrayed New Zealand as 'the long pink cloud'. Pākehā–Māori relations featured in Sinclair's history, but Pacific Islanders, Asia, and women did not. Instead, new interdependencies between town and country brought to the forefront the place of Māori in the nation.

MĀORI URBANISATION

The growth in migration among Māori in search of work intensified from the 1930s, propelled by population recovery and far too little land to support young people. At the same time, the long postwar boom demanded workers. The Second World War accelerated the 'silent migration' of Māori, raising hopes of work and a better life. Between 1945 and 1976 the Māori population transformed from predominantly rural (74 per cent) to urban (77 per cent). This was a radical change for both Māori and Pākehā, who had lived largely separate lives since the New Zealand Wars. After the Second World War, New Zealand underwent another round of cultural encounter. Again, shared spaces were in cities.

The postwar move by young Māori adults to the city and suburbs was viewed positively by Māori who were attracted to urban life and entertainment, and by settler governments. Auckland proved a popular 'destination of choice'. In Auckland, tribal villages became engulfed by suburban sprawl, because Pākehā policymakers viewed traditional pā (villages) as blots on the landscape. 'Modern' Māori were envisioned as urban and suburban, living in the suburbs, the twentieth-century opposite of the slum. In this context the Māori Women's Welfare League, formed in 1951, succeeded in having the booklet *Washday at the Pa* withdrawn from schools in 1964 because of its pre-modern portrayal of Māori life.

'Integration' replaced 'assimilation' as the preferred race-relations policy in response to rapid demographic change. For

Āpirana Ngata, earlier in the century, hapū (subtribes) belonged in rural New Zealand, within their tribal territory. His solution had been to assist them where possible to farm and develop their own land. But the Second World War mobilised young Māori for the war effort, both in the services and in production, and for many this entailed a shift to the cities. After the war, this move was highly orchestrated. From a full employment perspective, the state viewed Māori youth as a 'reserve of industrial labour' who should be transferred from 'uneconomic' areas to cities and towns. At the time, there were over 20 000 job vacancies. An official relocation scheme from 1960 until 1967, when costs were cut, provided support for families prepared to shift centres. Young Māori women were attracted to hotel and hospital work by cheap board and good pay, and into teaching and nursing, all viewed as suitable training for future wives and mothers. Young men, largely from the East Coast of the North Island, migrated to Christchurch for trade training. Between 1961 and 1967, of nearly 2700 young people relocated, 52 per cent moved to Christchurch as apprentices.

The Hunn Report of 1960 (published in 1961) recommended that Māori adopt a 'modern way of life'. Senior public servant J. K. Hunn defined the objective of integration: to 'combine (not fuse) the Maori and pakeha elements to form one nation wherein Maori culture remains distinct'. This implied 'some continuation of Maori culture' in addressing Māori issues. Critics, however, dismissed this policy as assimilation by another name. It assumed state leadership as a given and ignored lessons of the past that Māori problems needed to be solved by Māori themselves. In the interests of a 'one nation' policy, the government dismantled the Māori schools system by 1969. Some Pākehā groups did take more interest in indigenous culture. Importantly, 'integration' gave Māori room to negotiate – for example, to secure state support for building urban marae (meeting places).

The policies of integration and urbanisation transformed Māori citizenship. Negatively, people were uprooted by land loss and forced to move. Positively, the population recovery of the early twentieth century was succeeded by a rapid improvement in life chances. From the 1960s Māori experienced a health transition that showed up in falling fertility and death rates. Māori women's life expectancy doubled between 1901 and 1961, and the disparities with Pākehā began to close. As the move to the cities rearranged kin networks from extended to nuclear families, the importance of the home – represented by the detached suburban house – grew in creating the ideal Māori as well as European citizen. The Māori Women's Welfare League declared its focus to be 'the mother, the child and the home' and targeted the problem of overcrowded, substandard housing, especially in Auckland.

SUBURBAN ICONS

After the war, governments fostered a collective identity framed by domestic ideals, marriage, and the family. The detached suburban house with a clipped front lawn and a more relaxed backyard where children could play, a rotary clothes line, a vegetable patch, flowers for Mum, and a shed for Dad, came to denote a national way of life supposedly accessible to all New Zealanders. Suburban houses and decentralised industrial development led to the appearance of suburban shopping centres and supermarkets in the 1960s. Woolworths the supermarket chain spread to New Zealand from Australia in 1958, and Tom Ah Chee and partners started Foodtown in Otara, Auckland, the same year. In Christchurch, Hay's opened at Church Corner in 1960 and Riccarton Mall in 1965.

Suburbia spread with the baby boom of 1945–61, which resulted from a combined marriage boom, among couples who delayed getting married because of the Depression and those who wed during or at the end of the war. Family sizes increased, from little more than two up to four children on average by 1960, which crowded maternity hospitals, then kindergartens and primary schools. The baby boomers buoyed demand for home appliances, especially washing machines to ease the chore of washing nappies. By the time of the late arrival of television, in 1960, most homes had a washing machine and a refrigerator. Baby boomers boosted the market for children's toys and obliged fathers to build sandpits to encourage creative toddler play (see figure 8.2). The rules of childrearing had changed with the transformations in the economic and emotional value of children, as people lived longer and healthier lives. Indeed, healthier children allowed the transition in childcare

8.2 A toddler in a sandpit, Palmerston North, c. 1959. For the under-five set in a new house in a new subdivision, the sandpit took precedence over making a garden in an undeveloped backyard. Family collection

rules, from 'character' and physical health to 'personality' development, and so from Dr Truby King to the American Dr Spock as the baby authority.

New parents, having survived the Depression, world war, and a housing shortage, aspired to a suburban house and car. But they worried about the debt incurred to own the dream. Status was increasingly derived from home ownership, and the proportion of houses owned rather than rented rose rapidly to 70 per cent. Cold War politics combined with the spirit of free enterprise to promote state endorsement of home ownership and the sale of state houses to tenants. The National government increased the availability of state loans for house building and provided a plan service for aspiring owners. Labour – briefly in office from 1957 – added cheap home loans and a facility for parents to capitalise their children's family benefit as a house deposit. The ideal of a property-owning democracy resurfaced as a bulwark against the Cold War, or a third world war (believed imminent), and a device to contain communism and social pathology.

Ideals of womanhood centred on the suburban housewife, who was now expected to be an accomplished home cook. One test entailed baking a pavlova, the fluffy meringue cake claimed as the national dessert by both New Zealand and Australia. Pure, white, and feminine, and a cooking hazard that required a cast-iron stove for success, the pavlova, along with the feather-light cream sponge, signified the feminine cook's cultural worth and expertise in the kitchen. The pavlova had emerged by the 1930s from an Australasian tradition of dainty baking using staple ingredients, in this case eggs and sugar, with cream as an accessory. An early published recipe appeared in the Rangiora Mothers' Union *Cookery Book of Tried and Tested Recipes*, contributed by women of the Rangiora Anglican parish in the depths of depression in 1933. By contrast the 1950s and early 1960s were years of eggs and other produce in abundance, embellished by official marketing that 'everything tastes better with cream'.

Men's aspirations, on the other hand, came to be represented by adventurer Sir Edmund Hillary. His conquest of Mount Everest, with Sherpa Tenzing Norgay in May 1953, as a member of a British climbing expedition, and instant knighthood forged his place as the greatest living New Zealander. Hillary's triumph, immediately before the coronation of Queen Elizabeth II, gave the impression that he climbed the world's highest mountain both for the queen and for New Zealand. Hillary continues to encapsulate the masculine qualities celebrated in Kiwi culture, although he died in 2008. In 2025 his profile still featured on the $5 note. An imperial hero and pioneer, the first and the best, laconic and humanitarian, a gentleman with a larrikin streak, adventurous and practical, a philanthropist in Nepal – and, after Everest, a family man – Hillary strode across the globe, conquering everything from the highest mountain to the South Pole.

In his dash to the South Pole on modified Ferguson farm tractors, in January 1958, as a member of the Commonwealth Trans-Antarctic Expedition, Hillary proved himself an adventurer first, and more a nationalist than an imperialist by trumping the British leader of the expedition, Vivian Fuchs, when he beat Fuchs to the

South Pole by 16 days. As leader of the New Zealanders on the expedition, Hillary was to support Fuchs by establishing depots. In doing so, with his improvised 'tractor train' he cleared a route to the pole for his own party – and for Fuchs' Sno-Cats. Compounding his impertinence, Hillary topped up his tractor tanks with American instead of British Petroleum fuel and was flown back to the South Pole by the Americans to greet Fuchs for the benefit of American press coverage.

Hillary's warm embrace of the United States better reflected people's responses to American popular culture than did elite intellectual attitudes that denounced the 'flood' of American movies, music, and comics as depraved and inferior. There was little of the earlier condemnatory response to jazz and swing music when, in 1956, Elvis Presley records and *Rock around the Clock*, the rock-and-roll musical, arrived in New Zealand. Rock and roll was greeted dispassionately; parents had more to worry about than adolescent musical tastes (see figure 8.3).

By comparison the public greeted the queen with great excitement as the first reigning monarch to visit the Antipodes, in the summer of 1953–4. The royal tour heightened patriotism, while the royal presence at Christmas 1953 comforted a community reeling from natural disaster. On Christmas Eve, at Tangiwai, in the North Island, 151 people died when a lahar from the volcanic plateau washed away a rail bridge and, moments later, the night express train from Wellington to Auckland, packed with Christmas holiday-makers, crashed into the swollen river below. The young queen mothered the nation in her charge. At the public's insistence, busloads of school pupils turned out to greet her and display the nation's wholesome children.

As child-centredness intensified, so did concern that teenagers had not suffered wartime restraint and were growing undisciplined because of consumerism. While the National government promoted itself as the 'party of the new consumer age', youth culture in the 1950s engendered a moral panic about teenage sexuality and sybaritism in the new state-house suburbs. Following salacious newspaper comment, the Special Committee on Moral Delinquency in Children and Adolescents met in 1954 to investigate youth behaviour in suburban Wellington and Auckland. The

8.3 'The kids are already too radio-active'. A comment on parental anxieties about nuclear testing and wry tolerance of teenage music in the 1950s
Unknown cartoonist, *Christchurch Star-Sun*, 6 October 1956. Courtesy of *Christchurch Star* and Gary Whitcher

committee of worthies, including a headmaster of a leading boys' school and representatives of the National Council of Women and Catholic Women's League, blamed working mothers and 'over-sexed' girls for teenage hanky-panky at milk bars and in homes. No matter that rates of juvenile offending had remained unchanged for 20 years. The committee was alarmed that the 1950s heralded a new era, in which teenagers were rebelling: 'A generation gap was emerging. The commission members and some witnesses were alarmed by Coca Cola, motorbikes and girls in jeans'. The concept of what was best in New Zealand culture came under strain, as young people thought and behaved differently.

Education of the juvenile delinquents' younger siblings, the baby boomers, stretched public resources into the 1970s. Primary schools put up (and put up with) prefabricated classrooms to cope with swollen school rolls, while secondary-school enrolments doubled between 1945 and 1959, as more teenagers stayed at school. Tertiary education ballooned at technical institutes and universities. The University of New Zealand, a federal institution of provincial colleges, split into separate universities in 1961. Two new autonomous universities, Massey University and the University of Waikato, opened in 1964, while the University of Canterbury moved in stages to a new suburban campus that gave more room to engineering and the sciences. Even in this small society an era awaited of youth revolution, hippie flower power, and protest. Rebellion was in, thanks to global influences.

PROTEST MOVEMENTS

Mothers' lives were transforming too. It was not the contraceptive pill, introduced in 1962, changing the position of women and how society viewed them, that unstitched moral codes; the pill merely broke the class barrier in types of birth control uses and made contraception more assured. Women married and on average had fewer children at a younger age than in the past, and they lived longer. This altered life course allowed married women the space to move into paid work, where the economy needed them once their children started school. By 1966 nearly 20 per cent of married Pākehā women were in the paid workforce, compared to less than 8 per cent in 1945. They occupied a narrow range of jobs, often part-time, so that they could also remain housewives. The public service especially sought to attract skilled women as permanent and relieving schoolteachers of the baby boomers. A related shortage of hospital nurses persisted throughout the 1950s and 1960s.

Ironically the state led the way in promoting paid work for married women while simultaneously advocating domesticity. Equal pay in the public service came into effect from 1960. The private sector lagged for another 12 years, until the Equal Pay Act of 1972. In the late 1960s the faltering of the compulsory arbitration system, which had set the highest wage rate for skilled male workers, provided scope for equal pay arguments to gain ground.

Barmaids were finally allowed back behind hotel bars, and six o'clock closing ended in 1967, after half a century. The easing of licensing laws permitted pubs to open until a respectable bedtime of

10 p.m., at last allowing hotels and restaurants to develop to international standards. But first came 'pub liberations' in Auckland, Wellington, and Christchurch, in 1971, by an angry new wave of young feminists who demanded the right of women to drink in public bars, with their cheaper drinks than those in lounge bars that admitted women. This demand for drinking equality stood in stark contrast to the pro-temperance stance of first-wave feminism.

The Women's Liberation Movement burst onto the scene in 1970, in protest against women being sentenced to housework, which they saw as restrictive. Typical of the hippie counterculture, women's liberationists challenged the establishment and social norms, determined to change society through liberation, activism, language, and new ways of thinking. In 'a Germaine moment', in March 1972, the visiting celebrity feminist Germaine Greer was arrested in Auckland for use of the word 'bullshit' in a public address at the town hall. Greer attracted a following among young women, because she was a 'saucy feminist': naughty, smart, fun, sexy, and outrageous. Through marches, theatre, and public protest, the women's libbers fought for legal change, especially concerning illegal abortion and equal pay.

Late-twentieth-century feminism grew from the international civil rights movement and anti–Vietnam War protests and drew especially on American influences. Young, urban, educated baby boomers – anti-racist, anti-sexist, and socialist – campaigned for peace, the environment, and revolution, including in sex roles. Young women university students were mortified to discover sexism in the peace and civil rights movements, where young men expected their female peers to make the tea and provide sexual comforts while they fought to free the oppressed. Such first-hand experience of second-rate status resolved the women's libbers to free women everywhere from a sexist, patriarchal society.

Vietnam War protests revealed that the class divide in politics was undergoing realignment, as the baby boomers grew up to join a new left, progressive middle class, keen to end the reign of the establishment. The peace protesters formed part of a broader movement seeking liberation from the strictures of the Cold War. Around the world a rising tide of issues-based protests foreshadowed a new politics that rejected conservative social norms and prejudices and embraced new, more fluid identities. Locally, Vietnam marked the end of consensus on foreign affairs and split the country. Young, educated professionals rallied to the Labour Party rather than National, attracted by Labour's anti-Vietnam stance.

Meanwhile both Britain and the United States were preparing to pull out of Southeast Asia. Britain's decision to withdraw strategically from east of Suez in 1967 was greeted with dismay, especially since this announcement coincided with a second British bid to join the European Economic Community (which became the European Union), a move that spelt economic withdrawal from its former empire and, combined with the Suez strategy, its effective abandonment. The British completed their withdrawal in the 1970s, while the United States retreated to the Philippines and Okinawa, leaving a rump of Australian and New Zealand military in Singapore. In the context of this great-power retreat New Zealand withdrew from Vietnam by late 1971, leaving two training teams to be recalled by the incoming Labour government.

From 1972 expressing a moral voice in the world proved the hallmark of the Labour government, led by Norman Kirk until his premature death, in 1974. 'Big Norm', as a youthful pop song affectionately called him, a former engine driver and a self-educated intellectual, who was in poor health, renewed the Labour tradition of an independent and visionary 'moral' foreign policy. With the end of the Vietnam War, Kirk opened diplomatic relations with the People's Republic of China and the Soviet Union. By striding across the world stage, he also tackled the hippie generation's bête noire of the 'cultural cringe', combining nationalism with internationalism. Kirk was on the same wavelength as the youth revolution protagonists, who perceived themselves as global citizens. He saw the country's smallness and isolation as an opportunity to mediate between small countries and superpowers to whom New Zealand posed no threat, much as Peter Fraser had done at the United Nations.

Progressive youth delighted in the Kirk government's promotion of a nuclear-weapons-free zone in the South Pacific. The cartoon *Big 3 ANZUS meeting* (see figure 8.4) shows Norman Kirk advancing his case for a nuclear-free zone in the South Pacific in the face of a battery of American military hardware brought to the ANZUS table by a dominating United States general, while

8.4 Eric W. Heath, *Big 3 ANZUS meeting*, 1974. The caption reads, 'Is there some reason we can't all support a nuclear-free zone, gentlemen?'
Dominion, 27 February 1974. Alexander Turnbull Library, Wellington, C-132-124. Courtesy of Eric Heath

Australia's foreign affairs minister stands to one side, wearing a 'Woomera Rocket Club' badge. The New Zealand public had opposed nuclear-weapons testing in the South Pacific since the 1960s, especially tests by France at Moruroa Atoll, irrespective of support for the ANZUS alliance.

Philosophically, opposition to nuclear testing coalesced with the rise of the environment movement. The South Island's world heritage national parks, Fiordland and Mount Cook, were created during the baby boomers' childhoods, in 1953, as was Urewera National Park, in 1954. Feelings grew of attachment to the landscape as more families took car trips and mobile holidays, staying at caravan parks or in motels. Developments in transport, such as the completion, in 1965, of the road through the Haast Pass from Wanaka to Westland, encouraged the trend. 'Freedom walking' of the Milford Track without a paid guide began in 1964.

But how protected were these scenic wonders and holiday places where the baby boomers learnt to explore? It was simply fortuitous that much future heritage landscape survived. As families discovered their own country, concern mounted about logging, mineral exploration, and rampant development without regard for scenic or conservation values. The 'Save Manapouri' campaign of the late 1960s and early 1970s marked a major shift in public attitudes, away from colonising the land and towards conserving natural resources, in this case by not raising the beautiful Lake Manapouri, in Fiordland National Park, for hydroelectric power. From 1960 successive governments approved a deal by Comalco, then a British–Australian conglomerate, to provide cheap power from Lake Manapouri for an aluminium smelter near Bluff, the southernmost port in the South Island. The initial proposal entailed raising the lake by 30 metres, which would have drowned most of the lake's islands and damaged neighbouring Lake Te Anau. The protest campaign raised critical questions of conservation versus development, domestic versus overseas capital, multinational corporations' threat to sovereignty, the role of the state, and the very values underpinning Kiwi culture. In this case public pressure resolved what a commission of inquiry in 1970 could not: a petition of 265 000 signatures organised in 1970 by the Royal Forest and Bird Protection Society stopped the lake level from being raised.

ECONOMIC INTERDEPENDENCIES

Environmental concerns, however, had yet to encompass the third round of the grasslands revolution, in which Kiwi pilots conquered the last frontier of rugged hill country as pioneers of aerial top dressing. Hill country hitherto off limits to pasture was sprayed from the air with phosphate dug up from the island of Nauru, without regard for the consequences in either place. Research using radioactive cobalt had also shown up cobalt deficiencies in the soil. Aerial top dressing with cobalt extended the grasslands revolution to the pumice lands of the central North Island and overcame the problem of 'bush sickness' in sheep. The new technology reflected new interdependencies once modes of travel became airborne. With the use of aircraft in hill-country farming, sheep numbers rose nearly 40 per cent in the 1950s. A far-sighted teacher and author, H. C. D. Somerset, quoted the farmer who worried about the unknown effects on the land of this 'new pioneering' and 'new husbandry': 'For all we know we may be taxing it more than it will stand, even with all our manuring'. The scientific farmer was preparing to turn environmentalist.

Aircraft accelerated the process of globalisation, which strengthened ties and forged new links throughout the world. By 1970 the cost of air travel had fallen to the level of sea travel, with the effect that adventurers no longer had to spend a minimum of three months away from home. Jet aircraft arrived with their deafening engines in the 1960s, after the government bought out the Qantas shareholding in Tasman Empire Airways Limited. This company, subject to state supervision by Britain, New Zealand, and Australia, had begun using British flying boats across the Tasman Sea during the war. Both Australia and New Zealand opted for a national carrier that travelled internationally to address issues of security and remoteness. Air New Zealand emerged as the national airline, flying American Douglas aircraft, in 1965. It limited its ambitions before 1973 to the Tasman route and the Pacific, flying to Los Angeles, Hong Kong, and Singapore.

Economically, the country stayed committed to the old Commonwealth club, because that offered the best assurance of external stability. The Commonwealth economic network formed a tight sterling area after the Second World War, not always comfortable for being familial, but 'lubricated by trust', thanks to the tie of kinship. The United States was no friend in trade, unlike in defence, although it was certainly powerful, and increasingly so. Had Australia and New Zealand left the sterling area they would still have had to overcome United States agricultural protectionism, which was impossible.

Inevitably the sterling area started to unravel in the 1950s, commensurate with Britain's decline as a world power. Wartime bulk-purchase agreements ended in 1954, though New Zealand retained duty-free access for meat and dairy products until 1967. This shift in the power base of the world economy compelled a reordering of relationships with Britain and other countries, as did a change in tastes away from butter, cheese, and carcasses of frozen lamb and mutton. It was harder for New Zealand to adapt to changes in the international environment than it was for Australia, which diversified by mining minerals.

Boom prices for wool during the Korean War initially masked the brewing difficulties but also led to a drop in the proportion of exports going to Britain, as wool more readily found new markets than did butter fat. High wool prices also propelled the grasslands revolution and environmental overreach through aerial top dressing. Economic historians argue that the postwar boom ended at the wool sales during the 1966–7 season, when the wool price crashed and the Wool Commission, established in 1952, bought over 80 per cent of the wool at auction. Not merely the 'pastoral era' ended with a lurch, but also the long boom.

In many ways 1967 heralded the end of the years of prosperity. Faced with another balance-of-payments crisis, the National government responded in the customary 'stop-go' style with budget cuts. Not only the 'six o'clock swill' ended in 1967, but also the 'ten o'clock swill' of school milk, at the request of education boards. That was a relief for schoolchildren who disliked warm milk. More stressful (still more for adults) was the switch from imperial weights and measures to metric measures and decimal arithmetic. The beloved British system of ounces, pounds, feet, miles, and acres was bid goodbye; in came grams, kilograms, metres, kilometres, and hectares. Also in 1967, symbolic of power shifts, out went pounds, shillings, and pence, and in came decimal currency, the dollar reflective of the rise of the United States to global financial dominance.

Australia's decision to adopt decimal currency, in 1966, foreshadowed the break of the British tie. Moreover, the concept of the dollar was popular with the public. The democratic process produced a distinctive New Zealand coinage (see figure 8.5). All the hallmarks of populism were there: Captain Cook's *Endeavour* sailed across the 50 cent coin; the informal national emblem, the kiwi, featured on the 20 cents, with a fern backdrop; while a fern leaf furled around the 1 cent piece. A kowhai bedecked the 2 cent piece, a tuatara the 5 cent, and a tiki the 10 cent, the last of these satisfactory as a replacement for the popular Māori warrior on the old shilling. Except for the tuatara, which made the link to Gondwana, all these images had a marketing pedigree: Māori motifs, the silver fern on war graves, sports jerseys, and butter wrappers. The choice of symbols suggested identification with the environment.

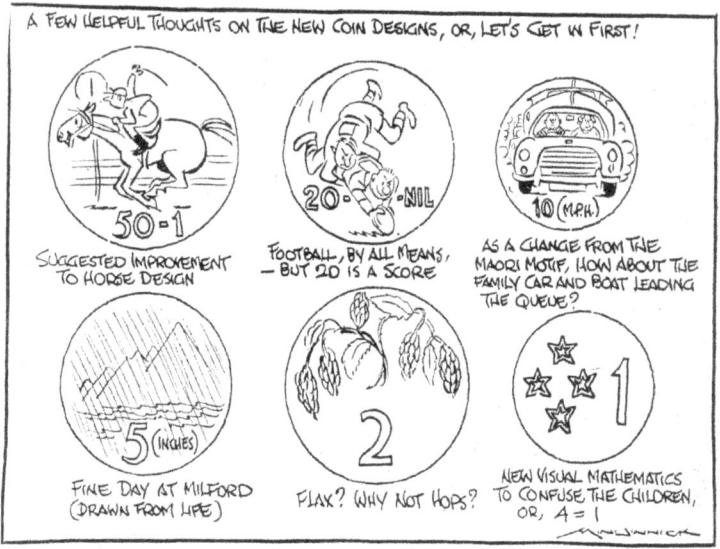

8.5 G. E. G. Minhinnick, *Tails you lose!*, 1966
New Zealand Herald, 3 February 1966. Courtesy of *New Zealand Herald*

Decimal currency also marked a commitment to closer ties with Australia. The New Zealand dollar was devalued, not by the British amount, but by nearly 20 per cent, which restored the parity with Australia lost in 1948. Parity with the Australian dollar increased competitiveness and made it possible for businesses to compete across the Tasman.

Britain's turn away from the Commonwealth towards Europe caused Australia and New Zealand to draw closer together. The crunch came in 1961 when Britain announced its decision to enter the European Economic Community and to abandon its colonial family of food producers for former enemies. New Zealand had few options in the face of such a threat. But for French president Charles de Gaulle's veto against Britain's entry to the Common Market, New Zealand's export economy would have suffered. Clearly Britain was looking after its own interests. The United States, too, was keen for Britain to join the European Economic Community. With the terms of trade in decline, the government used the breathing space from the breakdown in the British–European negotiations to reorder its trade relations with Australia. Policymakers saw salvation in freer trade and in closer relations with Asia (a future recognised by Australia first) and with each other.

New Zealand had studied the prospect of freer trade with Australia since 1956, when Prime Minister Sid Holland had negotiated greater access for New Zealand timber and newsprint. Forestry – specifically the pulp and paper industry – was one of the few industries capable of expanding exports to Australia. New Zealand also became an important market for Holden cars. After talks in 1960 the two governments resolved to tackle common problems by working together as closely as possible. They agreed to cooperate in dealing with the prospect of the loss of British trade privileges as Britain looked to enter the European Economic Community. Meetings of the Australia–New Zealand Consultative Committee on Trade in 1960, of ministers in 1961, and of a joint standing committee of officials from 1960 examined proposals for a free trade area. Britain tried, and failed, to block any agreement.

Expansion of the forestry industry contributed to strengthening trans-Tasman ties. Large plantations of radiata pine established between the wars in the central North Island were ready for harvesting from the 1940s. The state-owned Kaingaroa Forest and the Murupara project to which it gave rise were intended to diversify the export economy and to save millions of dollars by supplying Australia and New Zealand with a substitute for American newsprint. Loans from London and the United States financed the paper mills. In an entrepreneurial state rerun, the government established a joint venture with business – Fletchers – to create the carefully branded Tasman Pulp and Paper Company, whose manufacturing plant at Kawerau was in full swing by the late 1950s. A new town, Murupara, was built to house forestry workers, while power came from geothermal resources on the volcanic plateau. A new port was built at Tauranga for the forestry hinterland. Tasman became the country's single largest manufacturing export plant, contributing 50 per cent of manufactured exports by 1965 and 45 per cent of all exports to Australia.

The growing trans-Tasman community of interest in New Zealand pine plantations and wood pulp influenced the signing, in 1965, of the New Zealand–Australia Free Trade Agreement, which only partially espoused free trade. Two-way trade increased by over 50 per cent in the five years from 1965–6 to 1970–1. By the end of the decade Australia met all its import requirements for newsprint and pulp from New Zealand; 95 per cent of exports of newsprint were to Australia.

Australia also provided a model for postwar development of an insulated kind, which manufacturers adapted and used to justify a change of direction that built on the shared model of state development from the 1890s. Sir Woolf Fisher, of Fisher & Paykel whitegoods, led a trade mission to Australia in 1959. The economic nationalist Bill Sutch (who was probably a spy for the Soviet Union) and other officials also embraced the Australian model of development as a way of reducing imports. Sutch saw the need to broaden the narrow structure of the economy and to reduce vulnerability to fluctuations, perceiving the farm and financial sectors as wedded to colonial dependence.

Thus various trends converged to persuade Australia and New Zealand to adopt a pattern of managing a transformed position in the world, first by diversifying their economies and second by showing interest in their region and in each other. Because of ANZUS and British withdrawal from the Pacific, the two also behaved more as if they occupied a regional zone of defence. Trans-Tasman air travel had a big effect on popular culture, increasing the frequency of trans-Tasman sporting contests, the circulation of Australian magazines, and informal contacts.

In the end, Britain's withdrawal from empire and turn to Europe proved a nemesis. No longer could the United Kingdom's strategic interests be reconciled with the British Commonwealth as an economic community. The end of the British embrace generated a prolonged, anguished 'fight for survival'. Many older, better-off Pākehā New Zealanders considered as betrayal Britain's entry, in January 1973, to the European Economic Community. That was a fair judgment, given the enigmatic prospect of compulsory decolonisation, at speed, not of Pacific Islanders but of themselves.

9
Latest experiments 1973–1996

The final three decades of the twentieth century bore witness to the most violent ruptures since colonisation and the two world wars. Revolutions in economic, defence, and public policy altered how this small country related to the world, shook the political landscape into new patterns, and unsettled the settler society. New Zealanders found themselves gasping from the change of water in their fishbowl, their ways of life buffeted and transformed. Suddenly – but not inevitably – governments demolished institutions that had been political defining features. It was as if, overnight, everyone lived in another country, so radical were the shifts in values.

The Depression and war generations felt anxious about what they experienced as decolonisation. No such unease afflicted baby boomers, provided they were well educated and not in public service jobs. Late boomers were still at school in 1973. Apocalyptically, Britain's turn to Europe overlapped with the abandonment of the ideas embedded in the Australasian settlement. In the language of mateship common to the masculine worlds of sport and politics, not only the rules of the game but the game itself had changed. The worker and to a lesser extent the farmer, the sheep farmer especially, were no longer wanted on the team. The world economy shifted from dominance by agriculture and manufacturing to a post-industrial emphasis on the service sector. Changes in technology created new jobs and rendered old unskilled ones obsolete. Traditional jobs for working-class men disappeared, spawning a new problem, of low male-employment levels. In this context, the settler contract was redundant.

From the 1980s New Zealand faced the restructured world economy with a brand-new set of experiments devised by political leaders influenced by the counterculture and student radicalism. These new, young leaders embraced globalisation, which may be defined as the 'process of deepening and changing links throughout the global economy', and the spread of capitalist economic relations. Here the focus is on economic integration; refreshed cultural links are addressed in chapter 10.

Three disturbing events in the 1970s confirmed the end of the 'golden weather' bestowed by greater postwar prosperity and foreshadowed a sequence of extreme responses to the transformed global environment. Britain's entry to the European Economic Community, in January 1973, was the most symbolic disturbance for people who had grown comfortable supplying the British dinner table, although New Zealand's exports and trade relationships were diversifying before 1973, which suggested there was no need to panic. Another event was the end of the Bretton Woods system of fixed exchange rates, after which the New Zealand dollar was 'pegged' to a basket of currencies. The first 'oil shock', of 1973–4, marked a third radical change, as oil producers in the Middle East formed a cartel and increased prices dramatically. Though the first oil shock, followed by a second, in 1979, caused by the Iranian Revolution, did not prove permanent, the steep rises in oil prices shocked the country. They induced sharp tremors in the balance-of-payments deficit, which jumped from 0 to 14 per cent of gross domestic product in 1974–5, compelled a resort to borrowing, and depressed the national mood. After 1974 New Zealand routinely recorded balance-of-payments deficits. With the oil crises, suddenly all the country's major markets contracted, hobbling the strategy to boost economic growth by diversifying exports.

At the same time alarm grew that New Zealand's economic performance and standards of living had slipped below averages in the Organisation for Economic Co-operation and Development (OECD). As with health statistics earlier in the century, this ignominious placement on a global league table clashed with the national image of natural abundance. New Zealand slid from the top five among OECD countries to nineteenth by 1980 as global

Latest experiments 1973–1996 223

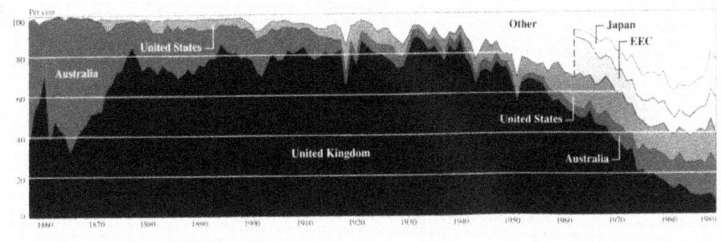

9.1 Trading partners. Proportion of total exports going to different markets, 1860–1989
Department of Statistics, *New Zealand Official 1990 Yearbook*, Wellington, 1990, 599
Note: Year ending 31 December to 1961, then 30 June. EEC: European Economic Community.

demand for its primary products ebbed. Especially galling was the fall in average real incomes relative to those in Australia. To add to economic woes, a rare combination of rising unemployment and high inflation, the latter of which rocketed to 18 per cent in 1976, baffled economists and policymakers. New Zealand, like most countries, had to restructure its economy and attempt to control overseas debt. Painfully, the country metamorphosed from Britain's farm to an exporter around the Pacific Rim and beyond, especially to Australia and Asia.

This transition was well under way by the 1970s, if not by that point incorporated in national types and myths. The underlying trend in the percentage of exports going to Britain, Australia, and elsewhere shows that export market and product diversification had proceeded steadily since the Second World War (see figure 9.1). The evenness of the underlying trend is striking in the decline of Britain as New Zealand's major trading partner during the second half of the twentieth century. The rate of change quickened briefly around 1973 but slowed for the remainder of the 1970s and 1980s, demonstrating that a long-run process was at work.

Some historians argue that 1973 marked the pivotal moment in national life, with the end of revived dependence on Britain. A 'misdiagnosis' of this change, a blinkered failure to see it as the core problem facing the country, led subsequent governments down the wrong path. However, the economic evidence used to promote it, illustrated in figure 9.1, does not support this interpretation.

Common sense suggests that 1973 and 1984, the latter a year of instant globalisation under the fourth Labour government, were both turning points in New Zealand history, the former due especially to the first oil shock. Both spelt moments of drama when domestic politics were thrown into turmoil by global and regional pressures. Both, moreover, exposed the underlying dilemma of how to manage size and remoteness. New Zealand and Australia experienced rapid and extensive economic liberalisation, not unlike that in Central Europe, in the 1980s and 1990s. New Zealand provides the more extreme example, because its reforms were faster and wider ranging. Further, the New Zealand reforms followed an era that is commonly associated with 'big government'. It is therefore necessary to examine the lurch from regulation to deregulation mindful that it is not a diagnosis that leads to certain outcomes in terms of policy change but a political process of ideas, leaders, and institutions.

MULDOONISM

In New Zealand culture, the package of ideas, leaders, and institutions in the era of the National government from 1975 to 1984 is named 'Muldoonism', after Robert Muldoon, the prime minister and minister of finance, who first rose to prominence for directing the changeover to decimal currency. An accountant, he distrusted the free market, believing in the tradition of managing the economy and society so that ordinary people could benefit from capitalism and be 'protected from its excesses'.

Although he was short (about 5 feet 4 inches, or 160 centimetres), Muldoon intimidated people with his laser-cold blue eyes and learnt as a child to use his sharp tongue to defend himself. The first politician to use television to his advantage, he expressed his philosophy in a distinctive growl on screen and recorded his views for posterity in multiple autobiographies. 'For my part I look back to Britain', he asserted in 1981. Muldoon held to a 1950s view of the 'New Zealand way of life'. Raised by his mother and grandmother in Auckland, he knew too well the stigma and hardship that accompanied the loss of a male breadwinner and held unwaveringly to the belief that social security was a right.

Muldoon's legacy is mixed and has been disparaged by successive governments. His generous and expensive non-contributory national superannuation scheme for senior citizens aged over 60 years, which initially pegged payments at 80 per cent of the average wage, manifested 'political ageing': a shift from youth to old age as a priority of social policy. Its chief beneficiaries, Muldoon's peers, have been called the 'welfare generation', because the welfare system changed to suit them at every stage of their lives. The super scheme was affordable only because high inflation pushed taxpayers into higher income-tax brackets (the top rate was then 66 per cent) and it was non-contributory, payable out of the government's consolidated fund. New rules operated subsequently for the baby boomers and their children, the latter of whom faced student loans from the 1990s.

To many people Muldoon stood for 'divide and rule' politics, hostility to the world, and totalitarianism. The prime minister's closest colleagues described him as a 'genuine, combative, populist demagogue'. 'Rob's mob' – his key supporters – represented the conservative, ordinary bloke of middling New Zealand, from the returned serviceman to the Māori gang member. Groups scorned by such politics, on the other hand, protesters of all sorts (including educated Māori, the women's movement, peace movement, civil rights movement, and conservationists), revolted against Muldoonism as a regime of colonialism continued (see chapter 10).

In turn, Muldoon (nicknamed 'Piggy' for his looks and style) launched further attacks on the counterculture. He regulated the economy and society through the abuse of executive power. If interest rates soared too high with inflation, he regulated them downwards. A supplementary minimum-price scheme to subsidise farmers encouraged unwarranted growth in sheep numbers. The second oil shock produced a perverse short-term regime of 'car-less days', for which motorists nominated a day – indicated by a sticker on their car's windscreen – when they would not drive. Rising unemployment mingled with a sense of oppression, divisiveness, gloom, and doom stirred thousands of young people to respond by departing for Australia in search of opportunities and a brighter future. Those who left found that they had to apply to the Reserve Bank to take their savings out of the country. A price and wage freeze imposed by exploiting the eccentric 1948 Economic Stabilisation Act crowned the edifice of controls in 1982.

According to critics, the traditional mixed economy accordingly lapsed into a 'command economy'. A series of Think Big development projects to reduce dependence on imported energy sources appeared to confirm that judgment. They included methanol and ammonia–urea plants and a synthetic-fuel plant, expansion of the national oil refinery and of New Zealand Steel (established in the 1960s), and a fast-tracked hydroelectric project: the Clyde Dam, completed in 1988. Recent scholarship, however, has disputed whether the New Zealand economy under Muldoon was uniquely 'highly regulated'. Alongside the Think Big schemes, the Muldoon government abolished food subsidies and price controls and relaxed financial controls before the freeze.

In this context of ad hoc responses, it is striking that Muldoon signed the free trade agreement in December 1982 that underwrites New Zealand's economic relations with Australia: the Australia–New Zealand Closer Economic Relations Trade Agreement (CER), implemented in January 1983. 'With his backing' the agreement 'was bound to succeed'. Doug Anthony, the Australian deputy prime minister, who led the negotiations, recalled that his hardest job was handling the respective prime ministers, because Muldoon and Australia's Malcolm Fraser disliked each other. Figure 9.2 suggests why, from Muldoon's perspective. His attitude to Australia is captured in the joke made by a columnist that the exodus of New Zealanders to Australia raised the IQ of both countries. Importantly, Muldoon had a rapport with Anthony, while Fraser related well to Brian Talboys, the diplomatic New Zealand deputy prime minister. Together, in 1978 Fraser and Talboys issued the landmark Nareen statement (named for Fraser's rural property), which affirmed that Australia and New Zealand were linked by 'deep ties of common origin and shared ideas and institutions'. This logically suggested that they would face new global circumstances together and encourage closer relations with each other. Their prime ministers had met annually since the 1960s, and numerous links had developed under the New Zealand–Australia

9.2 Robert Muldoon (right) and Malcolm Fraser, 1980
Copyright unknown

Free Trade Agreement, helped by improved communications. But that agreement became bogged in detail. Anthony's proposal for a 'closer economic association', to take advantage of new opportunities, especially in Asia, followed Talboys' initiatives to work together internationally and in the region and set in train the process that led from the earlier (1965) to the later (1983) agreement.

At the end of the Muldoon years the Australia–New Zealand Closer Economic Relations Trade Agreement shone as the major positive legacy of the Muldoon National government. Two-way trade expanded 500 per cent. The agreement, initiated quietly, proved a big success, helped by a historically integrated labour market. Capital markets were also linked. Australia became New Zealand's biggest trading partner, while New Zealand was Australia's fifth largest market and, importantly, often the first export market for Australian business. Economically the countries integrated rapidly in unprecedented ways. Any shopping trip demonstrated this, whether to buy clothing, furniture, or food, in both countries, using Australian banking facilities. The two economies had integrated and moved so closely together by the beginning of the twenty-first century that the New Zealand and New South Wales economies marched in lock step.

Consequently, the Australia–New Zealand Closer Economic Relations Trade Agreement is celebrated as the most comprehensive, effective, and mutually compatible free trade agreement in the world. This confounds any analysis of the Muldoon era as being associated solely with big government. The trade agreement is routinely not associated with Muldoonism, which is synonymous with regulation, cynical abuse of democracy, and dictatorship; yet it shares that lineage.

ROGERNOMICS

The package of ideas, leaders, and institutions associated with the economic liberalisation experiment that followed Muldoonism and used its worst features as an excuse came to be known as 'Rogernomics'. These reforms were named for Roger Douglas, the minister of finance in the fourth Labour government, which swept into office in a snap election in July 1984. A new generation of policymakers keen to end the reign of the establishment – and to become the establishment – formed 'arguably, the most radical government in New Zealand's history'. It was also the best educated and dominated by lawyers. Several ministers were still in their thirties, and members of the leadership in their early forties. The new prime minister, David Lange, a 'complicated and gifted man' who loved India and fun parks, delighted the public with his witty intelligence, his quips, and his humanism. While Lange operated among the many, his henchman, Douglas, who grew up in a state house, was an ideologically enthusiastic and uncompromising neoliberal. An atmosphere of energy, free of Muldoon, surrounded the new government, in whom the people placed great expectations, unaware of the path ahead.

An aura of crisis created the opportunity for Douglas and his supporters in Lange's Cabinet to launch the swathe of economic reforms. Rogernomics reformers believed that the 'jerry-built economic structure' required 'drastic restructuring' as a 'matter of urgency'. More immediately, New Zealand suffered a costly run on the dollar before and after the snap election. The enduring image of crisis was of Muldoon himself, announcing the election on television with slurred speech, while he was drunk, and refusing after the election to devalue the dollar, against the advice of the incoming government. This violated constitutional conventions. A currency crisis therefore bred a constitutional crisis, cementing convictions that Muldoon had pitched the country headlong into economic chaos.

The devaluation crisis and its threat to the country's reputation for political stability justified, but did not determine, the shape of the reforms that followed. Long-run justifications for the Rogernomics revolution included the decline in economic performance relative to the OECD average, the massive balance-of-payments deficit, rampaging inflation, the expensive national superannuation scheme, excessive regulation, the Think Big projects, and the general failure to adjust to changing realities. Allegedly the body politic had become infected with all the problems said to be poisoning capitalism, such as import and capital controls, strong trade unions, a large state sector, and a redistributive welfare state. New Zealand, the neoliberal reformers argued, had still not adjusted to Britain's abandonment of empire, thanks to Muldoon's intransigence, and had immediately to catch up with the rest of the world. Salvation lay with the free market.

Rogernomics has been likened to a 'blitzkrieg', because the reforms proceeded so fast and so extensively, with all the zeal of a crusade. Lange's Cabinet intoned the motto 'We will do the right thing', bonded by a sense of crisis and the 'audacity' of its policy directions. Twenty years later, ministers insisted they did do 'the right thing'. This creates a philosophical problem, because to assume that you know what the right thing is indicates a conviction of rightness, that there is a right way and a wrong way, and that people who disagree with you are wrong: 'there is no alternative', in the contemporary catchphrase. There is always an alternative, as the Australian case shows. (Australia enjoyed better outcomes from less radical reforms.)

In pursuit of change, an inner circle of reformers in the Cabinet, the Treasury, and the Reserve Bank demolished the Australasian model of state development that their forebears had created in response to similar global forces 90 years earlier and supplanted it with an Anglo-American neoliberal orthodoxy associated with Margaret Thatcher and Ronald Reagan. The speed and extent of reforms depended much on thinking that Treasury and Reserve Bank advisers had already done. Reformers resolved to return the country to this orthodoxy, citing examples of economic mismanagement that ranged from the Margarine Act 1908 (designed to protect butter) to Muldoon's misuse of the Economic Stabilisation Act 1948 to regulate the economy.

Moreover, the reformers intended that their revolution would be irreversible. So concerned were the change agents with their place in history that they ignored lessons contained in institutional memory and traditions created by their reformist forebears. The ideology of the free market would brook no competition from a historical set of 'state experiments'. Rather, a new set would take their place, and the workingman's paradise would be pensioned off, the old compromise of social protection against vicissitudes of the market abandoned. A pioneering heritage demanded no less.

While the Labour Party membership and the public knew that change was necessary, the proposed means of change provoked an ideological struggle between the parliamentary Labour Party and the Cabinet and, most destructively for the party, between Lange and Douglas. Some argue that change became the end, not the means. For his part, Douglas did not wait to consult beyond his inner circle, because he believed that consultation would thwart his goals. His Treasury advisers shared this mindset, because the government lacked a consensus over whether the proposed economic reforms represented the appropriate way forwards.

In up-ending historic state experiments, the comprehensive reform package embraced globalisation. Disciples could market Rogernomics as another 'New Zealand experiment' and even the 'great experiment' precisely because the lurch to neoliberalism was so extreme and abrupt. New Zealand presented the ideal field trial for structural reform. In the late twentieth century, furthermore, a single house of parliament that could push through reforms added gloss to the laboratory conditions. Continuities were not merely rhetorical; New Zealand again created an edifice of liberal 'state experiments' to manage global forces. Only the new set eagerly accepted globalisation without cushioning it and threw out the old set. While it is disputed how far some outcomes were unintended, traditional icons and labour values were relegated to the rubbish tip as deviant and obsolete.

The market's icon was not the worker but the consumer, presented with an alluring choice of things to buy, from clothing made in China to cars made in Japan. The worker turned into a tradeable commodity. Finance capital outstripped industrial capital, and power transferred to people and institutions with access to international finance. That debt should bestow power, not shame, illustrated the shift in values. Restructuring related directly to transformed global links. Unemployment and structural change in the economy from industry to services and information technology also helped unravel old accommodations. Henceforth neoliberals strove to expose the economy to external shocks to make it more adaptable and resilient.

From 1984, therefore, New Zealand underwent 'a theory driven revolution' derived from neoclassical, theoretical economics and New Right philosophies, including (but not confined to) the monetarism of Milton Friedman and the Chicago School, public choice and agency theory, and the new institutional economics. A small elite of strategically placed individuals in the Cabinet, the Treasury, and the Reserve Bank introduced the changes, supported by the Business Roundtable, whose members comprised CEOs drawn from the 200 largest companies. Within this circle, Douglas worked with the Treasury before running ideas past his associate finance ministers, lawyers Richard Prebble and David Caygill, followed by lawyers David Lange and his deputy Geoffrey Palmer. Three finance ministers were appointed because of the amount of work the reforms generated. The group – which has been described as an 'elected dictatorship' – then persuaded the Cabinet. Leaders of the inner circle and their friends had been graduate students in the United States. Embarrassed by the smallness and parochialism of their quaint country, they returned home yearning to drag New Zealand into the global village.

Local circumstances, however, made the changes that New Zealanders experienced faster, more extensive, and closer to theoretical purity than those elsewhere. It is now accepted that New Zealand's reforms occurred in the wrong sequence, with labour market reform last in the series; the ideal ordering of initiatives was impossible to implement. The first economic reforms introduced financial deregulation. Following Australia, the Labour government floated the exchange rate, deregulated banking, and abolished exchange and price controls. It dismantled trade barriers and removed import licensing, while farmers faced the sudden removal of agricultural subsidies, because the government believed that international market signals should guide resource use. It targeted inflation and held the Reserve Bank responsible for maintaining the inflation rate between 0 and 2 per cent, which became a requirement under the Reserve Bank Act 1989 (the upper bound was 3 per cent from 1996). Tax reform followed, to broaden the tax base: within two years (in 1986) Labour introduced a goods and services tax of 10 per cent on all domestic spending except financial services, before raising it to 12.5 per cent in 1989. Marginal income-tax rates flattened; the top tax rate slid from 66 per cent to 33 per cent by 1988. The government also introduced a tax surcharge on national superannuation.

Public sector reforms made familiar institutions unrecognisable. Service arms of government had business mores imposed on them, damaging the values and quality of the core public service by use of language that expressed the ethos of cost-cutting and competition. In one critic's view, 'the new order turned the public service inside out'. Policy split from delivery functions and funders from providers. To reflect on strategy, for example, New Zealand established a defence ministry separate from the defence force, which reported separately to ministers. The State Sector Act 1988 applied a commercial model to government departments, shifting emphasis from policy advice to responsibility for the management of resources by the restructured public sector.

The Department of Labour and the State Services Commission fared better, because they restructured themselves. Labour market reform proved to be the only instance in which interest groups were consulted. While the ripple effect of wage adjustments under the old arbitration system ceased in 1984, under the Labour Relations Act 1987 a labour court and voluntary arbitration commission replaced the historic system of compulsory arbitration. Capital and labour ceased to be at the core of state development.

Reforms to government trading arms achieved the most success in efficiency terms. From 1987 state-owned enterprises were legislatively required to act as businesses and pursue the profit motive. The State-Owned Enterprises Act, passed in October 1986, established nine state-owned corporations, including three split from the dismembered post office: NZ Post, Postbank (previously the Post Office Savings Bank), and Telecom. State sector unions that opposed restructuring, suspicious that it would lead to state asset sales, were assured that the reforms represented the 'answer', not the 'road to privatisation', and that no one would lose their job.

For the unions, deception comprised the Rogernomics means of change, since, from one obscurantist word and process to another, corporatisation did lead rapidly to privatisation. Public asset sales extended from Telecom, Postbank, and State Insurance to the Think Big projects. Government mortgages, the Rural Bank, cutting rights in state forests, Air New Zealand, and the railways were all sold. Thus, the public infrastructure created over the previous century was outfitted in corporate clothing and put up for tender. Big business did well out of the sales of public assets, while the merchant bankers who brokered the sales did best of all. Fletcher Challenge acquired Think Big projects, and Business Roundtable members enjoyed appointments as chairmen of state-owned enterprises. In this sense the tradition of the entrepreneurial state continued. Scandal attached to the fate of the Bank of New Zealand, which had to be rescued, in a story that paralleled the 1890s. Saved by the taxpayer after it had been partly privatised by merchant bankers, the flagship bank was sold to the National Australia Bank.

Social costs were high. Rather than slashing short-term costs, the reforms maximised them for those affected. Transaction costs were huge. A career public service disappeared. The Cabinet overlooked the effects of multiple restructurings on small communities: small towns lost their local post offices (432 in total), defining institutions that had eased remoteness since the nineteenth century. More importantly, every step in the restructuring program produced a wave of redundancies. Former post office employees and workers in the forestry industry in the central North Island – often Māori – were particularly hard hit. One affected community was the coal town of Huntly, between Hamilton and Auckland. Huntly suffered a severe blow from the corporatisation of state coal mines in 1987 under the State-Owned Enterprises Act. Miners and their families had little time to prepare for job losses. Over half the workforce (484 employees) were laid off just 19 days after the public announcement at the Huntly rugby grounds that staffing levels would shrink from 1728 in State Coal to 892 in CoalCorp. Policies developed in Wellington to address redeployment and redundancy proved inappropriate for such communities, in which restructuring imposed the biggest impact.

Despite public resistance to Rogernomics by the late 1980s, a National government from 1990 picked up the reform policies and pursued yet more change. The Employment Contracts Act 1991 radically deregulated the labour market and adopted individual contracts in employment. For the union movement the cycle had returned to the nineteenth century. Ironically, individuals such as Jim Bolger, the National prime minister from 1990 and previously associated with the Muldoon era, extended more-market reforms to social policy.

This agenda dictated severe welfare cuts in 1991. Ruth Richardson, representative of the 'new broom' New Right as the first woman minister of finance, set out to shift responsibility for family welfare from the state to the individual under a regime that equated self-reliance with personal responsibility and paid work. She is remembered for her 'mother of all budgets', in 1991, which slashed government spending across the board. Policymakers expressed faith in the claim that economic growth would 'deliver jobs and reduce welfare dependency'. Thus, successive governments embraced orthodox, neoliberal approaches to rising welfare expenditure.

CONTINUITIES

Striking continuities exist between Muldoonism and Rogernomics, because the streamlined Westminster system in the second half of the twentieth century allowed a concentration of power in the

Cabinet that was 'enormous' and 'intolerable'. Both Muldoonism and Rogernomics illustrated extremes in the use and misuse of executive power by an inner circle of strong personalities who dominated policymaking in a small society. If Muldoon's attempt to manage the postmodern dilemmas of the late twentieth century was short term and ad hoc, while the approach pursued by Rogernomics aimed to be long term and coherent, the country's small scale made possible both swings of the pendulum.

Each exploited the absence of checks and balances found in larger democracies. New Zealand's unicameral political system was simple: without an upper house, there were no parliamentary checks on executive power; the first-past-the-post voting system ensured that the Cabinet controlled the legislature. No written constitution stood silently sentinel to collective values. Rather, the rules that made up the New Zealand constitution were found in law, conventions, and practice. In a perceived crisis, it was easy for missionary reformers to pursue their beliefs, while a village-like culture reinforced the dearth of debate.

Law reformer and Deputy Prime Minister Geoffrey Palmer moved to check this 'unbridled power' by drafting the Constitution Act 1986, motivated by the constitutional crisis of July 1984, precipitated when Muldoon refused to devalue the currency. The 1986 Act was more a tidy-up than an experiment. Significantly, this law finally 'patriated' the constitution, removing the United Kingdom's residual powers to make law for New Zealand at the request of the New Zealand parliament.

By itself the Constitution Act was not enough to check executive power. Briefed about the grim economic outlook after the 1990 election, the National government, led by Jim Bolger, a Waikato farmer, pressed on with reforms in health, the labour market, immigration, social welfare, and education, among other areas of public policy. A case study of continuities is given by the 1990s health reforms. Statistics showed that the health system before the reforms performed well by OECD standards; ideology, however, judged that public hospitals, which consumed about 70 per cent of the health budget, were inefficient. In 1988 a hospital taskforce, chaired by businessman and head of one of the new state-owned enterprises Alan Gibbs, decided restructuring was the panacea for the public hospital system's alleged woes. The Gibbs Report, *Unshackling the Hospitals* (1988), asserted that the traditional triumvirate of matron, medical superintendent, and administrator stifled leadership in hospitals and led to weak hospital management by allowing medical professionals undue influence. Instead, nurses, doctors, and administrators should be responsible to a CEO, and hospitals should be run competitively as businesses.

The Bolger National government duly introduced wide-ranging market-oriented health reforms based on the previous government's Gibbs Report, which transformed the culture of healthcare delivery. No other country with a public health system introduced such unfettered market reforms. Neither the health sector nor the public was consulted, on the assumption that health professionals would capture the process; collective memory and expertise were pilloried. The forcing of a managerial model on health destroyed the hospital career path for nurses, so that many of the most experienced health workers left. Events soon disproved the theories.

Scholars have since confirmed what practitioners in public hospitals knew: that market approaches to the delivery of health care have 'major limitations'. The health experiments were unsustainable. From 1993 the belief that funders should be split from providers justified dividing the country into four different health systems, each with its own contractual arrangements and standards of care. Imposing a competitive model on the public health system polarised clinicians and managers and had to be abandoned in 1996 as untenable. The greatest lesson learnt was in what not to do. Structural change itself – four times in a decade – was demonstrated to be 'an impediment for the health sector'.

Through the politics of experiment, New Zealand transformed from one of the most regulated to one of the freest economies in the world. Old institutions vanished. New identities emerged, many informally and some forcefully. Few lamented the abandonment of the historic compromise shared with Australia, because of its rigidities. The speed and mode of change were the problem, along with the neglect of people's wellbeing, including a replacement for the settler contract, and not listening. If the rush to deregulate seemed headlong in Australia compared with New Zealand, in the former, at least, the federal political system ensured a more selective and gradual approach to reform.

Arguably the greatest benefits of free trade derived not from Rogernomics but from the Australia–New Zealand Closer Economic Relations Trade Agreement, which prepared New Zealand to be internationally competitive and developed business confidence. The agreement was extended from goods to services in 1988, and remaining barriers were removed by 1990, five years ahead of schedule, although areas of cultural sensitivity such as television broadcasting remained exempt. The economy grew more resilient from embracing globalisation, but many of the gains moved offshore.

Socially, the prosperity promised to 'trickle down' to the nation failed to eventuate. Income inequality grew more rapidly than in any other country in the OECD, as real incomes of low-income households fell between 1984 and 1996. Inevitably the winners were the educated and affluent, whose lives were enriched by choice and opportunities. The language of class itself became a casualty as global capitalism triumphed over labour.

From the 1990s, however, gross national product per capita began to recover, prompting the Treasury to infer from long-term trends that the institutional and policy reforms of the 1980s were responsible. The shopper, not the worker, benefited from the open economy once the farmer and the worker were no longer the focus and rationale of state development. From the 1980s cafe culture arrived. Rusty cars vanished from the roads and were replaced by late-model imports. Trans-Tasman retail chains graced rebuilt shopping malls. Food, wine, and the hospitality industry grew more cosmopolitan, and life more interesting and varied for those with purchasing power.

Underneath the technicolour consumerism, however, lurked a problem evident from the early twentieth century: technological advances and productivity were crucial to economic growth. Technological innovation was not the focus of this experiment, which centred in practice on abandonment of the past and on cutting costs. For this reason Rogernomics could not deliver to low-income and ordinary people what its apostles promised.

Globalisation, on the other hand, demanded new approaches to issues at the heart of how people identified with place and community. New Zealanders accepted the need for change, if not such radical change. Despite the pain of constant experiment, they generally embraced the process as a way of adjusting to their country's size, remoteness from the rest of the world, and slim resources. Globalisation encouraged a broader outlook. Many options lie between the poles of parochialism and globalism, and nowhere are these more evident than in defence policy.

NUCLEAR-FREE NEW ZEALAND

The transformed face of the country extended to foreign affairs and alliance relationships. Assertion of a nuclear-free identity coincided with the last stage of the Cold War and spelt the end of dependence on the United States. For many the pronouncement of a nuclear-free nation amounted to a declaration of independence – if it also 'made explicit the role of power in New Zealand's foreign relations', by pitting New Zealand as a metaphorical David against the Goliath of the United States. In contrast to its economic reforms, the fourth Labour government possessed a mandate to oppose nuclear weapons, and nuclear power as well by the mid-1980s; but it did not have a mandate to scuttle the ANZUS alliance.

A decade earlier, Norman Kirk's Labour government had assumed power on a pledge to promote a nuclear-weapons-free zone in the South Pacific (see chapter 8). Kirk made a principled stand against nuclear-bomb tests in French Polynesia. In June 1973 he despatched a naval frigate to Moruroa Atoll with a cabinet minister, journalists, and a National Radiation Laboratory physicist on board to witness and monitor French atmospheric nuclear tests. A second frigate followed to relieve the first, in a gesture that attracted world media attention. In 1973 Australia and New Zealand also took France to the International Court of Justice. France duly ceased atmospheric tests but commenced an underground nuclear-weapons program from 1975, after which New Zealand scientists found they could monitor the explosions by way of the seismograph recordings used to detect earthquakes.

The Muldoon government's priorities shifted abruptly from Labour's to support for the ANZUS alliance. No United States nuclear-powered cruisers or submarines visited New Zealand from 1965 through to 1975. Ten visited under Muldoon, who believed a ban on nuclear-ship visits was foolhardy and a threat to ANZUS, and whose provocativeness broadened support for the peace and environment movements.

Anti-nuclear sentiment triggered the snap election in July 1984, in the context of campaigns to promote world peace through disarmament stirred by mounting Cold War tensions between the United States and the Soviet Union. Locally, the increased frequency of United States naval visits – three in 1983 alone – attracted protests and publicity. In June 1984 Labour member of parliament Richard Prebble introduced a nuclear-free New Zealand bill (one of a series since 1976) to ban not only nuclear-armed and nuclear-powered ships but also nuclear reactors and waste. Since the National government had a majority of one, Muldoon warned that he saw the vote as a matter of confidence. The bill failed by one vote. Muldoon called an early election on the pretext that the feminist anti-nuclear stance adopted by Marilyn Waring, a young National member of parliament who sought to represent women and youth, undermined his ability to govern. More likely, he could not create a credible budget.

The critical moment in New Zealand–United States relations came early in 1985, when New Zealand refused a request for a visit from the elderly destroyer USS *Buchanan* on the grounds that it could carry nuclear weapons. Controversy still exists as to how New Zealand defied its major ally and was ejected from the American alliance. Labour entered office intent on declaring New Zealand nuclear-free but campaigned on a compromise policy of a nuclear-free nation within an updated ANZUS alliance, which it proposed to renegotiate to accommodate the nuclear-free concept. This compromise acknowledged that public opinion supported the non-nuclear policy but also favoured continued membership of ANZUS. In practice the hope to update the alliance was unrealistic.

In practice, too, the policies of New Zealand and the United States were irreconcilable. The United States stuck rigidly to its principle of neither confirming nor denying whether its vessels were nuclear armed or powered, while New Zealand stated that ships were welcome provided they were not nuclear powered and did not carry nuclear weapons.

Responsibility for the critical decision to refuse a visit by *Buchanan* is still disputed in detail, because processes were in train on several different fronts after the 1984 election, and the separate initiatives did not develop in concert. American advisers United States Secretary of State George Shultz and his assistant, Paul Wolfowitz, liaised privately with Lange when they visited Wellington for an ANZUS council meeting two days after the election. While there is dispute over what transpired, the sole other person present recalled that Lange did not undertake to allow a naval visit but asked for time to talk to his party. He was given six months to resolve the impasse. In turn, 'Mr Shultz heard what he wanted to hear'. In the meantime, a select group of New Zealand officials led by the chief of defence staff obtained approval to negotiate with the United States admiral in charge of the Pacific to ensure that the ship proposed was 'the least nuclearish ship available'. Serendipitously, the chosen vessel, *Buchanan*, was a 'clapped-out old destroyer on which no one in his right mind would put nuclear weapons'. In opaque diplomatic language, the Defence and Foreign Affairs officials cited evidence that showed 'beyond reasonable doubt' that *Buchanan* was neither nuclear propelled nor nuclear armed and therefore conformed with the government's policy on ship visits. Lange, however, did not send the prepared papers to the Cabinet, so ministers knew nothing about this course of events and lacked the background to digest the papers' subtleties.

Meanwhile, peace protests mounted against naval visits and for declaring New Zealand nuclear-free. Problematically for the government, one anti-nuclear group, the Coalition Against Nuclear Warships, named *Buchanan* on a blacklist of nuclear-armed destroyers, because it could launch nuclear charges. Worse, the *Sydney Morning Herald* leaked news of an impending ship visit. Immediately the American request to send *Buchanan* arrived, in January 1985, Lange left for the Pacific on a planned visit to Tokelau, a New Zealand territory of three atolls north of Samoa, travelling the second leg of his journey by boat, which rendered communication difficult.

In Lange's absence Geoffrey Palmer, the acting prime minister, stepped in. According to his biographer, Palmer 'believed the decision had to be made on essentially legal grounds. On the balance of proof, could the government conclude that the *Buchanan* was free of nuclear weapons?' In Palmer's legal interpretation, the officials' reports could not satisfy the Cabinet that the destroyer was not nuclear armed. He judged that he could not decide within the terms of the test proposed for Labour's future legislation to declare New Zealand nuclear-free. Despite wanting to avoid this impasse, the Cabinet could not escape it in a politically acceptable way. Palmer's biographer argues that 'Palmer effectively decided the matter' and made New Zealand nuclear-free.

A former Labour minister has since claimed that Lange was out-manoeuvred by 'in-house critics' over the nuclear-ships issue. The alleged 'atom splitters' were the Labour Party executive, specifically Helen Clark, the future prime minister, and Margaret Wilson, the future attorney-general (then the party president), both peace activists and opponents of Rogernomics. In this critique Clark and Wilson wielded influence through tightening the language of party policy, removing the ambiguity desired by diplomats and the United States that allowed room to negotiate visits.

For the party executive, Wilson saw the anti-nuclear policy as 'a test of principle'. The party opposed visits by 'nuclear-weaponed and nuclear-powered ships', even if the Cabinet might be prepared to shift ground to conserve the ANZUS alliance. Wilson believed most party members also wanted New Zealand to withdraw from ANZUS, as part of a more independent foreign policy appropriate for a small nation in the South Pacific. The party executive saw the episode as tests of the democratic process and of sovereignty in the face of opposition by the United States as the global superpower. Wilson reminded Palmer in January 1985 that,

> unless there was clear proof that the ship was neither nuclear powered nor nuclear armed, its visit would be in breach of the policy. He said the ship was not nuclear powered but that the United States would not break its policy of neither confirming nor denying the presence of nuclear weapons. I then established that the ship was capable of carrying nuclear weapons.

This posed the problem. The party executive therefore reaffirmed its strong support for the nuclear-free policy and urged the government to refuse entry. On his return from the Pacific, Lange took the issue to the caucus, as the executive requested, leaving Labour members of parliament to understand there would be no visit.

By this account, then, Wilson and the party's executive, as well as Palmer, demonstrated clear leadership. If we piece together the strands of evidence, we see that Lange's habit of avoiding conflict created a space for women's politics. From this chaotic process the landmark non-nuclear stance emerged.

Labour women hailed the non-nuclear policy's implementation as a 'triumph for democracy'. This was a principled view consistent with the party's lineage, updated by feminist counterculture politics designed to challenge centres of power. Such politics advocated not isolationism but the agency of the global citizen, active in the international peace and women's movements, determined on behalf of New Zealand to make a stand for peace.

Lange subsequently claimed the nuclear-free mantle as his own. In his account, on his return to Wellington, he 'supported Palmer's assessment and the cabinet agreed'. But Lange insisted he had 'already made' the key decision while in the Pacific and would 'not let the allegation pass that [he] was somehow pressured into refusing the visit of the *Buchanan*'. It was he who publicised the nuclear-free policy on the world stage and stirred nationalism at home, by making headlines a month later with a debate at the Oxford Union. 'There is no moral case for nuclear weapons', Lange told his Oxford audience in March 1985. 'Rejecting nuclear weapons is to assert what is human over the evil nature of the weapon; it is to restore to humanity the power of decision; it is to allow true moral force to reign supreme.'

The predicted effect of the *Buchanan* incident on the ANZUS alliance – a breakup – is illustrated in figure 9.3. Note the paddle power of the New Zealand waka (canoe) in contrast to the space-age technology of the United States vessel and Australia's weaponry and telecommunications as New Zealand goes it alone after the split. The United States retaliated strongly, declared ANZUS 'inoperative' in relation to New Zealand and severed ties, imposing a freeze on high-level contacts.

In August 1986 the United States took the formal step of suspending its security commitment under the alliance, demoting New Zealand from 'ally' to 'friend'. New Zealand's Cold War was over. The cartoon in figure 9.3 elucidates a further theme in this small country's relations with its allies: New Zealand's absence, but not its presence, attracts comment.

9.3 Eric W. Heath, *ANZUS*, 1985
Dominion, 5 February 1985. Alexander Turnbull Library, Wellington, B-143-009. Courtesy of Eric Heath

In addition to a clash of principles, the row highlighted differences in perception of nuclear deterrence and in attitudes to security among the alliance partners. In the United States' view, New Zealand had to choose between ANZUS and its nuclear-free policy. From New Zealand's perspective, nuclear weapons were irrelevant to the defence of the South Pacific. Australia took the contrasting view that membership of ANZUS implied that Australia should not contest the 'neither confirm nor deny' policy. After the rift, Australia worked hard to preserve its relations first with the United States and second with New Zealand. Australian diplomats were especially concerned to retain ANZUS, which they viewed as superior to any bilateral alternative.

While New Zealand sought to limit the damage already done, realpolitik – American power – prevailed. If, for the United States, the moment of breach came when *Buchanan* was rejected, locally, 'the breach came when the United States took measures against New Zealand'. The suspension by the United States of its security obligations when the alliance did not provide for suspension of a member only increased popular support for Lange and the Labour government.

A second defining incident, involving France, assured public celebration of the nuclear-free policy. Three French secret agents bombed the Greenpeace flagship *Rainbow Warrior* in Auckland Harbour in July 1985 (figure 9.4), killing a photographer. In classic 'whodunnit' style, Auckland police exposed two of the agents with assistance from an army of sleuths supplied by the public, who were shocked as the French operation was unveiled. The French government attempted a cover up before admitting responsibility and provoked further outrage when it broke an agreement reached on the detention of the perpetrators. The French factor affirmed ancient Anglo–French prejudices and exacerbated tensions with the United States over a nuclear-free Pacific. New Zealanders would not tolerate being bullied and bombed in an act of 'state terrorism' executed not by an enemy but by an ally, whom New Zealanders had defended in two world wars.

Together, the *Buchanan* and *Rainbow Warrior* incidents assured the passage in 1987 of the Nuclear-Free Zone, Disarmament and

9.4 The stricken *Rainbow Warrior* in Auckland Harbour, 1985 *New Zealand Herald*, 10 July 1985. Courtesy of *New Zealand Herald*

Arms Control Act, which declared New Zealand nuclear-free. They also assured the revival of plans for a nuclear-free zone in the South Pacific proposed by Kirk in the early 1970s. The Treaty of Rarotonga in August 1985 created a zone that stretched from the Equator to the Antarctic and west of Papua New Guinea to Easter Island. No nuclear weapons were to be tested in this vast area, although the protocol did not affect the passage of nuclear vessels, because of rights under international law to 'freedom of the seas'. This sequence of events encouraged an enhanced focus on and identification with the South Pacific and faith in the idea that a small, isolated nation set a moral example to the world. As we have seen, both these elements of a new nationalism that imagined the country to be a moral Pacific paradise had precedents. So did the image of the alien ship in the harbour as a threat to the body politic.

The report of the Defence Committee of Enquiry, named the Corner committee for chairman Frank Corner, a retired diplomat, in July 1986 disclosed the results of its inquiry into popular attitudes towards the ANZUS alliance and a nuclear-free stance. Its other members comprised a left-wing academic, a woman scientist, and a retired Māori army general, who surprised Lange with their unanimous conclusions. The inquiry's poll results are summarised in table 9.1.

As the table shows, New Zealanders were evenly divided between the desire 'to be in an alliance with larger countries' and the desire to be nuclear-free. The majority wanted the impossible: to be nuclear-free *and* to remain in ANZUS. Further, 92 per cent (identical to the proportion who opposed nuclear weapons) thought Australia was important to New Zealand's defence and security. Strengthening ties with Australia, the committee concluded, was 'the most promising option left open to New Zealand'. Not only did closer relations with Australia stand in the 'mainstream tradition' of policymaking, but the results would focus on 'New Zealand's own region, the South Pacific', and the possibility of a return to ANZUS in the future.

Thus, the nuclear-free idea, while annoying Australia, propelled New Zealand closer to its neighbour. The defence imbroglio boosted the success of the Australia–New Zealand Closer Economic Relations Trade Agreement while affirming that New Zealand

Table 9.1 *New Zealander votes on ANZUS alliance or nuclear-free New Zealand, 1986*

Options	Votes (%)
Against nuclear weapons	92
Against nuclear weapons and in favour of nuclear-free New Zealand	73
In favour of alliances with larger countries	72
In favour of ANZUS alliance	71
In favour of nuclear-free New Zealand within ANZUS alliance	**80**
Stay in ANZUS alliance and ban nuclear ships	44
Stay in ANZUS alliance and allow nuclear ships	37
If being nuclear-free within ANZUS is impossible:	
New Zealand should stay in ANZUS and allow nuclear ships which may or may not be nuclear armed or powered	52
New Zealand should withdraw from ANZUS and ban nuclear ships	44

Compiled from Defence Committee of Enquiry, *Defence and Security: What New Zealanders Want*, Wellington, 1986

identity was not Australian. In a significant change, Canberra decided, after lively debate, that Australia's interests would be best served by strengthening the defence relationship with New Zealand. Both Australia and New Zealand therefore resolved to strengthen ties in the second half of the 1980s. Despite deep differences over the nuclear issue, the Anzac defence relationship grew closer, culminating in a joint project to build a series of new Anzac frigates, to enable the two allies to act alone and in tandem in the South Pacific.

But the ANZUS crisis left a legacy of unresolved tension in the trans-Tasman relationship. Defence had been a key motive for Australia to support the 1983 trade agreement, and it resurfaced as the bugbear in otherwise warm relations in the late twentieth century, because of simmering resentment that New Zealand was not pulling its weight in defence. After 1985 New Zealand tried to fit into an Australian model of strategic interests; but it failed to meet neighbourly expectations, both because it lacked resources and because New Zealanders had a distinctive strategic outlook. While they shared solidarity of kinship and purpose, New Zealanders had a different idea of what constituted the Pacific and historically felt less exposed to threats that, real and imagined, appeared from Southeast Asia.

Overall, the most important outcomes of the ruptures in economic and defence policies from the 1970s proved to be the United States' disgruntled attitude towards New Zealand and the refashioned relationship with Australia, which was left as the small nation's sole ally. At the same time the ANZUS issue lurked as a potential confounder of relationships. Anzac Day, the shared sacred day, acquired new layers of meaning. The funereal Anzac tradition and late discoveries in the 1980s of the men's actual experiences of war, learnt through interviews before they died, accommodated the concept of a nuclear-free nation. A dual tradition developed that encompassed remembrance of war and peace and so held meaning for everyone.

Nuclear-free New Zealand was a woman's as well as a man's country. A new generation, born in the postwar years and raised in New Zealand, entered positions of power and influence. This generation contained a new class of professionals determined to attack the cultural cringe. Importantly, their counterculture convictions could be accommodated by existing myths. This urban, educated generation, reared to question standards and norms, embraced the youth revolution that made them global citizens. Simultaneously, they donned a 'made in New Zealand' identity in their passage to adulthood.

A transfer of political power between generations helps explain the lurch from Muldoonism to Rogernomics. It also resolves the apparent paradox of how nuclear-free New Zealand shared a heritage with enthusiasm for an Anglo-American neoliberalism. Both the nuclear-free principle and Rogernomics were crusades that made the country a model for the world and created aspirations to set a moral example. Both were represented as state experiments. The nuclear-free experiment enjoyed majority support, if complicated by regret over the demise of ANZUS, and sought and found meaning in the geographic facts of smallness and isolation. The economic experiment, on the other hand, undermined the fourth Labour government's credibility, because it hurt so many ordinary people.

The neoliberal crusade split the Labour Party, due to a fundamental philosophical dispute over the nature of fairness, especially to those least able to cope, the people without personal wealth or power. Jim Anderton, a disenchanted Labour stalwart, left to form the NewLabour Party in 1989. The 'crash through' or 'blitzkrieg' approach also undermined the legitimacy of the political system, because it was fundamentally undemocratic. To impose some control on executive power, New Zealanders turned to electoral reform.

By referendum in 1993 the people changed the method of voting from first past the post to mixed-member proportional representation, under which people cast two votes: one for a political party and one for an electorate member of parliament in their local or Māori electorate. Percentages of party votes determined the number of members of parliament on a party list (a list of candidates) elected to parliament. This change in the electoral system made it less likely that a single political party would hold a majority of seats in parliament, the hope being that this would be fairer and introduce checks and balances in the system through more consensual policymaking.

A National–New Zealand First coalition government led by Jim Bolger assumed power in 1996 in a new parliament, based on this form of proportional representation. Not only would a new multi-party democracy constrain the executive, people hoped, but a more representative parliament could better speak for diverse identities and an expanding citizenship. What no one foresaw was how minority parties in the future might exploit new opportunities to overrule the will of the people.

10

Treaty revival 1973–1999

Expanding citizenship characterised New Zealand in the late twentieth century, when ruptures in the very meaning of New Zealandness obliged people to adapt to new ideas about who belonged to the nation and what belonging entailed. The country reshaped political institutions to reflect that its people and culture had grown more diverse and connected to the world and to accommodate the concept of biculturalism.

THE TREATY COMES ALIVE

Internally the Treaty of Waitangi's return to public life drove these changes. The wairua (spirit) of the Treaty made it unique in the world, determined its place in history, and shaped national myth-making in the late twentieth century. Gradually a Māori narrative of the Treaty seeped into public awareness. Māori had consistently called for the Crown to honour the Treaty; pronounced a 'simple nullity' by the courts in 1877 (see chapter 4), its spirit stirred 100 years later not just in Māoridom but in the body politic, changing assumptions entrenched since 1840 about the importance of land and food resources to Māori and of the need for fresh decision-making about paths ahead.

Lobbied by the Rātana movement to make 6 February a national day, the second Labour government declared Waitangi Day a day of thanksgiving and commemoration in 1960. Under the New Zealand Day Act 1973, the third Labour government declared 6 February a public holiday. Prime Minister Norman Kirk sought to create a national day distinctive for its remembrance not of a revolution or war but of a peaceful agreement between two peoples who had grown into a nation of many peoples. But the name change to New Zealand Day was short lived. Prime Minister Robert Muldoon reverted to the name Waitangi Day in 1976, because he disliked the motive behind the invention of a New Zealand day, to prepare for a multicultural future. Conversely, some Māori opposed having Waitangi Day whitewashed. The renaming returned the day's focus to policy on Māori issues and made 6 February more prone to gestures of angry defiance by protesters, especially youth.

Amid rapid social change from the 1960s, Māori population recovery and urbanisation spurred debate about the place of Māori in modern society. Renewed culture contact, this time in cities, and a high rate of intermarriage (half of Māori marriages were with Pākehā, European New Zealanders) made indigenous disadvantage more obvious. Internationally, emphasis intensified on equal rights to citizenship. Young, educated, urban Māori, alert to the American civil rights movement and the United Nations' advocacy of human rights, demanded a fairer share of resources and to have their status as tangata whenua (people of the land) acknowledged. Schooled in counterculture values at university, notably the University of Auckland, this new class of dynamic leaders called for the decolonisation of New Zealand.

Māori youth also lost patience with their conservative elders. But Māori leadership itself was shifting ground. The New Zealand Māori Council, appointed by the Holyoake National government in 1962 from iwi (tribe) notables to balance the Rātana movement's influence on the four Māori seats (held by Labour), provided advice to the government which expressed conservative Māori views. Yet council members were as ready to resist National's land reform policies as were their younger, more radicalised relations. By the late 1960s concerns to retain the last vestiges of ancestral, collectively owned land rose alongside youth protest, magnified by migration to the cities.

In Auckland, youthful activists joined progressive movements, such as the Māori Organisation on Human Rights, established in 1968, with some embracing Marxist beliefs that indigenous rights went hand in hand with class struggle. Radicals and university students seeking mana motuhake (self-determination) joined the 'young warriors' of Ngā Tamatoa, a group modelled on the American Black Power movement, whose members, dressed in black, staged protests at Waitangi Day ceremonies from 1971 – the United Nations' year for the elimination of racial discrimination – and declared 6 February a day of mourning. Ngā Tamatoa drew attention to the loss of the Māori language and denounced the Treaty as a fraud, calling for a boycott of the annual celebrations. Increasingly, tensions erupted every Waitangi Day, due to a clash of Māori and settler Treaty narratives.

Struggles for land resurfaced in the 1960s, as a series of National governments persisted in believing that Māori land was not effectively used and that this hindered the country's economic development. By contrast, university student activists asserted in 1966 that Māori lands were for Māori use. A series of statutes in 1967 incited waves of protest. Land policy had changed little since the 1840s; and 1967 marked the culmination of official attempts to force Māori land into European law. By this time the intent was less to transfer collectively owned land into European ownership and control than to change the nature of title, so that Māori land could be managed in a way that allegedly made it more financially useful for owners. The government baulked at the complicated process of managing Māori land under the individualised system created for collectively owned land overseen by the Māori Land Court. To the Māori Council, the proposed legislative changes were misguided; the council wanted a policy of land development with youth-training programs, so that young Māori could occupy ancestral land. The Māori Affairs Amendment Act 1967 did nothing new in extending the dictum of 'use it or lose it' (see chapter 5). Predictably, this attitude was universally condemned by Māori, who likened the government's plans to another round of confiscations.

Campaigners against the legislation frequently referred to the Treaty of Waitangi. Supposed equality had not allowed Māori collectively or as tribes to engage with the modern economy and the state as their ancestors had expected when they signed the Treaty. 'Maori people were fed up', not merely with 'the sense of being left on the margins of a Pakeha-dominated economy' but with being ignored and patronised.

In response, Māori of all ages and politics – Ngā Tamatoa, kaumātua and kuia (elders), and radicals – together joined the Māori Land March in 1975 to alert Pākehā and the government to the issues and to fight the 'last land grab', represented by the 1967 Act, as well as other laws passed about rates, public works, and local government schemes which allowed the taking of collectively owned land. The protesters' slogan echoed the Kīngitanga (King movement) call: 'Not one more acre of Māori land'. Led by 80-year-old Whina Cooper, the foundation president of the Māori Women's Welfare League, the protesters walked and drove from the far north of the North Island to Wellington. On the last day, they marched to parliament silently, in the rain, to deliver their message not merely about grievances over the loss of ancestral land – which had grown more important to people pushed off, who had no other choice than to move to cities – but also that the government should finally acknowledge property rights under the Treaty of Waitangi.

Recourse to the Treaty required Māori to educate Pākehā, since the latter either did not know about the Treaty's history, or dismissed the covenant as a historic relic, or assumed that – in the English version – its tenets had been upheld. In response to the land march and calls from Māori leaders, the third Labour government, led by Bill Rowling after Kirk's untimely death, passed the Treaty of Waitangi Act 1975. This law was the initiative of Matiu Rata, Minister of Māori Affairs, who strongly opposed the measures of 1967. Rata proposed establishing a tribunal empowered to deal with modern Treaty grievances as a corollary to the concept of 6 February as a national day. The Waitangi Tribunal was duly established under the Treaty of Waitangi Act. The tribunal grew to be an iconic institution. While it could only listen to grievances and make recommendations, in the wording of the statute it marked the 'observance' and 'confirmation' of the 'principles of the Treaty of Waitangi', leaving the principles to be interpreted in the future through its inquiries. Principles of the Treaty incited controversy 50 years later (see chapter 12).

However, the Bastion Point protest, in Auckland, in 1977–8, aroused more public consciousness than the land march had done, through the medium of television. By this time about 1.3 million hectares of land remained with tribes. Ōrakei, Bastion Point's original name, was the home of Ngāti Whātua, who had sold Auckland in 1840 to Lieutenant-Governor William Hobson. The 1977 protest, the first to gain publicity, because it broke the law, followed numerous court actions, as was the pattern with most Māori grievances. Dispute had simmered since 1869, when the Native Land Court had determined the Ōrakei block of 280 hectares was owned by three hapū (subtribes); in 1873 it had issued a certificate of title to 13 members of these hapū, effectively disinheriting the rest of the tribe. The title had a rider that the land was inalienable by sale or lease, but in 1886 the state took land under the Public Works Act for defence purposes, on the pretext of a Russian naval scare. In 1898 the 13 trustees were declared 'owners' with power to alienate the remaining land. Between 1914 and 1928 the state purchased the remainder of the block except for 1 hectare which contained the marae (meeting house). Sidney Holland's National government compulsorily acquired the last sliver of land, except for the cemetery, in 1951 and moved the residents to nearby state rental houses. As workers moved in to demolish the ancestral meeting house, members of Ngāti Whātua torched the building themselves to prevent its demolition by the government.

For Ngāti Whātua who had watched the burning of their ancestral place and grew up poor in state housing, the final insult was Robert Muldoon's government's decision to sell the remaining land at Bastion Point, with its harbour views, to developers for upmarket houses. A group led by Joe Hawke, later a Labour member of parliament, challenged the Crown's ownership. Bastion Point symbolised the social aspects of Muldoonism, since, after a 506-day occupation, Muldoon sent in police and the army to remove the protesters. Television viewers were shocked to watch the Riot Act read and 222 people arrested. Through the prolonged dispute the public learnt about creeping dispossession and plain unfairness, and how tangata whenua were forced into state housing while the government proposed to sell the last of their ancestral heritage for an expensive subdivision.

At the same time the politics of racism and anti-racist protest, local and global, spilt over into the sport of rugby, the national game. The first South African Springbok rugby team to visit

New Zealand, in 1921, had offended Te Arawa in Rotorua by accepting the tribe's formal welcome and then, disgusted at having to play a 'native' team, turning their backs while a New Zealand Māori side (precursor of the Māori All Blacks) performed the haka (posture dance, accompanied by a song). That offence set the tone for subsequent protests, especially given the capitulation to apartheid by the New Zealand Rugby Football Union, which agreed not to send Māori players to South Africa from 1928, including George Nēpia. Protests were relatively low key at first. Non-Māori All Black and Springbok rugby tours of South Africa and New Zealand took place in 1949 and 1956 respectively, oblivious to objections from Māori members of parliament and the Māori Women's Welfare League.

From the 1960s, however, 'No Māori, No Tour' protests featured in national life. South Africa was expelled from the Olympic Games because of apartheid, and in 1973 Kirk ordered the rugby union to cancel the scheduled Springbok tour to New Zealand, after violence during an earlier tour of Australia. In contrast, Muldoon let South Africa play its game while he played his; he did nothing to stop the 1981 Springbok tour of New Zealand (and arranged a royal tour by Queen Elizabeth II immediately afterwards), to ensure his party won that year's election. His appeal to law and order secured the National government a majority of one. The tour both damaged the interests of rugby and unleashed protest on a scale unparalleled since the 1860s.

The Springbok tour of 1981 rallied protesters with a variety of agendas, from Treaty activists and gang members to university students, women, the churches, homosexuality-law reformers, and urban middle-class people. In many respects the rugby tour protests signified a popular uprising against this blatant case of Muldoonism. Once on the streets, worthy citizens were stunned by the police response to their protests. Peaceful demonstrators encountered rings of barbed wire around rugby fields and the violence of the Red Squad (an elite riot squad wearing helmets and bearing batons), whose culture 'was as alien to many New Zealanders as was apartheid'. Urban, educated people came face to face with riot police for the first time and found the confrontation and sense of menace frightening, dramatic, and formative. The experience politicised younger people, while earlier Vietnam and civil rights protests conditioned older ones to join the marches. Thousands flocked to the anti-tour movement, which enjoyed worldwide coverage after protesters stopped the first game at Hamilton, in July, by invading the pitch. To Nelson Mandela watching in South Africa, it felt as if the sun had come out.

Violence escalated during the tour. In September 1981, the scion of a Marxist family halted the test in Auckland by dropping leaflets and smoke bombs from a light plane, just clearing the goal posts. Families were riven by conflict, and the entire country felt split. The tour exposed deep rifts in New Zealand society, shattering its image as a peaceful nation with harmonious race relations. Protesters heard Māori activists denounce not just apartheid in South Africa – by chanting 'Free Nelson Mandela'– but injustice at home. At stake were competing ideas of New Zealand, its image, identity, and future.

Meanwhile the Department of Māori Affairs established the Tū Tāngata (stand tall) program. Senior women prominent in the Māori Women's Welfare League created the idea of kōhanga reo (language nests) organised as preschools to nurture and save the Māori language through immersive methods. Kōhanga reo mushroomed from 1982, outpacing officials who rushed to draft the necessary policy and regulations.

Simultaneously, the Waitangi Tribunal, established in 1975, came to life under (Sir) Edward Taihākurei Durie (see figure 10.1), the first person of Māori descent to be appointed chief judge of the Māori Land Court. As chairman of the Waitangi Tribunal from 1981, Durie set about redressing Treaty injustices and educating Pākehā about the meaning and significance of the Treaty of Waitangi. Durie himself symbolised a bicultural New Zealand. In 1983 he and the tribunal attracted public notice with a decision for Te Āti Awa of Taranaki on the Motunui Synthetic Fuels Plant, a Think Big project, which required a sewage outfall to pump effluent into the Tasman Sea. The tribe claimed that the outfall would pollute their fishing reefs, and the tribunal agreed.

This decision represented a direct challenge to Muldoonism and won the support of the environmental movement. Indigenous rights in alliance with environmentalist politics saw the outfall proposal

10.1 Justice Sir Edward Taihākurei Durie, Chair of the Waitangi Tribunal, 1981–2003, c. 2003
Courtesy of Donna Durie Hall

dropped. For the first time since 1877, the Treaty was 'brought to life', transformed to the status of a constitutional instrument under the Treaty of Waitangi Act 1975, and Māoridom was abuzz.

With past land claims and disputes handled at a political level, results had been inevitably uneven and unfair. In 1985, therefore, by making the Waitangi Tribunal's jurisdiction retrospective to 1840 under the Treaty of Waitangi Amendment Act, the radical fourth Labour government opened the way for hundreds of historical claims about breaches of the Treaty by settler governments. Koro Wetere, Minister of Māori Affairs, introduced the bill to address rising tensions about outstanding grievances. From that moment, iwi and hapū shifted tactics from protest over land claims to litigation, as an expanded tribunal began to channel generations of anger and despair over official wrongs. This transfer of energy also defused extremism and instilled hope for long-sought equality.

For some, lodgement of Treaty claims suggested a means to the goal of advancement of the people through self-determination and establishment of an economic base for tribes. The change also called for a national review of indigenous rights.

In 1986 the Waitangi Tribunal recommended that, under article 2 of the Treaty, the Māori language have the status of a taonga (treasure), which the state should guarantee to preserve. Consequently, the Māori Language Act 1987 made Māori an official language of New Zealand, alongside English, and efforts accelerated to save te reo from extinction. Māori immersion schools that taught in Māori continued the work of preschool language nests, and from there students could progress to tertiary education. Māori radio stations began broadcasting, while state-supported Māori television, designed to appeal to the youthful population of Māori descent, finally screened in 2004.

Critically, questioning of the bases of citizenship by Māori leaders and the formal hearing of Treaty claims led to a rewriting of New Zealand history to include Māori, a process begun by Keith Sinclair and others in the 1950s but vastly extended in the 1980s to social history and writing by Māori authors. Evidence gathered by the tribunal challenged settler narratives and undermined assumptions that governments had extinguished indigenous property rights honourably, through full consent and fair processes of purchase. Further, Rogernomics challenged Māoridom to check settler politicians' continued abuse of executive power. Tribal resistance to the dismemberment and sale of public assets attracted widespread support, because of alarm about the speed and undemocratic nature of the fourth Labour government's reform agenda.

The State-Owned Enterprises Act 1986 triggered a court battle to prevent the privatisation of state assets. The Act prepared for the transfer of public assets into private ownership, out of reach of Treaty claims by tribes and beyond inclusion in any compensatory settlement packages to redress land loss. The Māori Council challenged the State-Owned Enterprises Act in the famous case *NZ Maori Council v. Attorney-General* of 1987 – known as the 'Lands case' – on the grounds that section 9 declared, 'Nothing in this Act shall permit the Crown to act in a manner that is inconsistent with the principles of the Treaty of Waitangi'. Through their ruling the justices on the Court of Appeal elevated the Treaty's legal status, as they declared that any transfer of assets to state enterprises 'without establishing any system to consider ... whether such transfer would be inconsistent with the principles of the Treaty of Waitangi would be unlawful'.

The Lands case proved a turning point in defining 'Treaty principles', since politicians had not defined them in the Treaty of Waitangi Act 1975 or since. Rather, the Waitangi Tribunal and the courts interpreted the Treaty concepts of 'kāwanatanga' (governance or government) and 'te tino rangatiratanga' (unqualified chieftainship), and the document's broader meaning, for modern New Zealand. The Court of Appeal outlined seven Treaty principles, of which the first was 'partnership', an idea developed in the Anglican Church and in Waitangi Tribunal reports before 1987. But the Lands case represented a step in comprehension, because the five justices agreed unanimously that the Treaty established a partnership between Māori people and the Crown. The Court of Appeal found that the principles of the Treaty overrode everything else in the State-Owned Enterprises Act. Above all, the partners had a duty to act reasonably and in good faith towards each other. While the principles of the Treaty did 'not authorise unreasonable restrictions' on government policy, the Crown also had a duty of 'active protection' of Māori people in the use of their lands and waters, to 'remedy past breaches', and to consult with Māori, who retained their rangatiratanga.

The justices determined that under article 1, chiefs 'ceded rights of government in exchange for guarantees of possession and control of their lands and precious possessions for so long as they wanted to retain them'. Thus New Zealand justices, like the Waitangi Tribunal, embraced the Māori narrative of the Treaty as a 'living, breathing, vital thing'. They saw the purpose of partnership as advancing the welfare of all New Zealanders, subject to the special condition of preserving the integrity of Māoridom. For the Waitangi Tribunal, now reinforced by the courts, the core issues revolved around Crown breaches of the Treaty in the struggles over land. Conversely, land loss for Māori entailed loss of mana (prestige) and their place in the nation. If the state were to honour the Treaty, the Pākehā–Māori relationship had to be transformed.

Major Treaty settlements in the 1990s laid bare the issues facing the country. The two biggest settlements were with Tainui, in the North Island, the Waikato iwi most affected by the New Zealand Wars and massive confiscations; and with Ngāi Tahu, in the South Island, which involved redress for a different history of dispossession, through purchase of a vast territory, loss of food-gathering places, and denial of reserves. The Ngāi Tahu claim, filed in August 1986, reflected long-standing grievances not addressed by the earlier political settlement in 1944 that concerned only the single, massive Kemp purchase in 1848. Initially, the claim highlighted the failure to provide tenths sections for Māori in the Otago settlement at Dunedin, unlike in Wellington, where tenths were drawn in the town plan and surveyed. Subsequently the claim developed into a broad review of all the Ngāi Tahu grievances since the 1840s. In particular, the Crown had acquired title to nearly all the tribe's vast territory between 1844 (the purchase for Dunedin) and 1860. Yet the state had neglected to make adequate reserves – that is, to set aside selected areas from sale – ignoring the wishes of hapū to retain substantial blocks – for example, on the Canterbury plains. Crown agents insisted on taking 'title to the whole of an area' whereas the Treaty authorised only purchase of land that 'Māori freely wished to sell'. This resulted in the 'extinguishment' of customary title and denial of access to vital food-gathering places that were guaranteed in deeds of purchase. Excluded from favourite food-gathering sites, Ngāi Tahu were left in poverty, landless, and marginalised.

By contrast, the basis of the claim by Waikato iwi in 1987 was that Tainui had their land unjustly confiscated after the Waikato War of the 1860s. Whole communities had suffered for the actions of a few, while the government had seized the best land, irrespective of whether the owners were 'loyal' Māori or supposed 'rebels' (the 1995 settlement refuted this label). This injustice not only ensured the continued vigour of Kīngitanga claims but hobbled Tainui's participation in national life.

Divergent tribal experiences produced similar outcomes of dispossession, poverty, and reduced life chances, with accompanying loss of mana. Guided by Jim Bolger's minister for Treaty negotiations, (Sir) Douglas Graham, these initial major claims resulted in apologies from the Crown – for Tainui, from the queen – and

Treaty settlements of $170 million respectively to Tainui in 1995 and to Ngāi Tahu in 1997, finalised by legislation in 1998.

As part of the Ngāi Tahu Treaty settlement, significant places regained their te reo names. Mount Cook, renamed Aoraki Mount Cook in the 1998 Ngāi Tahu Claims Settlement Act, returned to the tribe; but on the same day, Ngāi Tahu, their mana restored and acknowledged, gave the mountain to the nation. The tribe quickly developed its new capital base and became an engine of economic growth in the South Island, active in property development, tourism, agriculture, and global business.

While native title in land had largely been extinguished, customary rights remained unclear over fisheries. In 1986, as part of the Rogernomics reforms, the fourth Labour government introduced a quota management system to ensure that New Zealand's fisheries were sustainable. The government argued its case in environmental terms: it was necessary to control the allowable catch of fish species under stress because of overfishing. Effectively, the quota management system privatised rights in fish by transferring to big companies the property rights in fishing that existed under the Treaty. Many small and part-time fishers missed out, especially in Northland. Māori leaders warned that the system breached article 2 of the Treaty of Waitangi. In 1987 the Ministry of Agriculture and Fisheries nonetheless began to issue fishing quotas. Māori who had lodged claims with the Waitangi Tribunal moved to halt this process, and applications for an injunction succeeded in the High Court.

From 1986 the courts, influenced by decisions in Canada and the United States, revived common law doctrine about customary rights by declaring that native title in land might have been extinguished, but not in fish. In the case *Te Weehi v Regional Fisheries Officer*, in defence against a charge of possessing undersized paua (abalone), Tom Te Weehi successfully argued that he took shellfish for his family in the customary way, and Justice J. Williamson, rejecting earlier denials of Māori customary law, found that customary fishing rights exercised in a customary manner continued to exist if recognised in legislation. Soon after, the quota management system itself was held to conflict with section 88(2) of the Fisheries Act 1983, which said, 'Nothing in this Act shall affect any Maori fishing rights'. When the High Court agreed that the quota management system contravened people's rights to fish, the government was obliged to negotiate.

From 1989, through the Māori Fisheries Commission, Māori once more became major players in the fishing industry. Ironically, an instrument of empire, the common law concept of native title, helped to recover Māori mana and control over resources. The wider community was still adjusting to the idea that article 2 of the Treaty was enforceable in the present when Māori fisheries negotiators, among them the member of parliament Matiu Rata and (Sir) Tipene O'Regan of Ngāi Tahu, plus National ministers, seized a one-off opportunity to deliver fishing quota to iwi. In 1992 they persuaded the government to provide $150 million to the Māori Fisheries Commission to buy a half-share in New Zealand's largest fishing company, Sealord Products, as a way of settling fisheries claims. This became known as the 'Sealord's deal'. The Treaty of Waitangi Fisheries Commission was established to manage the block-of-fish quota acquired through the deal – about a quarter of the national total – and the half-share of Sealord's capital and expertise in fish processing and marketing. The commissioners also had to decide how to distribute an asset worth $500 million by 1998. By 1999, Māori owned 50 per cent of New Zealand's commercial sea fisheries. How to allocate these fisheries assets remained bitterly contested until settled by statute in 2004.

'A WOMAN'S RIGHT TO CHOOSE'

The Women's Liberation Movement similarly sought 'a place to stand' in the 1970s. The year of the Treaty of Waitangi Act, 1975, was also International Women's Year. As a social movement, second-wave feminism developed from shifting family relations and the altered status of women, as girls increasingly acquired a tertiary education, while married as well as single women moved into the paid workforce. Feminism's time had come to liberate women from 'patriarchy' and address women as 'Ms', not 'Miss' or 'Mrs', to avoid defining them by marital status. Family structures and the nature of marriage were changing; 1973 saw the arrival of the domestic purposes benefit for single parents over the age of 16 with dependent children, and 1975 that of no-fault divorce. The economy needed women and girls, both to fill jobs in an expanded tertiary sector and for the traditional task of unpaid work in the home. Families also needed mothers to undertake paid work, since costs of home ownership and raising children could no longer be met by a single breadwinner wage.

The objectives of New Zealand's women's lib paralleled those of the international movement. Activists demanded equal pay, won in legislation in 1972; liberation from the role of 'housewife'; sexual freedom and equality, including freedom from 'sex roles'; and autonomy for women over their own bodies and lives. Motherhood and domesticity were no longer imagined as empowering. On the contrary, women's lib portrayed the home as a prison. To claim the self, therefore, feminists strove to transform society to free women from the bonds of home and family. The demand for access to safe, legal abortion proved to be the most contentious issue in the 1970s, because it divided the feminist movement while being opposed strongly by lobby groups like the Society for the Protection of the Unborn Child, which had political influence. When it became difficult for women to have abortions after the Muldoon government passed the Contraception, Sterilisation and Abortion Act 1977, feminist groups in New Zealand and Australia cooperated to fly women to Sydney clinics. This restrictive law demonstrated the social conservatism of the Muldoon years. Doctors interpreted the law more liberally by the 1980s, yet the feminist campaign failed to have abortion removed from the Crimes Act.

Management of childbirth, on the other hand, delivered a feminist success with the return of the independent midwife from 1990. Achieved through consensus between midwives, middle-class women's organisations, and the fourth Labour government, the return to the idea of birth as a normal physiological process resulted from changes in the 'political opportunity structure' that favoured midwives over doctors. In contrast to doctors' 1930s domination of the management of childbirth, in 1988 the medical profession's power and influence were challenged following a cervical cancer inquiry chaired by Dame Silvia Cartwright, who subsequently became New Zealand's first woman High Court judge and the second woman governor-general. The Cartwright inquiry endorsed patients' rights and intensified public questioning of medical authority. The midwife's moment arrived with the Nurses Amendment Act 1990, whereby the midwife regained autonomy as an independent practitioner and won the right to the same pay as a doctor who practised obstetrics.

Rogernomics helped in the return of the midwife. State sector reforms redefined birthing women as 'clients', giving extra weight to patients' rights and to feminist demands that women regain control of birth. Both feminist and economic rationalist agendas favoured the midwife. As Helen Clark (see figure 10.2), then minister of health, later prime minister, observed in 1990, 'Even the Treasury could see merit in increased autonomy'. Midwives provided competition for doctors, and midwife-attended births were expected to cut costs. In fact, competition increased, but costs soared, since many women opted for care shared by a doctor and a midwife. This unintended outcome led to the Lead Maternity Carer scheme, from 1996, which obliged the mother to choose a midwife *or* a doctor, who was paid a capped fee. The scheme was introduced to save money, not to provide choice. By the end of the twentieth century most mothers had a midwife-managed birth with a brief stay in hospital, much like mothers in the early 1900s. A review of maternity services in 1999 reported the highest levels of satisfied customers among mothers cared for by midwives.

By the late twentieth century nearly half the female population aged 16 to 64 were in paid employment. An independent working life now featured in women's life histories. More married women returned to the workforce or did not ever leave it, and by 1990 most married women were earners for their families. While equal pay and wealth remained elusive, a United Nations report concluded that New Zealand had one of the highest rankings of gender equality in the world.

A historical question therefore arises of how a country whose first-wave feminists extolled motherhood and domesticity appointed women leaders by the end of the twentieth century. New Zealand attained two women prime ministers in rapid succession: Jenny Shipley, in 1997, when she toppled Jim Bolger from the leadership of the National coalition government; and Helen Clark, who became the first elected woman prime minister when Labour won

10.2 Prime Minister Helen Clark on Hochstetter Dome, Aoraki Mount Cook National Park, with southerly clouds spilling over the Main Divide, 2003
Photographer Gottlieb Braun-Elwert. Courtesy of Anne Braun-Elwert

the 1999 election. Tellingly, the public did not think it odd to have women running the country.

The major continuities over time are of a liberal feminism, in which women worked within the system to influence policymaking and law-making, supported by democratic political institutions; and of prominent mother figures (or aunts). The Green Party had a woman co-leader, Jeanette Fitzsimons, from 1995 until 2009, while the chief justice and attorney-general were both women at the end of the twentieth century. New Zealand appointed the first woman governor-general, Dame Catherine Tizard, in time for the country's sesquicentennial, in 1990. A popular figure who had appeared on a long-running television program, Dame Cath was also the first woman mayor of Auckland.

Until the 1970s, women who entered parliament did so through family networks, as did Iriaka Rātana, who was elected the first Māori woman member of parliament in 1949, after her husband died. Women's engagement with politics rose in the early 1980s, spurred by protests against Muldoonism, when the number of women members of parliament rose from four to eight. One of them was Helen Clark, who entered parliament in 1981.

By the centennial of women's suffrage, in 1993, women comprised 21 per cent of the members of parliament, and the figure rose to 30 per cent in the first mixed-member proportional representation parliament, in 1996. The dramatic change in the voting system from the traditional first past the post to mixed-member proportional representation was intended to align each party's share of seats in parliament with its share of the vote. This both ensured fairness and increased the likelihood of coalition governments, since minority parties won more votes and influence.

In parallel, history recovered women's 'herstory'. Unlike the gothic history of gender relations in Australia, coloured by convictism, New Zealand women's history was likened to 'standing in the sunshine'. Historians rediscovered Kate Sheppard, the national leader of the women's suffrage campaign, and the colonial suffragists as heroines, though the movement's leaders were ambivalent models for young women who sought to escape the domestic constraints imposed on their mothers and grandmothers. Celebrated as a representative activist for women's citizenship, Sheppard became the first woman other than Queen Elizabeth II to be portrayed on a New Zealand banknote.

By the 1990s mother stereotypes featured alongside warrior stereotypes in university lectures, books, and commemorations, just as the figure of Zealandia stood beside a Māori warrior on the national coat of arms and women began to find a place in the Anzac legend. Women were gaining more space in the public world. But many social structures were yet to adapt.

DIVERSITY IN FILM AND ART

In New Zealand films by the 1990s, blokes as lead characters, and having blokey adventures, were succeeded by strong and quirky women – for example, in *The Piano* (1993), directed by Jane Campion; and in Peter Jackson's *Heavenly Creatures* (1994), which recreated the infamous Parker–Hulme murder case, of 1954, in Christchurch. *War Stories Our Mother Never Told Us* (1995), a feature film documentary by filmmaker Gaylene Preston, brought to life the stories of 'seven old ladies' who talked about their experiences during the Second World War. Preston paid tribute to her mother, who divulged her life secrets, that she had married because of a pregnancy, an unspoken yet common experience, and had an affair during the war but resumed her marriage for her son's sake.

New Zealand film also had gothic elements. It often starred the landscape, as if the environment were a character; for instance, Lee Tamahori's *Once Were Warriors* (1994) opens with a classic New Zealand scene: a billboard in a grubby urban setting. This movie reflected the evolution of Kiwi culture to include women and Māori. Based on the grim novel by Alan Duff, son of a Pākehā father and Māori mother, the film shocked audiences but resonated in the national psyche through its gritty portrayal of urban Māori and domestic violence. *Once Were Warriors* resulted from the deregulation of broadcasting. Tamahori was a commercial-television producer with a reputation for slick advertisements who progressed to Hollywood and filming James Bond movies.

If cultural pluralism marked these films, so did a fresh creativity and confidence that farewelled the cultural cringe. Globalisation provided funding for local products and local stories while recruiting a worldwide audience for stories of universal human interest. A resident creative class emerged that made film in New Zealand, but with international money, and produced a new cultural economy.

From the 1970s there was also a flowering of art expressing Māori and Pacific identity that blossomed into a renaissance. From Ralph Hotere's combining art and poetry to protest nuclear testing to Julia Morison's postmodern paintings and to Michel Tuffery, who gave sculptural shape to New Zealand's place in the Pacific, New Zealand art was distinguished by diversity, internationally celebrated yet located here. Shane Cotton drew on Māori history, spirituality, prophet movements, and themes of colonialism and biculturalism to explore colonisation, nationhood, and identity. Euan Macleod's figures walked through expressionist landscapes, while Bill Hammond portrayed the archipelago as a land of richly clothed birds, capturing in his paintings the sense of remoteness for birds as for humans.

The *Te Māori* exhibition (1984–7) was a landmark in showcasing Māori art and culture and the first time that Māori art was respected as art, not as ethnographic objects. However, the exhibition omitted weaving, which was largely but not exclusively a women's art form. Initiated by the Metropolitan Museum in New York and a New Zealand diplomat, the exhibition was seen by iwi leaders not only as an opportunity to celebrate Māori culture and show how much taonga meant to tangata whenua but also as a way of reviving the language. *Te Māori* triumphed from its opening in New York, in 1984, after which selected works toured the United States into 1986 and New Zealand in 1986–7. This was also the first time that museums and government officials engaged fully in the public display of taonga, guided by iwi.

By 1990 New Zealand had become officially bicultural and 1840 was celebrated as the birth date of the nation, symbolised by the signing of the Treaty of Waitangi, not by the beginnings of organised white settlement. The spirit of the Treaty emanated from Archives New Zealand in Wellington, where the Treaty documents lay on public display in a constitution room from 1991 until their move to the National Library. Government and the courts were making conscious efforts to provide redress for land improperly acquired, to listen to and accommodate Māori hopes, and to ensure fairness in the future. Historians joined artists in reflecting on the emergence of national identity, on Waitangi and Anzac, on biculturalism, on being Pākehā and being Māori.

Was New Zealand still colonial or was it postcolonial? Was Kiwi culture bicultural in practice, just as New Zealand speech was becoming, by adopting Māori words? Did national institutions deal fairly with minorities? Race trumped gender as a concern, because it always had done. The nation's history still pivoted around settler–indigenous relations, and so did sesquicentennial modes of remembrance. In 1990 a Māori filmmaker, Merata Mita, made the official film *Mana Waka*, a documentary that rediscovered forgotten footage of a project, initiated by Te Puea Hērangi for the centennial, in 1940, to build carved replicas of ancestral waka (canoes) that had brought the first people to Aotearoa. By filming the waka construction process Mita realised Te Puea's vision of restoring pride in Māori traditions. As her daughter recognised, in her work she 'decolonised the screen'.

THE SLOW DEATH OF WHITE NEW ZEALAND

It took longer for New Zealand to shift to multiculturalism, which it did from the 1980s in law and policy, and effectively from the 1990s. Federal Canada coined the term 'multicultural' to defuse historic tensions with the province of Quebec, whose relations with English Canada in practice followed a bicultural model. Unlike Māoridom, however, Quebec was governed by its own parliament. Some public figures warned that the Treaty of Waitangi created difficulties for multiculturalism. They advised that before politicians could imagine New Zealand as a melting pot, like the United States or multicultural Australia, they should settle Treaty grievances and accord the indigenous people proper acknowledgement. New Zealand therefore had first to adopt a bicultural model of state development before it could contemplate multiculturalism.

The new national museum, Te Papa Tongarewa (our place), on the Wellington waterfront, opened in 1998 and presented a history that focused on Māori–European interactions. Since the Treaty of Waitangi had acquired constitutional status culturally and gained some status in law (though not in a written constitution), Te Papa showcased the dual texts of the Treaty and acknowledged the first people as tangata whenua, the people of the land. The public accepted this recovery of the Treaty and the recognition of Māori. But there was outcry at the museum's placement of a painting by Colin McCahon alongside a 1950s refrigerator. The debate about the place of popular culture in culture showcased as 'national' touched raw nerves.

Some things stayed the same. As in the past, migrants to this distant and isolated archipelago sought a better life, a hope often expressed by the search for a secure, healthy place to raise their families. Migrant aspirations reinforced the idea of New Zealand as a good place to bring up children that was already embedded in national mythology. But the context changed from the colonial idea of a British nursery to the international concept of a clean, green New Zealand that provided an ideal environment in which to rear flexible, skilled, global citizens.

Increasingly from the 1970s, waves of New Zealanders became migrants themselves, seeking a better life in Australia, as a relative gap in gross domestic product opened between the countries. People continued to move freely both ways across the Tasman Sea, as they had done since the nineteenth century. From 1973 the citizens of each country could visit, live, and work in either country without a passport or visa; passports were introduced for trans-Tasman travel only in 1981. Australia continued to be the second largest source of newcomers to New Zealand after Britain. By contrast, the increasing volatility of long-term movement by New Zealanders and the growth in numbers departing for Australia were such that by the turn of the century New Zealanders comprised Australia's second largest overseas-born group. Trans-Tasman migration, significant since the 1800s, remained a substantial part of international arrivals and departures for both countries. The distinguishing features from the late twentieth century were that more and more New Zealanders left for Australia, the swings in arrivals and departures grew more volatile, and trans-Tasman people movement represented 'little more than another form of interregional migration within a single labour market'.

New Zealand became more integrated with Australia just when their populations were growing more diverse. New Zealand's growing Pacific identity owed much to history, accentuated by a postwar focus on the Pacific Islands as a source of labour and a site of development assistance. Through the 1950s and 1960s Pacific Islanders provided cheap labour for manufacturing industry, and immigration authorities tended to ignore those overstaying their work permits. Numbers of Pacific Islanders in New Zealand grew substantially, to over 200 000 in 1996, assisted from the 1970s by the building of airstrips in the Cook Islands, Niue, and Samoa. From the 1970s, however, their labour was in less demand. Successive governments launched crackdowns on overstayers, and the Muldoon government became notorious for this when the police launched dawn raids on the homes of Islanders suspected to carry expired permits.

Samoan New Zealanders also ran into difficulty. In a special case, the Privy Council in the United Kingdom appeared to confirm that Western Samoans born in Samoa when it was administered by New Zealand as a mandated territory could hold New Zealand citizenship. In 1982 Muldoon warned of the risk that Samoans would head to New Zealand in a mass exodus after this ruling. His government thought they were being generous in their response by granting New Zealand citizenship to all Samoans already in the country. Some Samoans had a different view of the Citizenship (Western Samoa) Act 1982. In their understanding, when New Zealand citizenship was introduced, in 1948, Western Samoans automatically became New Zealand citizens, and this remained the case when Western Samoa gained independence. So did Cook Islanders, because the Cook Islands were legally part of New Zealand from 1901 to 1965. The Privy Council supported that view.

From 1987 a change in immigration policy about family reunion allowed extended family members to join kin in New Zealand, so that by the 1990s most Pacific Islanders gaining residence who were not automatically New Zealanders were doing so not as workers but as family. By the end of the century Pacific Island New Zealanders were no longer migrants; they were New Zealanders, with multiple identities. They were also transnational citizens, with families spread across the Pacific in New Zealand (mainly Auckland), Australia (Sydney), and the United States (especially Los Angeles). Among Samoans the transnational diaspora overtook the population of Samoa. Twice as many Cook Islanders lived in New Zealand as in the Cook Islands, while the bulk of Niueans had left the coral outcrop for New Zealand. Scholars described Pacific Island extended family networks as 'transnational corporations', because of the significance of remittances sent to relatives in the islands. Reciprocal flows and obligations were further aspects of Pacific transnationalism that bound extended family members whose multicultural heritages and kin relationships crossed the Pacific.

Islanders travelled the pathways of their ancestors but at the same time created a new trans-Pacific constituency, the largest segment of which became New Zealand residents and citizens. Through mobility they acquired new layers of identity, while their resettlement altered New Zealanders' views of themselves. From hip-hop to the classical drum-driven compositions of the composer Gareth Farr, New Zealand music resonated with a Pacific rhythm and a Pacific sound. Pacific themes embellished fashion stores, interior decor, and home gardens.

Externally, the White New Zealand policy yielded to pluralism rapidly and late, as globalisation swept aside old prejudices. Following Australia, New Zealand shifted from a policy of immigration restriction that shut out 'Asia' to one of active encouragement of Asian business migrants and recruitment of international students. In keeping with the new links to Asia and the northern Pacific in the 1980s, in population and cultural flows, in the economy, travel, and consciousness, immigration policy shed race criteria from 1987 and replaced race barriers with benchmarks of skills and money. Rogernomics, economic integration, and transformed links required new rules that opened the nation to business migrants from Asia and an 'Austral-Asian' future.

Ruptures in total net migration set in by the 1970s, once the era of classical British migration ended and the country was exposed to new global pressures that pulled New Zealanders overseas, especially to Australia, and attracted newcomers to New Zealand, this time from Asia. The onset of significant migration swings, reflecting changes in economic conditions and government policy, is shown in figure 4.2. A flow of departures in the late 1970s resulted from Muldoonism and better opportunities across the Tasman, while a wave of arrivals in the 1990s stemmed from changed global circumstances and economic priorities that accepted Asian migrants who brought skills and capital. Forty per cent of newcomers were Asian, predominantly from North Asia, by 1999, while in 1999, as in the 30 years previously, most permanent and long-term expatriates (57 per cent) were in Australia.

After the first election under the mixed-member proportional representation system, in 1996, the New Zealand First Party, headed by Winston Peters, a populist politician of Māori descent, expressed anxieties about Asian immigration. Peters played the power broker in the fragile National–New Zealand First coalition government. Racist rhetoric targeted the migrants with the highest profile, who came from Asia. At the same time, minority voices began to be heard in politics and the media. The first member of parliament of Asian ethnic origin, Pansy Wong, entered parliament in 1996. The number of Asian people who migrated to New Zealand between 1986 and 1998 was 162 000, comprising over half (52 per cent) of the total net gain in non–New Zealanders. This was by no means an 'Asian invasion', as Peters claimed. The 1990s peak did not become a trend. Most new arrivals continued to be white, from Australia, the United Kingdom, or South Africa.

People with global interests and marketable skills increasingly led lives characterised by mobility and travel. If Pacific and Chinese people were transnational citizens, so were entrepreneurial and educated Māori and Pākehā. For over 200 years Sydney had been a Māori town as well as an alluring, metropolitan carnival and market. Australia served as an extension of home for those who sought new lives, brighter lights, and freedom to be themselves. Descendants of a mobile settler society behaved as if they were still following their migrant forebears. While Sydney remained the region's metropolitan centre, Auckland was New Zealand's fast-growing hub for migrants and economic activity, the most Australian of its cities with its low-density sprawl, the biggest home to Māori and Pacific Islanders from the 1960s, and the national centre of business and finance. Three out of 10 New Zealanders lived in greater Auckland by the end of the twentieth century.

Transnationalism and cultural globalisation showed in sport, turned by media into spectacle. National heroes, popularly represented by Sir Edmund Hillary, were men of the outdoors: adventurous, frontier types who strode across – and, some historians maintain, colonised – the landscape. They were men of the land but also of the sea. Increasingly women sailors and rowing crews navigated to success in the Olympic Games, proving they were heroes too. The America's Cup, offered in a yachting competition for rich entrepreneurs, became the trophy that New Zealand ought to have, especially once Australia had won it. By implication the nation's mariners were great navigators by birthright, idealised as the heirs of Captain Cook and Polynesian seafarers. Sir Peter Blake, the sailor who masterminded New Zealand's America's Cup wins in 1995 and 2000 (and was murdered by pirates on the Amazon), embodied the imperial type of hero. When his successors lost the cup and decamped to Switzerland, some read as betrayal the Kiwi sailors' status as yachting mercenaries.

The commercialisation of sport revived the image of rugby, by tailoring it for television. Fast-growing Pacific Island and Māori populations, the cult of the market, and the reality that team sports are less expensive strengthened Polynesian prominence in men's and women's teams, notably in rugby, rugby league, and netball. Selection for the All Blacks or for the Silver Ferns, the national netball team, offered a chance for talented youth to get on. Sports hero Jonah Lomu, a Tongan New Zealander, was a giant wing player who became a global brand. Rugby union's premier competition, Super 12 (later Super 15), comprising provincial teams from New Zealand, Australia, and South Africa, and a tri-nations test series between the three countries, generated new teams of rugby heroes in the 1990s. In Christchurch, it was no surprise that the local franchise should be called the Crusaders, that their Otago rivals should adopt the name Highlanders, or that Auckland would be home to the Warriors: colonial paths crisscrossed rugby fields. In such multifarious ways, global forces strengthened local identities.

By the twenty-first century, trade with the Pacific Rim dominated New Zealand's exports and imports. The country's major trading partners were Australia, the United States, and Japan. The United Kingdom, the Republic of Korea, the People's Republic of China, Hong Kong, and Germany ranked fourth to eighth after this trade triumvirate, and a shift to more focus on trade with China, the most populous world power, was in the air.

At a time of regional instability, in 1999, a 'defining moment in identity creation' occurred when Jenny Shipley, the first woman prime minister, chaired in Auckland the annual ministerial meeting for the economic forum APEC (Asia-Pacific Economic Cooperation). Ten years after its founding, in Canberra, APEC had grown to 21 member economies around the Pacific Rim. In Auckland, the focus of the meeting was not the removal of trade barriers, as suggested by the agenda, but the political and security question of violence in Timor-Leste (East Timor), whose people had voted for independence from Indonesia only days before. Indonesia had invaded the former Portuguese colony in 1975. As the APEC chair, New Zealand brokered an agreement to organise a United Nations peacekeeping force commanded by an Australian general, who, for the multinational operation, chose a New Zealand deputy whom he knew; such is the nature of defence force relationships.

New Zealand troops worked with Australians as peacekeepers in Bougainville from 1997 to 2003 and in Timor-Leste from 1999 to 2002 and, in response to further violence, from 2006 to 2012. The truce monitors organised by the New Zealand army in Bougainville displeased Australian officers who read New Zealand brokerage as interference in 'their' Pacific (since Bougainville is part of Papua New Guinea), but the friendly rivalry proved instructive. Māori soldiers mediated with locals and in doing so extended the country's reputation for harmonious race relations. New Zealand's warrior peacekeepers were much in demand with the United Nations, to the extent that the government could not keep up with requested commitments. The myth of harmonious relations between Māori and Pākehā might have been only partly true, but people believed it wherever the New Zealand army served well, with positive results. At home, the Anzac legend enjoyed a revival. Myths may inhibit but can also help in the search for common ground.

11

Shaky ground 2000–2016

Globalisation has always shaken the kaleidoscope of connections between people into new patterns. In the greatest global shift of power since the United States assumed Britain's former role in the world, China and India returned to global supremacy in the twenty-first century. By 2000, China loomed on the horizon as the next global juggernaut. Half a millennium after Europe rose to dominance, the world witnessed a fundamental rebalancing of West and East from the developed countries to the developing powers of North and South Asia. This metamorphosis in economic and power relations reshaped New Zealand's export economy.

WEST TO EAST

In a mere five years, the league table of trade relationships transformed. China, which ranked sixth in New Zealand's list of trading partners in 2000, overtook the United Kingdom by 2003. One of the world's biggest economies 'and one of the fastest growing', China rose rapidly to be New Zealand's third largest trading partner by 2008, when the two countries of vastly different sizes signed a free trade agreement: the first between China and a Western country. At this point, China emerged as New Zealand's second most important two-way trading partner, after Australia, followed by the United States and Japan.

The New Zealand–China Free Trade Agreement of 2008 proved life-changing for New Zealand, which was fortunate to be a partner, even if it qualified by being small and unthreatening. A success for both countries, despite their contrasting sizes and power, the agreement encouraged cooperation, created opportunities, and quadrupled New Zealand's goods exports to China over the next 15 years. That New Zealand was first in the West to obtain an agreement was a historic moment for New Zealand–China relations. Chinese premier Wen Jiabao praised Labour prime minister Helen Clark for her 'far sightedness' and emphasised that three of the four 'firsts' in New Zealand's relations with China were achieved under her leadership: New Zealand was the first country to agree to China's becoming a member of the World Trade Organization, the first to recognise China as a market economy, the first to open free trade negotiations with China, and the first to conclude them. The agreement eliminated tariffs, secured better market access, and increased exports and imports.

In 2001 New Zealand had secured a trade agreement with Singapore; in 2005 it obtained one with Thailand and another, jointly, with Chile, Singapore, and Brunei, the latter as part of the Trans-Pacific Strategic Economic Partnership. In 2010 New Zealand also signed a closer economic partnership agreement with Hong Kong and an agreement with Malaysia; in the same year New Zealand and Australia's free trade agreement with the Association of South-East Asian Nations entered into force. Significantly, diplomats also signed a free trade agreement with Korea that came into force in December 2015. These new relationships reoriented the community from a familiar Europe towards an unfamiliar Asia and redefined the meaning of 'Asia' for New Zealanders. In the early twenty-first century New Zealand's Asia stretched in an arc from Afghanistan, where army peacekeepers were stationed, through South and Southeast Asia to Timor Leste, and across the China Sea to major trading partners and sources of migrants in North Asia and East Asia, from China to Korea and Japan.

Simultaneously, demographic change altered the face of New Zealand. The percentage of people classified in the 2006 census as 'Asian' was larger than that of Pacific Islanders for the first time, with Asian people replacing Pacific people as the third largest group. The total labelled 'Asian' exceeded 400 000 (the two biggest groups being Chinese, at 148 000, and Indian, at 105 000), while the numbers of people of mixed descent had increased significantly. The Asian community engaged more actively with New Zealand society in general, in turn reshaping national culture through food, fashion, household goods, cars, and trains ordered for Kiwi Rail (which the government bought back after privatising the railways failed). Items labelled 'made in China' multiplied, most noticeably clothes.

South of Indonesia, Australasia continued to re-emerge, only without that name. China's rise clarified that New Zealand's closest relationship was with Australia. The Tasman neighbours were more integrated than at any other time in their history, even though Australia no longer ranked first as a trading partner. New Zealand sometimes behaved as an Australian state and at other times as an independent, sovereign nation, a status it enjoyed politically. A loose federalism operated in trans-Tasman political and economic relations through New Zealand's participation in ministerial councils and forums within the Council of Australian Governments, the intergovernmental structure in which the Australian federal, state, and territory governments met. New Zealand politicians and officials worked within the Australian federal model to the extent that doing so advanced the national interest and participated in Council of Australian Governments meetings from 1992, when the council was established, until 2020, when it was dismantled due to the Covid-19 pandemic.

Trans-Tasman relations grew closer despite a social welfare agreement in 2001 that restricted New Zealanders' eligibility for welfare in Australia, an agreement that was revised once injustices came to light in the wake of natural disasters. Australia and New Zealand also agreed to disagree on security policy. Business and government strove to advance the novel agenda of a Single Economic Market and of collaborating to mutual advantage. The finance ministers Michael Cullen (Labour) and Peter Costello (Liberal) announced the objective of a Single Economic Market in 2004 and established the Australia New Zealand Leadership Forum, of political and business leaders, to advance this goal. The degree of integration in spheres of law and policy was uneven but increased in 2010 with the creation of a trans-Tasman judicial area under Trans-Tasman Proceedings Acts passed in both parliaments. Keeping the relationship in good heart demanded political effort, which generated a near-domestic experience for travellers flying across the Tasman Sea, in the form of combined passport queues at airports and electronic SmartGate technology to speed processing through customs. Moments of alignment could pass quickly, however, with global shifts or changes of government. A quarter of New Zealanders surveyed in a poll in 2010 favoured another look at the question of whether New Zealand should become an Australian state, while 41 per cent thought the idea was worth debating. At heart, New Zealanders cherished their independence, which they were unlikely to sacrifice unless overwhelmed by a cataclysmic event.

At the same time, New Zealanders expected to retain their right of free entry to Australia under the Trans-Tasman Travel Arrangement. The big change in the flows of people occurred in the late 1960s, after the wool price crash, when more people were migrating from New Zealand to Australia than the other way. Migration to Australia surged in waves during every decade from the late 1970s to the late 2000s, driven by increasing gaps in real earnings and employment. Consequently, a high proportion of New Zealanders were living in Australia. By 2006, for every 100 New Zealanders in New Zealand, 15 people born in New Zealand were living in Australia. Many who lived in New Zealand visited Australia regularly as tourists or to see Australian family. Almost all Māori had whanau (extended family) across the Tasman, conspicuously on Queensland's Gold Coast, a popular holiday and retirement destination for New Zealanders and Australians.

Overlaying trade and migration flows, a new strategic zone emerged as the United States turned again to the Pacific, in response to the rise of China. In that context, the world changed on 11 September 2001, with the terrorist attacks on New York and Washington, DC. Yet again, there were advantages in being insignificant, perceived as safe, and not a threat to anybody. For New Zealand, the most likely terrorist threat was a pathogen that breached biosecurity. 'Security' held more meaning than 'defence' to a small country whose remoteness shaped its strategic outlook and threat perceptions. The Iraq War in 2003 illustrated how much had changed in New Zealand's outlook since the United

States had ended New Zealand's membership of the ANZUS alliance: Helen Clark's Labour-led government refrained from joining its historically great and powerful friends, the United States and the United Kingdom, in invading Iraq, sending only engineers to help with reconstruction efforts. The Clark government refused to commit troops, because the invasion did not have the backing of the United Nations.

Although Australia and New Zealand differed over the Iraq conflict, New Zealand committed troops to Solomon Islands alongside Australian forces in 2003. A revived Anzac spirit pervaded regional peacekeeping missions in Bougainville, where a peace agreement was signed in 2001, followed by the commitments in Timor-Leste and Solomon Islands. By 2010, a government white paper on defence policy expressed a global outlook with a focus on peace and security in the Asia-Pacific, mindful that New Zealand belonged to 'a region which is changing as the Asian powers grow'. The paper listed national security interests as a 'safe and secure New Zealand', a 'rules-based international order', development of strong international links, and a 'sound global economy underpinned by open trade routes'. Australia remained most important for security as the country's closest relationship and sole ally.

New Zealand's security relationship with the United States began to thaw despite disagreement about the conflict in Iraq. The inaugural United States–New Zealand Partnership Forum, in Washington, DC, in 2006, signalled attempts to improve the relationship for both sides. To the public's astonishment, cables later released by WikiLeaks divulged that full intelligence cooperation with the United States was restored in 2009. New Zealand's nuclear-free identity remained reflective of a common purpose, though questions began to be asked about the policy's relevance in a post–Cold War world. In an ideological turnaround, the president of the United States Barack Obama invited the New Zealand prime minister John Key to the 2010 Nuclear Security Summit, in Washington, DC. Nuclear-free New Zealand fitted with Obama's campaign for global nuclear disarmament. These developments merged in the Wellington Declaration, signed by United States secretary of state Hillary Clinton during her first visit to New Zealand, in 2010, which named New Zealand a 'strategic partner', including in the South Pacific, where the United States finally ratified the South Pacific Nuclear-Free Zone, which had generated such dissent in the 1980s.

MONEY, MORALS, MARKETS

Fortunately, the power shift from the United States to China helped New Zealand weather the global financial crisis from 2008, the most serious economic event since the Depression. The country's markets in East Asia and Australia were much less affected. New Zealand benefited from China's and India's influences on regional growth and, more directly, from the strong Australian recovery. It was a blessing that New Zealand was closely integrated with Australia. While New Zealand supplied primary products to Asia, Australia remained its biggest market in food and manufacturing exports. The crisis was 'widespread', originating from the banking sector, and struck the housing market 'particularly hard'. A series of financial companies collapsed like dominoes, evaporating retirement savings: Bluechip, Hanover Finance, Bridgecorp. New Zealand entered recession late in 2008, unlike Australia, reaching a trough in 2009. Failures flowed on into 2010, when the crisis toppled the South Island's richest philanthropist. But in New Zealand, as in other countries, Keynesian-style fiscal stimulus helped to cushion the economy. This time, New Zealand was protected by the Australian banking system. Asian trading partners were also differently positioned from New Zealand in the world economy.

Labour-government initiatives to cater for an ageing population proved timely. Though compulsory superannuation was politically unpalatable, in 2001 Clark's Labour-led government had established the New Zealand Superannuation Fund (popularly named the 'Cullen fund', after its creator, the minister of finance Michael Cullen) to make superannuation more affordable in the long term. Savings increased, encouraged by the KiwiSaver scheme, launched in 2007. The goods and services tax rose to 15 per cent in 2010: a more modest effort to address the budget deficit than those made in indebted European countries.

During Clark's prime ministership social and liberal reforms accumulated in pursuit of human rights and towards a more pluralistic, peaceful society. Clark apologised to Samoa in 2002 for its treatment under New Zealand colonial rule and to the New Zealand–born Chinese community for discrimination under the White New Zealand policy. There was greater acceptance of diversity in intimate relationships and sexuality as social attitudes grew more tolerant. Homosexual-law reform by the fourth Labour government, in the 1980s, had legalised sex between males over 16, reducing prejudice. Subsequently, in 1993, an amendment to the Human Rights Act outlawed discrimination based on sexuality. A new round of debate over sexuality and morality in the new century relaxed traditional codes of conduct. The Prostitution Law Reform Act 2003 legalised prostitution, removed the double standard of morality whereby sex workers, but not their clients, were criminalised, and gave workers rights. Law reform also reframed ideas of relationships between couples, in the Civil Union Act 2004, which allowed state-registered civil unions an equivalent status to marriage, regardless of gender.

Some dismissed these reforms, together with 'anti-smoking' and 'anti-smacking' legislation, as social engineering. From December 2004 smoking was not allowed in passenger vehicles or terminals, indoors in hotels or restaurants, in school grounds or at childcare centres, or in the workplace. Green member of parliament Sue Bradford's anti-smacking legislation, in 2007, which removed the statutory defence in the Crimes Act that parents could use 'reasonable force' to discipline a child, proved most controversial of all. Both measures reflected international trends. The anti-smacking law answered criticism from the United Nations' Committee on the Rights of the Child that New Zealand was the only country with legislation that allowed parents to use reasonable force to discipline children. Detractors, however, condemned the measure as continuing the nanny state and attempted, unsuccessfully, to overturn the law change by referendum.

In every culture, people walk along paths taken by their ancestors. At times the ground moves, rendering old paths perilous, and nowhere is this more clearly seen than in oral traditions. For Pākehā (European New Zealanders), Captain James Cook and Sir Edmund

Hillary shared 'a common narrative of discovery and exploration'. The nation honoured Hillary with a state funeral when he died, aged 88, in 2008. As the locus of interest shifted to Asia, however, Hillary began to be remembered not just as a 'British' hero who climbed Mount Everest at the time of Queen Elizabeth II's coronation but as a pioneer of relations with South Asia, through his philanthropic work building schools and hospitals in Nepal, and in the 1980s as David Lange's government's ambassador to India.

New heroes materialised in sport with the arrival of football ('soccer' in New Zealand) in national consciousness. The All Whites captained by Ryan Nelsen delighted the nation by being undefeated in the 2010 FIFA World Cup. The 'tournament's plucky minnows' defended 'like giants' in a draw against the world champions, Italy. Still, the All Blacks stood supreme in sporting affections and in hopes of hosting the 2011 Rugby World Cup.

Women as heroes grew more prominent, and in an era of assumed gender equality, Cook's and Hillary's attributes as people of action and outstanding merit applied to women too. The erstwhile colony chose ordinary people who achieved great heights and world firsts to be its heroes. Hillary was popularly remembered as saying, 'In some ways I believe I epitomise the average New Zealander. I have modest abilities, I combine these with a good deal of determination and I rather like to succeed'. Helen Clark followed this tradition, both as prime minister and in her post-political roles as head of the United Nations Development Programme in New York and as patron of the Helen Clark Foundation. A heritage of colonial stereotypes did not equate to continued colonialism when qualities such as ingenuity and quiet achievement, along with philanthropy, were reinterpreted to meet circumstances in modern life.

The filming in New Zealand of the film adaptation of J. R. R. Tolkien's *Lord of the Rings* trilogy, by director Peter Jackson and screenwriter Fran Walsh, suggested some possibilities, both for the United Kingdom's use as a historical reference point and for embellishing myths and ideas of New Zealand. The three films, launched respectively in 2001, 2002, and 2003, employed a cast of thousands. In New Zealand's village culture, just about everyone had some degree of association with the movies. The country became Middle Earth during filming, its varied landscape digitally enhanced for special effects. As intended, the environment performed as a character: 'something beautiful belonging to the land', identified by the artist Colin McCahon, finally belonged to its peoples and achieved a marketing coup. That New Zealand could pose as Middle Earth confirmed the power of inherited mythology.

It also reflected and reinforced a new environmental awareness, as did New Zealand's success in winning the 2004 Chelsea Flower Show. Winning the Best Show Garden award, the picturesque indigenous garden was embellished by a recreated geothermal landscape of the lost Pink and White Terraces as a historical reference (the terraces near Rotorua were destroyed by a volcanic eruption in 1886). Te Arawa, mana whenua (those with tribal authority) in the geothermal area, contributed tree ferns and carvings, continuing their people's role as providers of the indigenous element in national trademarks. The New Zealand Pavilion at the Shanghai Expo in 2010 similarly associated the landscape and the idea of a garden with national identity. Symbolic of the new relationship with the People's Republic of China, the pavilion stood on a prime site near the Chinese National Pavilion, its sloping roof garden landscaped with tussock at the top, descending through bush to a sculptured pohutukawa tree at ground level.

CHANGING CLIMATES

New Zealand's strength in dairy farming was less advantageous when the country competed with market segments in agriculture that were the most protected in the world. To achieve economies of scale, a new company, Fonterra, was created in 2001 from a merger of the New Zealand Dairy Board and the two largest dairy cooperatives, owned by about 96 per cent of dairy farmers. Consequently, China invited New Zealand to help introduce food-safety standards across the Chinese dairy industry and encouraged joint ventures to develop agricultural technologies that addressed climate change.

Locally, the growth of dairying intensified conflict over the pollution of waterways and water allocation. Voices rose to demand protection of the country's self-image as 'clean and green'. The pollution of the Manawatū River, which runs through former bushland long converted to grassland for dairy farming, was symptomatic of a national problem. The concept of 'improvement', it seemed, had reached its environmental limit. No longer could people take for granted the environmental advantages of a small population and abundant fresh water. New Zealand may have had the clearest natural fresh water in the world – in national parks. But intensive dairy farming had degraded lakes, rivers, and streams. Disputes over water were heated in the province of Canterbury, where dramatic changes in land use since the 1990s had seen the dry plains turn green with irrigation for intensive dairy farming and the braided rivers and groundwater dwindle. Environmentalists reminded governments that for water quality to improve and for water use to be sustainable their priorities ought to shift to economic sustainability. 'All flesh is as grass' required a rethink, due to environmental overreach.

Inevitably conflict erupted between environmental and recreational groups on the one hand and farming and business lobbies with water interests on the other. In a controversial move, John Key's National coalition government passed the Environment Canterbury (Temporary Commissioners and Improved Water Management) Act 2010, which sacked the elected members of the regional council responsible for water policy (Environment Canterbury) and replaced them with appointed commissioners. A public outcry ensued against this loss of power to the people, with protesters fearful that they had lost their voice's power as a brake on development and that Christchurch's pure, artesian water supply was at risk. The commissioners duly implemented the water-management strategy devised by Environment Canterbury, which shifted water management from a user-based system driven by applications for individual consents to an integrated approach towards sustainable management based on water-management zones. The commissioners exercised their new powers to impose moratoria on two over-allocated rivers, the Hurunui and Waiau, which halted water consents.

New Zealand's agricultural economy was most at risk from climate change in terms of sustainability, more severe weather, and distance from markets. Uniquely among developed countries, New

Zealand acquired a greater percentage of energy from renewable resources, principally hydroelectric power, and its greenhouse-gas emissions needed to be reduced in agriculture more than in industry. To protect the 'clean and green' brand and to meet the country's obligations under the Kyoto Protocol, the National coalition government announced that New Zealand would lead research to reduce agricultural emissions and introduced an emissions trading scheme, launched in 2010, that placed a price on carbon in fishing, industry, and forestry. Because farmers hotly contested the scheme, agriculture's entry was deferred until 2015. But some farmers began planting forests, and deforestation reversed. (The National coalition government led by Christopher Luxon backtracked from agreed targets when it removed agriculture from the emissions trading scheme in November 2024.)

Previously the country had showed leadership through the appointment of a New Zealand diplomat as chair of the Kyoto Protocol at the United Nations Climate Change Conference in Cancún, Mexico, in 2010. The hope was that the predicted higher temperatures would be moderated by New Zealand's geography, as an archipelago of islands deep in the South Pacific. Sea-level rise was the most obvious danger. While major earthquakes or the circulation patterns of oceans might override the impact of rising sea levels, in the long term rising seas and higher tides were expected to increase the erosion of beaches and the coast, breaching coastal defence systems and threatening seaside suburbs and settlements.

The coast itself was shaky ground politically in the early twenty-first century, when the beach again played host to cross-cultural encounters. A furore erupted because local Māori wanted to take up marine farming in the Marlborough Sounds, and local government refused to cooperate. In 2003 the Court of Appeal decided that Marlborough iwi (tribes) were entitled to test their claims to the foreshore and seabed in the Māori Land Court on the grounds that customary title continued to exist until specifically extinguished by law. Alarmed by this decision and fearing it undermined parliament's understanding that the Crown owned the foreshore and seabed, the Clark Labour government drafted a Foreshore and Seabed Bill – widely denounced by Māoridom – that legislated for Crown ownership on behalf of all New Zealanders. While the government insisted on asserting the supremacy of parliament, the country's top judges supported the Māori perspective, backed by Treaty jurisprudence since the 1980s about the principle of 'partnership'.

Unexpectedly, this debate brought to a head disagreements not only over ownership of the coast but also over the beach as a place central to Pākehā as well as Māori identities. The clash fired activist responses by the Māori sovereignty movement on one side and the Coastal Coalition on the other, the latter refusing to believe the guarantees given by the government and iwi leaders to free public access.

Somehow, New Zealanders needed to find common ground. A divisive speech at the Orewa Rotary Club by Dr Don Brash, leader of the opposition, in January 2004, suggested that finding common ground would require superior leadership. 'We are one country with many peoples', he expounded, adapting William Hobson's phrase from 1840. Effectively, Brash presented an article 3 reading of the Treaty of Waitangi, which suggested a swing away from the article 2 interpretations (see chapter 3) dominant since the 1980s. Explicit in Treaty settlements with tribes were agreements that Māoridom would participate in shaping the nation's future. Instead, Brash denounced Māori 'privilege'.

On the contrary, statistics told a story of Māori inequality and suggested specific measures were required to improve outcomes. For example, the seven Māori seats in parliament had proved necessary to ensure that proportional representation was working. By the 2002 election the mixed-member proportional electoral system had ushered into parliament 20 people of Māori descent, who held 15 per cent of the total 120 seats – approximately the proportion of Māori in the total population. These included members of parliament in Māori electorates, which increased from four to seven in number under mixed-member proportional representation, in proportion to the number of voters registered on the Māori roll.

From the complicated debate over the foreshore and seabed emerged a new political force: the Māori Party, established in 2004 to repeal the Foreshore and Seabed Act and regain the right of tribes to have their claims heard in court. Led by Tariana Turia, a former Labour member of parliament who left the Labour government over the issue, in partnership with Dr Pita Sharples, a distinguished educationalist who had participated in the *Te Māori* exhibition, the Māori Party opposed both the Act (passed in November 2004) and Brash's political dog-whistling. It therefore astonished the country when the Māori Party joined the conservative National coalition government after the November 2008 election. Equally surprisingly, the National Party led by John Key, a former foreign exchange dealer, promised to repeal the Foreshore and Seabed Act as part of a confidence-and-supply agreement with the Māori Party. This swerve by National towards a partnership with Māori sealed the new prime minister's reputation as a deal maker, just as the confidence-and-supply agreement with a non-Labour government marked a shift in Māori politics.

The Marine and Coastal Area (Takutai Moana) Act replaced the Foreshore and Seabed Act in March 2011, redefining the foreshore and seabed as a common space: the marine and coastal area. While some saw little difference between Crown ownership and the idea of the coast as a common space, owned by no one, which could never be sold, the Māori Party believed it had expunged the wrong of Crown ownership, which in its view amounted to another confiscation.

In such ways the coast served as a flashpoint for disputes over what was, in the main, common ground. The beach again became a site of exchange in the early twenty-first century, a place of new beginnings, uncertainty, and danger, where the extraordinary might happen. Efforts to rename and reclaim the foreshore as part of a 'common marine and coastal area' highlighted the dangers; 'beach' was too loaded a word, integral to competing identities.

A spectrum of Treaty settlements continued the work to quieten settler–indigenous tensions. Two involved iwi whose ancestors had not signed the Treaty of Waitangi. First, the Waitangi Tribunal's Central North Island inquiry heard claims by tribes living on the North Island's volcanic plateau. Seven tribes established the Central North Island Forests Iwi Collective, which obtained the largest of all Treaty of Waitangi settlements with the government: the 'Treelords deal', so named to rhyme with the 'Sealord's deal', on sea fisheries. Dr (Sir) Tumu Te Heuheu, paramount chief of Ngāti Tūwharetoa, had continued his forebears' leadership by initiating this agreement, when he proposed in 2007 that the

Labour-led government use the vast state forest lands in the region to settle historical Treaty claims. Assisted by Crown facilitators, he negotiated the terms with Michael Cullen, Deputy Prime Minister and Minister in Charge of Treaty of Waitangi Negotiations. The Treelords settlement, signed in 2008, was worth over $400 million, including Crown forest land, forestry rentals, and carbon credits under the emissions trading scheme. It transferred most state forests in the region to the seven iwi, including Kaingaroa Forest, the base of the postwar pulp and paper industry, which made the collective members the largest single forestry owner in the country. As Te Heuheu announced at the signing, the agreement represented 'an extraordinary example of what can be achieved when we focus on a clear vision for our future, establish a climate of trust and goodwill and maintain a determination to succeed'.

By contrast, a major Treaty settlement with Ngāi Tūhoe – one of the tribes in the Central North Island Iwi Collective – stalled in 2010 when Prime Minister John Key vetoed returning ownership of the 212 672-hectare Te Urewera National Park. At the heart of the disagreement rested Tūhoe's long-standing grievance at being disconnected from 'the exercise of authority over and within their homelands': the park *was* their homeland, carved from the 1896 Urewera District Native Reserve (see chapter 6). The tribe did not give up; Tūhoe held firm on the demand for internal self-government.

A country still adjusting to the accord between the National Party and the Māori Party, which lasted from 2008 to 2017, had yet to absorb such ideas. Previous Treaty settlements had returned only small parcels of conservation estate; and iwi had gifted back any significant sites to the nation, as when Ngāi Tahu returned Aoraki Mount Cook. This failure to reach a settlement showed how a national park, like the foreshore, held value and meaning for various identities.

The rebuff to Tūhoe exposed anxieties about the tribe's history of resistance to the settler state. The public knew little of this history; it knew only of Tūhoe and their prophet Rua Kēnana as suspect rebels. In the context of the twenty-first-century war on terror, it was easy to recast Tūhoe activism as terrorism. Media coverage of armed-police raids in the Urewera to uncover and apprehend an alleged terrorist network in 2007 evoked bitter memories for Tūhoe of the police raid to arrest Rua in 1916. This time, though, the veteran activist and artist Tame Iti was arrested. Missing was a climate of trust between the state and iwi in which issues of ownership and control of land could be resolved in an innovative way. Yet a successful model of how to solve the problems of ownership, control, and competing identities already existed at Bastion Point, in Auckland, a former site of protest. Since 1991 Bastion Point had not been Crown land but vested in Ngāti Whātua, managed by the iwi and Auckland City Council, with public access assured. Here was a precedent for finding common ground in the nation's largest city.

Auckland revised its governance in 2010, through local-government restructuring, to create an Auckland super-city. A single Auckland Council replaced four city councils and three district councils to lower costs and make the country's biggest city more liveable. This experiment raised questions about the balance of power between Wellington and Auckland, given Auckland's growth had far exceeded that of the other main cities, and whether Auckland would be more manageable or demand a greater share of the country's resources. Central and local government agreed on the aim to make Auckland, as the sole metropolis, a world-class city. But they disagreed over strategies for growth and investment in road or rail transport to solve Auckland's traffic problems. While the Auckland Council advocated a rail loop to service a compact, sustainable, denser city, the National-led government opposed this in favour of highways, as had its predecessors. Path dependence was significant.

What made Auckland exceptional among New Zealand cities was not just the rate at which it grew and decentralised after the Second World War but the speed at which Aucklanders took to driving cars because of the infrastructure decision in the 1950s to build highways on the United States model. Consequently, the proportion of trips by public transport in Auckland plummeted, from 58 per cent in the 1950s to 2 per cent by 2000, resulting in traffic gridlock and another round of debate over cars or rail.

Auckland's future mattered, because one in three people lived in the Auckland region. The country was home to 4.4 million

11.1 Meadowlands Shopping Centre, Howick, South Auckland, 2011
Photographer Jessica Mein Smith

people by 2010, of whom 1.4 million lived in Auckland. As the largest city Auckland attracted the most migrants, and ethnic diversity was increasing rapidly. Reflective of that diversity, Manukau and Māngere, in South Auckland, were areas in which the processes of cultural mixing and globalisation came together (see figure 11.1).

For New Zealand as a whole by 2010, the United Kingdom remained the commonest source of migrants, and towards one in four residents (23 per cent) were born overseas. But in Manukau the proportion of people born overseas was 41 per cent, for whom the most common birthplace was Samoa; while in Auckland city, 40 per cent of people were born overseas, and newcomers were most likely to have come from China. Two-thirds of Asian residents and two-thirds of Pacific people lived in the Auckland region: double the proportions in the total population. Rather than biculturalism giving way to multiculturalism, the two ideas coexisted in Auckland.

Global forces obliged New Zealanders to reorient themselves. The shift from West to East, momentous in world history, presented new answers to the questions of *what* and *where* New Zealand was and whether 'Aotearoa' was a better name for the remade community. Yet there were limits, which showed in attitudes to constitutional change. New Zealand was still a constitutional monarchy. Queen Elizabeth II was the queen of New Zealand and her other realms, and, courtesy of Henry VIII, the defender of the faith – roles inherited by her son King Charles III. Only with the establishment of the Supreme Court, which sat for the first time in 2004, did New Zealand sever the last residual ties with the United Kingdom, by ending the right of appeal to the Privy Council. Prince William nonetheless opened the Supreme Court's new building, in Wellington, which some found quaint and others, anachronistic.

Constitutional review made up part of the relationship accord and confidence-and-supply agreements between the National Party and the Māori Party in 2008 and 2011. John Key's National coalition government announced a review of constitutional arrangements and appointed a bicultural advisory panel of distinguished citizens, who duly reported on areas on which the public widely agreed in 2013. That prompted the government to settle on the easiest and least electorally risky option, of asking New Zealanders to consider a new flag, and to sidestep questions about the role of the Treaty of Waitangi and whether to move to a written constitution, which were included in the review's terms of reference, and whether the nation should become a republic, which was excluded.

Revising the flag was the most practical option, given each parliament had a short term, of three years, to introduce reforms. Key promoted a new flag for international branding purposes, and two referenda were held, in 2015–16, the first to choose a new design and the second to decide between the new design and the existing flag. The old flag won, despite its similarity to its Australian cousin. Evidently it did not matter to most voters that the current flag, adopted by colonial New Zealand in 1902, was based on the British Blue Ensign, with a Union Jack in the upper hoist corner. New Zealanders had a long attachment to their flag's blue background, symbolising the Pacific Ocean, and the four red stars, representing the Southern Cross.

The referenda results revealed that citizens were not ready to shed the monarchy, nor were they ready for a written constitution. Instead, people remained content with the one found in various statutes, legal documents, court decisions, and conventions, as explained in the government's Cabinet Manual. The manual also declared that the New Zealand constitution acknowledged the Treaty of Waitangi as a founding document of government that could limit majority decisions. A national emergency might be necessary, then, to spark constitutional change.

EARTHQUAKES

A series of calamities in 2009–11 called for Anzac qualities of mateship, solidarity, and bravery, and a new attribute: resilience, a word heard often in the next decade. Deadly bushfires in Victoria in 2009 were followed in 2010 by massive floods in the Australian eastern states and, in New Zealand on 4 September 2010, a magnitude 7.1 earthquake centred near Christchurch. Miraculously, no one died, since the city was asleep, though damage was widespread. In November, an explosion at the Pike River coal mine, on the South Island's West Coast, killed 29 miners, exposing lapses in safety.

It was therefore a shock when a more devastating earthquake struck Christchurch on 22 February 2011, at 12.51 p.m., when adults were at work and children were at school. An aftershock of the September earthquake, the February 2011 rupture measured less on the Richter scale (6.3) but was far more extreme in its ground acceleration, shaking, and destructive fury. It ripped and shook the land, buildings, and people, killing 185, injuring thousands, and destroying 10 000 homes. Australian and New Zealand emergency teams responded in concert, while specialist search-and-rescue volunteers, police, firefighters, and medical personnel raced from one disaster zone to the next.

Compared to stretches of geological time, New Zealand's brief human history suddenly seemed insignificant to those affected, standing on that shaky ground. Beneath the sediments of the Canterbury plains, two hitherto unknown faults ruptured into life after, perhaps, 10 000 years of inactivity, the first to the city's west and the second beneath the Port Hills, in the city's south. Such was the degree of ground movement that the land had to be resurveyed afterwards. The September 2010 earthquake caused ground displacement of between 1 and 5 metres, while the extraordinary shaking and acceleration in February 2011 thrust the Port Hills 40 centimetres higher. By contrast, in some eastern suburbs the ground sank permanently, due to liquefaction, and continued sinking along the coast well into the 2020s.

'Solid as rock' held no meaning for locals when hill homes built on rocky outcrops and spurs in Port Hills suburbs toppled and crumbled, rockfalls tumbled from cliff faces, and historic stone buildings collapsed, especially churches. Christchurch's heritage architecture lay in ruins, including the magnificent provincial government buildings and Christ Church Cathedral, the symbolic heart of the city (see figures 11.2 and 11.3).

Natural icons crumbled too. Locals mourned the collapse of Shag Rock Rapanui, a sea stack of volcanic origin, which stood

11.2 Before the earthquake. Christ Church Cathedral, Christchurch, 2006
Photographer Mark Tremewan

11.3 After the earthquake. Christ Church Cathedral, Christchurch, after 22 February 2011. Dean Peter Beck stands in the foreground.
Courtesy of Christ Church Cathedral

sentinel on Sumner beach, at the entrance to the estuary of the Avon and Heathcote rivers. Tangata whenua (people of the land) likewise mourned the rock named by their ancestors. With Rapanui reduced to a mound reminiscent of a fallen chimney stack, locals affectionately rechristened it 'Shag Pile'. Life for Cantabrians would never be the same again, made more alert to the environment as they were by the forces of nature. Their history changed forever, and so did the future they had anticipated.

New Zealanders learnt about themselves from these experiences. Residents discovered their strength as survivors and modelled unity and community spirit. The mayor spread confidence and hope. A new politics took shape, organised online through the new social media: groups such as the Canterbury Communities Earthquake Recovery Network and the Student Volunteer Army of university students rallied to help, communicating by way of blogs, forums, Twitter, and Facebook. The 'Farmy Army' of farmers drove into town with water tankers and bulldozers to clear silt from streets and gardens, a job the Student Volunteer Army also tackled enthusiastically with shovels.

Sadly, the community's global connections showed in the names of the dead: international students from Japan, China, Korea, and the Philippines perished when their language school collapsed. Search-and-rescue teams hastened from overseas to assist with the rescue and recovery effort, from Australia, the United Kingdom, the United States, Mexico, Japan, and China. While the visiting Singaporean military stayed to patrol the cordoned-off 'red zone' alongside New Zealand army colleagues, medical specialists rushed from a conference venue in the city to help rescue the injured from damaged buildings, and the Australian army set up a field hospital. The widespread support was etched into collective memory.

So were the tragedies. The worst building disaster, the collapse of the CTV building, killed 115 people, including the language students. The collapse resulted from poor engineering design. Among older buildings, the commonest flaw proved to be unreinforced concrete facades, which crashed onto pavements, endangering lives. The central city, with its stock of elderly brick buildings, was particularly hard hit.

As a constitutional monarchy, New Zealand received a visit from a member of the British royal family. Before his wedding, in 2011, Prince William flew from the United Kingdom as family representative to comfort earthquake-ravaged Christchurch and the Pike River mineworkers' grieving families, as well as flood-affected Queensland (see figure 11.4). The visit delighted many. Cries of 'God save the king!' rang out around Hagley Park as the prince greeted the public after the earthquake memorial service in March.

Residents knew the aftermath called for patience, adaptability, and hard work. But they were yet to discover that they would live through 10 000 tremors during the Canterbury Earthquake Sequence of 2010–12. Neighbourhood ties and communities strengthened; people's resilience shone amid sadness, trauma, and

11.4 Prince William greeting locals on his visit to Sumner, a quake-hit seaside suburb of Christchurch, 18 March 2011
Photograph by author

discomfort. 'Courage and understated determination have always been the hallmark of New Zealanders', Prince William reassured the public on his grandmother's behalf.

REBUILD

In the 15 years following the earthquakes, Christchurch succeeded in rebuilding a vibrant community and a renewed city with energy and an ambience that attracted young people. It took time for the new mood to be obvious. Residents who suffered severe damage or whose homes were demolished might have felt aghast had they known that rebuilding would take a decade or more, because of insurance technicalities. Repairs were quicker. Fortunately, locals learnt to cope. The phrase 'Kia Kaha!' (stay strong), used by the Māori Battalion, bestowed comfort in disaster, which seemed unceasing, as earthquakes rocked the South Island from 2013 and the North Island from 2014 to 2021.

A magnitude 7.8 earthquake at Kaikōura, on the South Island's east coast, in November 2016 irreparably damaged infrastructure and buildings and killed two people. This time 20 faults ruptured, triggering not just the earthquake but a tsunami, landslides, and slips that closed the main coastal highway and railway line. Strikingly, the coastline rose between 0.5 and 2.0 metres and up to 5.5 metres in places. This disrupted the local seal population, which was finally recovering from the slaughter by sealers 200 years earlier, because the uplift of rocky shoreline displaced the seals from their breeding grounds.

In every affected location, people shared the goal to build back better after the earthquakes. One question was whether to restore a severely damaged building or demolish it and start again. After some controversy, the 1972 Christchurch Town Hall, designed by establishment architects Warren and Mahoney, was restored to better than the original, strengthened to 100 per cent of the building code, and reopened in 2019. New landmarks appeared in the city centre, such as a public library, a convention centre, a replacement Court theatre, a sports stadium, and a sports complex. An Edwardian theatre was saved through refurbishment. The colonial inner grid of streets in the 'old town', which were named after bishoprics of the British Empire, was embellished by a series of precincts, all with new architecture, a cluster of laneways for boutique shopping, and the tempting seven-day Riverside Market. Like new developments in hospitality and housing, these initiatives owed their genesis mostly to enterprise in the private sector. Such enhancements heralded the old town's replacement by a 'new city' that was more lively and diverse.

The local iwi, Ngāi Tahu, emerged as the new city's new powerbrokers. Leaders actively shaped the design of 'new', multicultural Christchurch, providing a set of tribal narratives to guide the rebuild. It was they who rescued the toppled statues of Queen Victoria and Captain James Cook from the ignominy of permanent removal as colonial relics and had them reinstalled in Victoria Square, named for Queen Victoria, in a new context of indigenous stories told through art, etched into the surrounding paving. Ngāi Tahu had honoured Victoria since their ancestors signed the Treaty of Waitangi. The tribe also gifted names for rebuilt institutions, such as pools and schools, as well as streets and subdivisions.

Nor did colonial Christchurch resurface from the post-quake landscape of boarded-up ruins dotted around the city that were owned by private investors, because, where wrecked buildings remained, graffiti artists covered them with street art, while sleek new architecture increasingly outshone remnants of the old. The rebuild took a decade or more in zones of severe damage, often by waterways and in the city's east. In the central city, owners mothballed or paused the restoration of prominent heritage buildings, including two most esteemed: Christ Church Cathedral and the Provincial Council Chambers, the latter built between 1859 and 1865 to house the nineteenth-century provincial government. Both examples of neo-Gothic architecture, these landmarks raised questions about how feasible it was to restore cultural heritage, given unaffordable costs, and about how to estimate the opportunity costs of not starting afresh with new buildings that could be designed to tell a heritage story. The Catholic cathedral was demolished, despite its outstanding architectural significance, to be replaced, eventually, by a new cathedral on the same secondary site.

The Christ Church Cathedral rebuild proved most controversial, because the cathedral was central to the identity of the 'old city'. The Anglican Church initially decided to demolish the cathedral and, from the skeleton of the old, build a new one, designed by Sir Miles Warren, who had co-designed the town hall. But a powerful reinstatement group led by wealthy, retired, 'old town' politicians blocked the path to an affordable, on-site replacement by taking the church to court, and the Anglican Synod backed down. With inadequate insurance and without government funding, the expensive rebuild could not proceed. In the meantime, on the site of one of its inner-city stone churches destroyed by the earthquakes, the Anglican Diocese erected a transitional cardboard cathedral designed by Japanese architect Shigeru Ban, a specialist in disaster architecture. The cardboard cathedral was cheap, attractive, undoubtedly fit for purpose, and built merely two years after the February 2011 earthquake. The city learnt lessons from this outcome.

Courtesy of the earthquakes, Christchurch experienced 'an abrupt rupture from the past', sidestepping the task of transitioning from a colonial to a postcolonial city. It shed its staid reputation and acquired a funky one from increasing numbers of young people. The 'old town', which originated in the Canterbury settlement of the 1850s, found itself outclassed by the 'new city' of 'creatives, students, hipsters and yo-pros' and by the youth in services and trades doing the rebuilding. But enough heritage survived to create a distinctive blend.

12

Beached 2017–2025

Uncertainty and disaster lurked despite New Zealand's remoteness, for danger lay within. In March 2019, mass shootings at two Christchurch mosques shocked the country and the world. New Zealand was supposed to be a peaceful place; it enjoyed a reputation for peace, not violence. Terrorism and mass murder were alien, except for episodes in the colonial New Zealand Wars or the invasion of Parihaka, a forerunner of passive resistance, in 1881 (see chapter 4).

On 15 March 2019, an unforgettable autumn day, a lone Australian gunman inflicted his right-wing, racist, white supremacist, Islamophobic views on worshippers at the Al Noor Mosque (Masjid Al Noor), opposite South Hagley Park, in Christchurch, during Friday prayers, shooting dead the elderly gentleman who welcomed him at the entrance and then firing at the congregation. Heavily armed with military-style weapons, the gunman then drove at speed to the Linwood Islamic Centre, where he murdered more innocent people before a plucky mosque member hurled objects at him and chased him off. In a brief time, the terrorist shot and killed 51 people and injured many more. Compounding the crime, he live-streamed his murderous rampage at Al Noor on Facebook.

Prime Minister (later Dame) Jacinda Ardern, the youngest woman head of government in the world after the 2017 election, immediately moved to calm the populace. She made international headlines with her compelling rhetoric and for covering her head with a scarf out of respect for Islam. As leader of the Labour-led coalition government, Ardern called for unity. 'They are us', she said, a slogan both praised and criticised, since some New Zealand Muslims felt othered more than included by Ardern's unifying phrase. Imam Gamal Fouda of Al Noor Mosque, however, declared the prime minister's response extraordinary, because she not only led the country but stood as a friend with the Muslim community. Most of the public agreed that the prime minister showed exceptional, compassionate leadership.

The government responded to this horrific episode in three main ways. First, gun reform targeted the loophole through which the terrorist had obtained a gun licence in a government buyback scheme under which the police collected prohibited firearms. Second, Ardern adopted a global strategy and organised the Christchurch Call to Action Summit, held in May 2019, in Paris, two months after the shootings, in partnership with France's president, Emmanuel Macron. The Christchurch Call aimed to stop the use of social media internationally to facilitate violent, extremist content online. Third, the government established a royal commission of inquiry to investigate the actions of the offender, the police, and other agencies, and to recommend changes that might prevent such terrorist attacks in future. The commission reported five years later. It found that ethnic and religious communities, especially Muslim communities, consistently reported discrimination. The rhetoric of right-wing politicians did not help. New Zealanders in general, however, were friendly and welcoming to newcomers, while people noticed a warming in attitudes after the attacks.

In Christchurch, the outpouring of empathy and concern for the victims reinforced the feeling of unity in crisis. Stunned that such an awful event could occur in their peaceful community, the public laid bouquets of flowers, accompanied by written words of sympathy and comfort, en masse along the fence beside the Botanic Gardens (see figure 12.1). Others gathered to offer condolences and read the messages left for the victims' families. Artwork popped up around town, including 51 white chairs painted by volunteers in remembrance of the victims (martyrs in Islam). Particularly powerful was the Muslim call to prayer and the following prayers led by the imams from the two mosques held in Hagley Park one week later, introduced by Ngāi Tahu. Pākehā

12.1 Bouquets and messages for the victims of the Christchurch massacre, Botanic Gardens, Rolleston Avenue, Christchurch, 2019 Photographer Philippa Mein Smith

women (European New Zealand) mourners sitting in the park covered their heads out of respect, like the prime minister. People at the open-air call to prayer were deeply affected, as were those who attended a subsequent outdoor remembrance service.

After this profound shock, it felt cataclysmic when the World Health Organization declared a worldwide health emergency in January 2020 and the Covid-19 pandemic reached New Zealand in late February. The Ardern-led government decided that protecting public health was the premier economic and health approach to the pandemic, consistent with international best practice. It imposed a nationwide lockdown from late March to May, including a 'stay at home' order in March–April, and a system of managed isolation to prevent community transmission. These evidence-based strategies, combined with clear communication by public health professionals, were successful. Three experts proved unflappable. The director-general of health (Sir) Ashley Bloomfield stood at a podium alongside the prime minister to give daily briefings for television, academic Dr Siouxsie Wiles explained the science of the pandemic to the public, and Professor Michael Baker advocated eliminating Covid-19 rather than trying to 'flatten the curve'.

Ardern the communicator coined the phrase 'team of five million' to convey the idea that New Zealanders would address the Covid-19 threat together as a united community. Covid-19 was eliminated in New Zealand by August 2020, and Ardern's popularity soared. She and the Labour Party were rewarded with a historic majority in the 2020 election. For the first time since the mixed-member proportional voting system was introduced, the winning party won sufficient votes (50 per cent) to govern alone. However, public unity soured after a second lockdown, in August 2021, in response to community cases of a new Covid variant in Auckland and Wellington. Though restrictions were eased, they ended only in August 2023, leaving many people hurt economically.

The strategies chosen were highly successful from a health perspective. International media praised Ardern's swift and effective response, especially her skill in persuading New Zealanders to accept elimination as a strategy, which reduced the number of potential deaths. The Bloomberg Covid Resilience Ranking placed New Zealand second, behind Singapore, for its pandemic action. It could have ranked first if not for its slower vaccination rates.

But the virus was not eliminated in the long term. Covid became endemic despite the introduction of vaccines from late 2020. Vaccine mandates divided opinion. Economically the lockdowns left their mark, because so many businesses had to close. As usual, the most disadvantaged struggled the most. New Zealand's economy entered a recession in the final quarter of 2023, less than 18 months after a previous economic contraction. Market watchers attributed the downturn to interest rates, which had increased in response to inflation after the pandemic. Ardern's government itself proved a major casualty. Despite having been rewarded with a large majority in 2020, the Labour government was ousted in the October 2023 election, after the mood of the electorate reversed dramatically, illustrating the impact of economic distress, and uncertainty and disillusionment, especially about the cost of living. Ardern's announcement before the election that she was leaving parliament added to the mix, as did some controversial policy proposals.

CONSTRAINTS ON THE TREATY

A previous period of economic crisis, under the fourth Labour government in the 1980s and the Bolger National government in the 1990s, both neoliberal converts, provided the context for the beginnings of the Treaty of Waitangi settlements process between iwi (tribes) and the Crown, in which the Waitangi Tribunal heard claims by tribes, and the government apologised for Treaty breaches and negotiated redress. The settlement of claims continued through the 2020s. By this time the Treaty was widely accepted as the nation's founding document of government, central to its history, identity, and future. Such had been the shift in attitudes and understanding since the 1980s that, with te reo Māori (the Māori language) in recovery, some New Zealanders preferred to call their country Aotearoa New Zealand, or simply Aotearoa.

In this context, it is telling that just three – half – of the six political parties in parliament after October 2023 committed to honour the Treaty of Waitangi and acknowledged its status as the founding document in their party principles: the Labour Party, the Greens, and Te Pāti Māori (the new name for the Māori Party from 2023). At the time, these parties were in opposition. The three parties conspicuous for their silence on the Treaty were National, ACT, and New Zealand First: coalition partners from October 2023 in the right-wing government led by Prime Minister Christopher Luxon of the National Party. This split reflected the state of the nation and marked an abrupt change in the tenor of parliamentary politics.

Under the Luxon-led coalition, the political climate veered from sympathy and support for Treaty edicts and claims to imposing limits on the Treaty. On the pretext of cost-cutting, the government abolished both the Office for Māori Crown Relations (established by the Ardern government to oversee Treaty settlements and applications for customary rights to the coast, foreshore, and seabed) and the Māori Health Authority. Budget cuts affected Māori more than any other group, increasing inequality. Water-management legislation diminished Māori input into water services. Accusing the public service of overusing te reo Māori, the government introduced an English-first policy, which targeted allegedly unnecessary use of Māori names and language.

As a condition of the minority ACT party's support for the coalition agreement, needed for National to secure power, Prime Minister Luxon agreed to a first reading of a Principles of the Treaty of Waitangi Bill championed by David Seymour, the leader of ACT. Like Don Brash before him, Seymour alleged that the Treaty of Waitangi treated Māori as privileged participants in public decision-making. In the contrary view, the Treaty promoted equality; it was only fair to expect Māori to contribute to public judgments about Māori matters.

From the perspectives of iwi and the Waitangi Tribunal, the bill's proposals to constrain the Treaty and misinterpret its meaning were dangerous. Treaty principles already existed, created since the 1980s by the Waitangi Tribunal and the courts; those most familiar to the public were partnership, protection, and participation. Seymour's principles, on the other hand, appeared intended to revise the Treaty's meaning for political purposes. Previous National politicians claimed the bill was unnecessary and would remove indigenous rights, because it failed to reflect accurately the Treaty signed in 1840.

Outside parliament, 42 king's counsel (senior lawyers) called for the government to abandon the bill, since it directly attacked the Treaty and sought to change its meaning without consulting Māori. Moreover, it was not the government's place to 'reinterpret constitutional treaties' retrospectively. Protesters, among them 440 church leaders, reiterated that the Treaty embraced all New Zealanders. Anthropologist Dame Anne Salmond agreed, explaining that the Treaty was about relationships in a power-sharing arrangement in which the governor, and later the government, acted as mediator. The Treaty was a multilateral agreement that enabled deal making which respected indigenous values and provided a check on government power. The coalition resented any such check, while Seymour repeated the myth that the Treaty had to change because it created Māori privilege.

Iwi leaders strongly opposed the bill. The seventh Māori king, Tūheitia Pōtatau Te Wherowhero VII (2006-24), organised a national hui (meeting) for unity against government policies judged to harm Māori rights, which 10 000 people attended at short notice. The king so vigorously opposed the bill that he convened more hui to block what he recognised was an attempt to change the Treaty's meaning. He wanted people to focus on the words of the Treaty as written.

When the king died, on 29 August 2024, Pākehā learnt something about the Kīngitanga (King movement) and Māori burial practices, because the king's tangi (wake) was screened on television for a week. At his burial, his 27-year-old daughter, Ngā Wai Hono i te pō Paki, accompanied him up their tribe's sacred mountain, where he was laid to rest and she was anointed queen. The previous Māori monarchs, all buried on the mountain, included Dame Te Atairangikaahu, the first Māori queen, who was Ngā Wai Hono i te pō Paki's grandmother. The second queen was chosen to represent a youthful population who were increasingly fluent in te reo.

With her retinue the new queen soon joined one of the largest marches ever seen in New Zealand, Te Hīkoi mō te Tiriti (the march for the Treaty), in November 2024, to oppose the Treaty Principles Bill and the reversal of Māori rights (see figure 12.2). The hīkoi, which travelled the country, conveyed the message of unity within a festival atmosphere by including groups such as Asians for te Tiriti as well as Pākehā supporters. After nine days on

12.2 Te Hīkoi mō te Tiriti (the march for the Treaty), Hastings Hīkoi, 16 November 2024. The banner stating 'Toitū te Tiriti' (uphold the Treaty) was carried all the way to Wellington. Photographer Paul Taylor

12.3 Te Hīkoi mō te Tiriti (the march for the Treaty), Wellington, 19 November 2024. Protesters rest outside the Beehive, which houses Cabinet ministers.
Photographer Kevin Peng

the road, on 19 November the protesters rallied outside parliament (see figure 12.3). An estimated 42 000–50 000 people, possibly more, crowded into parliament grounds chanting, 'Kill the bill!'

The public response to the government select committee process on the Treaty Principles Bill illustrated the degree of feeling. Over 300 000 people submitted on the bill early in 2025, crashing the official website. Of the submitters, over 90 per cent opposed the bill; only 8 per cent were in support. Iwi leaders stated passionately that they would not allow the Treaty to be undermined. Former prime minister Sir Geoffrey Palmer rebuked the government for not following correct process and for wasting time and money, while

National's Dame Jenny Shipley, who had been the nation's first woman prime minister, described the bill as 'unconscionable' for diverging from the 'innovative relationship' created by the Treaty.

In April 2025, the divisive bill was roundly defeated in parliament, by 112 votes to 11. This result was consistent with the loud 'no' from submitters to the select committee.

CUSTOMARY TITLE

The renewed debate over indigenous issues extended to customary title. As the Treaty settlements process rolled on, the focus of claims shifted from land to waterways, and customary marine title, the latter previously termed 'title to the foreshore and seabed'. In the Māori world view, rivers, lakes, and springs were taonga (treasures) vital to wellbeing and ways of life. Waterways were resources, each with a distinctive character. They were living entities of spiritual significance in which various hapū (subtribes) held separate interests. Lakes traditionally could be divided into family plots to show the extent of each group's fishing rights, just as European surveyors marked out blocks of land.

Treaty settlements from the 1990s incorporated the right of ownership to natural resources including fisheries, forests, and aquaculture, as per article 2 of the Treaty. Despite Waitangi Tribunal recommendations that governments acknowledge tribal proprietary rights to rivers of special significance, parliament generally balked at granting iwi ownership or political authority over any sort of fresh water. Nor did various parliaments appreciate the tribunal's decision in 2014 that the Ngāpuhi chiefs who first signed the Treaty of Waitangi in northern New Zealand did not cede political authority.

There was chagrin, then, when in 2024 the Luxon government, in defiance of the courts, supported a proposal from the ACT party to tighten criteria for claiming customary marine title under the Marine and Coastal Area (Takutai Moana) Act 2011. ACT sought to erase the effects of a Court of Appeal judgment that had reduced the threshold for recognition of customary title. As well as introducing the idea that the foreshore and seabed belonged to no one, the 2011 Act had restored rights to pursue customary title that the Foreshore and Seabed Act 2004 had extinguished, while assuring public access to the coast and beaches. Iwi could seek to protect uses of waterways or claim customary title over part of the coast, but the statutory tests were strict, for iwi had to show that rights had been passed down the generations, uninterrupted, since 1840.

In 2017, the New Zealand Māori Council and 166 Māori groups won support from the Waitangi Tribunal for their claim that existing law failed to accommodate Māori proprietary interests in fresh water. Former chair Sir Edward Taihākurei Durie explained how family groups held exclusive-use rights and control over waterbodies, and so owned them, while the government believed the opposite: that the Crown owned water, and tribal interests were limited to care of waterways. Governments knew Māori connections with lakes, rivers, and springs so assumed Māori had a responsibility to care for them. But a duty of care was only one side of the equation. The other concerned iwi proprietary rights, because groups with ancestral ties to water sources received no legal benefits.

PERSONHOOD FOR NATURE

Novel solutions for the care of rivers and other significant environmental features emerged via some Treaty settlements. When parliament granted personhood to New Zealand's second longest river, the Whanganui, in 2017, it was the first in the world to pass a special statute that acknowledged a river as a person and a living whole. Reverence for the river was pivotal to the Whanganui Treaty settlement, a process led by Chris Finlayson, the attorney-general and minister of Treaty of Waitangi negotiations in the National-led coalition government. According to a popular saying among tribes, 'The Great River flows from the Mountains to the Sea; I am the River and the River is me'. The successful campaign by Whanganui Māori to protect their river reflected wider cultural renewal and gave impetus nationally to value nature. It helped that lawyers had no difficulty viewing a river as a person, because in law a limited liability company is treated as a separate legal entity.

Te Urewera, the Ngāi Tūhoe homeland, was the first rainforest to gain personhood status, and it did so before the Whanganui River. After John Key's prime ministerial veto on the park's return to the tribe, the personhood concept, as an alternative to ownership, secured Ngāi Tūhoe's Treaty settlement, in 2013. Tūhoe ancestors had refused to sign the Treaty of Waitangi and suffered indiscriminate confiscation of their ancestral territory, which the government redesignated as Te Urewera National Park in 1954. The tribe suffered years of scorched-earth warfare and was denied a self-governing reserve. By making Te Urewera a legal entity, the Crown recognised the forest as a being. It agreed that Tūhoe and the Department of Conservation would manage the park in partnership. Similarly, Taranaki Maunga (Mount Taranaki) gained legal personhood under a settlement reached with eight Taranaki iwi in January 2025, in which the Crown apologised for confiscating most of Taranaki province.

Legal recognition as a living entity assumed another form for New Zealand's longest river, the Waikato, and its tributary the Waipa. A new institution, the Waikato River Authority, was established in 2014 under two Treaty Settlement Acts, with tribes in the combined river catchments tasked with restoring and protecting the river's health and wellbeing so that it would sustain 'abundant life and prosperous communities'. Using a co-governance model, equal numbers of iwi and Crown representatives shared responsibility for management and care and were required to make decisions by consensus.

The Waikato River was central to the Tainui settlement. As the river's guardian, the Waikato River Authority was obliged to know about the impacts of the Waikato War, which had resulted in mass land confiscations (see chapter 4). Impacts included rapid development and associated environmental harm to land and water.

In these ways, Treaty settlements boosted efforts to restore cherished waterways and other environmental features. Thanks to tribal initiatives to protect aspects of nature important to them, New Zealand presented internationally as an innovator in devising indigenous-led policies to return major rivers and mountains to health.

ECOLOGICAL RESTORATION

In the twenty-first century public attitudes to conservation transformed, alongside legislative reform and growing collaboration between iwi and non-Māori. The ecological transformations achieved within a generation were revolutionary. Reflective of these changes, in 2020 a national biodiversity strategy was produced to preserve and protect unique species. The strategy sought to protect, restore, and use biodiversity sustainably, to ensure better use of land and sea, underpinned by the idea that 'when nature is in trouble, so are people'. With New Zealand having lost an estimated 70 per cent of its forest cover, the Department of Conservation, working with Treaty partners, local government, and community groups, aimed to recloak the natural landscape with native trees, shrubs, and grasses, and to care for the marine environment. Around the country, volunteers and ecologists activated networks to plant seeds and seedlings, to remove weeds, and to trap predators. In selected places birds were left to sow native seeds. Rivers, lakes, and streams, as well as estuaries and wetlands, began to recover more quickly than expected, and critically endangered species benefited from initiatives to protect them.

Engagement with tribes confirmed that catches of seafood had declined in numbers and diversity since the 1970s. For Māori, smaller coastal catches entailed both ecological and cultural losses. Iwi therefore sought to restore the health of food-gathering sites on the coast as well as inland, in the interests of cultural and ecological revival.

Outcomes of restoration efforts were striking, culturally and ecologically, in Christchurch's former red zone, where thousands of houses were demolished after the earthquakes. Communities expressed local identities by launching individual projects but also contributed ideas for the red zone's future design, including a pathway from the city to the sea for walkers and cyclists. This city-to-sea pathway, along with a coastal pathway ending at Sumner beach, instantly became a favourite amenity.

Nationally, projects to conserve and restore native bush and plant cover and to protect and encourage wildlife proliferated. Some ecological initiatives were new, while others begun in the 1970s were revived 50 years later, due to anxieties about the climate crisis. Public-driven change included restoration of the freshwater Travis Wetland by volunteers, with support from the city council and Ngāi Tahu, who valued the wetland as a food resource. Known in the twentieth century as Travis Swamp, it became a refuge for waterbirds and a nature park. On the other hand, privately managed land included Hinewai Reserve, on Banks Peninsula, established in 1987, owned by a native forest trust, and cared for by a respected botanist. Its success in restoring native bush was achieved partly through the discovery that gorse is a useful nursery plant for native seedlings.

Zealandia Te Māra a Tāne (the garden of Tāne), in the suburb of Karori, in Wellington, showed what was possible in cities. Established in 1995, Zealandia was the first urban ecosanctuary to be fully fenced. Arranged around an old reservoir, it featured water from a stream and regenerating bush. Once protected, the forest attracted growing numbers of rare birds, including kaka (bush parrot) and takahe, the largest flightless bird to survive in New Zealand. The long-term vision of the community trust managing the ecosanctuary was to connect people with nature by restoring the forest and freshwater ecosystems to how they were before humans arrived. Thanks to Zealandia, Wellington became alive with birdsong, and its inhabitants were entertained and educated by native birds (see figure 12.4).

Elsewhere, ecological reserves and sanctuaries run by trusts increased forest cover and improved water quality, allowing bird numbers to increase. By 2020 there were 80 ecosanctuaries in New Zealand, all working to eliminate predators and restore native plants and wildlife. The reserve on Tiritiri Matangi Island, in the Hauraki Gulf, gave visitors from Auckland, New Zealand's largest city, the opportunity to encounter takahe, spotted kiwi, and little blue penguins, among other rare species, in a native bush and beach setting. By the early 2020s the largest wildlife reserve in the country was Sanctuary Mountain Maungatautari, in the Waikato, an hour's drive from Hamilton and Rotorua. Reflective of its size, its predator fence was the largest in the world.

Outside cities, Pūkaka Mount Bruce National Wildlife Centre, sited in a restored forest in the Wairarapa, provided a breeding sanctuary for rare wildlife. The reserve's most famous resident was Manukura (2011–20), the first pure-white kiwi born in captivity, whose feathers taught children it was fine to be different. Orokonui Ecosanctuary, near Dunedin, opened in 2007 as a predator-free ecological island, with a community trust working

12.4 Zealandia Te Māra a Tāne (the garden of Tāne), Karori, Wellington, 2024
Photographer Jeff Mein Smith

in collaboration with local iwi to restore the forest and encourage wildlife. As concern grew about the effects of climate change, New Zealanders learnt to cherish reserves and ecosanctuaries which, like national parks, served as refuges for wildlife and humans.

CLIMATE EMERGENCY

The rapidity of global warming had generated sufficient alarm by 2019 for Jacinda Ardern's government to pass the Climate Change Response (Zero Carbon) Amendment Act, which established a framework for moving to a low-carbon economy and adapting to climate change effects. The Climate Change Commission, created under the Act, was led initially by Dr Rod Carr, a lateral-thinking former banker and university vice-chancellor, who warned that world leaders must act immediately to reduce carbon emissions, because global temperatures were already increasing, and weather events were growing more extreme because there was more energy in the atmosphere. For New Zealanders accustomed to a temperate, if vigorous, climate, the damage wreaked by the tropical cyclone Gabrielle, in February 2023, warned of the dangers ahead. Cyclone Gabrielle stunned the North Island: 10 000 people lost their homes or were displaced, and the storm triggered flooding and landslips, showing how slips posed a risk to homes, infrastructure, and the environment. In the south, glaciers were melting fast and snow levels rising, endangering rivers and wildlife. Rising sea levels posed a particular risk, with New Zealand being surrounded by ocean.

Scientists predicted that in terms of risks, floods would be overtaken by sea-level rise later in the twenty-first century. By how much would depend on the West Antarctic ice sheet. On the other hand, the ozone hole above Antarctica, discovered in 1985, was expected to close by the middle of the twenty-first century. The Montreal Protocol, which banned ozone-depleting gases in the 1980s, appeared to be working and to show that humanity had the capacity to reduce carbon emissions (greenhouse gases). However, political parties disagreed over responses to climate change. The Luxon-led government supported mining in pursuit of economic growth and in 2025 reversed a ban on oil and gas exploration enacted by Ardern's government in 2018 to encourage use of renewable energy.

For over 100 years, Forest and Bird, the country's leading conservation charity since 1923, defended the environment and birdlife against short-sighted, short-term political policies – famously, during the campaign to save Lake Manapouri when public protest achieved success. Activist groups such as Climate Liberation Aotearoa engaged in civil resistance during the 2020s to demand urgent climate action and oppose plans to renew mining. The climate emergency also worried children and young people who – following Swedish activist Greta Thunberg – joined the School Strike 4 Climate movement and participated in large rallies in 2019, with the goal of carbon neutrality by 2050, the aim of the Zero Carbon Act.

Researchers reasoned that reducing emissions was a more realistic approach to dealing with climate change than adaptation, since global warming was threatening the entire planet and much was already locked in. However, most politicians and local councils, keen to balance efforts to reduce emissions with responses to natural hazards, such as repeated storm damage and flooding, focused on adaptation. By the 2020s, flooding had become New Zealand's major form of property damage, notably in Auckland. Much of the water infrastructure, including drinking water, was vulnerable to flooding and sea-level rise. Therefore, four policy options gained favour nationally: to prevent development in areas at risk of sea-level rise; to reduce the potential for damage – for example, by raising floor levels in buildings; to protect beaches and sand dunes; and to retreat – that is, to relocate people, buildings, infrastructure, and sites of cultural significance.

New Zealand already had experience of successful relocation after earthquakes, but that did not extend to indigenous infrastructure. Māori ancestral sites and communities were highly vulnerable to climate change, because 80 per cent of marae (public meeting places) were in low-lying coastal areas or beside rivers susceptible to floods. In 2022–3 an official working group devised a set of objectives and principles for funding relocation, including a Treaty-based approach to adaptation, which was necessary for the policy to be effective.

All New Zealand's cities developed climate plans. The largest, Auckland, was the most car-dependent city (see chapter 11). Consequently, Auckland appeared more Australian in style than the other main centres, because of the scale of its suburban sprawl. A more compact shape is part of the agenda for climate action, since dependency on cars and the predominance of low-density housing make it difficult to reduce greenhouse gas emissions. Auckland City Council declared a climate emergency in 2019 and joined the global network of cities committed to addressing climate change. But emissions reduction proved elusive.

Urban researchers recognised that for suburbanites to move from standalone houses to city townhouses and apartments would require frequent, rapid, and affordable public transport, along with cycleways and walkways, and the greening of inner-city neighbourhoods to ensure they were attractive as well as convenient to live in. Investment in parks, reserves, rivers, streams, bush, and wetlands would also reduce emissions. Increasingly, the role of nature and the geography of each city, as well as local rather than imported culture, played larger parts in urban design, enhancing cities' distinctiveness.

CULTURAL CHANGE

Novel proposals for turning cities into places that reflected Māori and Pacific values and a shared Pacific heritage included architect Anthony Hōete's idea in 2024 of a 'transcolonised' city that 'work[ed] with what exists'. He suggested that this could involve building new forms of marae above flood level and hapū-relevant architecture that encouraged people to socialise. The Pacific diaspora, too, was reinterpreting and creating a distinctive urban culture, starting in South Auckland.

A national day to commemorate the New Zealand Wars was introduced in 2017, initiated by 186 high-school students from the Waikato after they took a field trip and as a result petitioned parliament for a day of remembrance and for the history of the wars to be taught in schools. The government approved a national day of 28 October, the date northern chiefs signed the Declaration of Independence in 1835. Consequently public awareness rose about the wars, and the declaration grew more visible.

Māori rituals and practices long strengthened biculturalism. The revival of te reo facilitated a wider cultural renaissance and changed New Zealand English, starting with young people's speech. In parallel, the New Zealand Geographic Board Ngā Pou Taunaha o Aotearoa in 2023 added over 800 te reo names to geographical features and places and corrected others. Some official renaming derived from Treaty settlements. In response the Labour government – led by Chris Hipkins after Jacinda Ardern resigned – planned to install bilingual road signs for those not already in English and Māori. Bilingual naming extended to government departments, hospitals, and schools.

The public's growing familiarity with Māori culture and tikanga (customs, protocols) provided the context for selected practices to be adopted nationally. From 2022, the Māori New Year, associated with both harvesting and planting, gained its own public holiday, marking when the star cluster Matariki (the Pleiades) rises in the dawn sky at the beginning of winter. In 2024, crowds celebrated the third official Matariki holiday with festivals, feasts, and stargazing events. As a public occasion, Matariki further enhanced knowledge of Māori culture.

Popular culture also changed, with the rise in the stature and significance of women's sport. In 2022 the New Zealand team won the women's Rugby World Cup for the fifth time, against England, in a competition delayed by the Covid-19 pandemic. More surprisingly, at the Paris Olympic Games of July–August 2024 New Zealand representatives won 10 gold medals, 8 of which were won by women athletes. Dame Lisa Carrington, a canoeist of Māori descent, won 3 of the gold medals, becoming the first Māori woman to win an Olympic gold medal. The Olympics also provided an opportunity for athletes to showcase New Zealand culture, with its highly visible Māori component, which attracted a global audience. International media commented how New Zealanders punched above their weight – a characteristic New Zealanders expected of themselves.

POLITICAL REALITIES

Within parliament, women members of parliament were in the majority for the first time in 2022. Māori achieved proportional representation in 2023, when Māori members of parliament made up 17 per cent of politicians and Māori constituted about 18 per cent of the population. This marked another form of political equality and resulted from the choice Māori had to vote either in one of the seven Māori electorates or in their local general electorate; people who identified as Māori (and had Māori ancestry) could register either on the Māori or on the general electoral roll. Some considered this choice unfair, when in fact it ensured electoral justice. Other ethnic groups were represented in parliament but not yet proportionately, while Pākehā, who had declined to 68 per cent of the population, comprised 69 per cent of members of parliament.

Pasifika (a term used for Pacific people since the 1980s) made up 9 per cent of the population by 2023, making them the fourth largest ethnic group, after Pākehā, Māori, and Asian New Zealanders. Among Pasifika, the largest group were from Samoa. As discussed in chapter 10, Samoans who were born in Samoa after May 1924 and before 1949 held New Zealand citizenship from 1949 until the Citizenship (Western Samoa) Act, passed by Robert Muldoon's government in 1982, overturned this policy. People who had seen their citizenship revoked were pleased to have it restored later in their lives by the Samoan Citizenship Act 2024, which enjoyed unanimous support at the second reading. Two-thirds of Samoan New Zealanders were born in New Zealand by 2023; about 62 per cent lived in Auckland.

Pasifika identities involved loyalties to different small island states. These ranged from Samoa, which was independent yet connected historically to New Zealand, to the independent states of Tonga and Fiji and the tiny New Zealand dependencies of the Cook Islands, Niue, and Tokelau (see chapter 8). Identities also varied generationally between younger people born in New Zealand and their elders who were either island born or New Zealand born.

Pasifika players shone in sport, especially rugby, rugby league, and netball. New Zealand–born rugby wing Jonah Lomu, as one of the best players in the world, was claimed by New Zealand and Tonga long after his death. Olympic shot-putter Dame Valerie Adams and her brother, the basketballer Steve Adams, whose mother was Tongan, enjoyed high profiles. So did choreographer Tupe Lualua and artists and musicians including the founder of the popular band Fat Freddy's Drop, Christopher Faiumu, who died in 2025.

While talented individuals were recognised, Pasifika had yet to gain proportional representation in parliament. After the 2023 election, Pacific representatives occupied 3 per cent of seats. Their experience again illustrated the value of the Māori seats, which, together with the mixed-member proportional system, ensured just representation in parliament for Māori.

Elsewhere, all was not well socially, particularly among families who for generations had remained impoverished, ever since colonisation had taken away land and resources. The lengthy Royal

Commission of Inquiry into Abuse in Care reported in 2024, exposing long-term hurt and injustice dealt to children placed into the care of church and state from 1950 until 2019. Māori children were especially affected. Both church and state establishments had failed the country's most in-need children, denied them their human rights, and denied Māori children and young people their rights to protection under the Treaty of Waitangi.

The public were horrified by the extent of neglect and of abuse inflicted by institutions believed to be trustworthy. An estimated 40 per cent of the total number of children placed in care were abused or neglected, with Māori youth often targeted for their ethnicity. Evidence showed Māori and Pasifika were treated more harshly and denied access to cultural support. The royal commission recommended a lengthy series of actions from the culpable institutions, churches, and government. The prime minister and relevant public sector heads apologised in 2024, and Oranga Tamariki Ministry for Children undertook to transform the way it worked. In a new strategy the ministry pledged to build strong relationships with Māori, while the government said it would address past wrongs, 'make the current system safe', and 'empower those in care'.

GLOBAL SHIFTS

Externally, global pivots, lurches, and flip-flops characterised a new world order dominated by the largest powers. By the 2020s China had moved from the horizon to front and centre in New Zealand's thinking in diplomacy, trade, business, and international education. Partly this new regard was due to China's remarkable rise in power and wealth. More immediately, esteem grew from familiarity – that is, building relationships. New Zealand felt privileged to be a partner in the first free trade agreement China signed with a Western country. A success for both countries, despite the disparities in their size and influence, the 2008 trade agreement created opportunities and quadrupled New Zealand's goods exports to China over the next 15 years. China grew to be New Zealand's major source of international students, a market for tourism, and a source of foreign investment.

By 2021 all imports from China could enter New Zealand tariff free. An update to the agreement in 2022 incorporated the latest policies and practices in trade and ecommerce, environmental areas, and government procurement. All New Zealand exports became tariff free, apart from dairy products and selected other goods, while remaining tariffs ended in 2024. Red tape diminished; cooperation multiplied on environmental and ecommerce problems; and New Zealand service providers, such as in education, and businesspeople gained easier access to China. Such was the agreement's impact that in 2023 China overtook Australia as New Zealand's largest trading partner, confirming how much New Zealand's world had altered shape.

While trade had been a zone of harmony with China before Donald Trump assumed the presidency of the United States for a second term, in January 2025, security continued to be an area of likely tensions in relationships. Given the South China Sea was a hotspot for flare-ups between China, Japan, the United States, and Australia, New Zealand was startled – if not as much as Australia – when three Chinese warships conducted live-fire drills in the Tasman Sea off New South Wales and Tasmania, and south of Australia, in February 2025. New Zealanders, too, were unaccustomed to such activity in 'their' backyard, though the Chinese vessels sailed in international waters. Some commentators thought the naval exercises signalled China's intention to change the world strategic order by establishing a permanent military presence in the Pacific; others, that drills in international waters were nothing unusual.

China also signed a memorandum of understanding with the Cook Islands that included an agreement about seabed mining. This caused concern, because the Cook Islands' prime minister did not consult New Zealand beforehand. As well as the lack of transparency, it was uncertain whether the agreement would enable China to establish a strategic presence, because the Cook Islands were still part of New Zealand's realm.

As a small country, New Zealand remained committed to multilateralism. In trade, this principle manifested in membership of the Regional Comprehensive Economic Partnership, launched in 2022, which New Zealand's top trade partners, China and

Australia, also joined. The partnership grouping, of 15 countries, included the large Asian economies of Japan, Indonesia, and South Korea, as well as poorer countries such as Vietnam, Cambodia, Thailand, and Laos. China was expected to take the lead in the Asia-centred partnership. New Zealand may have seemed an outlier but had long participated in meetings of the Association of Southeast Asian Nations, which spawned the partnership to strengthen itself economically.

By the twenty-first century, attitudes in New Zealand to Asian immigration had transformed. New Zealand was a multicultural society, and Chinese people, who historically formed the largest group from Asian countries, made a significant contribution to multiculturalism. According to the 2023 census, nearly 279 000 people identified as Chinese: 5 per cent of the population. Most lived in the Auckland area.

The census revealed, however, that the number of Indian New Zealanders had narrowly overtaken the number of Chinese New Zealanders by 2023. India itself surpassed China's population size in 2023, a change poised to affect strategies in the Indo-Pacific region, because it made India the largest country in the world. For several reasons, New Zealand aspired to build a stronger strategic relationship with India, despite New Zealand's small population (5.33 million in 2025). Given its support for the United Nations, its British heritage, and its democracy, let alone its growth in power, India was a logical friend to consult on shared problems and interests, while hopes for a trade agreement received a boost from the positive experience with China.

Popular culture also sustained New Zealand–India relations, particularly rivalry in cricket. The unexpected victory over India by the New Zealand men's team in the inaugural World Test Championship, in 2021, and the unprecedented 3–0 Test series win in India in 2024 were two of New Zealand's greatest sporting achievements. A Kiwi Indian, Ajaz Patel, fittingly helped the Black Caps win through his spin bowling.

Cricket was Australia's national game, and while Australia's national team routinely expected to beat New Zealand, New Zealanders still compared themselves with Australians in sporting contests. Australia remained New Zealand's closest partner and sole ally. In the 2020s politicians described the two countries not just as friends but as family, which had not been the case 50 years earlier. The family metaphor surfaced in response to increasing migration westwards, as well as intensifying cultural traffic, trade, and family ties. From the late 1960s, New Zealanders had been the main drivers of trans-Tasman people movement. An annual net migration loss to Australia became the norm. In 2023, the net loss amounted to 27 000 people, as New Zealanders left in search of more employment choice and better pay. In 2024, the net loss jumped to 47 000. By that point, 15 per cent of New Zealanders, including Māori, were still based across the Tasman.

The degree of integration was high even as international shocks rattled the architecture of official relationships. One surprise for New Zealand occurred in 2020 when the Australian federal government responded to the Covid-19 pandemic by dismantling the Council of Australian Governments, through which New Zealand representatives engaged with their counterparts in Australia's federal, state, and territory governments. At the same time, the pandemic drew the countries closer – for example, when senior health officials participated in the Australian health protection apparatus. The National Cabinet system that replaced the Council of Australian Governments allowed for intergovernmental collaboration in a more flexible manner, although New Zealand's role was less formalised than previously. New Zealand obtained seats at the food ministers' meeting (since the food-safety system was trans-Tasman) and the data and digital ministers' meeting, among others.

In 2023, New Zealand celebrated the 40th anniversary of the Closer Economic Relations Trade Agreement, which remained both countries' most comprehensive free trade treaty; 2023 was also the 50th anniversary of the Trans-Tasman Travel Arrangement, which, since 1973, had made it straightforward for each country's citizens to live and work in the other country. To mark these anniversaries, the countries announced they aimed to move beyond the trade agreement by making the conduct of business as easy as possible, a goal discussed at the annual Australia New Zealand Leadership Forum. They also agreed to promote joint scientific research and indigenous collaboration.

Just as New Zealand was suspended from the ANZUS alliance, it was excluded from AUKUS, an Anglo-American security partnership between Australia, the United Kingdom, and the United States, signed in September 2021. The main purpose of AUKUS was to equip Australia with nuclear-powered attack submarines for use in the Indo-Pacific alongside the United States. Secondarily, Australia would acquire military technology, including cyber technology. Occasionally there was talk of inviting New Zealand to participate in this second strand, since the United States had re-admitted New Zealand to intelligence sharing in 2009, but the AUKUS focus on nuclear submarines conflicted with the country's anti-nuclear policy. Non-membership also smoothed relations with China. Unpredictable United States behaviour early in Trump's second term confirmed that non-membership was prudent.

A volte-face by Britain in trade policy after Brexit (Britain's withdrawal from the European Union, in 2020) granted New Zealand preferential access to Britain's consumer market for the first time since that country had joined the European Economic Community. This was what New Zealand trade negotiators had always wanted. The vehicle for market access was the New Zealand–United Kingdom Free Trade Agreement 2023. Like AUKUS, this agreement provided a means for Britain to return to the Indo-Pacific region 50 years after its strategic withdrawal from east of Suez. New Zealand was happy for the former imperial mother country to show interest, especially since the agreement allowed most New Zealand goods to enter the United Kingdom duty free. The aim was eventually to remove all customs duties. Duties remained on cheese and butter for 5 years and meat for 15 years to protect British farmers, an issue New Zealanders were familiar with historically.

The United Kingdom agreement was unique in the priority given to Māori interests. While New Zealand trade agreements in the first quarter of the twenty-first century all contained a clause to ensure that the government fulfilled its obligations under the Treaty of Waitangi, the agreement with the United Kingdom went further, with a focus on issues important to Māori, such as intellectual property. History played its part. The free trade agreement also supported women's empowerment economically and contained provisions on the environment.

There was a quid pro quo for British largesse, however; the United Kingdom viewed the agreement as a package with its accession to the Comprehensive and Progressive Agreement for Trans-Pacific Partnership, a move New Zealand supported. The partnership was a multilateral agreement of 12 members by 2025, including Australia, New Zealand, Canada, Chile, Singapore, and Vietnam. New Zealand favoured diverse membership to strengthen the group's resilience against external shocks. The United Kingdom's entry served as an additional instrument to assist its return to the Indo-Pacific region.

PRECARIOUS WORLD

As we have seen, global volatility in the late nineteenth and early twentieth centuries led settler governments to manage global forces through a set of state experiments intended to protect Pākehā settlers and their standard of living, which increased the hunger for Māori land. In the late twentieth century, again in response to global shocks, Labour and National governments abandoned the century-old Australasian model of state development for an Anglo-American neoliberal orthodoxy of free-market capitalism, deregulation, and reduced state influence in the economy, which upended old ways of life. Renewed prosperity was not forthcoming, however; instead, economic stagnation set in. Among the negative outcomes, neoliberal policies worsened inequality for Māori and devalued the worker.

New Zealand governments actively pursued free trade agreements early in the twenty-first century, because they expanded export markets and ensured that the economy remained one of the freest in the world. The world, however, suffered from economic and political instability from unexpected sources in the 2020s, while local disasters reduced New Zealand's capacity for big reform compared with that of the 1980s. The paucity of checks and balances in the political system made decision-making easier but harmed the quality of decisions. More oversight was imperative, as were more ways of making governments accountable.

An erosion of democracy aided the growth in government power. Locally, democracy suffered due to internal and external shocks from 2010 onwards, from earthquakes that governments responded to with top-down governance and curtailed civil liberties, to emergency powers exercised during the Covid-19 pandemic (though this outcome was unintended), unregulated lobbying, and a conspicuous unwillingness to consult. Increasingly, governments, especially right-leaning coalitions, appeared less capable of formulating timely and innovative ideas that protected New Zealand's outstanding environment and improved ordinary people's lives. Likewise, a long-term vision essential to prepare for climate change languished politically. Instead, local governments took up this mantle.

In the twenty-first century institutions and people outside parliament, such as the Kīngitanga, Waikato high-school students, and more than 300 000 submitters to the justice select committee, demonstrated potential to hold governments accountable, just as trade unions once did. The many initiatives in ecological restoration relied on the work of dedicated volunteers who were likewise capable of taking a stand on behalf of the environment and human rights. By exercising agency, individuals and groups, mostly local, drove collective efforts that addressed gaps or deficits in government policies. When trust in politicians eroded in the 2020s people stood up and spoke up. Since colonisation, and especially since suffrage, New Zealanders had expected to have a say, just as there were Māori protocols for speaking on marae, which came to be widely adopted.

As for the Treaty of Waitangi, in 2024–5 the public communicated its respect for it when the coalition government neglected to do so by delegating excessive power to a minor partner. The magnitude of protest on the Treaty's behalf demonstrated how support had soared for its message and spirit.

Demographic change reinforced that trajectory by reshaping New Zealand's population. Auckland was increasing in size while regions were generally in decline. The population was growing older, due to ageing baby boomers. It was also becoming more Māori, as Māori families were having more children than other groups. Pākehā fertility declined markedly, because couples were having fewer children or no children. Consequently, Māori as a community were much younger than New Zealanders in general.

In a precarious world, it was wise to secure the historic free trade agreement with China, which gave access to new relationships and opportunities as well as China's massive market. Propitiously, this agreement and others with Asian countries were finalised well before the United States lurched towards isolationism on the re-election of President Donald Trump. It was unclear what the effects on world trade would be of the return to protection, marked in 2025 by the Trump administration imposing sweeping tariffs of on average over 50 per cent on imports from China, a blanket 25 per cent on those from India, and 10 per cent on those from Britain and Australia. A 15 per cent tariff surprised New Zealand. Within months, the world was forcibly shunted away from decades of multilateral work on behalf of free trade and trade rules by strongman politics emanating from the world's oldest democracy.

From the beginning, New Zealand's story was shaped by its geography, as an archipelago of islands in the Pacific, and by its dynamic environment. It was distinguished by people's absence before the late thirteenth century and by a history of late settlement, first by East Polynesians and then, centuries later, by colonising Europeans. The small population nurtured a village culture. New Zealand began and was periodically refashioned as a colonial experiment. Indeed, 'experiment' entered the country's DNA with the arrival of the first people in Aotearoa. Capacity for revolutionary change, if unintended, was embedded in the body politic.

The picturesque environment remained alive in New Zealand life – though destroyed, 'improved', conserved, exploited, and restored over time – all the while expanding in people's consciousness to mean far more than a character in films. It is exhilarating to live immersed in the Pacific Ocean Te Moana-nui-a-Kiwa on islands that span from the mountains to the sea. Yet it has grown perilous to cross beaches in an era of rising seas and global hazards. During heightened uncertainty, New Zealanders may find their history will help them to navigate exceptional tides.

GLOSSARY OF MĀORI WORDS

Aoraki	Mount Cook (cloud piercer)
Aotearoa	New Zealand (long white cloud)
ariki	high chief, priest
haka	posture dance, accompanied by a song
hapū	clan, subtribe, extended family, kin group
He Whakaputanga o te Rangatiratanga o Nu Tireni	The Declaration of Independence of the United Tribes of New Zealand
hi iwi tahi tātou	we are now one people; we are peoples together
hīkoi mō te Tiriti	march for the Treaty
hokonga	sale and purchase of land that chiefs were willing to sell
hui	gathering, meeting
iwi	tribe
kai	food
kai-tangata	cannibalism
kainga	home, village
kainga nohoanga	seasonal occupation site
katoa	all, whole
kaumātua	elders
kauri	*Agathis australis*, a forest tree

kāwanatanga	governorship, governance, government, authority
kia kaha	be strong, stay strong
Kīngitanga	Māori King movement
kōhanga reo	language nest(s), preschools where lessons are in Māori
Kororāreka	Russell, historic port in the Bay of Islands
kotahitanga	unity
kuia	woman elder, grandmother
kumara	sweet potato
kūpapa	'friendlies', troops who fought on the government's side; or independent, neutral (some Māori used the term to state their neutrality)
mahinga kai	In the North Island this meant cultivations, gardens; in the south it had a wider meaning, of traditional food and natural resources including food-gathering places
mana	influence, prestige, power, psychic force
mana motuhake	self-determination
mana whenua	(those with) tribal authority within a region
Māori	indigenous people of New Zealand
marae	courtyard, space in front of a meeting house; meeting ground, including buildings
maunga	mountain
mere	club
moko	tattoo, design on the face or body done according to strict protocols; traditionally applied to male facial tattoos

Moriori	indigenous people of the Chatham Islands
Nu Tireni, Nu Tirani (also Niu, Nui)	New Zealand (transliteration)
pā	stockade, fortified village
Pākehā	person of European descent
pohutukawa	*Metrosideros excelsa*, New Zealand Christmas tree
ponga	tree fern, silver fern
pounamu	greenstone, New Zealand jade
Rakiura	Stewart Island
rangatira	chief, well-born person
rangatiratanga	chieftainship
Rohe Pōtae	King Country, territory united in support of the Māori king; can also apply to the Urewera, meaning 'encircling boundary'
tahi	together, all
taiaha	long club
Takutai Moana	marine and coastal area
tangata	men (nineteenth-century definition), people, humans
tangata whenua	people of the land, indigenous people, first peoples
tangi	wake, funeral ceremony
taonga	treasure(s), treasured possession(s)
tapū	under religious restriction, sacred
taua	war expedition, war party
Te Ika-a-Māui	North Island (the fish of Māui)
Te Moana-nui-a-Kiwa	the Pacific Ocean (great ocean of Kiwa)
te reo Māori	the Māori language
Te Riu-a-Māui	Zealandia (the hills, valleys, and plains of Māui)
Te Tiriti o Waitangi	the Māori text of the Treaty of Waitangi

Te Waipounamu	South Island (waters of greenstone)
Te Waka o Aoraki	South Island (canoe of Aoraki) – a Ngāi Tahu name
Te Waka-o-Māui	South Island (canoe of Māui)
Te Whanga nui a Tara	Wellington Harbour (the great harbour of Tara)
tī-kōuka	*Cordyline australis*, cabbage tree
tikanga	custom, the right way of doing things, customary law
Tū Tāngata	stand tall, stand together
tupuna (tūpuna)	ancestor(s), grandparent(s)
utu	repayment, return, reciprocity; to make response, whether by way of payment, blow or answer
wairua	spirit
waka	canoe(s)
waka hourua	voyaging canoe(s)
waka taua	war canoe(s)
wānanga	seminar, conference, form of open discussion
whakapapa	genealogy, lineage
whanau	extended family, family group
whare	house
whenua	land

TIMELINE

1250–1300	Evidence of first Polynesian settlement
1642	Abel Tasman visits without landing
1769–70	James Cook visits for first time, stays six months
1769	Jean-François Marie de Surville visits
1772	Marion du Fresne visits
1773–4	Cook's second visit
1777	Cook's third visit
1793	Māori relations with governors of New South Wales established
	Antoine Bruni d'Entrecasteaux searches for Jean-François Galaup de La Pérouse
1808	Sealing rush in Foveaux Strait
1814	Anglican missionaries arrive from Sydney
1815–40	Musket wars and associated migrations
1820	Hongi Hika visits London and King George IV
1827	Bay whaling; shore whaling stations commence
1828	Hongi Hika of Ngāpuhi dies, marking power shift in wars
1827–8, 1829	Ngāti Toa invade South Island
1830–2	Te Rauparaha's main southern assault
1833	James Busby, the British resident, arrives at Bay of Islands
1834	New Zealand flag selected for trans-Tasman Māori shipping
1835	He Whakaputanga Declaration of Independence signed by chiefs from United Tribes of New Zealand
	Taranaki Māori invade Chatham Islands

1837	New Zealand Association formed; renamed New Zealand Company in 1838
1838	Catholic missionaries arrive
1839	New South Wales extends its boundaries to include any ceded lands in New Zealand
1840	Wellington settled; Auckland established; French settle in Akaroa
	British Empire annexes New Zealand as part of Colony of New South Wales; William Hobson, the lieutenant-governor, arrives
	Treaty of Waitangi
1841	New Zealand achieves Crown colony status; William Hobson becomes governor; Auckland established as the capital
	Whanganui and New Plymouth settled by New Zealand Company
1842	Nelson settled by New Zealand Company
1843	Robert FitzRoy becomes governor
	Wairau dispute
1844	Hōne Heke chops down flagstaff at Kororāreka (Russell) for first time
1845–6	Northern war
1845	George Grey becomes governor (remains until 1853)
1846–7	Conflicts in Wellington region and Whanganui
1846	Te Rauparaha arrested
1848	Otago settled (Dunedin); Canterbury block purchased by Kemp's Deed
1850	Canterbury settled (Christchurch and port of Lyttelton)
1852	New Zealand Constitution Act allows the colony to establish representative government
1853	First elections of provincial councils; male property vote established
1854	Part-elected national parliament meets for first time in Auckland
1855	Thomas Gore Browne becomes governor
	Earthquake of magnitude 8.2 elevates Wellington

1856	Responsible government formed; sequence of short-term premiers
1858	Pōtatau Te Wherowhero becomes first Māori king; Kīngitanga (King movement) established
1860–72	New Zealand Wars
1860–1	First Taranaki War
	Kohimarama conference
	European population overtakes Māori
1861	Gold discovered in Otago
	Sir George Grey reappointed as governor (recalled 1868)
1863–4	Waikato War
1863	Frederick Whitaker becomes premier
	New Zealand Settlements Act allows taking of land for public purposes and governor to establish settlements for colonisation in North Island
1864	Gold discovered on West Coast
	Frederick Weld becomes premier
	Battle of Ōrākau; Rewi Maniapoto's last stand
1865	Native Land Court established after Waikato War to individualise title to Māori land and enable its transfer to European settlers
	Government (and capital) transferred from Auckland to Wellington
	Edward Stafford made premier for second time
	Kīngitanga land in the Waikato and Taranaki land confiscated
	Chinese miners invited to Otago from Victoria
1867	First Māori members of parliament elected; male Māori vote established
	'Native schools' begin
1868	Riwha Titokowaru victorious in battle for south Taranaki
	Te Kooti Arikirangi Te Turuki escapes from Chatham Islands
1869	William Fox becomes premier for third time
	First university college founded, in Otago
1870	Secret ballot introduced

1872	Te Kooti Arikirangi Te Turuki takes refuge in King Country
	Edward Stafford becomes premier for third time
1873	William Fox becomes premier for fourth time; he is succeeded by Julius Vogel
	Government offers free fares to migrants from Europe to New Zealand
1876	Provincial government ends
	Sir Julius Vogel becomes premier for second time; he is succeeded by Harry Atkinson
	Telegraph cable joins New Zealand to Australia
1877	Sir George Grey appointed premier
	Chief Justice James Prendergast dismisses Treaty of Waitangi
	Free, compulsory, secular primary education introduced
	Kate Edger is first woman to graduate from university in New Zealand
1879	Full manhood suffrage established
	John Hall becomes premier
1879–95	Long Depression
1881	Thermal Springs District Act gives government monopoly on purchase and lease of areas with hot springs
	Government sends troops to assault Parihaka; Te Whiti, Tohu Kākahi, and followers imprisoned; King Tāwhiao makes peace
1882	First shipment of frozen New Zealand meat to Britain
	Frederick Whitaker becomes premier for second time
1883	Harry Atkinson becomes premier for second time
	Te Whiti and prisoners released; Te Kooti pardoned
1884	King Tāwhiao sails to London to petition Queen Victoria but is refused access
	Harry Atkinson becomes premier for third time; he is both preceded and succeeded by Sir Robert Stout

	Married Women's Property Act allows wives to own property separately from their husbands
1885	Women's Christian Temperance Union founded
1886	Mount Tarawera erupts, burying Pink and White Terraces
1887	Sir Harry Atkinson becomes premier for fourth time
1888	Tariffs on imports introduced
	Immigration restriction imposed against Chinese people
1889	Plural voting abolished
1890	Australasian Federation Conference, Melbourne
	Australasian Maritime Strike
1891	John Ballance (Liberal) becomes premier
	Australasian Federation Convention, Sydney
1892	Kotahitanga (unity) movement founded
1893	Richard Seddon becomes premier
	Women's suffrage enacted
1894	Industrial Conciliation and Arbitration Act introduces compulsory arbitration and conciliation
	Advances to Settlers Act awards government loans for land to settlers
	Āpirana Ngata is first Māori to graduate from university
	Tongariro National Park established, courtesy of Ngāti Tūwharetoa
1895	Kotahitanga movement boycotts Native Land Court
1896	Brunner Mine disaster on West Coast kills 65 miners
	National Council of Women established
	Māori population is at lowest point since Europeans' arrival
	Poll tax on Chinese migrants increases from £10 to £100
1898	Old age pension introduced
1899	First contingent of New Zealand troops departs for South African War

1901	New Zealand annexes Cook Islands and Niue
	Department of Tourist and Health Resorts and Department of Public Health established
1902	Richard Seddon is first premier to use the title 'prime minister'
	New Zealand flag given statutory recognition
1905	State maternity (St Helens) hospitals established
1906	William Hall-Jones (Liberal) and Sir Joseph Ward (Liberal) respectively become prime minister
1907	New Zealand acquires Dominion status
1908	Population reaches one million
	Chinese people are denied citizenship
	Main trunk line from Auckland to Wellington completed
	Blackball coalminers' strike on West Coast
	United States' Great White Fleet visits
1909	Native Land Act removes restrictions on land sales
	Compulsory military training introduced
1911	Home-ownership rate reaches 50 per cent
	HMS *New Zealand* launched
1912	Waihi goldminers' strike
	Thomas Mackenzie (Liberal) and William Massey (Reform) respectively become prime minister
1913	Red Feds call general strike
1914–18	First World War
1914	New Zealand soldiers take German Samoa
1915	Gallipoli landings
	Wartime coalition, termed 'National government', formed of Reform (under Prime Minister William Massey) and Liberals (opposition leader Joseph Ward)
1916	Labour Party founded
	Conscription introduced
	Rua Kēnana arrested
1917–67	Six o'clock closing
1918–19	Influenza pandemic
1918	T. W. Rātana begins religious and political movements

1919	Women gain right to enter parliament
	William Massey retains prime ministership in general election
1920	Health Act reforms public health system in response to pandemic by consolidating statutes, remodelling Department of Health, and clarifying responsibilities of the department and local authorities
	Native Trust Office formed to manage remaining Māori land; funds land-development schemes
	New Zealand joins League of Nations, accepts mandate over Western Samoa
1922	Meat Producers' Board formed
1923	Dairy Export Control Board established
1925	J. G. (Gordon) Coates (Reform) becomes prime minister
1926	Balfour Declaration instigates equal status (in theory) for United Kingdom and Dominions
1928	Sir Joseph Ward (United) becomes prime minister
1929–33	Āpirana Ngata's Māori land-development schemes
1929	Arthurs Pass National Park established
1930	George Forbes (United) becomes prime minister
1930–4	Depression trough
1931	New Zealand gains legislative independence under Statute of Westminster but delays signing
	Napier earthquake
	George Forbes retains prime ministership and forms coalition government
1932	Ottawa Agreements establish a system of imperial trade preferences
1933	Elizabeth McCombs becomes New Zealand's first woman member of parliament
1934	Reserve Bank established
	First public remembrance of Treaty of Waitangi
1935	Michael Joseph Savage (Labour) becomes prime minister

1936	Guaranteed prices introduced for dairy farmers
	Compulsory arbitration restored
	National Party formed
1937–67	National school-milk scheme
1937	State-housing scheme begins
1938	Import licensing introduced
	Social Security Act improves age pension, introduces unemployment benefits
1939–45	Second World War
1939–40	*New Zealand Centennial Exhibition*, Wellington
1939	Social Security Act introduces free public hospital care and free childbirth (maternity benefit)
1940	Treaty of Waitangi centennial
	Peter Fraser becomes prime minister
1941	Japanese attack Pearl Harbor, Hawaii
1942	First official New Zealand representation in United States
	Fall of Singapore naval base; arrival in New Zealand of American forces
1943	New Zealand High Commission opens in Canberra
1944	Australia–New Zealand Agreement (Canberra Pact)
	Poll tax on Chinese migrants abolished
1945	New Zealand joins United Nations as 'New Zealand'
	Māori Social and Economic Advancement Act
	Universal family benefit introduced
1946	Samoa becomes a New Zealand Trust Territory
1947	New Zealand ratifies Statute of Westminster, attaining independence over its own laws
	South Pacific Commission established
1948	New Zealand nationality created and citizenship defined
1949	Iriaka Rātana becomes first Māori woman member of parliament; Sidney Holland (National) becomes prime minister
1950	Legislative Council abolished

	New Zealand troops deploy to Korea
	Colombo Plan established
1951	Waterfront dispute
	ANZUS alliance formed
	Māori Women's Welfare League founded
1952	Population reaches two million
1953	Edmund Hillary and Tenzing Norgay become first climbers confirmed to reach summit of Mount Everest
	Tangiwai rail disaster
	Queen Elizabeth II and Prince Philip, Duke of Edinburgh, conduct royal tour
1954	Southeast Asia Treaty Organization formed through Southeast Asia Collective Defense Treaty
1956	New Zealand troops deploy to Malaya
	Rock and roll arrives
1957	Keith Holyoake (National) and Walter Nash (Labour) respectively become prime minister
1959	Antarctic Treaty reserves the continent for peaceful purposes and scientific research; New Zealand is a signatory
1960	Equal pay in public service comes into effect
	Keith Holyoake (National) becomes prime minister for second time
1961	New Zealand joins International Monetary Fund
1962	Western Samoa gains independence
	New Zealand Māori Council appointed as a national body
	New Zealand troops deploy to Malaysia
1964	Cook Strait power cable laid
1965	New Zealand–Australia Free Trade Agreement
	New Zealand artillery battery deploys to Vietnam
	Vietnam War protests
	Cook Islands self-government begins
1967	Wool price crisis and collapse
	Metric system and decimal currency adopted
	Six o'clock closing of hotels ends

1968	*Wahine* sinks, becoming New Zealand's worst modern maritime disaster
1969	Māori schools system dismantled
1970	'Save Manapouri' petition gains 260 000 signatures opposing raising of Lake Manapouri for hydroelectric power
	Women's liberation movement begins
1971	Ngā Tamatoa group protests at Waitangi Day ceremonies against racial discrimination and breaches of the Treaty
1972	John (Jack) Marshall (National) and Norman Kirk (Labour) respectively become prime minister
	Equal Pay Act extends equal pay provisions from public to private sector; aims to achieve equal pay for work of equal value
1973	Britain joins European Economic Community
	New Zealand opposes French nuclear testing in French Polynesia
	Population reaches three million
1974	Voting age lowered from 20 to 18
	Prime Minister Norman Kirk dies; he is succeeded by Wallace (Bill) Rowling (Labour)
1975	Māori Land March
	Treaty of Waitangi Act establishes Waitangi Tribunal
	Robert Muldoon (National) becomes prime minister
1977	National Superannuation scheme begins
	Bastion Point protest
1979	Air New Zealand plane crashes into Mount Erebus, Antarctica
1981	South Africa's Springboks rugby tour and associated protests
1982–4	Wage and price freezes
1982	Australia–New Zealand Closer Economic Relations Trade Agreement signed
	First kōhanga reo (language nest) established

1983	Australia–New Zealand Closer Economic Relations Trade Agreement implemented
1984	Waitangi Day march and protest (one of many over years)
	David Lange (Labour) becomes prime minister
	New Zealand dollar devalued by 20 per cent
1985	New Zealand refuses request for visit by USS *Buchanan*
	Rainbow Warrior sunk in Auckland Harbour by French agents
	Treaty of Rarotonga creates nuclear-free zone in South Pacific
	New Zealand dollar floated
	Waitangi Tribunal empowered to hear Treaty grievances dating back to 1840
	Sir Paul Reeves becomes first Māori governor-general
1986	Constitution Act removes United Kingdom's residual powers to make law for New Zealand
	Goods and services tax introduced
	Māori tribes lodge first Treaty claims
	United States expels New Zealand from ANZUS
	White New Zealand immigration policy ends
1987	New Zealand Māori Council's challenge in Court of Appeal stops state-owned enterprises from selling land or other public assets required for iwi Treaty settlements, giving Treaty an explicit place in New Zealand jurisprudence
	Māori Language Act makes Māori an official language of New Zealand
	Nuclear-Free Zone, Disarmament and Arms Control Act makes New Zealand legally nuclear-free
1988	State Sector Act applies commercial model to government departments
	Over 100 000 people are unemployed
1989	Labour Party splits, and NewLabour Party forms; Geoffrey Palmer becomes prime minister

	Tomorrow's Schools education reforms devolve decision-making to individual schools
	Local-government reforms
	Māori Fisheries Act establishes Māori Fisheries Commission to help Māori into the fishing industry and decide how to allocate fisheries assets to tribes
1990	New Zealand sesquicentennial
	Dame Catherine Tizard becomes first woman governor-general of New Zealand
	Mike Moore (Labour) and Jim Bolger (National) respectively become prime minister
	Remaining barriers removed under Australia–New Zealand Closer Economic Relations Trade Agreement
	Forestry cutting rights sold
1991	Alliance Party formed; National government in power
	Employment Contracts Act deregulates labour market and adopts individual contracts in employment
	Resource Management Act consolidates over 50 laws to provide a streamlined framework for sustainable environmental management
	Over 200 000 people are unemployed; welfare benefits are cut under National's 'mother of all budgets'
1992	Sealord's (fisheries) deal
	Health and state-housing reforms
1993	Referendum changes voting method to mixed-member proportional system
	National government elected without a majority
1995	America's Cup victory
	Waikato Raupatu Claims Settlement Act is the first act providing for a major historical Treaty settlement for the Waikato-Tainui iwi
1996	First mixed-member proportional representation election held; National–New Zealand First coalition government formed

1997	Jenny Shipley becomes first woman prime minister of New Zealand
	Bougainville Peace Agreement
1998	National minority government formed
	Ngāi Tahu Claims Settlement Act enforces the 1997 deed of settlement and provides for transfer of assets and property
	New Museum of New Zealand Te Papa Tongarewa opens
1999	Peacekeeping troops deploy to Timor-Leste
	Asia-Pacific Economic Cooperation ministerial meeting, Auckland
	Helen Clark becomes first elected woman prime minister of New Zealand, leading Labour government coalition with Alliance and Green Parties
2001	New Zealand Superannuation Fund (Cullen fund) commences as a sovereign wealth fund
	Government rescues Air New Zealand from risk of failure precipitated by Australian subsidiary Ansett
	Fonterra forms from merger of New Zealand Dairy Board and two largest dairy cooperatives
2002	Labour government in coalition with Progressives (rump of Alliance)
2003	Foreshore and seabed judgment that Marlborough iwi are entitled to test their claims
	Prostitution Law Reform Act legalises prostitution and introduces workers' rights
2004	Right of appeal to Privy Council ends
	First Australia New Zealand Leadership Forum
	Māori Party formed
	Foreshore and Seabed Act declares Crown owns foreshore and seabed on behalf of all New Zealanders; Civil Union Act allows state-registered civil unions equivalent status to marriage regardless of gender
2005	Trans-Pacific Strategic Economic Partnership with Chile, Singapore, and Brunei

2006	Inaugural United States–New Zealand Partnership Forum
	Sir Anand Satyanand becomes first New Zealand governor-general of Indian and Pacific ancestry
	Percentage of people classified as 'Asian' outnumber percentage classified as 'Pacific Islander' for first time
2007	KiwiSaver scheme launched
	'Anti-smacking' legislation introduced
2008	Treelords deal transfers most state forests in the central North Island to seven iwi
	John Key (National) becomes prime minister
	Free trade agreement with China
2009	SmartGate processing introduced at airports for trans-Tasman travel
2010	United Nations Declaration on the Rights of Indigenous Peoples
	All Whites are undefeated in FIFA World Cup
	Environment Canterbury (Temporary Commissioners and Improved Water Management) Act replaces elected members of regional council responsible for water policy with appointed commissioners; emissions trading scheme launched in fishing, industry, and forestry
	Auckland super-city created
	Wellington Declaration signals thaw in United States–New Zealand relationship
	Pike River coal mine disaster
	Earthquake of magnitude 7.1 in Canterbury
2011	Earthquakes in Christchurch, largest of magnitude 6.3; Canterbury Earthquake Recovery Authority established
	Marine and Coastal Area (Takutai Moana) Act redefines foreshore and seabed as common space owned by no one
	New Zealand hosts and wins Rugby World Cup
	John Key (National) retains prime ministership
2012	Legal drinking age kept at 18

Timeline

2013	Same-sex marriage legalised
	Powerful earthquakes hit central New Zealand
	Population reaches four million
2014	John Key (National) retains prime ministership
	Te Urewera rainforest granted legal personhood
	Earthquake of 6.5 magnitude near Gisborne
2015	All Blacks win Rugby World Cup in England
	Trans-Pacific Partnership trade deal
	First flag referendum
	Gallipoli landings centennial
2016	Earthquake of magnitude 7.8 at Kaikōura
	John Key resigns prime ministership and is replaced by Bill English
	Second referendum retains existing flag
2017	Cyclones and flooding
	Jacinda Ardern (Labour) becomes prime minister, in coalition with Winston Peters (New Zealand First)
	Crown apologises at Parihaka and pardons Tūhoe's prophet Rua Kēnana
	America's Cup win
	Whanganui River gains legal personhood
2018	First national day held to commemorate New Zealand Wars
	Hottest summer on record
	Earthquake of magnitude 6.2 in North Island
2019	Terrorist attack on Christchurch mosques
	Whakaari White Island erupts
2020	Covid-19 reaches New Zealand, forcing nationwide lockdown
	Population reaches five million
	Labour wins majority of seats in parliament
2021	Warmest year on record
	Second national lockdown, due to new Covid-19 variant
2022	Increase in Covid-19 deaths and easing of restrictions; more international tourists readmitted
	First Matariki public holiday

2023	Cyclone Gabrielle
	Economic recession
	Jacinda Ardern resigns prime ministership and is replaced by Chris Hipkins; election sees swing to National-led coalition with New Zealand First and ACT; Christopher Luxon becomes prime minister
2024	Māori king Tūheitia Pōtatau Te Wherowhero VII dies; his daughter Ngā Wai Hono i te pō Paki is anointed queen
	Te Hīkoi mō te Tiriti opposes Treaty Principles Bill
	New Zealand athletes win 10 gold medals at Paris Olympics; third America's Cup win
2025	Mount Taranaki gains legal personhood
	Treaty Principles Bill rejected by parliament

SOURCES OF QUOTATIONS

Full source details can be found in the 'Guide to further reading' section, listed by chapter.

1 WAKA ACROSS A WATERY WORLD

'South Polynesia' from Anderson, 'Origins, Settlement and Society'; and applied in Williams, *Polynesia*. Story of Te Arawa canoe from Evans, *Discovery of Aotearoa*, 47. 'Mental maps' of Polynesian world from O'Regan, 'Ngai Tahu and the Crown', 2–3. 'Spirit of his god and ancestors' and 'establishing the "mental world"' from Tau, 'Tirohia atu nei ka Whetū Rangitia', 20. 'Ancestral genetic trail' from Howe, *Quest for Origins*, 82. 'Inconclusive' evidence from Anderson, 'Te Ao Tawhito', 25. New model for late colonisation of East Polynesia and 'in one major pulse' from Wilmshurst et al., 'High-Precision Radiocarbon Dating'.

Quotation about whakapapa from Tau, 'Ngāi Tahu and the Canterbury Landscape', 41; 'gods' and 'heroes' from Tremewan, *Traditional Stories*, xxi; 'archetypal images' from Tau, 'Ngāi Tahu and the Canterbury Landscape', 50; 'rolled up our legends' from O'Regan, 'Ngai Tahu and the Crown', 1–2. Paikea story from Walker, *He Tipua*, 20–1. 'Lost tribes of Israel' from Sorrenson, *Maori Origins and Migrations*, 16.

'Sacredness of nature' from Schama, *Landscape and Memory*, 18. Quotation on 'magico-religious world view of the environment' from New Zealand, Waitangi Tribunal, *Manukau Report*, 38–9; 'introduced to rules' from New Zealand, Waitangi Tribunal, *Ngai Tahu Report*, vol. 2, 201; vol. 3, 879–83. 'Optimal foragers' from Anderson, 'Fragile Plenty', 20; 'hunter-gardeners' from Belich, *Making Peoples*, 47. 'Avifauna has been decimated' from Worthy and Holdaway, *Lost World of the Moa*, 565. 'Festive fare' and 'added value' from Leach, 'In the Beginning', 23.

2 BEACHCROSSERS 1769–1839

The author developed the concept of 'beachcrossing' concurrently with Dening, *Beach Crossings*. Tasman's instructions and views from Salmond, *Two Worlds*, 72; also the encounter, 81–2. Cook as hero of free trading from Smith, *Imagining the Pacific*, 230. 'Mechanical tinkerers' from Jones, *European Miracle*, 65. 'Humanist myth' from Obeyesekere, *Apotheosis of Captain Cook*. Cook quoted in Beaglehole, *Life of Captain James Cook*, 698, 696–714. 'Global village' from Smith, *Imagining the Pacific*, 240.

Sinclair, *History of New Zealand*, 1st edn; Beaglehole, *Life of Captain James Cook*; Salmond, *Two Worlds*; and Belich, *Making Peoples* all cite the Horeta Te Taniwha story; this version from Salmond, *Two Worlds*, 88. The written source is 'Account Given by Hore-Ta-Te-Taniwha', in White, *Ancient History of the Maori*, 121–8. Du Fresne's story from Salmond, *Two Worlds*, 387. 'Series of blunders' from Owens, 'New Zealand before Annexation', 30. Governor King's comments about Māori from King Papers, 2 January 1806, in McNab, *Historical Records of New Zealand*, 267; also Salmond, *Between Worlds*, 351–2, 356, 516.

Whalers as 'agents of contact' from Belich, *Making Peoples*, 137. On sealers and the built environment see Mein Smith, 'Sealing Industry'. Te Pahi blamed for killings from Salmond, *Between Worlds*, 386–94; also 'friendly chief' and 'treacherous cannibal', 387; Moon, *Te Ara ki te Tiriti*, 49. 'Very treacherous race' from Governor Macquarie to Viscount Castlereagh, 12 March 1810, quoted in Salmond, *Between Worlds*, 387.

Samuel Marsden was known as the 'flogging parson'; on Marsden and Māori, see Salmond, *Between Worlds*, 429–31; Cloher, *Hongi Hika*, 69–91. 'Pocket Parramatta' from Clunie, 'Kerikeri', 24. 'Land wars' from Ballara, *Taua*, 17; wars as 'modern catastrophe for Māori' from Head, 'Pursuit of Modernity', 102.

'Maintenance of tranquillity' and Busby as 'watch-dog without teeth' from Hill, *Policing the Colonial Frontier*, 58, 60. 'Clearer racial hierarchy' from Bayly, *Imperial Meridian*, 149; also 'independency', 151; 'freeborn Englishmen', 207. The contents of the Declaration of Independence are reprinted in Davidson, *Introducing He Whakaputanga*, 15–16; also 'rangatiratanga', 14; 'collective capacity', 15; 'friendship and protection', 11, 16. 'Magna Carta of New Zealand Independence' and meeting of chiefs from Busby to Bourke, 10 October 1835, quoted in Raeside, *Sovereign Chief*, 115. 'Fatal impact' from Moorehead, *Fatal Impact*. Imperialism and humanitarianism 'march[ed] together' from Sinclair, *History of New Zealand*, 5th edn, 70. On 'fatal necessity' see Adams, *Fatal Necessity*. De Thierry criticised in Vaggioli, *History of New Zealand*, 63; and quoted in Raeside, *Sovereign Chief*, 183.

'Accumulating evils' from Busby, quoted in Owens, 'New Zealand before Annexation', 41; British superiority from Porter, *Oxford History of the British Empire*, 208. On 'notorious and visionary' Wakefield see

Temple, *Sort of Conscience*. Hobson's instructions quoted in Hill, *Policing the Colonial Frontier*, 89. The meeting with 'Warri Podi' and 'Pooni' on Wellington Harbour from William Mein Smith, 'Journal of a Voyage on Board the Barque *Cuba* from London to New Zealand', 5–6 January 1840, copy in private possession, original in Alexander Turnbull Library, Wellington, qMS-1840-1844, vol. 3.

3 CLAIMING THE LAND 1840–1860

Tareha quoted in Orange, *Story of a Treaty*, 31; Māori debate before Treaty signing discussed in New Zealand, Waitangi Tribunal, *Muriwhenua Land Report*, 111. 'Battle of words' summarised in Orange, *Story of a Treaty*, 31–5; also Hobson's first words in Māori, 38; Fletcher, *English Text*, 337. 'We are peoples together' from Margaret Mutu, quoted in Healy, McCreanor, and Nairn, 'Hobson's Actual Pledges'. Panakareao's motives assessed in Belgrave, *Historical Frictions*, 102–13; quotation from 108; Panakareao quoted by W. Shortland to Lord Stanley, 18 January 1845, cited in Ward, *Unsettled History*, 16. Panakareao's speech also in Orange, *Illustrated History*, 38.

The Treaty's newly found legal status reviewed in Kawharu, *Waitangi*. 'New myth' from McHugh, 'Australasian Narratives', 114. For Treaty in original English and Māori see New Zealand, Lieutenant Governor, *Te Tiriti o Waitangi / The Treaty of Waitangi*. Article 2 quoted in Ward, *Unsettled History*, 14; Māori text from New Zealand, Lieutenant Governor, *Facsimile*; Orange, *Illustrated History*, 257. English translation of Māori text of the Treaty reproduced from Coleman, 'Literal Translation'. 'Individual capacity', 'collective capacity', 'governmental power', and 'internal tribal authority' from Busby, quoted in Fletcher, *English Text*, 502. Context of Williams' Māori translation explained in Head, 'Pursuit of Modernity', 106; also 'friends' as opposed to 'enemies', 110–11. Meaning of Treaty analysed in Fletcher, *English Text*, 487–529.

'Civilisation' from Pawson, 'Confronting Nature', 63; Locke quoted in Denoon and Mein Smith, *History*, 120. 'Mixture of all classes' from Temple, *Sort of Conscience*, 127. 'Natural abundance' from Fairburn, *Ideal Society*. Wakefield quoted in Condliffe, *New Zealand in the Making*, 17; and Wakefield, Ward, and Wakefield, *British Colonization of New Zealand*, 28–9. 'Sufficient price' from Prichard, 'Wakefield Changes His Mind about the "Sufficient Price"'.

'Morals and manners' from Dalziel, 'Men, Women and Wakefield', 83–4; Wakefield to Godley, 6 May 1851, quoted in Temple, *Sort of Conscience*, 419; also 'standard of morals and manners', 132. Description of New Zealand Company lottery of 29 July 1839 from *Spectator*, 3 August 1839. William Mein Smith's report is 'Last Report of W. M. Smith as Surveyor-General', Wellington, 4 April 1842, enclosure in Principal Agent to Secretary, New Zealand Company, Wellington, 27 August 1842,

National Archives, London, CO 208/100, no. 128; his personal views from 'Journal of a Voyage on Board the Barque *Cuba* from London to New Zealand', 9 January 1840, copy in private possession, original in Alexander Turnbull Library, Wellington, qMS-1840-1844, vol. 3. Settler numbers from Borrie, *European Peopling of Australasia*, 95. Kitsets to 'hasten the process' from Schrader, 'Bi-cultural Townscape', 12.

'Southern New Zealand' from Tremewan, *French Akaroa*. 'Forgotten forty-niners' from Amodeo, *Forgotten Forty-Niners*. 'Advance guard of empire' and 'colonial capitalist class' from McAloon, *No Idle Rich*, 23.

Governor as ruler from Francis, *Governors and Settlers*, 213; appeasement of the 'savage' from McAloon, *Nelson*, 35. Hōne Heke's letter quoted in Kawharu, 'Heke Pokai'. 'Show of justice' from Ward, *Show of Justice*. Browne quoted in Orange, 'Covenant of Kohimarama', 65.

4 REMOTER AUSTRALASIA 1861–1890

British 'small wars' from Belich, *New Zealand Wars*, 335. New Zealand's 'Great War' from O'Malley, *Great War for New Zealand*, 9. Browne depicted as a scapegoat in Dalton, 'Browne, Thomas Robert Gore'; and Bohan, *Climates of War*, 90–1. 'Deliberate war of conquest' from O'Malley, *New Zealand Wars*, 104. Cowan's account of Rewi's story from 'Famous New Zealanders'.

New Zealand Settlements Act 1863 as 'just the beginning' from Boast, '"Expensive Mistake"', 145. Numbers of acres purchased from Ward, *National Overview*, 8. Resisters as 'rebels' from O'Malley, *Invasion of Waikato*, 166, 173. Native Land Court's objectives outlined in New Zealand, *Parliamentary Debates*, vol. 9, 29 August 1870, 361 (Sewell). Boast's view of court's purpose from Boast, *Buying the Land*, 42, 93.

Description of colonial forest rangers from Cowan, *New Zealand Wars*, vol. 1, 266. New Zealand, Waitangi Tribunal, *Turanga Tangata Turanga Whenua*, found 'there was no rebellion in Turanga [Poverty Bay]'; also Te Kooti's story, chap. 5. East Coast 'had its own war' from Oliver and Thomson, *Challenge and Response*, 86. Confiscation of 'rebel' Māori's land for allocation to military settlers and 'loyal' Māori from New Zealand, Waitangi Tribunal, *Turanga Tangata Turanga Whenua*, xx–xxi; Map of confiscated areas in Spoonley, 'Ethnic and Religious Intolerance'. 'Tenants in common' as form of title from New Zealand, House of Representatives, *Appendix to the Journals of the House of Representatives*, 1891, G-01a, 19, reproduced in Boast, *Buying the Land*, 105. On 'aboriginal title' see Parsonson, 'Fate of Maori Land Rights', 185. Quotations from Prendergast judgment, *Wi Parata v Bishop of Wellington* [1877], 3 NZ Jur (NS) 72. Te Whiti and Tohu 'walked to captivity' from Scott, *Ask That Mountain*, 117. Invasion of Parihaka reconsidered in Buchanan, 'Beating Shame'.

Māori numbers from Pool, *Te Iwi Maori*; dispossession, population decline, health, and wellbeing discussed in Durie, *Whaiora*; and Boast, *Buying the Land*, 254–60. British migration statistics from Borrie, *European Peopling of Australasia*; number of gold-seekers to the West Coast from Australia in 1865–7 from May, *West Coast Gold Rushes*, 845, 884. 'Material abundance' from Fairburn, *Ideal Society*, chap. 1; also Arcadianism as a fallacy, 236. 'Disproportion of the sexes' from Macdonald, 'Too Many Men'. Millions spent on 'progressive colonisation' from Belich, *Making Peoples*, 351. Russell and Whitaker from Hunt, *Rich List*, 80–7; Russell's 'clandestine negotiations' from Stone, *Makers of Fortune*, 177. Male Māori vote from Atkinson, *Adventures in Democracy*, 50. 'Share in the fruits of progress' from Macintyre, *Concise History of Australia*, 115. Alternative given Māori children from Pope, *Health for the Maori*. 'Gendered script' from Daley, *Girls & Women*. Macmillan Brown quoted in Gardner, *Colonial Cap and Gown*, 71; also percentages of women graduates, 110. Self-help and 'shiftless' from Thomson, *World without Welfare*, 5, 17, 29. Expectation that women should be 'economically dependent' on men discussed in Brookes, *History of New Zealand Women*, 108. 'Undeserving' from Thomson, *World without Welfare*, 30–1.

'Boiling Water Land' from Wevers, *Country of Writing*, 174. Debate over Te Heuheu's gift of volcanic peaks summarised in New Zealand, Waitangi Tribunal, *Closing Submissions*; 'practical sovereignty' from Boast, *Generic Submissions*, 7. Tumu Te Heuheu quoted in New Zealand, Waitangi Tribunal, *Closing Submissions*, 5.

'Deep natural Exchequer' from Hursthouse, *Australasian Republic*. Definition of 'Australasia' from Morris, *Austral English*, cited in Denoon, 'Re-membering Australasia', 293; Russell's remarks on federation quoted in Mein Smith, 'New Zealand Federation Commissioners', 312, 313. 'Crimson thread' from Mein Smith, 'New Zealand', 402. 'Distinct national type' from Russell, quoted in Australasian Federation Conference, *Official Record*, 125. On 'colonial nationalism' see Jebb, *Studies in Colonial Nationalism*, 327; 'dismemberment' from Denoon, 'Re-membering Australasia', 297.

Definition of 'depression' from Hawke, *Making of New Zealand*, 82–3; 'frenzy of private borrowing' from Simkin, *Instability of a Dependent Economy*, 151. Growth of 'new unionism' from Nolan, 'Maritime Strike'.

5 MANAGING GLOBALISATION 1891–1913

'State experiments' from Reeves, *State Experiments*; 'Australian Settlement' from Kelly, *End of Certainty*; 'domestic defence' from Castles, *Australian Public Policy*. New Zealand as 'Māoriland' from Sinclair, *Destiny Apart*. Belich elaborates his thesis in *Paradise Reforged* and extends it to the Anglo world in *Replenishing the Earth*.

'Natural resource benefits' from Ville, *Rural Entrepreneurs*, 7. McLean and Cheviot Hills from Hunt, *Rich List*. Māori land loss from Ward, *National Overview*, 246–7; Brooking, *Lands for the People?*, 134, 140. Loans as 'special reward' from Reeves, *State Experiments*, vol. 1, 330. 'New urban frontier' from Frost, *New Urban Frontier*; Hamer, *New Towns*.

'Man's country' from Phillips, *Man's Country?*; Woman's Christian Temperance Union of New Zealand, *Sixteen Reasons*; 'pure and temperate fathers' from Stout, 'New Woman'.

Reeves' debt to Kingston traced in Gardner, *Prelude to Arbitration*. 'Free, prosperous and contented people' from Macintyre, 'Neither Capital nor Labour', 186; Ballance quoted in Hamer, *New Zealand Liberals*, 53. 'Hold the balance' from Martin, *Holding the Balance*. 'Living wage' from Holt, *Compulsory Arbitration*, 105. On Red Feds see chapters by Eric Olssen and Len Richardson in Fry, *Common Cause*; 'battle over democracy' from Nolan, '1913 in Retrospect', 34, 35.

'Penultimate Maori land grab' from Brooking, *Lands for the People?*, 134; also 'bursting up', chap. 8; homestead blocks, 142. Attitudes of Reform Party supporters from *New Zealand Herald*, 15 May 1906; land in Māori ownership from New Zealand, House of Representatives, *Appendix to the Journals of the House of Representatives*, 1911, G-6, 1–4. Native Land Act 1909 from Ward, *National Overview*, 380. 'Blended New Zealander' from Lange, *May the People Live*, 56; also Young Māori Party quotation, 122–3. Tregear's 'long and adventurous past' and 'Aryan of the West' quoted in Howe, *Quest for Origins*, 168, 169–70.

New Zealanders as non-Australians from Sinclair, 'Why New Zealanders Are Not Australians'. Wood's views on 'waffle' in 'Why Did New Zealand Not Join'; dissenting voice was Chan, 'New Zealand'. Belich suggested 'Tasman world' ended in 1901 in *Paradise Reforged*, 30–1, 52; counterargument in Mein Smith, Hempenstall, and Goldfinch, *Remaking the Tasman World*. Barton quoted in New Zealand, House of Representatives, *Appendix to the Journals of the House of Representatives*, 1901, A-4, 479; also W. Curzon-Siggers, 109. Hall quoted in Australasian Federation Conference, *Official Record*, 175.

Chinese as 'archetypal alien' from Ip, *Unfolding History*, xi; 'did not swim with the mainstream' from Price, *Great White Walls*, 254. Ideal society as 'real enemy' from Moloughney and Stenhouse, '"Drug-Besotten, Sin Begotten"', 64.

Seddon on South African War quoted in Hawdon, *New Zealanders and the Boer War*, 5; also 'fraternal terms', 260. On the 'Learned Eleventh' see Ellis, 'New Zealand Women and the War', 140; on New Zealand's 'long-term interests' see McGibbon, 'Origins', 10. Colonies as 'white men's country' from McGibbon, *Path to Gallipoli*, 165.

'Our best immigrant' from New Zealand, House of Representatives, *Appendix to the Journals of the House of Representatives*, 1925, H-31, 3.

'Mother's mutiny' from Belich, *Paradise Reforged*, 181; 'Sacredness of the Body' from Royal New Zealand Society for the Health of Women and Children, annual reports, various years from 1908, Hocken Collections Uare Taoka o Hākena, University of Otago, Dunedin; 'educational health mission' from 'Vesta' (a New Zealand journalist), 'Women to Women'. 'Broad hips' from Mein Smith, *Mothers and King Baby*, 95. Patriotic scouts from Esplin, 'Cossgrove, David', 117.

6 'ALL FLESH IS AS GRASS' 1914–1929

'All flesh is as grass' quotation from McCormick, *Making New Zealand*, 2; 'ecological imperialism' from Crosby, *Ecological Imperialism*. 'Most traumatic event' from McGibbon, *New Zealand Battlefields*, 1.

Stretcher bearers' heroism and 'Bloody Beach Bay' from Fenwick, *Gallipoli Diary*, 14. See also Fewster, Basarin, and Basarin, *Gallipoli*. 'Expression of sorrow' from New Zealand, Manatū Taonga Ministry for Culture and Heritage, 'Sacred Holiday'; 'greatest of all causes' from *Press* (Christchurch), 11 December 1914; 'splendid conduct and bravery' from Auckland Weekly News, *New Zealand's Roll of Honour*, 1.

'Neat dress' from C. E. W. Bean (Australia's war historian), *Story of ANZAC*, 129, cited in McGibbon, *Path to Gallipoli*, 255; on quiet New Zealanders see Burton, *Silent Division*; 'Digger and cobber' from H. S. B. R., 'War Friends'; 'Anzacs together' from Inglis, *Sacred Places*, 84.

Chunuk Bair as 'central' from Shadbolt, *Voices of Gallipoli*, 9; later New Zealand role from Pugsley, *Gallipoli*, 358; 'Daredevil Dan' quoted in Shadbolt, *Voices of Gallipoli*, 49; Buck quoted in Gardiner, *Te Mura o te Ahi*, 19; Wilson quoted in Harper, *Massacre at Passchendaele*, 10. Tremewan's mother notified of his death in Captain Ernest Harston, France, to Mrs [Mary] Tremewan, 20 September 1916, private collection; his obituary is in *Wanganui Chronicle*, 31 October 1916. Shakespeare's Volumnia quoted in Triggs, 'New Zealand Mothers', 73.

Te Puea quoted in King, *Te Puea*, 78; and Baker, *King and Country Call*, 213; 'mothers of the world' from Hutching, '"Mothers of the World"'. Foljambe, *Her Excellency's Knitting Book*, quoted in Coney, *Standing in the Sunshine*, 312. *New Zealand Herald*, 27 April 1925, quoted in Worthy, 'Debt of Honour', 195. Memorial types from Phillips and Inglis, 'War Memorials', 187; Oamaru's memorial oak trees from Pawson, 'Trees as Sites of Commemoration'.

King's 'great wastage of ... life' quoted in *Argus* (Melbourne), 2 December 1919. '"Modern" women' from Bryder, *Voice for Mothers*, 80–1; King's 'betterment of the race' quoted in Mein Smith, *Maternity in Dispute*, 2. Gunn's 'crockery' order recalled by Barbara Smith (describing medical inspections at primary school in the Manawatū during the 1920s), interview, 1990s; 'fattening human stock' from Tennant, *Children's*

Health, 38; also Gunn's inspections, 39–40; portrayal of health camp from *Wanganui Chronicle*, 17 November 1922.

'Grasslands revolution' from Brooking, Hodge, and Wood, 'Grasslands Revolution Reconsidered'. 'Empire's Dairy Farm' from *New Zealand Dairy Produce Exporter*, 25 July 1925; films described in *New Zealand Dairy Produce Exporter*, 29 May 1926; also 'healthy stock', and butter for development. 'Economic and cultural landscape' from Barnes, *New Zealand's London*, 188. 'Housekeeping purse' from *New Zealand Dairy Produce Exporter*, 29 August 1925.

'Maximising farm income' from Fleming, 'Agricultural Support Policies', 351. '"Smash" the capitalist system' from King, *Penguin History of New Zealand*, 313. Prejudice about 'idle' land from Ward, *Unsettled History*, 159; Rātana quoted in Henderson, *Ratana*, 88. Nēpia described in Zavos and Bray, *Two Mighty Tribes*.

Urewera as 'bounded land' from Binney, *Encircled Lands*, 325; also Rua's imprisonment 'snuffed out' Tūhoe control, 569. On Urewera see also Boast, *Buying the Land*, 234–44. Sim Commission quotations from New Zealand, House of Representatives, *Appendix to the Journals of the House of Representatives*, 1928, G-7, 1–6 (terms of reference), 11 (Taranaki), 17 (Waikato), 20 (Tauranga), 22 (Bay of Plenty); also O'Malley, *Aftermath*, 9, 110–12, 130.

7 MAKING NEW ZEALAND 1930–1949

'No pay without work' from McClure, *Civilised Community*, 49; Depression myth from Simpson, *Sugarbag Years*; Park and 'unfair taxation' from Nolan, *Breadwinning*, 173. Cover of Gustafson, *From the Cradle*, illustrates the promise. Savage described as 'Christ-like figure' and 'ninny' by diplomat Sir Carl Berendsen, quoted in Hensley, 'Beyond the Battlefield: Peter Fraser at War', 105. Savage's joke in *Evening Post*, 16 June 1938, quoted in Gustafson, *From the Cradle*, 216. Labour's election manifesto from Gustafson, *From the Cradle*, 165; and Hanson, *Politics of Social Security*, 37. Breadwinner wage from H. T. Armstrong, interviewed by Mrs E. Freeman, 23 April 1936, Archives New Zealand, Wellington, L1 3/3/564-1, R18784256 (restricted).

'Workers' welfare state' from Castles, *Working Class and Welfare*; also 'wage security for the worker', 87; standard of living people 'ought to have' from Nash, quoted in McClure, *Civilised Community*, 80. 'Painless maternity' from Society for the Protection of Women and Children, Committee of Inquiry into Maternity Services, Auckland, evidence, 6 September 1937, Archives New Zealand, Wellington, Evidence, H3 3/7; 'fullest degree of pain-relief' from New Zealand, House of Representatives, *Appendix to the Journals of the House of Representatives*, 1938, H-31A, 107.

Government expenditure from McIntyre, *New Zealand Prepares for War*, 259; 'independent' and 'moral' foreign policy from Crawford and Watson,

Sources of quotations 355

'"Most Appeasing Line"', 75, 91. 'Loyal opposition' from McKinnon, *Independence and Foreign Policy*, 45; Savage's attitude to war from McIntyre, *New Zealand Prepares for War*, 237; Savage's broadcast quoted in Wood, *New Zealand People at War*, 11. 'Air came first' from Peter Fraser to William F. Halsey, 30 August 1943, quoted in Wood, *New Zealand People at War*, 260. Number of war dead from Crawford, *Kia Kaha*, 3. Fraser's cable to Churchill, 15 June 1940 (about Britain's withdrawn promise to defend Singapore naval base), quoted in Wood, *New Zealand People at War*, 194; McIntyre, *New Zealand Prepares for War*, 241.

'Real settlement' from New Zealand, Department of Tourist and Publicity, *New Zealand Centennial*; exhibition outlined in *Evening Post Centennial Number*, 7 November 1939. Āpirana Ngata, speech delivered at Waitangi celebrations, 6 February 1940, transcript at Archives New Zealand, Wellington, 14987489 (formerly IA 1, 62/25/6), and quoted in Walker, *He Tipua*, 352. Māori Battalion information from Gardiner, *Te Mura o te Ahi*, 31.

New Zealand 'geographically part of the Pacific' from Wood, *Understanding New Zealand*, 217. Australia–New Zealand cooperation from Kay, *Australian–New Zealand Agreement*, 146; 'territorial integrity' from Wood, *New Zealand People at War*, 376. 'Government's objective' from New Zealand, House of Representatives, *Appendix to the Journals of the House of Representatives*, 1939, E-1, 2–3. Profile of a good migrant from McKinnon, *Immigrants and Citizens*, 1–17, 99. 'Every man springs from the soil' from Duff, *New Zealand Now*, 14. 'Intellectual stagnation' from Condliffe, *Eye of the Earth*, 102; 'mother-complex' from Condliffe, *New Zealand in the Making*, 431. 'So-called mother complex' from Wood, *Understanding New Zealand*, 194; also foreign policy as 'drama', 195. 'Dual dependency' from McIntyre, 'From Dual Dependency'.

8 GOLDEN WEATHER 1950–1972

'This *golden weather*' from Mason, *End of the Golden Weather*, 12–13. McCahon quoted in Docking, *Two Hundred Years*, 184. *Freedom* was the National Party's monthly newspaper; Weston information from Carol Shand (granddaughter), pers. comm., April 2004.

'Anzac dilemma' coined in Wood, 'Anzac Dilemma'; McIntosh quoted in McIntosh, 'Origins', 21; 'dual dependence' from Kennaway, *New Zealand Foreign Policy*, chap. 2; New Zealand, *Parliamentary Debates*, vol. 305, 24 March 1955, 11–26 (Holland).

Ross Dependency under New Zealand jurisdiction from Templeton, *Wise Adventure*, chaps 2–3; United States and New Zealand as 'neighbours' from Rear Admiral George Dufek, United States navy, from Stephen Hicks, pers. comm., 2004.

Waterfront dispute's structural causes explained in Green, *British Capital*, 153. 'Nuclear playground' from Firth, *Nuclear Playground*;

uranium rush and 'atoms for peace' from Priestley, *Mad on Radium*, 106–12, 155; also New Zealand's sole nuclear reactor, 179.

Migration statistics from McKinnon, *Immigrants and Citizens*, 39. 'Free association' from Campbell, *Worlds Apart*, 284;'long pink cloud' from W. H. Oliver, pers. comm., 1983. 'Silent migration' from Broughton et al., *Silent Migration*. Auckland a 'destination of choice' from Harris, 'Māori Affairs', 395. 'Reserve of industrial labour' from *Labour and Employment Gazette*, February 1952, quoted in Woods, 'Dissolving the Frontiers', 119; apprenticeship scheme from Woods, 'Integrating the Nation', 77–8, 195–6. Definition of 'integration' from New Zealand, House of Representatives, *Appendix to the Journals of the House of Representatives*, 1961, G-10, 15–16; Māori Women's Welfare League quoted in Brookes, 'Nostalgia', 212.

Rangiora pavlova recipe from Teal, 'Recipes for the Renovations'; cream advertising in New Zealand Milk Board, *Everything tastes better with cream* [poster], 1960s, Archives New Zealand, Christchurch, R16953892.

Hillary's 'tractor train' from Hicks, 'Commonwealth Trans-Antarctic Expedition', 230. '"Flood" of American culture' from Whitcher, '"More than America"' (quoting *Star-Sun*, 14 October 1946); also reception of rock and roll.

'New consumer age' from Brickell, 'Politics', 138. 'Oversexed' girls from New Zealand, Special Committee on Moral Delinquency in Children and Adolescents, *Report*, 63–8; 'generation gap' from Coney, *Standing in the Sunshine*, 174–5. 'Pub liberations' from Cook, 'Women's Movement'. On Greer's impact see Brookes, 'Germaine Moment'; 'saucy feminist' from 'Saucy Feminist That Even Men Like' [anchorage text], *Life* magazine, 7 May 1971, cover.

Farmer quoted in Somerset, *Littledene*, 126, 220; 'lubricated by trust' from Singleton and Robertson, *Economic Relations*, 11. Wool price crash and auction from Easton, *Not in Narrow Seas*, 350, 362–5; and Gould, *Rake's Progress?*, 113–14; 'pastoral era' from Easton, *Not in Narrow Seas*, 362; 'stop-go' from Gould, *Rake's Progress?*, 113. 'Fight for survival' from Marshall, *Memoirs*, 61.

9 LATEST EXPERIMENTS 1973–1996

Definition of 'globalisation' from Le Heron and Pawson, *Changing Places*, 22. Balance-of-payments deficit from Dalziel and Lattimore, *New Zealand Macroeconomy*, graph 2.4. Fall in real incomes from New Zealand, Treasury, *New Zealand Economic Growth*; 'misdiagnosis' from Belich, *Paradise Reforged*, 460; 'big government' from Bassett, *State in New Zealand*, 324.

Muldoon's wanting people 'protected from [capitalism's] excesses' from Gustafson, *His Way*, 6; 'I look back to Britain' from Muldoon, *My Way*, 9; 'New Zealand way of life' from Muldoon, *Rise and Fall*, 197. 'Political ageing' and 'welfare generation' from Thomson, *Selfish Generations?*, 28, 105, 215. 'Genuine, combative, populist demagogue' from Templeton, *All Honourable Men*, 224; 'command economy' from Bassett, *State in New Zealand*, 17. Challenge to view that New Zealand's economy was uniquely 'highly regulated' from Goldfinch and Malpass, 'Polish Shipyard', 118–19. Muldoon's backing for the Australia–New Zealand Closer Economic Relations Trade Agreement from Mein Smith, 'Did Muldoon Really "Go Too Slowly"', 175. Fraser and Muldoon's relationship from Anthony, '20 Years of Trans-Tasman CER'. Nareen statement from Andre, Payton, and Mills, *Negotiation*, 1–4; also 'deep ties', 2; Anthony, 5–7.

'Most radical government' from Cullen, 'Opening Remarks', 9; Lange described in Palmer, 'Working with David Lange'; and Henderson, 'Warrior Peacenik', 136–9, 142–3. 'Jerry-built economic structure' from Bassett, *State in New Zealand*, 23; 'blitzkrieg' from Easton, *Not in Narrow Seas*, 489. 'The right thing' from Bassett, 'Cabinet Making', 43–4; and Douglas, 'How We Did It', 56; Margarine Act example from Caygill, 'Industry Policy', 76; change as end, not means, from Cullen, 'Opening Remarks', 11.

'Theory driven revolution' from Goldfinch, *Remaking New Zealand*, 37. 'Elected dictatorship' from Easton, *Not in Narrow Seas*, 489. Reforms in the wrong order from Hawke, 'New Zealand', 244. Quoted critic is Kelsey, *Rolling Back the State*, 60–1. Assurance that reforms represented the 'answer' recalled by Ron Burgess (former head of Combined Service Unions), in a comment made at Conference on the First Term of the Fourth Labour Government, 1 May 2004. Huntly case study from Dillon, 'Rogernomics and Rupture'.

'Deliver jobs' from Davey, *Another New Zealand Experiment*, 9; 'enormous' and 'intolerable' concentration of power from Palmer, 'Working with David Lange'. 'Unbridled power' from Palmer and Palmer, *Bridled Power*, 9; also Constitution Act, 6–9; 'patriated', 6. 'Major limitations' from Barnett and Barnett, 'Back to the Future?', 137, 145; 'impediment for the health sector' from Gauld, *Revolving Doors*, 214.

Independence and 'role of power' from McKinnon, *Independence and Foreign Policy*, 278. Data on nuclear-ship visits from Priestley, *Mad on Radium*, 225. Lange government's conduct of foreign policy from Norrish (secretary of Ministry of Foreign Affairs and Trade, 1980–9), 'Lange Government's Foreign Policy'; also Shultz's response, 151. 'Least nuclearish ship' from Richards, *Palmer*, 21; 'clapped-out old destroyer' from Norrish, 'Lange Government's Foreign Policy', 153; also 'beyond reasonable doubt'. Palmer's judgment from Richards, *Palmer*, 27; also assessments of Palmer's role, 29.

'Atom splitters' from Bassett, 'Atom Splitters'. 'Test of principle' from Wilson, *Labour in Government*, 55; also 'unless there was clear proof', 64. Caucus understanding from Richards, *Palmer*, 30; 'triumph for democracy' from Clark, 'Politician's View', 18. Lange quotations from Lange, *My Life*, 204, 205; Lange, '"Nuclear Weapons"', 15, 16, 21.

ANZUS declared 'inoperative' from McIntyre, 'From Dual Dependency', 535; 'the breach came' from McMillan, *Neither Confirm nor Deny*, 88; 'state terrorism' from *Times*, Leader, 9 July 1986; on 'freedom of the seas' see treaty extracts in McMillan, *Neither Confirm nor Deny*, 168. Quotations from New Zealand, Defence Committee of Enquiry, *Defence and Security*, 73, 67, 73. 'Crash through' from Goldfinch, *Remaking New Zealand*, 215.

10 TREATY REVIVAL 1973–1999

On Waitangi Day see Orange, 'Waitangi Day 1960s' and 'Waitangi Day 1970s'. 'Māori people were fed up' from Ward, *National Overview*, vol. 1, 137. 'Last land grab' from Walker, *Ka Whawhai Tonu Matou*, 207; Harris, *Hikoi*, 24; 'not one more acre' quoted by Walker, 'Māori People since 1950', 513. Bastion Point protest from Walker, *Ka Whawhai Tonu Matou*, 216–18; for details see New Zealand, Waitangi Tribunal, *Report*.

Red Squad culture and Mandela from Richards, *Dancing on Our Bones*, 223; Te Āti Awa's opposition to pollution of fishing reefs from *Evening Post*, 6 April 1983. Treaty 'brought to life' from Temm, *Waitangi Tribunal*, 40. Treaty principles from Hayward, 'Appendix'. Māori 'ceded rights' according to Justice Maurice Casey, quoted in Temm, *Waitangi Tribunal*, 96; also Treaty as 'living, breathing, vital thing', 97.

Ngāi Tahu claim from O'Regan, 'Ngāi Tahu Claim', 242–3; Ngāi Tahu's fate from Tau, 'Ngai Tahu', 222–5. Fishing rights from Ward, *Unsettled History*, 46–8; Brookfield, *Waitangi and Indigenous Rights*, 129. Sealord's deal from Anderson, Binney, and Harris, *Tangata Whenua*, 131. Māori sea fisheries ownership from Ward, *Unsettled History*, 48; on dispute over distribution of fisheries assets, compare account in Ward, *Unsettled History*, 47–51, with that in Walker, *Ka Whawhai Tonu Matou*, 295–9.

'Woman's right to choose' from Brown, '"Woman's Right to Choose"'; 'place to stand' from Macdonald, 'Place to Stand', 206; abortion campaign from Brown, '"Woman's Right to Choose"'. 'Political opportunity structure' from theorist Charles Tilly, quoted in Mein Smith, 'Midwifery Re-innovation', 178. Treasury's view of midwives' autonomy from Clark, 'Opening Address'. 'Standing in the sunshine' from Sandra Coney's book and television series *Standing in the Sunshine*, produced for women's suffrage centennial, 1993. Preston quoted in Shepard, *Reframing Women*, 172. 'Decolonised the screen' from Mita, *Merata*.

Trans-Tasman travel arrangements from Mein Smith, Hempenstall, and Goldfinch, *Remaking the Tasman World*, 62–5. Trans-Tasman migration as 'interregional migration' from Bell, 'Comparing Population Mobility', 190–1. Citizenship (Western Samoa) Act 1982 discussed in McMillan, 'Developing Citizens', 282–4; Pacific transnationalism from Spoonley and Macpherson, 'Transnational New Zealand', 180–5. Multicultural heritages and trans-Pacific constituency from Nero, 'End of Insularity', 465, 467.

'Austral-Asia' from McLean, *Prickly Pair*, 307. 'Asian invasion' from Peters, quoted in Bedford, Ho, and Lidgard, 'International Migration', 55. APEC 1999 described as 'defining moment in identity creation' in O'Brien, 'Now Our First Big Summit Is Over'.

11 SHAKY GROUND 2000–2016

'Fastest growing' from China, Ministry of Commerce, and New Zealand, Ministry of Foreign Affairs and Trade, *Joint Study Report*, 13; Chinese premier quoted in O'Sullivan, 'Trade Agreement Just the Start'.

Demographic statistics from Bedford and Ho, *Asians in New Zealand*. Tasman migration from Mein Smith, Hempenstall, and Goldfinch, *Remaking the Tasman World*, 57–62; Australian Bureau of Statistics, 'New Zealanders in Australia'; Hamer, *Māori in Australia*.

'Region which is changing' from Ayson, 'New Zealand, Australia', 7; New Zealand, Ministry of Defence, *Defence White Paper*, chap. 1. Wellington Declaration from Jacobi, 'Forum Will Bolster Links'. Crisis as 'widespread' and 'particularly hard' on housing market from Bollard, 'The Recovery, the Aftershock', 1.

'Common narrative' from Pickles, 'Colonisation, Empire and Gender', 236. 'Plucky minnows' from Stuff, 'World Takes Notice'. Hillary quoted in Stuff, 'Tributes to Sir Edmund Hillary'; McCahon quoted in Docking, *Two Hundred Years*, 184.

Fonterra in China from O'Sullivan, 'So Long, Sanlu'. Canterbury water debate from Canterbury Mayoral Forum, *Canterbury Water Management Strategy*. Emissions trading scheme from Nick Smith, speech at Australia New Zealand Climate Change and Business Conference, Sydney, 11 August 2010.

Māori political representation from Durie, *Ngā Tai Matatū*, 219–20. 'Common marine and coastal area' from Marine and Coastal Area (Takutai Moana) Act 2011, no. 3, section 4 (1) (c). Treelords deal's official title is 'Deed of Settlement of the Historical Claims of the CNI (Central North Island) Forests Iwi Collective to Central North Island Forest Land', made on 25 June 2008; settlement's worth from 'Govt Signs $400 Million-Plus "Treelords" Deal'; Te Heuheu, 'Dr Tumu Te Heuheu's Speech'. Tūhoe's grievance from Tūhoe Claims Settlement Act 2014, section 8; overview also in Ngāi Tūhoe, 'Our History'. Bastion Point as a potential model from Williams, 'Be Bold and Talk'.

Public transport percentages from Coleman, 'Transport Infrastructure'. Auckland statistics from Stats NZ, 'Auckland Region'. Cabinet Manual at New Zealand, Cabinet Office, *Cabinet Manual*.

Prince William quoted in Earthquake Memorial Service, Christchurch, 18 March 2011. 'Abrupt rupture' from Pickles, *Christchurch Ruptures*. Concepts of 'old town', 'new city', and 'creatives, students, hipsters and yo-pros' from MacManus, 'Old Town'.

12 BEACHED 2017–2025

On 'they are us' see '"They Are Us" Voted New Zealand's Quote of 2019'. Christchurch Call from Christchurch Call website, www.christchurchcall.org. For 'team of five million' see, for example, Roy, 'Ardern Thanks "Team of 5 Million"'.

'Reinterpret constitutional treaties' from Stuff, 'Top Lawyers Tell PM'. Māori 'privilege' from Meihana, *Privilege in Perpetuity*, 7–12. Palmer's rebuke from Gabel, 'Treaty Principles Bill'; 'unconscionable' and 'innovative relationship' from Shipley, 'Treaty Principles Submission'; and Radio New Zealand, 'Treaty Principles Bill'.

'Abundant life' from Waikato River Authority, 'Te Ture Whaimana o Te Awa o Waikato'. 'When nature is in trouble, so are people' from Environment Foundation, 'National Policy Documents'.

'Transcolonised' city from Hōete, 'From the Māori', 60; ideas for Pacific urbanism from Tone, 'Pacific Urbanism', 84–5.

Oranga Tamariki strategy from New Zealand, Oranga Tamariki Ministry for Children, *Strategic Intentions*, 8; 'make current system safe' from New Zealand, Government, *Crown Response*, 4.

For media responses to peaks in New Zealanders moving to Australia see, for example, 'Why New Zealanders Are Migrating'.

GLOSSARY OF MĀORI WORDS

'Encircling boundary' translation of Urewera from Williams, *Dictionary of the Maori Language*.

GUIDE TO FURTHER READING

REFERENCE

Brown, Deidre, and Ngarino Ellis, with Jonathan Mane-Wheoki. *Toi te Mana: An Indigenous History of Māori Art*. Auckland: Auckland University Press, 2024.
McGibbon, Ian, ed., with Paul Goldstone. *The Oxford Companion to New Zealand Military History*. Auckland: Oxford University Press, 2000.
McKinnon, Malcolm, ed., with Barry Bradley and Russell Kirkpatrick. *New Zealand Historical Atlas*. Auckland: David Bateman / Historical Branch, Department of Internal Affairs, 1997.
New Zealand. Department of Internal Affairs. *The Dictionary of New Zealand Biography*. 5 vols, ed. W. H. Oliver and Claudia Orange. Wellington: Department of Internal Affairs, 1990–2000.
New Zealand. Manatū Taonga Ministry for Culture and Heritage. New Zealand History [website]. Accessed August 2025. https://nzhistory.govt.nz.
———. *Ngā Tāngata Taumata Rau Dictionary of New Zealand Biography*. Accessed August 2025. https://teara.govt.nz/en/biographies.
———. *Te Ara The Encyclopedia of New Zealand*. Accessed August 2025. https://teara.govt.nz/en.

GENERAL

Anderson, Atholl, Judith Binney, and Aroha Harris. *Tangata Whenua: An Illustrated History*. Wellington: Bridget Williams Books, 2015.
Belgrave, Michael. *Becoming Aotearoa: A New New Zealand History*. Palmerston North: Massey University Press, 2024.
Belich, James. *Making Peoples: A History of the New Zealanders, from Polynesian Settlement to the End of the Nineteenth Century*. Auckland: Allen Lane, 1996.
———. *Paradise Reforged: A History of the New Zealanders from the 1880s to the Year 2000*. Auckland: Allen Lane, 2001.

——. *Replenishing the Earth: The Settler Revolution and the Rise of the Anglo-World, 1783–1939*. Oxford: Oxford University Press, 2009.
Brookes, Barbara. *A History of New Zealand Women*. Wellington: Bridget Williams Books, 2016.
Byrnes, Giselle, ed. *The New Oxford History of New Zealand*. South Melbourne: Oxford University Press, 2009.
Coney, Sandra. *Standing in the Sunshine: A History of New Zealand Women since They Won the Vote*. Auckland: Viking, 1993.
Denoon, Donald, and Philippa Mein Smith, with Marivic Wyndham. *A History of Australia, New Zealand and the Pacific*. Oxford: Blackwell Publishers, 2000.
Docking, Gil. *Two Hundred Years of New Zealand Painting*. With additions by Michael Dunn. Rev. edn. Auckland: David Bateman, 1990.
Easton, Brian. *Not in Narrow Seas: The Economic History of Aotearoa New Zealand*. Wellington: Victoria University of Wellington Press, 2020.
Hawke, G. R. *The Making of New Zealand: An Economic History*. Cambridge: Cambridge University Press, 1985.
Keith, Hamish. *The Big Picture: A History of New Zealand Art from 1642*. Auckland: Godwit, 2007.
King, Michael. *The Penguin History of New Zealand*. Auckland: Penguin, 2003.
Rice, Geoffrey W., ed. *The Oxford History of New Zealand*. 2nd edn. Auckland: Oxford University Press, 1992.
Steel, Frances, ed. *New Zealand and the Sea: Historical Perspectives*. Wellington: Bridget Williams Books, 2018.

1 WAKA ACROSS A WATERY WORLD

Anderson, Atholl. 'A Fragile Plenty: Pre-European Maori and the New Zealand Environment'. In *Environmental Histories of New Zealand*, ed. Eric Pawson and Tom Brooking, 19–34. South Melbourne: Oxford University Press, 2002.
——. 'Origins, Settlement and Society of Pre-European South Polynesia'. In *The New Oxford History of New Zealand*, ed. Giselle Byrnes, 21–46. South Melbourne: Oxford University Press, 2009.
——. 'Te Ao Tawhito: The Old World'. In Anderson Atholl, Judith Binney, and Aroha Harris, *Tangata Whenua: An Illustrated History*, 16–131 (part 1). Wellington: Bridget Williams Books, 2015.
——. *The Welcome of Strangers: A History of Southern Māori*. Rev. edn. Wellington: Bridget Williams Books / Te Rūnanga o Ngāi Tahu, 2025.
——. *The Welcome of Strangers: An Ethnohistory of Southern Maori, A.D. 1650–1850*. Dunedin: University of Otago Press / Dunedin City Council, 1998.
Belich, James. *Making Peoples: A History of the New Zealanders, from Polynesian Settlement to the End of the Nineteenth Century*. Auckland: Allen Lane, 1996.

Binney, Judith. 'Maori Oral Narratives, Pakeha Written Texts: Two Forms of Telling History'. *New Zealand Journal of History* 21, no. 1 (1987): 16–28.
Bunbury, Magdalena M. E., Fiona Petchey, and Simon H. Bickler. 'A New Chronology for the Māori Settlement of Aotearoa (NZ) and the Potential Role of Climate Change in Demographic Developments'. *Proceedings of the National Academy of Sciences* 119, no. 46 (2022): 1–8.
Davidson, Janet. *The Prehistory of New Zealand*. 2nd edn. Auckland: Longman Paul, 1992.
Evans, Jeff. *The Discovery of Aotearoa*. Auckland: Reed, 1998.
Howe, K. R. *The Quest for Origins*. Auckland: Penguin, 2003.
Leach, Helen. 'In the Beginning'. In *Te Whenua, te Iwi: The Land and the People*, ed. Jock Phillips, 18–26. Wellington: Allen & Unwin / Port Nicholson Press, 1987.
New Zealand. Waitangi Tribunal. *Manukau Report*. Wai 8. Wellington: Government Printer, 1985.
———. *Ngai Tahu Report*. Wai 27. Vols 2–3. Wellington: GP Publications, 1991.
O'Regan, Tipene. 'Ngai Tahu and the Crown: Partnership Promised'. In *Rural Canterbury: Celebrating Its History*, ed. Garth Cant and Russell Kirkpatrick, 1–19. Wellington: Daphne Brasell Associates / Lincoln University Press, 2001.
Schama, Simon. *Landscape and Memory*. London: HarperCollins, 1995.
Sorrenson, M. P. K. *Maori Origins and Migrations: The Genesis of Some Pakeha Myths and Legends*. Auckland: Auckland University Press, 1979.
Tau, Rawiri Te Maire. 'Tirohia atu nei ka Whetū Rangitia'. In *Maranga! Maranga! Maranga! The Call to Māori History*, ed. Aroha Harris and Melissa Williams, 11–31. Wellington: Bridget Williams Books, 2024.
Tau, Te Maire. *Ngā Pikitūroa o Ngāi Tahu: The Oral Traditions of Ngāi Tahu*. Dunedin: University of Otago Press, 2003.
———. 'Ngāi Tahu and the Canterbury Landscape: A Broad Context'. In *Southern Capital: Christchurch*, ed. John Cookson and Graeme Dunstall, 41–59. Christchurch: Canterbury University Press, 2000.
Tau, Te Maire, and Atholl Anderson, eds. *Ngāi Tahu: A Migration History; The Carrington Text*. Wellington: Bridget Williams Books / Te Rūnanga O Ngāi Tahu, 2008.
Tremewan, Christine, trans. and ed. *Traditional Stories from Southern New Zealand: He Korero no Te Wai Pounamu*. Christchurch: Macmillan Brown Centre for Pacific Studies, University of Canterbury, 2002.
Walker, Ranginui. *He Tipua: The Life and Times of Sir Āpirana Ngata*. Auckland: Viking, 2001.
Walter, Richard, Halley Buckley, Chris Jacomb, and Elizabeth Matisoo-Smith. 'Mass Migration and the Polynesian Settlement of New Zealand'. *Journal of World Prehistory* 30 (2017): 351–76.
Williams, Madi. *Polynesia, 900–1600: An Overview of the History of Aotearoa, Rēkohu, and Rapa Nui*. Christchurch: Canterbury University Press, 2021.

Wilmshurst, Janet M., Terry L. Hunt, Carl P. Lipo, and Atholl J. Anderson. 'High-Precision Radiocarbon Dating Shows Recent and Rapid Initial Human Colonization of East Polynesia'. *Proceedings of the National Academy of Sciences* 108, no. 5 (27 December 2010), 1815–20. https://doi.org/10.1073/pnas.1015876108.

Worthy, Trevor H., and Richard N. Holdaway. *The Lost World of the Moa: Prehistoric Life of New Zealand.* Christchurch: Canterbury University Press, 2002.

2 BEACHCROSSERS 1769–1839

Adams, Peter. *Fatal Necessity: British Intervention in New Zealand, 1830–1847.* Auckland: Auckland University Press, 1977.

Ballara, Angela. *Taua: 'Musket Wars', 'Land Wars' or Tikanga? Warfare in Maori Society in the Early Nineteenth Century.* Auckland: Penguin, 2003.

Bayly, C. A. *Imperial Meridian: The British Empire and the World, 1780–1830.* London: Longman, 1989.

Beaglehole, J. C. *The Life of Captain James Cook.* London: Adam & Charles Black, 1974.

Belich, James. *Making Peoples: A History of the New Zealanders, from Polynesian Settlement to the End of the Nineteenth Century.* Auckland: Allen Lane, 1996.

Cloher, Dorothy Urlich. *Hongi Hika: Warrior Chief.* Auckland: Viking, 2003.

Clunie, Fergus. 'Kerikeri: A Pocket Parramatta'. *Historic Places*, no. 85 (May 2002), 24–7.

Crosby, R. D. *The Musket Wars: A History of Inter-iwi Conflict, 1806–1845.* 2nd edn. Auckland: Reed, 2001.

Davidson, Jared, ed. *Introducing He Whakaputanga.* Wellington: BWB Texts, 2023.

Dening, Greg. *Beach Crossings: Voyaging across Times, Cultures and Self.* Melbourne: Melbourne University Publishing, 2004.

Druett, Joan. *Tupaia: Cook's Polynesian Navigator.* Auckland: Random House, 2018.

Dunmore, John. 'French Navigators in New Zealand, 1769–1840'. In *New Zealand and the French: Two Centuries of Contact*, ed. John Dunmore, 8–19. Waikanae: Heritage Press, 1997.

Head, Lyndsay. 'The Pursuit of Modernity in Maori Society: The Conceptual Bases of Citizenship in the Early Colonial Period'. In *Histories, Power and Loss: Uses of the Past; A New Zealand Commentary*, ed. Andrew Sharp and Paul McHugh, 97–121. Wellington: Bridget Williams Books, 2001.

Hill, Richard S. *Policing the Colonial Frontier: The Theory and Practice of Coercive Social and Racial Control in New Zealand, 1767–1867.* Part 1, vol. 1. Wellington: Historical Publications Branch, Department of Internal Affairs, 1986.

Jones, E. L. *The European Miracle: Environments, Economies, and Geopolitics in the History of Europe and Asia*. 2nd edn. Cambridge: Cambridge University Press, 1992.

King, Michael. *Moriori: A People Rediscovered*. Auckland: Viking, 1989.

McNab, R., ed. *Historical Records of New Zealand*. Vol. 1. Wellington: Government Printer, 1908.

Mein Smith, Philippa. 'The Sealing Industry and the Architecture of the Tasman World'. *Fabrications* 29, no. 3 (2019): 317–33.

Moon, Paul. *Te Ara ki te Tiriti: The Path to the Treaty of Waitangi*. Auckland: David Ling Publishing, 2002.

Moorehead, Alan. *The Fatal Impact: An Account of the Invasion of the South Pacific, 1767–1840*. London: Hamish Hamilton, 1966.

Obeyesekere, Gananath. *The Apotheosis of Captain Cook: European Mythmaking in the Pacific*. Princeton: Princeton University Press, 1992.

Owens, J. M. R. 'New Zealand before Annexation'. In *The Oxford History of New Zealand*, 2nd edn, ed. Geoffrey W. Rice, 28–53. Auckland: Oxford University Press, 1992.

Porter, Andrew, ed. *The Oxford History of the British Empire*. Vol. 3: *The Nineteenth Century*. Oxford: Oxford University Press, 1999.

Raeside, J. D. *Sovereign Chief: A Biography of Baron de Thierry*. Christchurch: Caxton Press, 1977.

Salmond, Anne. *Between Worlds: Early Exchanges between Maori and Europeans, 1773–1815*. Auckland: Viking, 1997.

——. *The Trial of the Cannibal Dog: Captain Cook in the South Seas*. Auckland: Allen Lane / Penguin Books, 2003.

——. *Two Worlds: First Meetings between Maori and Europeans, 1642–1772*. Auckland: Viking, 1991.

Sinclair, Keith. *A History of New Zealand*. 1st edn. Auckland: Penguin, 1959; 5th edn. Additional material by Raewyn Dalziel. Auckland: Penguin, 2000.

Smith, Bernard. *Imagining the Pacific: In the Wake of the Cook Voyages*. Melbourne: Miegunyah Press, 1992.

Temple, Philip. *A Sort of Conscience: The Wakefields*. Auckland: Auckland University Press, 2002.

Vaggioli, Felice. *History of New Zealand and Its Inhabitants*, trans. John Crockett. Dunedin: University of Otago Press, 2000. (First published 1896.)

White, John. *The Ancient History of the Maori, His Mythology and Traditions*. Vol. 5: *Tai-Nui*. Wellington: Government Printer, 1888.

3 CLAIMING THE LAND 1840–1860

Amodeo, Colin, with Ron Chapman. *Forgotten Forty-Niners*. Christchurch: Caxton Press, 2003.

Belgrave, Michael. *Historical Frictions: Maori Claims and Reinvented Histories*. Auckland: Auckland University Press, 2005.

Borrie, W. D. *The European Peopling of Australasia*. Canberra: Demography, Research School of Social Sciences, Australian National University, 1994.

Coleman, J. N. 'A Literal Translation into English, Made in New Zealand, of the Maori Version of the Treaty'. In J. N. Coleman, *A Memoir of the Rev. Richard Davis, for Thirty-Nine Years a Missionary in New Zealand*, 455-6. London: J. Nisbet, 1865.

Condliffe, J. B. *New Zealand in the Making*. London: George Allen & Unwin, 1930.

Dalziel, Raewyn. 'Men, Women and Wakefield'. In *Edward Gibbon Wakefield and the Colonial Dream: A Reconsideration*, ed. Friends of the Turnbull Library, 77-86. Wellington: GP Publications / Friends of the Turnbull Library, 1997.

Denoon, Donald, and Philippa Mein Smith, with Marivic Wyndham. *A History of Australia, New Zealand and the Pacific*. Oxford: Blackwell Publishers, 2000.

Evison, Harry C. *The Ngai Tahu Deeds: A Window on New Zealand History*. Christchurch: Canterbury University Press, 2006.

Fairburn, Miles. *The Ideal Society and Its Enemies: The Foundations of Modern New Zealand Society, 1850-1900*. Auckland: Auckland University Press, 1989.

Fletcher, Ned. *The English Text of the Treaty of Waitangi*. Wellington: Bridget Williams Books, 2022.

Francis, Mark. *Governors and Settlers: Images of Authority in the British Colonies, 1820-60*. London: Macmillan, 1992.

Hamer, David, and Roberta Nicholls, eds. *The Making of Wellington, 1800-1914*. Wellington: Victoria University Press, 1990.

Head, Lyndsay. 'The Pursuit of Modernity in Maori Society'. In *Histories, Power and Loss*, ed. Andrew Sharp and Paul G. McHugh, 97-121. Wellington: Bridget Williams Books, 2001.

Healy, Susan, Tim McCreanor, and Ray Nairn. 'Hobson's Actual Pledges'. *E-Tangata*, 8 December 2024. www.e-tangata.co.nz/history/hobsons-actual-pledges/.

Hickford, Mark. *Lords of the Land: Indigenous Property Rights and Jurisprudence of Empire*. Oxford: Oxford University Press, 2011.

Kawharu, F. R. 'Heke Pokai'. In *The Dictionary of New Zealand Biography*, vol. 1, ed. W. H. Oliver, 184-7. Wellington: Allen & Unwin / Department of Internal Affairs, 1990.

Kawharu, I. H., ed. *Waitangi: Maori and Pakeha Perspectives of the Treaty of Waitangi*. Auckland: Oxford University Press, 1989.

McAloon, Jim. *Nelson: A Regional History*. Whatamango Bay: Cape Catley / Nelson City Council, 1997.

———. *No Idle Rich: The Wealthy in Canterbury and Otago, 1840-1914*. Dunedin: University of Otago Press, 2002.

McClintock, A. H. *Crown Colony Government in New Zealand*. Wellington: Government Printer, 1958.

McHugh, P. G. 'Australasian Narratives of Constitutional Foundation'. In *Quicksands: Foundational Histories in Australia and Aotearoa New Zealand*, ed. Klaus Neumann, Nicholas Thomas, and Hilary Ericksen, 98–114. Sydney: UNSW Press, 1999.

Moon, Paul. '"Amenable to Civil Power": The Influence of the Periphery on British Policy on New Zealand, 1831 to 1837'. *Journal of Imperial and Commonwealth History* 50 (2022): 478–97.

New Zealand. Lieutenant Governor. *Facsimile of the Treaty of Waitangi*. Wellington: Government Printer, 1976.

———. Te Tiriti o Waitangi / The Treaty of Waitangi. 1840. Text reproduced at Museum of New Zealand Te Papa Tongarewa. 'The Full Text of Te Tiriti o Waitangi / The Treaty of Waitangi'. Accessed August 2025. www.tepapa.govt.nz/discover-collections/read-watch-play/maori/treaty-waitangi/treaty-close/full-text-te-tiriti-o.

New Zealand. Waitangi Tribunal. *Muriwhenua Land Report*. Wai 45. Wellington: GP Publications, 1997.

Olssen, Erik. 'Wakefield and the Scottish Enlightenment, with Particular Reference to Adam Smith and His *Wealth of Nations*'. In *Edward Gibbon Wakefield and the Colonial Dream: A Reconsideration*, ed. Friends of the Turnbull Library, 47–66. Wellington: GP Publications / Friends of the Turnbull Library, 1997.

Orange, Claudia. 'The Covenant of Kohimarama: A Ratification of the Treaty of Waitangi'. *New Zealand Journal of History* 14, no. 1 (1980): 61–82.

———. *An Illustrated History of the Treaty of Waitangi*. Wellington: Allen & Unwin, 1990. (Rev. edn, 2004.)

———. *The Story of a Treaty: He Kōrero Tiriti*. Wellington: Bridget Williams Books, 2022.

Parsonson, Ann. 'The Challenge to Mana Maori'. In *The Oxford History of New Zealand*, 2nd edn, ed. Geoffrey W. Rice, 167–98. Auckland: Oxford University Press, 1992.

Pawson, Eric. 'Confronting Nature'. In *Southern Capital Christchurch*, ed. John Cookson and Graeme Dunstall, 60–84. Christchurch: Canterbury University Press, 2000.

Prichard, M. F. L. 'Wakefield Changes His Mind about the "Sufficient Price"'. *International Review of Social History* 8, no. 2 (1963): 251–69. https://doi.org/10.1017/S0020859000002315.

Schrader, Ben. 'A Bi-cultural Townscape: Wellington in the 1840s'. *Architectural History Aotearoa*, 11 (2014): 11–16.

Sharp, Andrew. *Justice and the Maori*. 2nd edn. Auckland: Oxford University Press, 1997.

Sharp, Andrew, and Paul G. McHugh, eds. *Histories, Power and Loss*. Wellington: Bridget Williams Books, 2001.

Stone, R. C. J. *From Tamaki-Makau-Rau to Auckland*. Auckland: Auckland University Press, 2001.
Temple, Philip. *A Sort of Conscience: The Wakefields*. Auckland: Auckland University Press, 2002.
Tremewan, Peter. *French Akaroa: An Attempt to Colonise Southern New Zealand*. 2nd edn. Christchurch: University of Canterbury Press, 1990. (Rev. edn, 2010.)
Wakefield, Edward Gibbon, John Ward, and Edward Jerningham Wakefield. *The British Colonization of New Zealand*. London: John W. Parker for the NZ Association, 1837.
Ward, Alan. *A Show of Justice: Racial 'Amalgamation' in Nineteenth Century New Zealand*. 2nd edn. Auckland: Auckland University Press, 1995.
——. *An Unsettled History: Treaty Claims in New Zealand Today*. Wellington: Bridget Williams Books, 1999.

4 REMOTER AUSTRALASIA 1861–1890

Atkinson, Neill. *Adventures in Democracy: A History of the Vote in New Zealand*. Dunedin: University of Otago Press, 2003.
Australasian Federation Conference. *Official Record of the Proceedings and Debates of the Australasian Federation Conference, 1890, Held in the Parliament House, Melbourne*. Melbourne: Government Printer, 1890. Copy in Papers of Alfred Deakin, National Library of Australia, MS 1540, 11/286.
Ballantyne, Tony, ed. *The Making and Unmaking of Australasia*. London: Bloomsbury Academic, 2024.
Belich, James. *'I Shall Not Die': Titokowaru's War, New Zealand, 1868–9*. Wellington: Allen & Unwin / Port Nicholson Press, 1989.
——. *Making Peoples: A History of the New Zealanders, from Polynesian Settlement to the End of the Nineteenth Century*. Auckland: Allen Lane, 1996.
——. *The New Zealand Wars and the Victorian Interpretation of Racial Conflict*. Auckland: Penguin, 1988. (First published 1986.)
Binney, Judith. *Redemption Songs: A Life of Te Kooti Arikirangi Te Turuki*. Auckland: Auckland University Press / Bridget Williams Books, 1995.
Boast, Richard. *Buying the Land, Selling the Land: Governments and Maori Land in the North Island, 1865–1921*. Wellington: Victoria University Press, 2008.
——. '"An Expensive Mistake": Law, Courts, and Confiscation on the New Zealand Colonial Frontier'. In *Raupatu: The Confiscation of Maori Land*, ed. Richard Boast and Richard S. Hill, chap. 7. Wellington: Victoria University Press, 2009.
——. *Generic Submissions Relating to the 'Gift' of the Peaks and the Establishment of Tongariro National Park*. Wai 1130, paper 3.3.23. Wellington: Waitangi Tribunal, 2007.

Boast, Richard, and Richard S. Hill, eds. *Raupatu: The Confiscation of Maori Land*. Wellington: Victoria University Press, 2009.

Bohan, Edmund. *Climates of War: New Zealand in Conflict, 1859–69*. Christchurch: Hazard Press, 2005.

Borrie, W. D. *The European Peopling of Australasia*. Canberra: Demography, Research School of Social Sciences, Australian National University, 1994.

Breward, Ian. *A History of the Churches in Australasia*. Oxford: Oxford University Press, 2001.

Brookes, Barbara. *A History of New Zealand Women*. Wellington: Bridget Williams Books, 2016.

Buchanan, Rachel. 'Beating Shame: Parihaka and the Very Long Sorry'. In *Maranga! Maranga! Maranga! The Call to Māori History*, ed. Aroha Harris and Melissa Williams, 173–95. Wellington: Bridget Williams Books, 2024.

Cowan, James. 'Famous New Zealanders – No. 5 – Rewi Maniapoto – The Story of Orakau'. *New Zealand Railways Magazine* 8, no. 4 (1933): 25–9.

———. *The New Zealand Wars: A History of the Maori Campaigns and the Pioneering Period*. Vols 1–2. Wellington: Government Printer, 1922. (Reprinted 1983.)

Daley, Caroline. *Girls & Women, Men & Boys: Gender in Taradale, 1886–1930*. Auckland: Auckland University Press, 1999.

Dalton, B. J. 'Browne, Thomas Robert Gore'. In *The Dictionary of New Zealand Biography*, vol. 1, ed. W. H. Oliver, 46–8. Wellington: Allen & Unwin, 1990.

Dalziel, Raewyn. *Julius Vogel: Business Politician*. Auckland: Auckland University Press / Oxford University Press, 1986.

Denoon, Donald. 'Re-membering Australasia: A Repressed Memory'. *Australian Historical Studies* 34, no. 122 (October 2003): 290–304.

Durie, Mason. *Whaiora: Maori Health Development*. 2nd edn. Auckland: Oxford University Press, 1998.

Eldred-Grigg, Stevan. *Diggers, Hatters & Whores: The Story of the New Zealand Gold Rushes*. Auckland: Random House, 2008.

Fairburn, Miles. *The Ideal Society and Its Enemies: The Foundations of Modern New Zealand Society, 1850–1900*. Auckland: Auckland University Press, 1989.

Fraser, Lyndon, ed. *A Distant Shore: Irish Migration and New Zealand Settlement*. Dunedin: University of Otago Press, 2000.

Gardner, W. J. *Colonial Cap and Gown: Studies in the Mid-Victorian Universities of Australasia*. Christchurch: University of Canterbury, 1979.

Hawke, G. R. *The Making of New Zealand: An Economic History*. Cambridge: Cambridge University Press, 1985.

Hill, Richard S. *The Colonial Frontier Tamed: New Zealand Policing in Transition, 1867–1886*. 2 vols. Wellington: Historical Branch / GP Books, 1989.

Hopkins-Weise, Jeff. *Blood Brothers: The Anzac Genesis*. Auckland: Penguin Books, 2009.
Hunt, Graeme. *The Rich List: Wealth and Enterprise in New Zealand, 1820–2000*. Auckland: Reed, 2000.
Hursthouse, Charles. *The Australasian Republic* [pamphlet]. 1869. Text reproduced in *Otago Witness*, 6 November 1869. Digitised at Papers Past, accessed August 2025. www.paperspast.natlib.govt.nz/newspapers/OW18691106.2.25.
Ip, Manying. *Dragons on the Long White Cloud: The Making of Chinese New Zealanders*. Auckland: Tandem Press, 1996.
Jebb, Richard. *Studies in Colonial Nationalism*. London: Edward Arnold, 1905.
Keenan, Danny. *Wars without End*. Auckland: Penguin Books, 2009.
Lovell-Smith, Margaret. *Easily the Best: The Life of Helen Connon (1857–1903)*. Christchurch: Canterbury University Press, 2004.
McAloon, Jim. *No Idle Rich: The Wealthy in Canterbury and Otago, 1840–1914*. Dunedin: University of Otago Press, 2002.
Macdonald, Charlotte. 'Too Many Men and Too Few Women: Gender's "Fatal Impact" in Nineteenth-Century Colonies'. In *The Gendered Kiwi*, ed. Caroline Daley and Deborah Montgomerie, 17–35. Auckland: Auckland University Press, 1999.
——. *A Woman of Good Character: Single Women as Immigrant Settlers in Nineteenth-Century New Zealand*. Wellington: Bridget Williams Books / Historical Branch, 1990.
Macintyre, Stuart. *A Concise History of Australia*. Melbourne: Cambridge University Press, 1999.
May, P. R. 'Gold on the Coast'. *New Zealand's Heritage* 3, no. 31 (part 1); no. 32 (part 2) (1971).
——. *The West Coast Gold Rushes*. Christchurch: Pegasus Press, 1962.
Mein Smith, Philippa. 'New Zealand'. In *The Centenary Companion to Australian Federation*, ed. Helen Irving, 400–5. Melbourne: Cambridge University Press, 1999.
——.'New Zealand Federation Commissioners in Australia: One Past, Two Historiographies'. *Australian Historical Studies* 34, no. 122 (October 2003): 305–25.
Morrell, W. P. *The Provincial System in New Zealand, 1852–76*. 2nd edn. Christchurch: Whitcombe and Tombs Ltd, 1964.
Morris, Edward E. *Austral English: A Dictionary of Australasian Words, Phrases and Usages*. London: Macmillan, 1898.
New Zealand. Waitangi Tribunal. *Closing Submissions of the Crown*. Wai 1130, paper 3.3.45. Wellington: Crown Law Office, 20 June 2007.
——. *Turanga Tangata Turanga Whenua: The Report on the Turanganui a Kiwa Claims*. Wai 814, vol. 1. Wellington: Legislation Direct, 2004.
Nolan, Melanie. 'Maritime Strike, Australasia, 1890'. In *St James Encyclopedia of Labor History Worldwide*, ed. Neil Schlager, vol. 1, 587–91. Chicago: Gale Group, 2003.

Oliver, W. H., and Jane M. Thomson. *Challenge and Response*. Gisborne: East Coast Development Research Association, 1971.
Olssen, Erik. 'Families and the Gendering of European New Zealand in the Colonial Period, 1840–80'. In *The Gendered Kiwi: Pakeha Men and Women, 1840–1990*, ed. Caroline Daley and Deborah Montgomerie, 37–62. Auckland: Auckland University Press, 1999.
O'Malley, Vincent. *The Great War for New Zealand: Waikato, 1800–2000*. Wellington: Bridget Williams Books, 2016.
——. *The Invasion of Waikato / Te Riri ki Tainui*. Wellington: Bridget Williams Books, 2024.
——. *The New Zealand Wars / Ngā Pakanga o Aotearoa*. Wellington: Bridget Williams Books, 2019.
——. *Voices from the New Zealand Wars / He Reo nō ngā Pakanga o Aotearoa*. Wellington: Bridget Williams Books, 2021.
Parsonson, Ann. 'The Challenge to Mana Maori'. In *The Oxford History of New Zealand*, 2nd edn, ed. Geoffrey W. Rice, 167–98. Auckland: Oxford University Press, 1992.
——. 'The Fate of Maori Land Rights in Early Colonial New Zealand: The Limits of the Treaty of Waitangi and the Doctrine of Aboriginal Title'. In *Law, History, Colonialism: The Reach of Empire*, ed. Diane Kirkby and Catharine Coleborne, 173–89. Manchester: Manchester University Press, 2001.
Pool, Ian. *Te Iwi Maori: A New Zealand Population Past, Present and Projected*. Auckland: Auckland University Press, 1991.
Pope, James H. *Health for the Maori: A Manual for Use in Native Schools*. Wellington: Government Printer, 1894.
Riseborough, Hazel. *Days of Darkness: Taranaki, 1878–1884*. Rev. edn. Auckland: Penguin, 2002.
Scott, Dick. *Ask That Mountain: The Story of Parihaka*. Auckland: Heinemann, 1975.
Simkin, C. G. F. *The Instability of a Dependent Economy: Economic Fluctuations in New Zealand, 1840–1914*. Oxford: Oxford University Press, 1951.
Simon, Judith, and Linda Tuhiwai Smith, eds. *A Civilising Mission? Perceptions and Representations of the Native Schools System*. Auckland: Auckland University Press, 2001.
Simpson, Tony. *The Immigrants: The Great Migration from Britain to New Zealand, 1830–1890*. Auckland: Godwit Publishing, 1997.
Spoonley, Paul. 'Ethnic and Religious Intolerance: Intolerance towards Māori'. In New Zealand, Manatū Taonga Ministry for Culture and Heritage, *Te Ara The Encyclopedia of New Zealand*, 2011. https://teara.govt.nz/en/zoomify/28137/land-confiscation-map.
Stone, R. C. J. *Makers of Fortune: A Colonial Business Community and Its Fall*. Auckland: Auckland University Press / Oxford University Press, 1973.
Tennant, Margaret. *Paupers and Providers: Charitable Aid in New Zealand*. Wellington: Allen & Unwin / Historical Branch, 1989.

Thomson, David. *A World without Welfare: New Zealand's Colonial Experiment*. Auckland: Auckland University Press / Bridget Williams Books, 1998.
Ward, Alan. *National Overview*. Vol. 1. Wellington: Waitangi Tribunal, 1997.
Wevers, Lydia. *Country of Writing: Travel Writing and New Zealand, 1809–1900*. Auckland: Auckland University Press, 2002.

5 MANAGING GLOBALISATION 1891–1913

Australasian Federation Conference. *Official Record of the Proceedings and Debates of the Australasian Federation Conference, 1890*. Melbourne: Government Printer, 1890. Copy in Papers of Alfred Deakin, National Library of Australia, MS 1540, 11/286.
Belich, James. *Paradise Reforged: A History of the New Zealanders from the 1880s to the Year 2000*. Auckland: Allen Lane, 2001.
———. *Replenishing the Earth: The Settler Revolution and the Rise of the Anglo-World, 1783–1939*. Oxford: Oxford University Press, 2009.
Brooking, Tom. *Lands for the People?* Dunedin: University of Otago Press, 1996.
Brooking, Tom, and Roberto Rabel. 'Neither British nor Polynesian: A Brief History of New Zealand's Other Immigrants'. In *Immigration and National Identity in New Zealand*, ed. Stuart W. Greif, 23–49. Palmerston North: Dunmore Press, 1995.
Castles, Francis G. *Australian Public Policy and Economic Vulnerability: A Comparative and Historical Perspective*. Sydney: Allen & Unwin, 1988.
———. *The Working Class and Welfare: Reflections on the Political Development of the Welfare State in Australia and New Zealand, 1890–1980*. Wellington: Allen & Unwin / Port Nicholson Press, 1985.
Chan, Adrian. 'New Zealand, the Australian Commonwealth and "Plain Nonsense"'. *New Zealand Journal of History* 3, no. 2 (1969): 190–5.
Crawford, John, and Ian McGibbon, eds. *One Flag, One Queen, One Tongue: New Zealand, the British Empire and the South African War, 1899–1902*. Auckland: Auckland University Press, 2003.
Daley, Caroline, and Melanie Nolan, eds. *Suffrage and Beyond: International Feminist Perspectives*. Auckland: Auckland University Press, 1994.
Dalziel, Raewyn. 'The Colonial Helpmeet: Women's Role and the Vote in Nineteenth-Century New Zealand'. In *Women in History: Essays on European Women in New Zealand*, ed. Barbara Brookes, Charlotte Macdonald, and Margaret Tennant, 55–68. Wellington: Allen & Unwin / Port Nicholson Press, 1986.
Ellis, Ellen. 'New Zealand Women and the War'. In *One Flag, One Queen, One Tongue: New Zealand, the British Empire and the South African War, 1899–1902*, ed. John Crawford and Ian McGibbon, 128–50. Auckland: Auckland University Press, 2003.

Esplin, M. 'Cossgrove, David; Cossgrove, Selina'. In *The Dictionary of New Zealand Biography*, vol. 3, ed. W. H. Oliver and Claudia Orange, 117–18. Wellington: Department of Internal Affairs, 1996.
Frost, Lionel. *The New Urban Frontier: Urbanisation and City-Building in Australasia and the American West*. Kensington, NSW: NSW University Press, 1991.
Fry, Eric, ed. *Common Cause: Essays in Australian and New Zealand Labour History*. Wellington: Allen & Unwin / Port Nicholson Press, 1986.
Gardner, W. J. *Prelude to Arbitration in 3 Movements: Ulster, South Australia, New Zealand, 1890–1894*. Christchurch: W. J. Gardner, 2009.
Greasley, David, and Les Oxley. 'Globalization and Real Wages in New Zealand, 1873–1913'. *Explorations in Economic History* 41, no. 1 (January 2004): 26–47.
Grimshaw, Patricia. *Women's Suffrage in New Zealand*. Auckland: Auckland University Press, 1987.
Hamer, David. *New Towns in the New World: Images and Perceptions of the Nineteenth-Century Urban Frontier*. New York: Columbia University Press, 1990.
———. *The New Zealand Liberals: The Years of Power, 1891–1912*. Auckland: Auckland University Press, 1988.
Hawdon, S. E. *New Zealanders and the Boer War; or, Soldiers from the Land of the Moa (By a New Zealander)*. Christchurch: Gordon and Gotch, c. 1902–3.
Holt, James. *Compulsory Arbitration in New Zealand: The First Forty Years*. Auckland: Auckland University Press, 1986.
Howe, K. R. *The Quest for Origins*. Auckland: Penguin, 2003.
Hunt, Graeme. *The Rich List: Wealth and Enterprise in New Zealand, 1820–2000*. Auckland: Reed, 2000.
Hutching, Megan. *Leading the Way: How New Zealand Women Won the Vote*. Auckland: HarperCollins, 2010.
Ip, Manying. *Dragons on the Long White Cloud: The Making of Chinese New Zealanders*. Auckland: Tandem Press, 1996.
———, ed. *Unfolding History, Evolving Identity: The Chinese in New Zealand*. Auckland: Auckland University Press, 2003.
Kelly, Paul. *The End of Certainty: The Story of the 1980s*. Sydney: Allen & Unwin, 1992.
Lange, Raeburn. *May the People Live: A History of Maori Health Development, 1900–1920*. Auckland: Auckland University Press, 1999.
McGibbon, Ian. 'Australia–New Zealand Defence Relations to 1939'. In *Tasman Relations*, ed. Keith Sinclair, 164–82. Auckland: Auckland University Press, 1987.
———. 'The Origins of New Zealand's South African War Contribution'. In *One Flag, One Queen, One Tongue: New Zealand, the British Empire and the South African War, 1899–1902*, ed. John Crawford and Ian McGibbon, 1–11. Auckland: Auckland University Press, 2003.

———. *The Path to Gallipoli: Defending New Zealand, 1840–1915*. Wellington: GP Books, 1991.
Macintyre, Stuart. 'Neither Capital nor Labour: The Politics of the Establishment of Arbitration'. In *Foundations of Arbitration: The Origins and Effects of State Compulsory Arbitration, 1890–1914*, ed. Stuart Macintyre and Richard Mitchell, 178–200. Melbourne: Oxford University Press, 1989.
Macintyre, Stuart, and Richard Mitchell, eds. *Foundations of Arbitration: The Origins and Effects of State Compulsory Arbitration, 1890–1914*. Melbourne: Oxford University Press, 1989.
Martin, John E. *Holding the Balance: A History of New Zealand's Department of Labour, 1891–1995*. Christchurch: Canterbury University Press, 1996.
Meaney, Neville. *The Search for Security in the Pacific, 1901–14*. Sydney: Sydney University Press, 1976.
Mein Smith, Philippa. *Mothers and King Baby: Infant Survival and Welfare in an Imperial World: Australia, 1880–1950*. Basingstoke: Macmillan, 1997.
———. 'New Zealand'. In *The Centenary Companion to Australian Federation*, ed. Helen Irving, 400–5. Melbourne: Cambridge University Press, 1999.
Mein Smith, Philippa, Peter Hempenstall, and Shaun Goldfinch. *Remaking the Tasman World*. Christchurch: Canterbury University Press, 2008.
Moloughney, Brian, and John Stenhouse. '"Drug-Besotten, Sin-Begotten Fiends of Filth": New Zealanders and the Oriental Other, 1850–1920'. *New Zealand Journal of History* 33, no. 1 (1999): 43–64.
Nolan, Melanie. '1913 in Retrospect: A Laboratory or a Battleground of Democracy?' In *Revolution: The 1913 Great Strike in New Zealand*, ed. Melanie Nolan, 21–40. Christchurch: Canterbury University Press, 2005.
———. *Breadwinning: New Zealand Women and the State*. Christchurch: Canterbury University Press, 2000.
Olssen, Erik. *Building the New World: Work, Politics and Society in Caversham, 1880s–1920s*. Auckland: Auckland University Press, 1995.
Phillips, Jock. *A Man's Country? The Image of the Pakeha Male: A History*. Rev. edn. Auckland: Penguin, 1996.
Price, Charles A. *The Great White Walls Are Built: Restrictive Immigration to North America and Australasia, 1836–1888*. Canberra: ANU Press, 1974.
Reeves, William Pember. *State Experiments in Australia and New Zealand*. 2 vols. London: George Allen & Unwin, 1902.
Ross, Angus. *New Zealand Aspirations in the Pacific in the Nineteenth Century*. Oxford: Clarendon Press, 1964.
Sinclair, Keith. *A Destiny Apart*. Wellington: Allen & Unwin / Port Nicholson Press, 1986.

——. 'Why New Zealanders Are Not Australians: New Zealand and the Australian Federal Movement, 1881-1901'. In *Tasman Relations: New Zealand and Australia, 1788-1988*, ed. Keith Sinclair, 90-103. Auckland: Auckland University Press, 1987.

——. *William Pember Reeves: New Zealand Fabian*. Oxford: Clarendon Press, 1965.

Stout, Anna P. 'The New Woman'. In *Women and the Vote*, ed. Hocken Library. Dunedin: Hocken Library, 1986.

'Vesta'. 'Women to Women: A School for Mothers'. *Argus* (Melbourne), 19 September 1917.

Ville, Simon. *The Rural Entrepreneurs: A History of the Stock and Station Agent Industry in Australia and New Zealand*. Cambridge: Cambridge University Press, 2000.

Ward, Alan. *National Overview*. Vol. 2. Wellington: Waitangi Tribunal, 1997.

Woman's Christian Temperance Union of New Zealand. *Sixteen Reasons for Supporting Woman's Suffrage*. Christchurch: WCTU, November 1891.

Wood, F. L. W. 'Why Did New Zealand Not Join the Australian Commonwealth in 1900-1901?' *New Zealand Journal of History* 2, no. 2 (1968): 115-29.

6 'ALL FLESH IS AS GRASS' 1914-1929

Auckland Weekly News. *New Zealand's Roll of Honour, 1915: The Auckland Weekly News, Illustrated List*. Auckland: Wilson & Horton Ltd, 21 October 1915.

Baker, Paul. *King and Country Call: New Zealanders, Conscription and the Great War*. Auckland: Auckland University Press, 1998.

Barnes, Felicity. *New Zealand's London: A Colony and Its Metropolis*. Auckland: Auckland University Press, 2012.

Bean, C. E. W. *The Story of ANZAC*. Brisbane: University of Queensland Press / Australian War Memorial, 1981. (First published 1921.)

Binney, Judith. *Encircled Lands: Te Urewera, 1820-1921*. Wellington: Bridget Williams Books, 2009.

Boast, Richard. *Buying the Land, Selling the Land: Governments and Maori Land in the North Island, 1865-1921*. Wellington: Victoria University Press, 2008.

Boyd, Mary. 'The Record in Western Samoa to 1945'. In *New Zealand's Record in the Pacific Islands in the Twentieth Century*, ed. Angus Ross, 115-88. London: Longman Paul, 1969.

Brooking, Tom, Robin Hodge, and Vaughan Wood. 'The Grasslands Revolution Reconsidered'. In *Environmental Histories of New Zealand*, ed. Eric Pawson and Tom Brooking, 169-82. South Melbourne: Oxford University Press, 2002.

Bryder, Linda. *A Voice for Mothers: The Plunket Society and Infant Welfare, 1907–2000.* Auckland: Auckland University Press, 2003.
Burton, Ormond. *The Silent Division: New Zealanders at the Front, 1914–1919.* Sydney: Angus & Robertson, 1935.
Coney, Sandra. *Standing in the Sunshine: A History of New Zealand Women since They Won the Vote.* Auckland: Viking, 1993.
Crosby, Alfred. *Ecological Imperialism: The Biological Expansion of Europe, 900–1900.* Cambridge: Cambridge University Press, 1986.
Daley, Caroline. *Leisure & Pleasure: Reshaping & Revealing the New Zealand Body, 1900–1960.* Auckland: Auckland University Press, 2003.
Fenwick, Percival. *Gallipoli Diary: 24 April to 27 June 1915.* Auckland: Auckland Museum, 1915.
Ferguson, Gael. *Building the New Zealand Dream.* Palmerston North: Dunmore Press / Historical Branch, 1994.
Fewster, Kevin, Vecihi Basarin, and Hatice Hurmuz Basarin. *Gallipoli: The Turkish Story.* 2nd edn. Crows Nest, NSW: Allen & Unwin, 2003.
Fleming, G. A. 'Agricultural Support Policies in a Small Open Economy: New Zealand in the 1920s'. *Economic History Review* 52, no. 2 (1999): 334–54.
Foljambe, Annette, Countess of Liverpool. *Her Excellency's Knitting Book.* Wellington: Ferguson and Osborn, 1915. Digitised at Wellington City Libraries, accessed August 2025. https://wellington.recollect.co.nz/nodes/view/8621.
Gardiner, Wira. *Te Mura o te Ahi: The Story of the Maori Battalion.* Auckland: Reed, 2002.
Gray, John H. *From the Uttermost Ends of the Earth: The New Zealand Division on the Western Front, 1916–1918; A History and Guide to Its Battlefields.* Christchurch: Willson Scott Publishing, 2010.
H. S. B. R. 'War Friends'. In New Zealand Division, *New Zealand at the Front: Written and Illustrated by Men of the New Zealand Division*, 180. London: Cassell and Co., 1917.
Harper, Glyn. *Dark Journey.* Auckland: HarperCollins, 2007.
———, ed. *Letters from the Battlefield: New Zealand Soldiers Write Home, 1914–18.* Auckland: HarperCollins, 2001.
———. *Massacre at Passchendaele: The New Zealand Story.* Auckland: HarperCollins, 2000.
Henderson, John. *Ratana: The Man, the Church, the Political Movement.* Wellington: A.H. & A.W. Reed / Polynesian Society, 1972.
Hutching, Megan. '"Mothers of the World": Women, Peace and Arbitration in Early Twentieth-Century New Zealand'. *New Zealand Journal of History* 27, no. 2 (1993): 173–85.
Inglis, K. S., assisted by Jan Brazier. *Sacred Places: War Memorials in the Australian Landscape.* Melbourne: Melbourne University Press, 1998.
King, Michael. *The Penguin History of New Zealand.* Auckland: Penguin, 2003.

———. *Te Puea: A Biography*. Auckland: Hodder and Stoughton, 1977.

Light, Rowan. *Anzac Nations: The Legacy of Gallipoli in New Zealand and Australia, 1965–2015*. Dunedin: Otago University Press, 2022.

Loveridge, Steven. *Calls to Arms: New Zealand Society and Commitment to the Great War*. Wellington: Victoria University Press, 2014.

McCormick, E. H., ed. *Making New Zealand: Pictorial Surveys of a Century*. Vol. 1, no. 11. Wellington: Department of Internal Affairs, 1940.

McGibbon, Ian. *New Zealand Battlefields and Memorials of the Western Front*. Auckland: Oxford University Press / History Group, Ministry for Culture and Heritage, 2001.

———. *The Path to Gallipoli: Defending New Zealand, 1840–1915*. Wellington: GP Books / Historical Branch, 1991.

McGibbon, Ian, and John Crawford, eds. *New Zealand's Great War: New Zealand, the Allies and the First World War*. Auckland: Exisle Publishing, 2007.

Mein Smith, Philippa. *Maternity in Dispute: New Zealand, 1920–1939*. Wellington: Historical Branch, Department of Internal Affairs, 1986.

New Zealand. Manatū Taonga Ministry for Culture and Heritage. 'New Zealand and the First World War'. New Zealand History, accessed August 2025. https://nzhistory.govt.nz/war/first-world-war.

———. 'A Sacred Holiday'. New Zealand History, updated 19 April 2021. https://nzhistory.govt.nz/war/anzac-day-1920-45.

O'Malley, Vincent. *The Aftermath of the Tauranga Raupatu, 1864–1981*. Wellington: Crown Forestry Rental Trust, June 1995.

Pawson, Eric. 'Trees as Sites of Commemoration: The North Otago Oaks'. Speech at New Zealand Historical Association Conference, Dunedin, 2003.

Phillips, Jock, and Ken Inglis. 'War Memorials in Australia and New Zealand: A Comparative Survey'. *Australian Historical Studies* 24, no. 96 (1991): 179–91.

Pugsley, Christopher. *The Anzac Experience: New Zealand, Australia and Empire in the First World War*. Auckland: Reed, 2004.

———. *Gallipoli: The New Zealand Story*. Auckland: Sceptre, 1990.

———. *Te Hokowhitu a Tu: The Maori Pioneer Battalion in the First World War*. Auckland: Reed, 1995.

Rice, Geoffrey W. *Black November: The 1918 Influenza Epidemic in New Zealand*. Wellington: Allen & Unwin / Historical Branch, 1988.

Shadbolt, Maurice. *Voices of Gallipoli*. Auckland: Hodder and Stoughton, 1988.

Tennant, Margaret. *Children's Health, the Nation's Wealth: A History of Children's Health Camps*. Wellington: Bridget Williams Books / Historical Branch, 1994.

Triggs, W. H. 'New Zealand Mothers and the War'. In *Countess of Liverpool's Gift Book of Art and Literature*, ed. Annette Foljambe,

Countess of Liverpool, and A. W. Shrimpton, 73–4. Christchurch: Whitcombe & Tombs, 1915.
Walker, Ranginui. *He Tipua: The Life and Times of Sir Āpirana Ngata.* Auckland: Viking, 2001.
Ward, Alan. *An Unsettled History: Treaty Claims in New Zealand Today.* Wellington: Bridget Williams Books, 1999.
Worthy, Scott. 'A Debt of Honour: New Zealanders' First Anzac Days'. *New Zealand Journal of History* 36, no. 2 (2002): 185–200.
Zavos, Spiro, and Gordon Bray. *Two Mighty Tribes: The Story of the All Blacks vs. the Wallabies.* Auckland: Penguin, 2003.

7 MAKING NEW ZEALAND 1930–1949

Bassett, Michael, and Michael King. *Tomorrow Comes the Song: A Life of Peter Fraser.* Auckland: Penguin, 2000.
Castles, Francis G. *The Working Class and Welfare: Reflections on the Political Development of the Welfare State in Australia and New Zealand, 1890–1980.* Wellington: Allen & Unwin / Port Nicholson Press, 1985.
Clark, Margaret, ed. *Peter Fraser: Master Politician.* Palmerston North: Dunmore Press, 1998.
Condliffe, J. B. *The Eye of the Earth: A Pacific Survey,* ed. Peter G. Condliffe and Michio Yamaoka. Tokyo: International Academic Printed, 2004.
———. *New Zealand in the Making: A Survey of Economic and Social Development.* London: Allen & Unwin, 1930.
Crawford, John, ed. *Kia Kaha: New Zealand in the Second World War.* Auckland: Oxford University Press, 2002.
Crawford, John, and James Watson. '"The Most Appeasing Line": New Zealand and Nazi Germany, 1935–40'. *Journal of Imperial and Commonwealth History* 38, no. 1 (2010): 75–97.
Duff, Oliver. *New Zealand Now.* Wellington: Department of Internal Affairs, 1941.
Gardiner, Wira. *Te Mura o te Ahi: The Story of the Maori Battalion.* Auckland: Reed, 2002.
Gustafson, Barry. *From the Cradle to the Grave: A Biography of Michael Joseph Savage.* Auckland: Reed Methuen, 1986.
Hanson, Elizabeth. *The Politics of Social Security.* Auckland: Auckland University Press / Oxford University Press, 1980.
Hensley, Gerald. *Beyond the Battlefield: New Zealand and Its Allies, 1939–45.* Auckland: Penguin / Viking, 2009.
———. 'Beyond the Battlefield: Peter Fraser at War'. In New Zealand Institute of International Affairs, *Celebrating 75 Years: New Zealand Institute of International Affairs,* vol. 1, ed. Brian Lynch, 103–18. Wellington: NZIIA, 2010.

Hill, Richard S. *State Authority, Indigenous Autonomy: Crown-Maori Relations in New Zealand/Aotearoa, 1900–1950*. Wellington: Victoria University Press, 2004.
Hilliard, Chris. 'Stories of Becoming: The Centennial Surveys and the Colonization of New Zealand'. *New Zealand Journal of History* 33, no. 1 (1999): 3–19.
Kay, Robin, ed. *The Australian–New Zealand Agreement 1944*. Vol. 1: *Documents on New Zealand External Relations*. Wellington: Historical Publications Branch, Department of Internal Affairs, 1972.
McClure, Margaret. *A Civilised Community: A History of Social Security in New Zealand, 1898–1998*. Auckland: Auckland University Press / Historical Branch, 1998.
McGibbon, Ian. *New Zealand and the Second World War: The People, the Battles and the Legacy*. Auckland: Hodder Moa Beckett, 2004.
McIntyre, W. D. 'From Dual Dependency to Nuclear Free'. In *The Oxford History of New Zealand*, 2nd edn, ed. Geoffrey W. Rice, 520–38. Auckland: Oxford University Press, 1992.
——. *New Zealand Prepares for War: Defence Policy, 1919–39*. Christchurch: University of Canterbury Press, 1988.
——. *The Rise and Fall of the Singapore Naval Base, 1919–1942*. London: Macmillan, 1979.
McKinnon, Malcolm. *Immigrants and Citizens: New Zealanders and Asian Immigration in Historical Context*. Wellington: Institute of Policy Studies, Victoria University of Wellington, 1996.
——. *Independence and Foreign Policy: New Zealand in the World since 1935*. Auckland: Auckland University Press / Historical Branch, 1993.
Montgomerie, Deborah. *The Women's War: New Zealand Women, 1939–45*. Auckland: Auckland University Press, 2001.
New Zealand. Department of Tourist and Publicity. *New Zealand Centennial, 1840–1940*. Wellington: Government Printer, 1938.
Nolan, Melanie. *Breadwinning: New Zealand Women and the State*. Christchurch: Canterbury University Press, 2000.
Simpson, Tony. *The Sugarbag Years*. 2nd edn. Auckland: Penguin, 1990.
Taylor, Nancy M. *The New Zealand People at War: The Home Front*. 2 vols. Wellington: Government Printer, 1986.
Walker, Ranginui. *He Tipua: The Life and Times of Sir Āpirana Ngata*. Auckland: Viking, 2001.
Wanhalla, Angela, Sarah Christie, Lachy Paterson, Ross Webb, and Erica Newman. *Te Hau Kāinga: The Māori Home Front during the Second World War*. Auckland: Auckland University Press, 2024.
Wood, F. L. W. *The New Zealand People at War: Political and External Affairs*, Wellington: War History Branch, Department of Internal Affairs, 1958.
——. *Understanding New Zealand*. New York: Coward-McCann Inc., 1944.

8 GOLDEN WEATHER 1950–1972

Brickell, Chris. 'The Politics of Post-war Consumer Culture'. *New Zealand Journal of History* 40, no. 2 (2006): 133–55.

Brookes, Barbara. 'A Germaine Moment: Style, Language and Audience'. In *Disputed Histories*, ed. Tony Ballantyne and Brian Moloughney, 191–213. Dunedin: Otago University Press, 2006.

——. 'Nostalgia for "Innocent Homely Pleasures": The 1964 New Zealand Controversy over *Washday at the Pa*'. In *At Home in New Zealand*, ed. Barbara Brookes, 210–25. Wellington: Bridget Williams Books, 2000.

Broughton, Agnes, et al., *The Silent Migration: Ngati Poneke Young Maori Club, 1937–1948; Stories of Urban Migration Told to Patricia Grace, Irihapeti Ramsden and Jonathan Dennis*. Wellington: Huia Publishers, 2001.

Campbell, I. C. *Worlds Apart: A History of the Pacific Islands*. 4th edn. Christchurch: Canterbury University Press, 2003.

Coney, Sandra. *Standing in the Sunshine: A History of New Zealand Women since They Won the Vote*. Auckland: Viking, 1993.

Cook, Megan. 'Women's Movement: The Women's Liberation Movement'. In New Zealand. Manatū Taonga Ministry for Culture and Heritage, *Te Ara The Encyclopedia of New Zealand*, 2011. https://teara.govt.nz/en/womens-movement/page-6.

Docking, Gil. *Two Hundred Years of New Zealand Painting*. With additions by Michael Dunn. Rev. edn. Auckland: David Bateman, 1990.

Easton, Brian. *In Stormy Seas: The Post-war New Zealand Economy*. Dunedin: University of Otago Press, 1997.

——. *The Nationbuilders*. Auckland: Auckland University Press, 2001.

——. *Not in Narrow Seas: The Economic History of Aotearoa New Zealand*. Wellington: Victoria University Press, 2020.

Firth, Stewart. 'A Nuclear Pacific'. In *The Cambridge History of the Pacific Islanders*, ed. Donald Denoon, Stewart Firth, Jocelyn Linnekin, Malama Meleisea, and Karen Nero, 324–58. Cambridge: Cambridge University Press, 1997.

——. *Nuclear Playground*. Honolulu: University of Hawaii Press, 1987.

Gould, J. D. *The Rake's Progress? The New Zealand Economy since 1945*. Auckland: Hodder and Stoughton, 1982.

Green, Anna. *British Capital, Antipodean Labour: Working the New Zealand Waterfront, 1915–1951*. Dunedin: University of Otago Press, 2001.

Guest, Morris, and John Singleton. 'The Murupara Project and Industrial Development in New Zealand, 1945–65'. *Australian Economic History Review* 39, no. 1 (1999): 52–71.

Gustafson, Barry. *The First Fifty Years: A History of the New Zealand National Party*. Auckland: Reed Methuen, 1986.

Harris, Aroha, with Melissa M. Williams. 'Māori Affairs, 1945–1970'. In *Tangata Whenua: An Illustrated History*, ed. Atholl Anderson, Judith

Binney, and Aroha Harris, 382–415. Wellington: Bridget Williams Books, 2015.

Hicks, Stephen. 'The Commonwealth Trans-Antarctic Expedition, 1955–1958' [PhD thesis]. University of Canterbury, 2015.

Ip, Manying. 'Redefining Chinese Female Migration: From Exclusion to Transnationalism'. In *Shifting Centres: Women and Migration in New Zealand History*, ed. Lyndon Fraser and Katie Pickles, 149–65. Dunedin: University of Otago Press, 2002.

Kennaway, Richard. *New Zealand Foreign Policy, 1951–1971*. London: Methuen, 1972.

McGibbon, Ian. 'Forward Defence: The Southeast Asian Commitment'. In *New Zealand in World Affairs*. Vol. 2: *1957–1972*, ed. Malcolm McKinnon, 9–39. Wellington: New Zealand Institute of International Affairs / Historical Branch, 1991.

———, ed. *Undiplomatic Dialogue: Letters between Carl Berendsen and Alister McIntosh, 1943–52*. Auckland: Auckland University Press / Ministry of Foreign Affairs and Trade / Historical Branch, 1993.

McIntosh, Alister. 'Origins of the Department of External Affairs and the Formulation of an Independent Foreign Policy'. In *New Zealand in World Affairs*, vol. 1, ed. Alister McIntosh et al., 11–35. Wellington: Price Milburn / New Zealand Institute of International Affairs, 1977.

McIntyre, W. D. *Background to the Anzus Pact: Policy-Making, Strategy and Diplomacy, 1945–55*. Basingstoke: St Martin's Press; Christchurch: Canterbury University Press, 1995.

McKinnon, Malcolm. *Immigrants and Citizens: New Zealanders and Asian Immigration in Historical Context*. Wellington: Institute of Policy Studies, Victoria University of Wellington, 1996.

———. *Independence and Foreign Policy: New Zealand in the World since 1935*. Auckland: Auckland University Press, 1993.

Marshall, John. *Memoirs*. Vol. 2: *1960 to 1988*. Auckland: William Collins, 1989.

Martin, John E., ed. *People, Politics and Power Stations: Electric Power Generation in New Zealand, 1880–1998*. Wellington: Electricity Corporation / Historical Branch / Bridget Williams Books, 1998.

Mason, Bruce. *The End of the Golden Weather*. Rev. edn. Wellington: Victoria University Press, 1970.

New Zealand. Special Committee on Moral Delinquency in Children and Adolescents. *Report of the Special Committee on Moral Delinquency in Children and Adolescents*. Wellington: Government Printer, 1954.

Nolan, Melanie. *Breadwinning: New Zealand Women and the State*. Christchurch: Canterbury University Press, 2000.

Pickles, Katie. 'Workers and Workplaces: Industry and Modernity'. In *Southern Capital Christchurch: Towards a City Biography, 1850–2000*,

ed. John Cookson and Graeme Dunstall, 138–61. Christchurch: Canterbury University Press, 2000.
Priestley, Rebecca. *Mad on Radium: New Zealand in the Atomic Age*. Auckland: Auckland University Press, 2012.
Rabel, Roberto. *New Zealand and the Vietnam War: Politics and Diplomacy*. Auckland: Auckland University Press, 2005.
Singleton, John, and Paul L. Robertson. *Economic Relations between Britain and Australasia, 1945–1970*. Basingstoke: Palgrave, 2002.
Somerset, H. C. D. *Littledene: Patterns of Change*. Enlarged edn. Wellington: New Zealand Council for Educational Research, 1974.
Teal, Jane. 'Recipes for the Renovations: Laurina Stevens and the Pavlova Cake'. *History Now* 9, no. 4 (2004): 13–16.
Templeton, Malcolm. *Standing Upright Here: New Zealand in the Nuclear Age, 1945–1990*. Wellington: Victoria University Press / New Zealand Institute of International Affairs, 2006.
———. *A Wise Adventure: New Zealand in Antarctica, 1920–60*. Wellington: Victoria University Press / New Zealand Institute of International Affairs, 2000.
Walker, Ranginui. *He Tipua: The Life and Times of Sir Āpirana Ngata*. Auckland: Viking, 2001.
Whitcher, Gary. '"More than America": Some New Zealand Responses to American Culture in the Mid-twentieth Century' [PhD thesis]. University of Canterbury, 2011.
Wood, F. L. W. 'The Anzac Dilemma'. *International Affairs* 29, no. 2 (April 1953): 184–92.
———. 'New Zealand Foreign Policy, 1945–1951'. In *New Zealand in World Affairs*, vol. 1, ed. Alister McIntosh et al., 89–113. Wellington: Price Milburn / New Zealand Institute of International Affairs, 1977.
Woods, Megan. 'Dissolving the Frontiers: Single Maori Women's Migrations, 1942–1969'. In *Shifting Centres: Women and Migration in New Zealand History*, ed. Lyndon Fraser and Katie Pickles, 117–34. Dunedin: University of Otago Press, 2002.
———. 'Integrating the Nation: Gendering Maori Urbanisation and Integration, 1942–1969' [PhD thesis]. University of Canterbury, 2002.

9 LATEST EXPERIMENTS 1973–1996

Andre, Pamela, Stephen Payton, and John Mills, eds. *The Negotiation of the Australia New Zealand Closer Economic Relations Trade Agreement 1983*. Canberra: Australian Department of Foreign Affairs and Trade; Wellington: Ministry of Foreign Affairs and Trade, 2003.
Anthony, Doug. '20 Years of Trans-Tasman CER: Where to Now?' Speech at Australia–New Zealand Closer Economic Relations Trade Agreement 20th Anniversary Luncheon, Sydney, 28 August 2003.

Barnett, Ross, and Pauline Barnett. 'Back to the Future? Reflections on Past Reforms and Future Prospects for Health Services in New Zealand'. *GeoJournal* 59, no. 2 (2004): 137–47.
Bassett, Michael. 'The Atom Splitters'. *National Business Review*, 8 August 2003.
———. 'Cabinet Making; Cabinet Breaking'. In *For the Record*, ed. Clark, 39–44.
———. *The State in New Zealand, 1840–1984: Socialism without Doctrines?* Auckland: Auckland University Press, 1998.
———. *Working with David: Inside the Lange Cabinet*. Auckland: Hodder Moa, 2008.
Belich, James. *Paradise Reforged: A History of the New Zealanders from the 1880s to the Year 2000*. Auckland: Allen Lane, 2001.
Castles, Frank, Rolf Gerritsen, and Jack Vowles, eds. *The Great Experiment: Labour Parties and Public Policy Transformation in Australia and New Zealand*. Auckland: Auckland University Press, 1996.
Caygill, David. 'Industry Policy'. In *For the Record*, ed. Clark, 66–78.
Clark, Helen. 'A Politician's View'. In *Nuclear Free Nation: A Case-Study of Aotearoa / New Zealand*, ed. Christian Conference of Asia, 15–18. Hong Kong: International Affairs, Christian Conference of Asia, c. 1985.
Clark, Margaret, ed. *The Bolger Years, 1990–1997*. Wellington: Dunmore Publishing, 2008.
———, ed. *For the Record: Lange and the Fourth Labour Government*. Wellington: Dunmore Publishing, 2005.
Cullen, Michael. 'Opening Remarks'. In *For the Record*, ed. Clark, 9–12.
Dalziel, Paul, and Ralph Lattimore, eds. *The New Zealand Macroeconomy: A Briefing on the Reforms and Their Legacy*. 4th edn. South Melbourne: Oxford University Press, 2001.
Davey, Judith A. *Another New Zealand Experiment: A Code of Social and Family Responsibility*. Wellington: Institute of Policy Studies, 2000.
Dillon, Helena. 'Rogernomics and Rupture: Huntly's Response to the Corporatisation of State Coal Mines in 1987' [MA thesis]. University of Canterbury, 2010.
Douglas, Roger. 'How We Did It'. In *For the Record*, ed. Clark, 56–9.
Easton, Brian. *The Commercialisation of New Zealand*. Auckland: Auckland University Press, 1997.
———, ed. *The Making of Rogernomics*. Auckland: Auckland University Press, 1989.
———. *Not in Narrow Seas: The Economic History of Aotearoa New Zealand*. Wellington: Victoria University Press, 2020.
Gauld, Robin. *Revolving Doors: New Zealand's Health Reforms*. Wellington: Institute of Policy Studies / Health Services Research Centre, Victoria University of Wellington, 2001.

Goldfinch, Shaun. *Remaking New Zealand and Australian Economic Policy*. Wellington: Victoria University Press, 2000.
Goldfinch, Shaun, and Daniel Malpass. 'The Polish Shipyard: Myth, Economic History and Economic Policy Reform in New Zealand'. *Australian Journal of Politics and History* 53, no. 1 (2007): 118–37.
Gustafson, Barry. *His Way: A Biography of Robert Muldoon*. Auckland: Auckland University Press, 2000.
Hawke, Gary. 'New Zealand: Developing and Sustaining Economic Liberalization'. In *The Asia-Pacific: A Region in Transition*, ed. Jim Rolfe, 239–58. Honolulu: Asia Pacific Center for Security Studies, 2004.
Hazledine, Tim. *Taking New Zealand Seriously: The Economics of Decency*. Auckland: HarperCollins, 1998.
Henderson, John. 'The Warrior Peacenik: Setting the Record Straight on ANZUS and the Fiji Coup'. In *For the Record*, ed. Clark, 136–43.
James, Colin. *The Quiet Revolution*. Wellington: Allen & Unwin, 1986.
Kelsey, Jane. *The New Zealand Experiment: A World Model for Structural Adjustment?* New edn. Auckland: Auckland University Press / Bridget Williams Books, 1997.
——. *Rolling Back the State: Privatisation of Power in Aotearoa / New Zealand*. Wellington: Bridget Williams Books, 1993.
Lange, David. *My Life*. Auckland: Viking, 2005.
——. '"Nuclear Weapons Are Morally Indefensible": Argument for the Affirmative during the Oxford Union Debate of 1 March'. In David Lange, *A Selection of Recent Foreign Policy Statements by the New Zealand Prime Minister and Minister of Foreign Affairs, Rt Hon. David Lange*, ed. Ministry of Foreign Affairs. Wellington: Ministry of Foreign Affairs, March 1985.
Le Heron, Richard, and Eric Pawson, eds. *Changing Places: New Zealand in the Nineties*. Auckland: Longman Paul, 1996.
McIntyre, W. D. 'From Dual Dependency to Nuclear Free'. In *The Oxford History of New Zealand*, 2nd edn, ed. Geoffrey W. Rice, 520–38. Auckland: Oxford University Press, 1992.
McKinnon, Malcolm. *Independence and Foreign Policy: New Zealand in the World since 1935*. Auckland: Auckland University Press, 1993.
McMillan, Stuart. *Neither Confirm nor Deny: The Nuclear Ships Dispute between New Zealand and the United States*. Wellington: Allen & Unwin / Port Nicholson Press, 1987.
Mein Smith, Philippa. 'Did Muldoon Really "Go Too Slowly" with CER?' *New Zealand Journal of History* 41, no. 2 (2007): 161–79.
Muldoon, R. D. *My Way*. Wellington: Reed, 1981.
——. *The Rise and Fall of a Young Turk*. Wellington: A. H. and A. W. Reed, 1974.
New Zealand. Defence Committee of Enquiry. *Defence and Security: What New Zealanders Want*. Wellington: Defence Committee of Enquiry, 1986.

New Zealand. Treasury. *New Zealand Economic Growth: An Analysis of Performance and Policy*. Wellington: Treasury, April 2004.
Norrish, Merwyn. 'Lange Government's Foreign Policy'. In *For the Record*, ed. Clark, 150–7.
Palmer, Geoffrey. 'Working with David Lange'. In *For the Record*, ed. Clark, 50–5.
Palmer, Geoffrey, and Matthew Palmer. *Bridled Power: New Zealand's Constitution and Government*. 4th edn. South Melbourne: Oxford University Press, 2004.
Priestley, Rebecca. *Mad on Radium: New Zealand in the Atomic Age*. Auckland: Auckland University Press, 2012.
Richards, Raymond. *Palmer: The Parliamentary Years*. Christchurch: Canterbury University Press, 2010.
Templeton, Hugh. *All Honourable Men: Inside the Muldoon Cabinet, 1975–1984*. Auckland: Auckland University Press, 1995.
Thomson, David. *Selfish Generations? How Welfare States Grow Old*. Rev. edn. Cambridge: White Horse Press, 1996.
Wilson, Margaret. *Labour in Government, 1984–1987*. Wellington: Allen & Unwin / Port Nicholson Press, 1989.

10 TREATY REVIVAL 1973–1999

Anderson, Atholl, Judith Binney, and Aroha Harris. *Tangata Whenua: An Illustrated History*. Wellington: Bridget Williams Books, 2015.
Bedford, Richard D., Elsie Ho, and Jacqueline Lidgard. 'International Migration in New Zealand: Context, Components and Policy Issues'. In *Populations of New Zealand and Australia at the Millennium: A Joint Special Issue of the Journal of Population Research and the New Zealand Population Review*, ed. Gordon A. Carmichael, with A. Dharmalingam, 39–65. Canberra: Australian Population Association; Wellington: Population Association of New Zealand, 2002.
Belgrave, Michael. *Historical Frictions: Maori Claims and Reinvented Histories*. Auckland: Auckland University Press, 2005.
Belgrave, Michael, Merata Kawharu, and David Williams, eds. *Waitangi Revisited: Perspectives on the Treaty of Waitangi*. Melbourne: Oxford University Press, 2005.
Bell, Martin. 'Comparing Population Mobility in Australia and New Zealand'. In *Populations of New Zealand and Australia at the Millennium: A Joint Special Issue of the Journal of Population Research and the New Zealand Population Review*, ed. Gordon A. Carmichael, with A. Dharmalingam, 169–93. Canberra: Australian Population Association; Wellington: Population Association of New Zealand, 2002.
Brookes, Barbara. 'A Germaine Moment: Style, Language and Audience'. In *Disputed Histories*, ed. Tony Ballantyne and Brian Moloughney, 191–213. Dunedin: Otago University Press, 2006.

Brookfield, F. M. (Jock). *Waitangi and Indigenous Rights: Revolution, Law and Legitimation.* Updated edn. Auckland: Auckland University Press, 2006.

Brown, Hayley M. '"A Woman's Right to Choose": Second Wave Feminist Advocacy of Abortion Law Reform in New Zealand and New South Wales from the 1970s' [MA thesis]. University of Canterbury, 2004.

Clark, Helen. 'Opening Address'. In *New Zealand College of Midwives Conference Proceedings*, ed. Karen Guilliland, 2–3. Dunedin: New Zealand College of Midwives, 1990.

Coates, Ken S., and P. G. McHugh. *Living Relationships: Kokiri Ngatahi; The Treaty of Waitangi in the New Millennium.* Wellington: Victoria University Press, 1998.

Dann, Christine. *Up from Under: Women and Liberation in New Zealand, 1970–1985.* Wellington: Allen & Unwin / Port Nicholson Press, 1985.

Denoon, Donald, Stewart Firth, Jocelyn Linnekin, Malama Meleisea, and Karen Nero, eds. *The Cambridge History of the Pacific Islanders.* Cambridge: Cambridge University Press, 1997.

Fisher, Martin. *A Long Time Coming: The Story of Ngāi Tahu's Treaty Settlement Negotiations with the Crown.* Christchurch: Canterbury University Press, 2020.

Harris, Aroha. *Hikoi: Forty Years of Maori Protest.* Wellington: Huia Publishers, 2004.

Hayward, Janine. 'Appendix'. In Alan Ward, *National Overview*, vol. 2, 477–9. Wellington: Waitangi Tribunal, 1997.

Kawharu, I. H., ed. *Waitangi: Maori and Pakeha Perspectives of the Treaty of Waitangi.* Auckland: Oxford University Press, 1989.

Macdonald, Charlotte. 'A Place to Stand: 1980s and 1990s'. In *The Vote, the Pill and the Demon Drink: A History of Feminist Writing in New Zealand, 1869–1993*, ed. Charlotte Macdonald, 206–53. Wellington: Bridget Williams Books, 1993.

———, ed. *The Vote, the Pill and the Demon Drink: A History of Feminist Writing in New Zealand, 1869–1993.* Wellington: Bridget Williams Books, 1993.

McLean, Denis. *The Prickly Pair: Making Nationalism in Australia and New Zealand.* Dunedin: University of Otago Press, 2003.

McMillan, Kate. 'Developing Citizens: Subjects, Aliens and Citizens in New Zealand since 1840'. In *Tangata Tangata: The Changing Ethnic Contours of New Zealand*, ed. Paul Spoonley, Cluny Macpherson, and David Pearson, 267–89. Melbourne: Thomson / Dunmore Press, 2004.

Mein Smith, Philippa. 'Midwifery Re-innovation in New Zealand'. In *Innovations in Health and Medicine: Diffusion and Resistance in the Twentieth Century*, ed. Jennifer Stanton, 169–87. London: Routledge, 2002.

Mein Smith, Philippa, Peter Hempenstall, and Shaun Goldfinch. *Remaking the Tasman World*. Christchurch: Canterbury University Press, 2008.
Mita, Hepi. *Merata: How Mum Decolonised the Screen* [documentary]. Arama Pictures, 2018.
Nero, Karen. 'The End of Insularity'. In *The Cambridge History of the Pacific Islanders*, ed. Donald Denoon, Stewart Firth, Jocelyn Linnekin, Malama Meleisea, and Karen Nero, 439–67. Cambridge: Cambridge University Press, 1997.
New Zealand. Waitangi Tribunal. *Report of the Waitangi Tribunal on the Orakei Claim*. Wai 9. Wellington: Tribunal, 1987.
O'Brien, Terence. 'Now Our First Big Summit Is Over, What Do We Do Next?' *New Zealand Herald*, 16 September 1999.
Orange, Claudia. 'Waitangi Day 1960s'. New Zealand History. Manatū Taonga Ministry for Culture and Heritage, updated 7 July 2014. https://nzhistory.govt.nz/politics/treaty/waitangi-day/waitangi-day-1960s.
——. 'Waitangi Day 1970s'. New Zealand History. Manatū Taonga Ministry for Culture and Heritage, updated 11 July 2025. https://nzhistory.govt.nz/page/waitangi-day-1970s.
O'Regan, Tipene. 'The Ngāi Tahu Claim'. In *Waitangi: Maori and Pakeha Perspectives of the Treaty of Waitangi*, ed. I. H. Kawharu, 234–62. Auckland: Oxford University Press, 1989.
Parsonson, Ann. 'Ngai Tahu – The Whale That Awoke: From Claim to Settlement (1960–1998)'. In *Southern Capital Christchurch: Towards a City Biography, 1850–2000*, ed. John Cookson and Graeme Dunstall, 248–76. Christchurch: Canterbury University Press, 2000.
Richards, Trevor. *Dancing on Our Bones: New Zealand, South Africa, Rugby and Racism*. Wellington: Bridget Williams Books, 1999.
Shepard, Deborah. *Reframing Women: A History of New Zealand Film*. Auckland: HarperCollins, 2000.
Spoonley, Paul, and Cluny Macpherson. 'Transnational New Zealand: Immigrants and Cross-Border Connections and Activities'. In *Tangata Tangata: The Changing Ethnic Contours of New Zealand*, ed. Paul Spoonley, Cluny Macpherson, and David Pearson, 180–5. Melbourne: Thomson / Dunmore Press, 2004.
Spoonley, Paul, Cluny Macpherson, and David Pearson, eds. *Tangata Tangata: The Changing Ethnic Contours of New Zealand*. Melbourne: Thomson / Dunmore Press, 2004.
Tau, Te Maire. 'Ngai Tahu: From "Better Be Dead and Out of the Way" to "To Be Seen to Belong"'. In *Southern Capital Christchurch: Towards a City Biography, 1850–2000*, ed. John Cookson and Graeme Dunstall, 222–47. Christchurch: Canterbury University Press, 2000.
Temm, Paul. *The Waitangi Tribunal: The Conscience of the Nation*. Auckland: Random Century, 1990.
Walker, Ranginui. *Ka Whawhai Tonu Matou: Struggle without End*. Rev. edn. Auckland: Penguin Books, 2004. (First published 1990.)

———. 'Māori People since 1950'. In *The Oxford History of New Zealand*, 2nd edn, ed. Geoffrey W. Rice, 498–519. Auckland: Oxford University Press, 1992.

Ward, Alan. *National Overview*. 3 vols. Wellington: Waitangi Tribunal, 1997.

———. *An Unsettled History: Treaty Claims in New Zealand Today*. Wellington: Bridget Williams Books, 1999.

11 SHAKY GROUND 2000–2016

Australian Bureau of Statistics. 'New Zealanders in Australia'. 4102.0: Australian Social Trends. September 2010. www.abs.gov.au/AUSSTATS/abs@.nsf/Lookup/4102.0Main+Features50Sep+2010.

Ayson, Robert. 'New Zealand, Australia and the Asia-Pacific Strategic Balance: From Trade Agreements to Defence White Papers'. *New Zealand International Review* 36, no. 1 (2011): 2–8.

Bedford, Richard, and Elsie Ho. *Asians in New Zealand: Implications of a Changing Demography*. Wellington: Asia New Zealand Foundation, 2008.

Binney, Judith. *Encircled Lands: Te Urewera, 1820–1921*. Wellington: Bridget Williams Books, 2009.

Bollard, Alan. 'The Recovery, the Aftershock, and the Economic Future'. Speech to Deloitte Tax Conference, 19 November 2010. Transcript at Reserve Bank of New Zealand, 19 November 2010. www.rbnz.govt.nz/hub/publications/speech/2010/speech2010-11-19.

Canterbury Mayoral Forum. *Canterbury Water Management Strategy: Strategic Framework November 2009 with Updated Targets, Provisional July 2010*. Christchurch: Canterbury Water, 2010.

China. Ministry of Commerce and New Zealand. Ministry of Foreign Affairs and Trade. *A Joint Study Report on a Free Trade Agreement between China and New Zealand*. MFAT, November 2004. www.mfat.govt.nz/assets/Trade-agreements/China-NZ-FTA/NZ-China-FTA-chinanzftastudy-November-2004.pdf.

Coleman, Andrew. 'Transport Infrastructure, Lock-Out and Urban Form: Highway Development in Auckland and the United States'. *Policy Quarterly* 6, no. 4 (2010): 23–7.

Docking, Gil. *Two Hundred Years of New Zealand Painting*. With additions by Michael Dunn. Rev. edn. Auckland: David Bateman, 1990.

Durie, Mason. *Ngā Tai Matatū: Tides of Māori Endurance*. South Melbourne: Oxford University Press, 2005.

'Govt Signs $400 Million-Plus "Treelords" Deal'. *National Business Review*. 25 June 2008.

Hamer, Paul. *Māori in Australia: Nga Māori i te Ao Moemoea*. Wellington: Te Puni Kokiri, 2007.

Jacobi, Stephen. 'Forum Will Bolster Links with US'. *Press*, 22 December 2010.

Joy, Mike. *Polluted Inheritance: New Zealand's Freshwater Crisis*. Wellington: BWB Texts, 2015.
MacManus, Joel. 'The Old Town and the New City: A Clash of Two Wellingtons'. *Spinoff*, 22 February 2024. https://thespinoff.co.nz/politics/22-02-2024/the-old-town-and-the-new-city-a-battle-of-two-wellingtons.
Mein Smith, Philippa, Peter Hempenstall, and Shaun Goldfinch. *Remaking the Tasman World*. Christchurch: Canterbury University Press, 2008.
New Zealand. Cabinet Office. *Cabinet Manual, 2023*. Department of Prime Minister and Cabinet, 2023. www.dpmc.govt.nz/sites/default/files/2023-06/cabinet-manual-2023-v2.pdf.
New Zealand. Ministry of Defence. *Defence White Paper, 2010*. Wellington: Ministry of Defence, 2010.
New Zealand. Ministry of Foreign Affairs and Trade. 'Free Trade Agreements'. Accessed August 2025. www.mfat.govt.nz/en/trade/free-trade-agreements.
——. 'NZ–China Free Trade Agreement'. Accessed August 2025. www.mfat.govt.nz/en/trade/free-trade-agreements/free-trade-agreements-in-force/nz-china-free-trade-agreement.
Ngāi Tūhoe. 'Our History'. Accessed August 2025. www.ngaituhoe.iwi.nz/our-history.
O'Sullivan, Fran. 'So Long, Sanlu'. *New Zealand Herald*, 2 May 2009.
——. 'Trade Agreement Just the Start – Clark'. *New Zealand Herald*, 7 April 2008.
Pickles, Katie. *Christchurch Ruptures*. Wellington: BWB Texts, 2016.
——. 'Colonisation, Empire and Gender'. In *The New Oxford History of New Zealand*, ed. Giselle Byrnes, 219–41. South Melbourne: Oxford University Press, 2009.
Stats NZ. 'Auckland Region'. Accessed August 2025. https://tools.summaries.stats.govt.nz/places/RC/auckland-region.
Stuff. 'Tributes to Sir Edmund Hillary'. 18 February 2009. www.stuff.co.nz/national/210644/Tributes-to-Sir-Edmund-Hillary.
——. 'World Takes Notice of All Whites'. 22 June 2010. www.stuff.co.nz/sport/fifa-world-cup/all-whites/3834701.
Te Heuheu, Tumu. 'Dr Tumu Te Heuheu's Speech at CNI Signing'. *New Zealand Herald*, 25 June 2008.
Williams, David. 'Be Bold and Talk about Benefits of Settlements'. *New Zealand Herald*, 17 June 2010.

12 BEACHED 2017–2025

Batchelor, David, and Bill McKay, eds. *Urban Aotearoa: The Future for Our Cities*. Wellington: BWB Texts, 2024.

Curtin, Jennifer, Lara Greaves, and Jack Vowles, eds. *A Team of Five Million? The 2020 'Covid-19' New Zealand General Election.* Canberra: ANU Press, 2020.
Environment Foundation. 'National Policy Documents: New Zealand Biodiversity Strategy'. Environment Guide, updated 21 January 2025. www.environmentguide.org.nz/issues/biodiversity/im:69761bac-28b7-434e-8e8c-af95ae89e73d/national-policy-documents/.
Gabel, Julia. 'Treaty Principles Bill: Former PM Sir Geoffrey Palmer Says Govt Process "Fundamentally Flawed"'. *New Zealand Herald*, 13 February 2025.
Hōete, Anthony. 'From the Māori to the Transcolonised City'. In *Urban Aotearoa: The Future for Our Cities*, ed. David Batchelor and Bill McKay, 49–67. Wellington: BWB Texts, 2024.
Meihana, Peter. *Privilege in Perpetuity: Exploding a Pākehā Myth.* Wellington: BWB Texts, 2023.
New Zealand. Government. *Crown Response to the Royal Commission into Historical Abuse in State Care and in the Care of Faith-Based Institutions.* Wellington: Crown Response Office, Te Kawa Mataaho Public Service Commission, 2025.
New Zealand. Oranga Tamariki Ministry for Children. *Strategic Intentions, 2024/25–2029/30.* Wellington: Oranga Tamariki, October 2024.
Radio New Zealand. 'Treaty Principles Bill "Inviting Civil War", Jenny Shipley Says'. 16 November 2024. www.rnz.co.nz/news/political/533944/treaty-principles-bill-inviting-civil-war-jenny-shipley-says.
Roy, Eleanor Ainge. 'Ardern Thanks "Team of 5 Million" as New Zealand Reopens Schools and Offices'. *Guardian*, 11 May 2020.
Salmond, Anne. *Tears of Rangi.* Wellington: Bridget Williams Books, 2020. (First published 2017.)
Shipley, Jenny. 'Treaty Principles Submission: Dame Jenny Shipley' [video], 20 February 2025. Kiwi Pulse / YouTube, 21 February 2025. www.youtube.com/watch?v=6NiEgLVW304.
Spoonley, Paul. *The New New Zealand: Facing Demographic Disruption.* Auckland: Massey University Press, 2021.
Stuff. 'Top Lawyers Tell PM to "Abandon" Treaty Principles Bill'. *Te Ao Māori News*, 14 November 2024.
'"They Are Us" Voted New Zealand's Quote of 2019'. *Massey [University] News*. 11 December 2019.
Tone, Lama. 'Pacific Urbanism within a Diverse Moana'. In *Urban Aotearoa: The Future for Our Cities*, ed. David Batchelor and Bill McKay, 68–85. Wellington: BWB Texts, 2024.
Waikato River Authority. 'Te Ture Whaimana o Te Awa o Waikato (Vision & Strategy)'. Accessed August 2025. https://waikatoriver.org.nz/visionandstrategy.

'Why New Zealanders Are Migrating to Australia in Record Numbers'. *Economist*. 6 March 2025. www.economist.com/asia/2025/03/06/why-new-zealanders-are-emigrating-in-record-numbers.

GLOSSARY OF MĀORI WORDS

Williams, Herbert H. *A Dictionary of the Maori Language*. 7th edn. Wellington: Government Printer, 1975.

INDEX

abortion, 168, 262
accent, New Zealand, 91
ACT Party, 305
Adams, Dame Valerie, 318
Adams, Steve, 318
aerial top dressing, 215
agriculture, 284
Air New Zealand, 216, 233
air travel, 185, 216, 220
All Blacks, 134, 142, 191, 254, 273, 282
America's Cup, 272
American Grand Fleet, 131, 180
Anderson, Atholl, 8
Anderton, Jim, 248
Anglo-Japanese alliance, 131
Anglo-Japanese commercial treaty, 129
Antarctica, 197, 208, 314
Anthony, Doug, 226
Anzac Day, 135, 138, 140, 247
Anzacs, 135, 137, 139, 140, 177, 179, 247
   legends of, 136, 137, 139, 140, 146, 179
   spirit of, 279
ANZUS alliance, 196, 197, 214, 220, 238, 239, 242, 245, 247, 323
Aoraki Mount Cook, 5, 260

Aotearoa, 1, 6, 7, 16, 17, 21, 36, 161, 267, 291, 304, 326
arbitration, 106, 116, 117, 118, 166, 171, 198, 211, 233
Arcadianism, 59, 65, 93, 108
architecture, 112, 155, 316
   indigenous, 65
   kitset cottages, 65
   sealing, 33
   Sydney, 33
Ardern, Dame Jacinda, 300, 303
arts, 266
   Te Māori exhibition, 267
Asia, 276
   exclusion of, 271
   migrants from, 271, 272, 276, 290
   trade agreements, 276
Asia-Pacific Economic Cooperation (APEC), 273
Aubert, Suzanne, 97
Auckland, 19, 38, 41, 54, 65, 67, 72, 73, 75, 78, 79, 81, 83, 88, 91, 95, 99, 104, 119, 120, 133, 154, 182, 184, 204, 206, 209, 212, 234, 244, 250, 252, 255, 264, 270, 272, 273, 289, 290, 312, 315, 316, 318, 321, 325
Auckland City Council, 289
Auckland Islands, 1

Index

AUKUS, 323
Australasia, 42, 43, 47, 67, 88, 103, 108, 117, 126, 127, 129, 138, 178, 180, 277
   meaning, 102
Australasian colonies. *See* Australasia
Australasian Federation Conferences, 102
Australia, 273, 275, 320
   competition with, 150, 321
   contrasts with, 61, 146, 149, 229
   cooperation with, 131, 185, 219, 322
   defence differences, 179, 243, 246, 279
   federation, 124, 126
   integration with, 118, 227, 228, 269, 277, 278, 280, 322
   links, 30, 32, 117
   migrants from, 269
   migration to, 225, 269, 271, 278, 322
   ties with, 127, 160, 169, 218, 219, 226, 245, 246, 322
   'white', 106, 126
Australia New Zealand Leadership Forum, 277, 322
Australia–New Zealand Agreement (Canberra Pact), 185
Australia–New Zealand Closer Economic Relations Trade Agreement (CER), 226, 227, 228, 237, 322

baby boom, 206, 210, 215
Baden-Powell, Sir Robert, 134
Ballance, John, 86, 106, 112, 117
Bank of New Zealand, 95, 233
banking system, 160, 169
Banks, Joseph, 24
Barton, Edmund, 126
Bastion Point, 252, 253
Baxter, Archibald, 147

Bay of Islands, 29, 30, 32, 33, 34, 35, 37, 43, 46, 48, 49, 54, 77
beach crossing, 26, 30. *See* Māori, early encounters with Europeans
Beaglehole, J. C., 26
Beeby, C. E., 186
Belich, James, 77, 107
Bennett, Agnes, 148, 183
Bennett, Rev. Frederick, 161
Best, Elsdon, 17
biculturalism, 249, 255, 267, 268, 290, 316
birds, 5, 6, 15
birth control, 132
Blake, Sir Peter, 272
Bledisloe, Charles Bathurst, Viscount, 181
Bloomfield, Sir Ashley, 302
Bolger, Jim, 234, 235, 248
Boswijk, Eelco, 202
Bourke, Governor Sir Richard, 45
Boyd, 33
Bradford, Sue, 281
Brash, Don, 286
Bretton Woods system, 222
Britain
   dependence on, 157, 160, 165, 176, 194, 195
   differences from, 175
   independence from, 176, 235
   loyalty to, 130, 137, 146, 176
   as market, 159, 172, 217, 218, 220, 223, 323
   migrants from, 95, 155, 201, 290
   New Zealand's 'mother complex', 190
   relations with, 216
British Empire, 26, 39, 43, 44, 45, 49, 53, 58, 96, 99, 108, 134, 139, 197, 220, 297
   in advertising dairy products, 157, 158
   end of, 213
   military, 78, 79, 82

British Medical Association, 173
Browne, Governor Thomas Gore, 74, 75, 78
Bryce, John, 84
Buchanan, 239, 240, 242, 244
Burton, Ormond, 139
Busby, James, 43, 44, 45, 46, 49, 50, 57, 58, 84, 181
Business Roundtable, 231, 233

Cameron, Lieutenant-General D. A., 79
Canterbury, 67, 68, 72, 166, 259, 284, 292
Canterbury Association, 67
capital city, 54
Carr, Rod, 313
Carrington, Dame Lisa, 317
Carroll, Sir James, 122, 142, 162
Cartwright, Dame Silvia, 262
Caygill, David, 231
centennial, 135, 181
  re-enactment of Treaty signing, 181
Chamberlain, Joseph, 129
Chapple, W. A., 132
Charles III, King, 291
Chatham Islands, 1, 8, 15, 20, 40, 83
  invasion of, 40
Chelsea Flower Show, 283
childbirth
  doctor service, 173
  management of, 154, 173, 262
  midwives, 262, 263
  pain relief, 173
  policy, 154, 173
children, 150
  'anti-smacking' legislation, 281
  child-rearing, 150
  health, 151, 152, 153, 171, 206
China, 8, 32, 46, 196, 213, 231, 275, 276, 280, 283, 290, 319, 320, 321, 326

  migrants from, 155, 202, 276, 321
  relations with, 319
Chinese
  denied citizenship, 129
  New Zealand–born, 281
Chinese gold-seekers, 91
Chisholm, Caroline, 68
Choie Sew Hoy, 91
Christchurch, 4, 67, 68, 148, 167, 198, 206, 212, 273, 292, 293, 301, 311
  rebuild, 296, 297, 298
Christchurch Call, 301
Christianity, 41, 46, 97
Chunuk Bair, 140, 141
citizenship, 183, 188, 203, 249, 257, 270, 318
civil unions, 281
Clark, Helen, 241, 263, 265, 276, 282
climate change, 283, 284, 285, 314, 315, 325
  cities, 315, 316
  School Strike 4 Climate movement, 314
  sea-level rise, 285, 314
  strategies, 315
Climate Change Commission, 313
Coates, J. G., 152, 160, 163, 169
Cold War, 192, 195, 198, 199, 207, 238, 239, 242
Colombo Plan, 196
Colonial Office, 42, 43
  strategy, 42, 45, 46
colonisation, 28, 93, 318
  military settlers, 80
Commonwealth, 196, 216, 218
  sterling area, 216
communications, 95, 194
Comprehensive and Progressive Agreement for Trans-Pacific Partnership, 324
compulsory military training, 134

Condliffe, J. B., 189, 190
Connon, Helen, 99
conscientious objectors, 147
conscription, 146, 176, 177
constitution, 235, 292
  review of, 291
  violation of, 229
  See also Britain, independence from
Constitution Act 1986, 235
consumerism, 194, 209, 231, 237
Cook Islands, 8, 128, 199, 203, 270, 318, 320
Cook, Captain James, 16, 19, 24, 26, 27, 28, 29, 33, 50, 87, 217, 264, 272, 281, 297
Cooper, Dame Whina, 252
Corner committee, 245
Cossgrove, David, 134
Cotton, Shane, 266
Council of Australian Governments, 277, 322
Covid-19 pandemic, 302, 303
  lockdowns, 302, 303
Crown right of pre-emption, 46, 56
Cuba, 48, 62
Cullen, Sir Michael, 277, 288
customary rights, 260. *See also* fisheries
customary title, 259, 260, 308
Cyclone Gabrielle, 314

Dairy Board, 159, 160, 170, 283
dairy industry, 110, 111, 157, 159, 162, 171, 283, 284
  marketing, 157
Davis, Richard, 56
Deakin, Alfred, 127, 131
decimal system, 217
Declaration of Independence He Whakaputanga, 44, 55, 84
defence policy, 137, 175, 279
democracy, 186, 207, 242, 248, 325
d'Entrecasteaux, Antoine Bruni, 28

Department of Conservation, 310, 311
Department of External Affairs, 185
depressions, 103, 104, 166
  1930s, 165
  effects, 167
  expenditure cuts, 166, 171
de Surville, Jean-François, 29
de Thierry, Charles, 45
devaluation, 169
Diggers, 139, 140
Domett, Alfred, 70
Dominion status, 131, 136, 186
Douglas, Sir Roger, 228, 230
dual dependency, 190, 195
du Fresne, Marc-Joseph Marion, 29
Dunedin, 4, 67, 91, 105, 127, 133, 259, 312
Durie, Sir Edward Taihākurei, 255, 309
Dutch community, 202

earthquakes, 165, 292, 293, 294, 295, 297, 299
  responses, 295
ecological restoration, 311, 312
economic reforms. *See* Rogernomics
economy, 104
  borrowing, 93, 95, 104
  controlled, 171, 172
  diversifying, 222, 223
  exports, 108, 109, 156, 223, 276
  global, 221
  restructuring, 105, 124, 222, 229, 230, 231
  structure of, 104
ecosanctuaries, 312, 313
Edger, Kate, 99
education, 97, 98, 210, 211
  Catholic, 97
  compulsory primary, 97
  Māori culture in, 187
  open-air schools, 152

education (cont.)
  outcomes, 97
  policy, 187
  school milk, 152
  secondary, 98, 99
Elizabeth, 39
Elizabeth II, Queen, 208, 209, 254, 282, 291
emissions trading scheme, 285
Employment Contracts Act, 234
employment, full, 193
English, New Zealand, 316
entrepreneurial state, 174, 219, 233
environment
  attitudes to, 14, 102, 283, 326
  conservation. *See* ecological restoration
  human impacts on, 15, 16
  pollution, 255
  predators, 16
Environment Canterbury (ECan), 284
environment movement, 214, 255
equal opportunity, 186, 188
eugenics, 128, 132, 149, 152
European Economic Community, 213, 218, 219, 220, 222
executive power, 235
  misuse of, 225, 231, 235, 236, 257

family wage, 118
Fat Freddy's Drop, 318
femininity, concepts of, 184, 208
feminism, 242, 264
  colonial, 113, 114
  second wave, 212, 261, 262, 263
Fenwick, Percival, 138
films, 158, 265, 266, 282
  Lord of the Rings, 282
Finlayson, Chris, 309
First World War, 136, 139
  casualties, 136
  expeditionary forces, 137

Gallipoli, 137, 138, 139, 140
  graves, 142, 149
  Great Sacrifice, 140, 145
  knitting, 148
  Lemon Squeezer hat, 141
  Māori Contingent, 141, 142
  Māori Pioneer Battalion, 141, 142, 147, 161
  Wellington Battalion, 141
  Western Front, 137, 142
  women in, 145, 148
Fisher, Sir Woolf, 220
fisheries, 260
FitzRoy, Governor Robert, 70
Fitzsimons, Jeanette, 264
flag, New Zealand, 44, 291
Fletcher Challenge, 233
Fletcher, James, 174
flora, 5, 6, 15, 283
Fonterra, 283
football, 282
  All Whites, 282
Forbes, George, 166
foreign policy, 175, 240, 241
Foreshore and Seabed Act, 285
foreshore and seabed debate, 285, 286, 287
forestry, 219, 288
Fouda, Imam Gamal, 301
Fox, Sir William, 101
France, 199, 238, 244
  nuclear tests, 238
  terrorism, 244
Fraser, Janet, 173, 183
Fraser, Malcolm, 226
Fraser, Peter, 147, 176, 178, 182, 185, 186, 194
French explorers, 28
Fuchs, Sir Vivian, 198, 208

Gallaher, David, 142
Ghormley, Vice-Admiral Robert L., 180
Gibbs Report, 236

Gibbs, Alan, 235
Gipps, Governor George, 47, 48
global financial crisis, 280
globalisation, 58, 222, 224, 230, 231, 237, 266, 272, 275
Godley, John Robert, 68
gold rushes, 93
  communities, 91
  geology, 89
  gold-dredging, 92
  miners from Australia, 89
  Otago, 88, 90
  West Coast, 88, 89
Gondwana, 4, 5, 217
Gore Browne, Governor Thomas. *See* Browne, Governor Thomas Gore
government
  Crown colony, 53, 72
  establishment of, 54, 69
  Māori seats, 96
  provincial, 72, 96
  representative government, 72
  responsible, 73
  structure of, 96, 194
Graham, Sir Douglas, 259
grasslands revolution, 135, 157, 215
Greer, Germaine, 212
Grey, Governor Sir George, 67, 71, 72, 77, 78
guaranteed prices, 170
Gunn, Elizabeth, 148, 152

Hall, Sir John, 114, 127
Hamilton, 79, 234, 255, 312
Hammond, Bill, 266
Hartley, Charles and Dinah, 70
Haumēne, Te Ua, 80
Hawaiki, 1, 7, 8, 12, 13, 121
Hawdon, Elizabeth, 130
Hawke, Joe, 253
He Whakaputanga Declaration of Independence, 44, 55, 84

health
  camps, 152
  in image of New Zealand, 101, 153
  Māori, 151, 161
  neoliberal reforms, 236
  resorts, 100
  school medical inspections, 152
Health, Department of, 151, 152
Herald, 53
Hillary, Sir Edmund, 208, 272, 282
Hobson, Captain William, 46, 47, 48, 49, 50, 54, 58
Hōete, Anthony, 316
Holland, Sidney, 194, 195, 219
Holyoake, Keith, 197
home ownership, 113, 156, 167, 173, 207
homosexual-law reform, 281
Hōne Heke, 71
Hongi Hika, 34, 35, 37, 38
hospitals, 93, 100, 132, 148, 235
hotel hours, 155, 212
Hotere, Ralph, 266
housing, 104, 112
humanitarianism, 45, 47, 54, 58
Hunn Report, 205
Huru, 30
hydroelectric power schemes, 173, 200, 226, 285
  cable, 201

identity, New Zealand, 14, 103, 107, 113, 136, 138, 139, 140, 141, 157, 191, 203, 217, 246, 247, 249, 255, 267, 270, 283, 288, 317
  nuclear-free, 238, 241, 244, 245, 247, 279
immigration, 95
  policy, 91, 93, 106, 128, 129, 155, 188, 202, 270, 271, 321
imperialism, 103, 106
import controls, 172

incomes, 237
　inequalities, 237
India, 275, 321
　migrants from, 155, 202, 276, 321
　relations with, 321
Indigenous Australians, 27, 30
Indo-Pacific, 321, 323, 324
infant mortality, 133, 150
infant welfare movement. See Plunket Society
inflation, 223
influenza pandemic, 151
Iraq War, 278
Islam, 300
Iti, Tame, 289

Jackson, Peter, 282
Japan, 128, 129, 131, 178, 190, 196, 231, 273, 275, 295, 320, 321

Kaikōura, 297
Kawiti, 71
Kemp, Henry Tacy, 67
Kendall, Thomas, 35
Kerikeri, 35
Kermadec Islands, 1, 128
Key, Sir John, 279
King Country, 80, 83, 86
King movement. See Kīngitanga
King, Governor Philip, 30
King, Sir Frederic Truby, 133, 149, 150, 151
Kingi, Wiremu, 78
Kīngitanga, 73, 74, 75, 78, 79, 80, 86, 121, 122, 147, 161, 162, 163, 252, 259, 306, 325
Kingston, Charles, 116
Kirk, Norman, 213, 249, 254
kiwi, 217, 312
kōhanga reo, 255
Kohimarama conference, 75
Korean War, 196, 198, 217

Kororāreka, 49
Kotahitanga, 121, 122
kumara, 12, 16, 18
kūpapa, 82, 83, 86, 87, 147
Kupe, 12
Kyoto Protocol, 285

La Pérouse, Jean-François Galaup de, 28
Labour governments
　first, 165, 169, 170, 177
　fourth, 228, 229, 231, 238, 247, 256, 260
　Labour-led (Ardern), 301, 302, 303
　Labour-led (Clark), 279, 281, 285, 288
　Labour-led (Hipkins), 316
　second, 207, 249
　third, 213, 238, 249
labour market, 234
labour market reforms, 232
labour movement. See unions
Labour Party, 147, 160, 170, 198, 230, 241
land
　alienation, 102
　confiscation, 70, 80, 81, 82, 83, 84, 86, 87, 95, 120, 147, 163, 164, 182, 251, 253, 287, 310
　leases, 85, 101, 111, 120, 162
　Māori reserves, 67, 120, 162, 163, 259, 288
　protests, 84, 251
　purchase, 67, 73, 74, 81, 111, 120, 121, 253
　purchase deed, French, 66
　purchase, Wellington, 62
　rights to, 59, 67, 75, 82
　speculators, 41, 61, 82, 95, 120
　state advances, 164
　views of, 59, 110, 111, 120

Lange, David, 228, 230, 240, 241, 242
Langlois, Jean François, 66
Lead Maternity Carer scheme, 263
League of Nations, 175, 185
Legislative Council, abolition of, 194
Liberal government, 106, 107, 109, 110, 128
liberalism, 106, 107, 117
life expectancy, 118, 193, 206
literature, 167
Liverpool, Lady Annette, 148
living wage. See family wage
Lomu, Jonah, 273, 318
Lord, Simeon, 32, 33
lunatic asylums, 93

Macleod, Euan, 266
Macmillan Brown, Helen. See Connon, Helen
Macmillan Brown, John, 99
Macquarie, Governor Lachlan, 34
Mahupuku, Hāmuera Tamahau, 121
Malayan Emergency, 197
Malone, Colonel W. G., 141
Manapouri, Lake, 215, 314
Manawatū, 70, 157
Mandela, Nelson, 255
Maniapoto, Rewi, 79, 80
Māori
  in Australia, 35, 278
  beliefs of, 7
  boarding schools, 97
  concepts of, 123, 124
  and Christianity, 76
  culture, 316
  definition, 17
  development, 121, 162, 164, 251
  diet, 18
  early encounters with Europeans, 23, 28
  education, 122, 205, 257
  health, 123
  housing, 175
  inequality, 175, 286
  infant mortality, 133
  land loss, 111, 119, 120, 121, 161, 250, 258
  land ownership, 94
  language, 20, 251, 255, 257
  members of parliament, 121, 122, 128, 142, 164, 254, 286, 317
  pā, 19
  poverty, 87, 119, 175
  reserves, 64, 85
  schools, 97
  status of, 205
  urbanisation, 204, 205, 250
  vote, 73
  weaving, 18
  wellbeing, 175
  in workforce, 234
  youth, 250
Māori Affairs, Department of, 255
Māori Council, 257, 309
Māori economy, 83, 87
Māori Fisheries Commission, 261
Māori land councils, 122
Māori Land Court, 251, 255
Māori Land March, 252
Māori New Year. See Matariki
Māori Organisation on Human Rights, 250
Māori parliaments, 121
Māori Party (Te Pāti Māori), 286, 287
Māori seats, 175, 250
Māori Social and Economic Advancement Act, 187
Māori tribes (iwi)
  Ngāi Tahu, 17, 33, 39, 39, 66, 67, 73, 78, 134, 259, 297, 301, 311
  Ngāi Tūhoe, 147, 162, 163, 288, 309

Māori tribes (iwi) (cont.)
  Ngāpuhi, 34, 37, 38, 41, 44, 50, 71, 181
  Ngāti Kahungunu, 17, 121
  Ngāti Mamoe, 17
  Ngāti Maniapoto, 81, 86
  Ngāti Mutunga, 40
  Ngāti Porou, 12, 82, 147, 162
  Ngāti Raukawa, 61
  Ngāti Tama, 40
  Ngāti Toa, 32, 37, 38, 39, 41, 61
  Ngāti Tūwharetoa, 53, 86, 101, 102, 121, 287
  Ngāti Whātua, 54, 253, 289
  Rongowhakaata, 83
  Tainui, 19, 147, 259, 310
  Te Arawa, 7, 13, 19, 53, 82, 87, 101, 147, 254, 283
  Te Āti Awa, 84, 255
  Waikato, 37, 53
  Whakatōhea, 164
Māori War Effort Organisation, 183
Māori Women's Welfare League, 204, 206, 252, 254, 255
Marine and Coastal Area (Takutai Moana) Act, 287, 308
Marquette disaster, 148
Marsden, Samuel, 34, 35, 50
masculinity, concepts of, 167, 184, 189, 208
Mason, Bruce, 193
Massey, William Ferguson (Bill), 137, 160
Matariki, 317
Māui, 7, 12, 24, 148
McCahon, Colin, 194
McCombs, Elizabeth, 116, 168
McIntosh, Alister, 195
McLean, Donald, 75, 96
McMillan, David, 173
Meat Producers' Board, 160
medical care, 173
Mein Smith, Captain William. *See* Smith, Captain William Mein

milk, 152, 153, 157, 171, 184, 210
  in schools, 171, 217
Miss New Zealand, 155
missionaries, 35, 45
  Anglican, 33, 34
  as Māori property, 35
  Roman Catholic, 45
  Wesleyan, 33
Mita, Merata, 267
Moehanga, 30
Montreal Protocol, 314
Moriori, 1, 8, 15, 20, 40
Morison, Julia, 266
mosque shootings, Christchurch, 300
  responses, 301, 302
Mother Mary Joseph. *See* Aubert, Suzanne
motherhood, 132, 133, 211
  in First World War, 149, 150
  maternal deaths, 153, 154
  safe maternity, 154
Muldoon, Sir Robert, 224, 225, 239, 250, 254
Muldoonism, 226, 234, 247, 253, 254, 265
Mulgan, John, 167
multiculturalism, 268, 321
Munro Ferguson, Lady Helen, 149
Murupara, 219
musket wars, 36, 38
  effects of, 38, 39, 40, 42
  European input, 39
  invasion of South Island, 40
  and migration, 38, 39, 40

Nahiti, 60
naming, 12, 260, 298, 304, 316
Nanto-Bordelaise Company, 66
Nash, Walter, 172, 178
national biodiversity strategy, 311
National Cabinet system, Australia, 322
National Council of Women, 115, 155, 210

National governments
  1950s–1960s, 198, 207, 209, 217, 251, 253
  1990s, 234
  Muldoon, 224
  National-led (Key), 284, 285, 287, 291
  National-led (Luxon), 285, 304, 308, 314
  National-led, 1990s, 248, 271
national parks, 101, 163, 214, 288, 310
National Party, 192, 194
nationalism, 208, 245, 249
  colonial, 123
  cultural, 165, 189
nationhood, 165, 190
Native Land Acts, 81, 122
Native Land Court, 70, 81, 83, 84, 86, 87, 95, 101, 111, 121, 122, 162, 253
Native Trust Office, 162
Nauru, 157, 215
navigators, Polynesian, 6, 14
Neill, Grace, 132
Nelson, 68, 69, 72
Nene, Tāmati Wāka, 50, 58, 71
neoliberalism, 228, 229, 230, 231, 234, 236, 247, 324
Nēpia, George, 161, 254
New Plymouth, 69, 72, 74, 78
New South Wales, 30, 32, 47
  trade with, 38
New Zealand, 131
New Zealand–Australia Free Trade Agreement, 219, 227
New Zealand–China Free Trade Agreement, 275, 320
New Zealand Company, 47, 48, 59, 61, 62, 69, 70, 96, 181
New Zealand Co-operative Dairy Company, 158
New Zealand Division, 137, 141, 142, 144, 146

New Zealand Federation of Labour, 118, 119, 147, 171, 198
New Zealand First Party, 271
New Zealand Insurance, 95
New Zealand Māori Council, 250
New Zealand Rugby Football Union, 254
New Zealand Settlements Act, 80, 84, 163
New Zealand–United Kingdom Free Trade Agreement, 323
New Zealand Wars, 71, 77, 82, 83, 96, 103
  effects, 86
  national day, 316
  Ōrākau, 79
  Taranaki, 74, 77, 78, 79
  Waikato, 78, 80, 81
  Waitara, 78
  wars of 1845–7, 71
Ngā Tamatoa, 251
Ngata, Sir Āpirana, 12, 122, 142, 162, 163, 164, 175, 181
Niue, 128, 203, 318
Nordmeyer, Arnold, 173
nuclear power, 200
nuclear weapons, 199, 200
  New Zealand stance on, 195, 213, 239, 245
  testing, 199

Oamaru, 149
oil shocks, 222, 224, 225
O'Malley, Vincent, 78, 79
O'Regan, Sir Tipene, 12, 261
Organisation for Economic Co-operation and Development (OECD), 222
Otago, 67, 68, 72, 173, 259
Ottawa Agreements, 169

Pacific Island New Zealanders, 270, 318
  in parliament, 318

Pacific Islands
  dependencies, 128, 203, 318
  migrants from, 202, 203,
    269, 290
  nuclear testing in, 199
  relations with, 203
Pacific transnationalism, 270
Pai Mārire, 80, 83
Paikea, 13
Paki, Ngā Wai Hono i te pō, 306
Palmer, Sir Geoffrey, 231, 235,
    240, 307
Panakareao, Nōpera, 51
Parata, Taare, 142
Parihaka, 84, 85, 86, 300
Park, Sir Keith, 177
Parramatta, 34, 35
pastoralism. *See* settler capitalism
Patel, Ajaz, 321
Pātuone, Eruera, 50, 58, 73
pavlova, 208
peace movement, 148, 199, 239,
    240, 242
peacekeeping, 274, 279
people power, 325
Peters, Winston, 271
petitions to British royalty, 43
pioneers
  heritage of, 181, 230
  mythology, 65
Plunket Society, 133, 134, 150, 151
Plunket, Lady Victoria, 133
police force, 93
  Red Squad, 254
Polynesia
  East, 1
  foods, 17
  South, 1
Pōmare, Lady Miria, 148
Pōmare, Sir Māui, 123, 142
Pompallier, Bishop Jean-Baptiste,
    46, 50
population, 188, 290, 325
  balance of sexes, 65, 88, 93
  decline, 86, 87
  diversity, 276
  European, 87
  fertility decline, 99, 132
  infant deaths, 87
  Māori, 77, 87, 161, 286, 325
  Māori and non-Māori, 94
  migration waves, 87, 88
  mortality, 132
  'native-born' Europeans, 103
  Pacific, 318
  urban, 113, 155
potatoes, 37, 38
Prebble, Richard, 231, 239
Prendergast, Chief Justice James, 84
Principles of Treaty of Waitangi
    Bill, 305
  opposition to, 305, 306, 307, 308
privatisation, 233
prophet movements, 80, 83, 84
prostitution law reform, 281
protection, 106, 172, 326
public health, 151
public sector reforms, 232
public works schemes, 166, 167

Queenstown, 91

race, views of, 14, 30, 43, 46, 60,
    91, 103, 124, 127, 128, 129,
    130, 131
radio, 156, 189, 257
railways, 86, 95, 120, 183, 233, 289
Rainbow Warrior, 244
Rata, Matiu, 252, 261
Rātana Church, 161
Rātana movement, 161, 175,
    249, 250
Rātana, Iriaka, 264
Rātana, T. W., 161
rationing, 184
Read, Gabriel, 88
Red Feds. *See* New Zealand
    Federation of Labour

redundancies, 234
Reeves, Maud, 116
Reeves, William Pember, 106, 108, 112, 116
Reform government, 155, 163
Reform Party, 119, 120, 160
refrigeration, 108, 109
Regional Comprehensive Economic Partnership, 320
Reserve Bank, 169, 171, 174, 226, 230, 231, 232
Reserve Bank Act, 232
Richardson, Ruth, 234
Ringatu, 83
Rogernomics, 233, 234, 237, 247, 263
Roosevelt, Franklin D., 131, 180
Ross, Hilda, 194
Rotorua, 13, 87, 101, 123, 163, 181, 254, 283, 312
   hot springs, 101
Rowling, Wallace (Bill), 252
Royal Commission of Inquiry into Abuse in Care, 319
Royal Forest and Bird Protection Society, 215, 314
Rua Kēnana, 147, 162, 288
Ruatara, 34, 35
rugby, 161, 253, 273, 282, 317, 318
   Springbok tours, 253, 254
Russell, Captain William, 102
Russell, Thomas, 95

Salmond, Anne, 30, 305
Samoa, 128, 137, 151, 185, 186, 203, 318
   apology to, 281
   migrants from, 270
Savage, Michael Joseph, 147, 170, 175, 176
scouting movement, 134
sealing, 30, 32, 33
'Sealord's deal', 261
seals, 297

Second World War, 176, 181
   28 (Māori) Battalion, 182, 183
   air force, 177
   deaths, 177
   expeditionary force, 177, 179, 180
   food production, 183
   imperial strategy, 178
   Pearl Harbor, 178
   Singapore naval base, 178, 179
   war effort, 177
   women in, 177, 184
   Women's War Service Auxiliary, 183
   women's auxiliaries, 183
Seddon, Richard, 91, 106, 121, 126, 130
settlement
   patterns, 117
   time of, 1, 8
settler capitalism, 67, 68, 73
settler contract, 109, 111, 112, 113, 117, 118, 119, 156, 187, 221, 236
Seymour, David, 305
Shanghai Expo, 283
Sharples, Pita, 286
sheep farming, 72, 111, 162, 170, 215, 221
Sheppard, Kate, 114, 265
Shipley, Dame Jenny, 263, 273, 308
Shultz, George, 240
Silver Ferns, 273
Sim Commission, 163
Sinclair, Sir Keith, 124, 257
Single Economic Market, 277
Smith, Adam, 60
Smith, Captain William Mein, 62, 63
smoking law reform, 281
social contract, 109, 116
social security, 170, 172, 175, 225
Social Security Act, 170, 172

soldier rehabilitation schemes, 156, 187
Somerset, H. C. D., 216
South African War, 130, 131
South Pacific Commission, 186
South Pacific Nuclear-Free Zone, 280
sovereignty
  British, 54
  Māori, 55
Spain, William, 69
sport, 253, 254, 272, 273, 318, 321
  women, 317
St Helens Hospitals, 132
state development
  Australasian model of, 106–7, 170, 171, 194, 221, 230
  entrepreneurial model of, 94, 96
  neoliberal model of, 232
state experiments. *See* state development, Australasian model of
state houses, 174, 187
state-owned enterprises, 233
State-Owned Enterprises Act, 233, 234, 257
Statute of Westminster, 189
Stephen, Sir James, 43, 58
Stewart, Captain John, 39
stock and station agents, 109
Stout, Anna, 114
Stout, Sir Robert, 114, 122
strikes
  general, 119
  Maritime Strike, 105
  miners, 118, 119
  waterfront dispute, 198
Strutt, William, 65
Student Volunteer Army, 294
suburbia, 112, 173, 206
superannuation, 172, 280
  KiwiSaver, 280
  New Zealand Superannuation Fund, 280

superannuation, national, 225
supermarkets, 206
surveyors, 48, 63, 64, 68, 84
Sutch, Bill, 220
systematic colonisation, theory of, 59, 60, 61, 62

Tāhiwi, Captain Pirimi, 143
Tāhiwi, Kingi, 187
Talboys, Brian, 226
Tama Te Kapua, 13
Tamahori, Lee, 266
Tama-ki-Hikurangi, Rēnata, 76
tangata whenua, 11, 12, 14, 19, 27, 29, 40, 41, 59, 250, 253, 267, 268, 294. *See also* Māori
Tangiwai disaster, 209
Taranaki, 37, 40, 157, 163, 255
Taranaki Maunga (Mount Taranaki), 310
Tareha, 50
Tasman Empire Airways Limited, 216
Tasman Pulp and Paper Company, 219
Tasman world, 126
Tasman, Abel, 23
Tau, Rawiri Te Maire, 7, 10
Tauranga, 219
Tāwhiao, 78, 86
taxation, 112, 168, 232, 280
Te Arawa Māori Trust Board, 163
Te Heuheu Tūkino II, Mananui, 53
Te Heuheu Tūkino IV, 102
Te Heuheu, Sir Tumu, 102, 287
Te Kooti Arikirangi Te Turuki, 82, 83, 87
telegraph, 79, 95, 183
television, 206, 224, 237, 252, 257, 273
Te Maiharanui, 39
Te Manihera, 72
Te Morenga, 37
Te Pahi, 30, 33

Te Papa Tongarewa, 268
Te Pāti Māori, 304
Te Pehi Kupe, 38, 39
Te Puea Hērangi, 147, 162, 182, 267
Te Puni, 48, 61
Te Rangi Hiroa (Sir Peter Buck), 14, 142
Te Rangihaeata, 69, 70
Te Rauparaha, 32, 37, 38, 39, 48, 69, 70, 71
te reo Māori, 257, 304, 316.
    See also Māori language
Terra Australis, 21, 22
Te Taniwha, Horeta, 27
Te Urewera, 83, 147, 162, 163, 309
Te Weehi, Tom, 260
Te Wharepouri, 40, 48, 61, 64
Te Wherowhero, 37
Te Wherowhero VII, Tūheitia Pōtatau, 305
Te Wherowhero, Pōtatau, 53, 73
Te Whiti o Rongomai, 84, 86
'Think Big' projects, 226, 233, 255
Thomas, Captain Joseph, 68
Tiramōrehu, Matiaha, 67
Titokowaru, Riwha, 82, 84
Tizard, Dame Catherine, 264
Tohu Kākahi, 84, 86
Toi, 13
Tokelau, 203, 240
Tory, 47, 48, 61, 62
tourism, 101, 167
trading partners, 273, 275, 319, 320, 323
traditions, 18, 21
    oral, 9, 10, 11
Trans-Pacific Strategic Economic Partnership, 276
Trans-Tasman Travel Arrangement, 278, 322
Treasury, 230, 231
Treaty of Rarotonga, 245

Treaty of Waitangi, 45, 48, 49, 56–7, 66, 81, 181, 255, 267, 268, 287, 292, 305, 323, 325
    articles, 55, 56, 57, 58, 75, 261, 286
    claims, 257
    documents, 52, 53
    legal status, 53
    Māori and English texts, 53, 55
    in Māori protests, 252
    meaning, 53, 55, 56, 57, 58
    principles, 252, 257, 258
    revival of, 249, 256
    split over, 304
Treaty of Waitangi Act 1975, 252
Treaty of Waitangi Amendment Act, 256
Treaty settlements, 259, 260, 287, 304, 308, 309
    Bastion Point, 289
    Ngāi Tahu, 259, 260
    Ngāi Tūhoe, 288, 310
    Tainui, 259
    Treelords, 288
    Whanganui, 309
Tregear, Edward, 14, 123
Tremewan, Captain H. S. (Spencer), 144
tribal settlements, 188
    Ngāti Tūwharetoa, 163
    Te Arawa Lakes, 163
Trump, Donald, 320, 326
Tuffery, Michel, 266
Tuki, 30
Tupaia, 26, 28
Turia, Tariana, 286
Tūwharetoa Māori Trust Board, 163

Underwood, James, 33
unemployment, 166, 223, 225
Union Steam Ship Company, 105
unions, 104, 105, 171, 198, 233, 234

United government, 166
United Nations, 186, 195
United States of America, 178,
    180, 194, 195, 196, 199, 209,
    239, 242, 243, 273, 275, 278,
    289, 320
  cultural influences, 209
  marines, 179, 184
  relations with, 195, 197, 198,
    200, 239, 243, 279
United–Reform coalition
  government, 166
universities, 99, 211, 250
uranium rush, 200
urbanisation, 205

Venus, 37
Victoria, Queen, 50, 73, 86,
    122, 297
Vietnam War, 197, 213
  protests, 212
Vogel, Sir Julius, 88, 91, 94
volcanoes, 4, 101, 283
  Tarawera eruption, 101
voting rights, 90
  Māori men, 96
  men, 96
  women, 114, 116
  See also women, suffrage
voting system, 235, 248, 265,
    286, 303
voyaging, reasons for, 9

wages, 118, 199, 226
  family, 171, 172
Waikato, 38, 95, 157, 163
Waikato River, 310
Waikato River Authority, 310
Wairarapa, 16, 18, 72, 121
Wairau dispute, 69, 70, 77
Waitangi Day, 249, 250, 251
Waitangi Tribunal, 15, 252, 255,
    257, 258, 304, 305, 308, 309
Waitara, 74, 75, 76, 77, 78
Wakefield, Captain Arthur, 69

Wakefield, Colonel William, 47,
    48, 63, 64, 69
Wakefield, Edward Gibbon, 47,
    54, 59, 64, 72
Walsh, F. P., 198
war memorials, 148, 149
Ward, Sir Joseph, 106, 131, 160
Waring, Marilyn, 239
waterways
  Māori views of, 308
  pollution of, 283, 284
  water management, 284
welfare, 100
  domestic purposes benefit, 261
  expenditure cuts, 234
  family allowances, 166
  family benefit, 187, 207
  old age pension, 166, 172
  self-help, 100
  unemployment benefit, 172
  'welfare generation', 225
  widows' pension, 166
Wellington, 16, 35, 37, 40, 41,
    48, 53, 54, 61, 62, 64, 66,
    68, 71, 72, 73, 95, 120, 121,
    185, 209, 212, 213, 234, 240,
    252, 259, 267, 268, 289, 291,
    307, 312
  planning of, 62, 63
  'tenths' reserves, 64
Wen Jiabao, 276
Weston, Agnes Louisa, 194
Wetere, Koro, 256
whakapapa, 11, 12, 18
whaling, 30, 31, 32, 33, 35, 48,
    54, 66
Whanganui, 68, 69, 97, 152, 161
Whanganui River, 309
Whitaker, Sir Frederick, 95
Wiles, Siouxsie, 303
William, Prince, 291, 295, 296
Williams, Henry, 49, 50, 55, 57
Wilson, Margaret, 241
women, 167, 242, 282
  as dependants, 172

education, 99
equal pay, 211
graduates, 99
helpmeets, 66
Māori, 205, 317
Māori women's property, 100
married women's property, 100
in parliament, 155, 265, 317
role of, 93, 113, 114, 148, 183, 208, 212
suffrage, 114, 116
in traditions, 12
Treaty signatories, 53
in trousers, 184
warriors, 79
wives, 33
in workforce, 172, 183, 193, 211, 261, 263

Women's Christian Temperance Union, 114
Women's International League for Peace and Freedom, 148
Women's Liberation Movement, 212, 261
Wong, Pansy, 272
Wood, F. L. W., 124, 185, 190
Wool Commission, 217
wool price crash, 217

Young Māori Party, 122
youth, 209, 213
youth revolution, 210, 211, 213, 222, 247

Zealandia, 3, 4, 5, 125, 189, 265, 313
Zealandia Te Māra a Tāne, 312

For EU product safety concerns, contact us at Calle de José Abascal, 56–1°, 28003 Madrid, Spain or eugpsr@cambridge.org.

www.ingramcontent.com/pod-product-compliance
Ingram Content Group UK Ltd.
Pitfield, Milton Keynes, MK11 3LW, UK
UKHW021628270326
469410UK00019B/338